QUE Bee

From Doubts to Distinction
Your ICSE 2026 Exams Partner

GIST OF THE TEXTBOOK
Crisp & Complete Theory - No need to go back to bulky textbooks!

ALL TYPES OF LATEST PATTERN QUESTIONS
MCQs | Case-based | Assertion-Reason; All in one place!

KEY WORDS HIGHLIGHTED
Important points and key words are neatly Underlined; Never miss what matters

10 YEARS' PYQS ANSWERS
Previous Year Questions with solutions

COUNCIL-STYLE ANSWERS
Write responses like an examiner expects

SAMPLE & SPECIMEN PAPER
Practice in real-exam mode. Perfect your timing, strategy, and confidence.

arihant
SUCCESS AND NOTHING LESS

ARIHANT PRAKASHAN
(School Division Series)

ADMINISTRATIVE & PRODUCTION OFFICES

Regd. Office
'Ramchhaya' 4577/15, Agarwal Road, Darya Ganj, New Delhi -110002
Tele: 011- 47630600, 43518550; Fax: 011- 23280316

Head Office
Kalindi, TP Nagar, Meerut (UP) - 250002, Tel: 0121-7156203, 7156204

SALES & SUPPORT OFFICES
Agra, Ahmedabad, Bengaluru, Bareilly, Chennai, Delhi, Guwahati, Hyderabad, Jaipur, Jhansi, Kolkata, Lucknow, Nagpur & Pune.

PO No : TXT-XX-XXXXXXX-X-XX

Published By Arihant Publications (India) Ltd.

For further information about the books published by Arihant, log on to www.arihantbooks.com or e-mail at info@arihantbooks.com

Follow us on

PRICE ₹ 250.00

PRODUCTION TEAM

Publishing Manager
Keshav Mohan

Project Head
Shivam Gupta

Cover Designer
Bilal Hashmi

Inner Designer
Ankit Tyagi

Page Layouting
Shivam Prajapati

Proof Reader
Priya Kumari

QUE Bee

ICSE
HISTORY & CIVICS
Class 10

Types of Questions & their Respective Number

Type of Questions	Total Number
Multiple Choice Questions (MCQs)	308
Assertion-Reason (A-R)	85
Very Short Answer Questions (VSA)	258
Short Answer Type Questions (SA)	100
Long Answer Type Questions (LA)	76
Structured Questions	52
TOTAL NO. OF QUESTIONS	**879**

Created by

Najmul Sahar
M.A, B.Ed.
38 Yrs. Experienced
PGT (History), Sophia Girls School

Contributor
Nazma Ansari

From Learner to Leader

Step-Into the Spotlight

QUE Bee is more than just a book - it's a platform for young achievers like you to guide future toppers. If you've cracked the code to smart study or have insights that can make learning easier for others, this is your moment to shine!

What Can You Share?

- Your study techniques, time management tips, or motivation hacks
- Feedback or suggestions to make QUE Bee even better
- Real experiences that can guide other students through the exam maze

What's in It for You?

- Your name will be featured in our exclusive Student Panel in the next edition
- Win exciting & surprise rewards for impactful suggestions
- **Get published** - your photo, Ideas-or even interviews can be featured in the book
- **Become a student icon** - recognized and followed by peers across schools

Let your learning become someone else's ladder.
Be remembered. Be featured. Be the guide.

SCAN TO SHARE YOUR IDEA

Index

Latest
Course Structure

There will be one paper of two hours duration carrying 80 marks and an Internal Assessment of 20 marks.

SECTION A : CIVICS

1. The Union Legislature

Meaning of the federal setup in India.

(i) Lok Sabha - Term, composition, qualifications for membership. Parliamentary procedures: a brief idea of sessions, quorum, question hour, adjournment and no-confidence motion. Speaker – election and functions.

(ii) Rajya Sabha – Composition, qualifications for membership, election, term, Presiding Officer.

Powers and functions of Union Parliament – (legislative, financial, judicial, electoral, amendment of the Constitution, control over executive). Exclusive powers of the two Houses.

2. The Union Executive

(i) The President: Qualifications for election, composition of Electoral College, reason for indirect election, term of office, procedure for impeachment.
Powers (executive, legislative, financial, judicial, discretionary and emergency)

(ii) The Vice-President: Qualifications for election, term of office and powers.

(iii) Prime Minister and Council of Ministers: Appointment, formation of Council of Ministers, tenure, functions - policy making, administrative, legislative, financial, emergency. Position and powers of the Prime Minister. Collective and individual responsibility of the members of the Cabinet. Distinction between the Council of Ministers and the Cabinet.

3. The Judiciary

(i) The Supreme Court: Composition, qualifications of judges, appointment, independence of judiciary from the control of executive and legislature; Jurisdiction and functions: Original, Appellate, Advisory, Revisory, Judicial Review and Court of Record. Enforcement of Fundamental Rights and Writs.

(ii) The High Courts: Composition, qualifications of judges, appointment; Jurisdiction and functions: Original, Appellate, Revisory, Judicial Review and Court of Record. Enforcement of Fundamental Rights and Writs.

(iii) Subordinate Courts: Distinction between Court of the District Judge and Sessions Court.

Lok Adalats: Meaning and advantages.

SECTION B : HISTORY

1. The Indian National Movement (1857 – 1917)

(i) The First War of Independence, 1857
Only the causes (political, socio-religious, economic and military) and consequences will be tested. [The events, however, need to be mentioned in order to maintain continuity and for a more comprehensive understanding.]

(ii) Factors leading to the growth of Nationalism – economic exploitation, repressive colonial policies, socio-religious reform movements (brief mention of contribution of Raja Ram Mohan Roy and Jyotiba Phule) and role of the Press.

Foundation of the Indian National Congress - the Indian National Association (Surendranath Banerjee) and the East India Association (Dadabhai Naoroji) as precursors. Immediate objectives of the Indian National Congress - the first two sessions and their Presidents should be mentioned.

(iii) First Phase of the Indian National Movement (1885-1907) - Objectives and methods of struggle of the Early Nationalists. Any two contributions of Dadabhai Naoroji, Surendranath Banerjee and Gopal Krishna Gokhale.

Second Phase of the Indian National Movement (1905-1916) - Brief mention of the causes of the Partition of Bengal and its perspective by the Nationalists. Brief mention of Surat Split of 1907; objectives and methods of struggle of the Radicals. Any two contributions of Bal Gangadhar Tilak, Bipin Chandra Pal and Lala Lajpat Rai. The Muslim League; Factors leading to the formation of the Muslim League and its objectives. Brief mention of the significance of the Lucknow Pact - 1916.

2. Mass Phase of the National Movement (1915-1947)

(i) Mahatma Gandhi:- Non-Cooperation Movement : causes (Khilafat Movement, Rowlatt Act, Jallianwala Bagh Tragedy), programme and suspension – Chauri Chaura incident and impact of the Movement; the Civil Disobedience Movement: causes (reaction to the Simon Commission, Declaration of Poorna Swaraj at the Lahore Session of 1929), Dandi March, programme and impact of the Movement, Gandhi-Irwin Pact and the Second Round Table Conference; the Quit India Movement: causes (failure of the Cripps Mission, Japanese threat), Quit India Resolution and the significance of the Movement.

(ii) Forward Bloc (objectives) and INA (objectives and contribution of Subhas Chandra Bose).

(iii) Independence and Partition of India – Cabinet Mission Plan (clauses only); Mountbatten Plan (clauses and its acceptance); and the Indian Independence Act of 1947 (clauses only).

3. The Contemporary World

(i) The First World War :
Causes (Nationalism and Imperialism, Armament Race, division of Europe and Sarajevo crisis) and Results (Treaty of Versailles, territorial rearrangements, formation of League of Nations).

(ii) Rise of Dictatorships :

Causes for the rise of Fascism in Italy and the rise of Nazism in Germany. A comparative study of Mussolini's Fascist and Hitler's Nazi ideologies.

(iii) The Second World War :

Causes (Dissatisfaction with the Treaty of Versailles, Rise of Fascism and Nazism, Policy of Appeasement, Japanese invasion of China, Failure of League of Nations and Hitler's invasion of Poland). Brief mention of the attack on Pearl Harbour and bombing of Hiroshima and Nagasaki. Consequences (Defeat of Axis Powers, Formation of the United Nations and Cold War).

(iv) United Nations
- (a) The objectives of the U.N. :
  The composition and functions of the General Assembly, the Security Council and the International Court of Justice.
- (b) Major agencies of the United Nations:
  NICEF, WHO and UNESCO - functions only.

(v) Non-Aligned Movement : Brief meaning; objectives; Panchsheel; role of Jawaharlal Nehru; Names of the architects of NAM.

Civics

THE UNION LEGISLATURE

Union Legislature is the body of people's representatives which has supreme power of governance in a Parliamentary form of democracy like India.

It consists of two houses: the Lok Sabha (House of the People) and the Rajya Sabha (Council of States).

The Constitution of India provides for a federal setup in India which means division of power between two levels of government like centre and state.

Lok Sabha

Lok Sabha is called house of the people where members are elected through universal adult franchise.

Term The Constitution provides a fixed term of 5 years for the Lok Sabha.

Composition At present, the Lok Sabha has 543 members. The maximum strength is fixed at 550.

Qualifications for Membership

- Should be an Indian citizen.
- Should be at least 25 years of age.
- Should not hold any office of profit under the government.
- Should have their name in the electoral rolls in some part of the country.

Speaker

The Speaker of the Lok Sabha is presiding officer of house who is elected from amongst its members soon after the newly elected House meets for the first time.

Functions of the Speaker

- Speaker receives all petitions and documents in the House.
- Speaker decides whether a bill is a Money Bill or not.
- Speaker is responsible for maintaining order in the House.
- Speaker decides on the matter of breach of privilege or contempt of House.

Rajya Sabha

Rajya Sabha is the upper house also known as council of states.

Composition Rajya Sabha has a maximum number of 250 members. 238 members represent states and Union Territories

- 12 members are nominated by the President.
- At present, Rajya Sabha has 245 members.

Qualifications For membership

- Minimum age to be appointed as a member in rajyasabha is 30 years.
- He/She should be an Indian citizen.
- He/She should have his name in the electoral rolls in some part of the country.
- He/She should not be a proclaimed criminal.

Election of Members elected by state legislative assembly through single transferrable vote.

Term Each member is elected for a period of 6 years and 1/3rd of the total members retire after every 2 years.

Presiding Officers Vice-President of India is the ex-officio Chairman of the Rajya Sabha.

Parliamentary Procedures

- **Sessions** Generally the Parliament meets thrice a year. The maximum gap between two sessions of Parliament cannot be more than 6 months.
  - (i) **Budget Session** *(February to May)* Focuses on presenting and passing the annual budget.
  - (ii) **Monsoon Session** *(July to September)* Discusses and passes key legislation.
  - (iii) **Winter Session** *(November to December)* Reviews and debates pending matters and policies.
- **Quorum** It means the minimum number of members required to run the business in the house. It is fixed at 1/10th of the total membership of each House.
- **Question Hour** The first hour on every working day of the House is the Question Hour where question of public interest are raised.
- **Adjournment Motion** It is laid to discuss a matter of urgent public importance.
- **No-Confidence Motion** This motion is a formal way for members of the Lok Sabha to express their lack of confidence in the Council of Ministers.

Powers and Functions of Union Parliament

Parliament of India

- **Legislative Powers** Both Houses have equal legislative powers in matters of seventh schedule lists and ordinary bills.
- **Financial Power** Parliament has the exclusive power to levy and collect taxes on subjects enumerated in the Union List (Article 246 and Seventh Schedule). Parliament also passes budget every year.
- **Judicial Powers** Parliament can remove the judges of both the High Court and Supreme Court, and members of any other constitutional body by following a special procedure.
- **Electoral Powers** The Lok Sabha and Rajya Sabha along with the state legislatures elects the President whereas only Lok Sabha and Rajya Sabha participate in the election of the Vice President.
- The Parliament along with the State Legislatures elects the President. Parliament by itself elects India's Vice President as well.
- **Power to Amend the Constitution** Procedure for amending the Constitution is mentioned under Article 368. Amendment bill can be introduced in either house and must be passed by 2/3 majority of members in each House.
- **Control Over Executive** The Parliament exercises control over the Executive through right of interpellation, adjournment motion and monetary controls.

Exclusive Powers of Lok Sabha

- A Money Bill can be introduced only in the Lok Sabha.
- Only Lok Sabha can introduce a no-confidence motion against the government.
- Only the Lok Sabha has the power to pass a resolution for the discontinuance of the national emergency.

Exclusive Powers of the Rajya Sabha

- A resolution seeking the removal of the Vice- President can originate only in the Rajya Sabha.
- A resolution to legislate on the matter of State List can only originate in the Rajya Sabha.
- Resolution for creation of New All India Service can initiate in Rajya Sabha only.

EXAM ORIENTED QUESTIONS

TYPE - 1 — 1 Mark

Multiple Choice Questions

Q.1 A ordinary bill passed by Lok Sabha has to be approved by the Rajya Sabha within .... months.

(a) two (b) three
(c) six (d) eight

Ans. (c) six

Q.2

Lok Sabha member term	5 years
Rajya Sabha member term	?

(ICSE Specimen 2023)

(a) 1 year (b) 2 years
(c) 4 years (d) 6 years

Ans. (d) 6 years

Q.3 Complete the given analogy.

Lok Sabha : Speaker :: Rajya Sabha : ? **(ICSE Specimen Semester I 2021)**

(a) Vice President
(b) Prime Minister
(c) President
(d) Chief Justice of India

Ans. (a) Vice President

Q.4 The interval between two sessions of the Parliament should not be more than .... **(ICSE Specimen 2023)**

(a) two months (b) three months
(c) four months (d) six months

Ans. (d) six months

Q.5 Who elect the Speaker of the Lok Sabha? **(ICSE Specimen Semester I 2021)**

(a) The President
(b) Only the members of the ruling party
(c) The Chairman of the Rajya Sabha
(d) The members of the Lok Sabha

Ans. (d) The members of the Lok Sabha

Q.6 The maximum composition of the Lok Sabha members is **(ICSE Specimen 2023)**

(a) 543 (b) 550
(c) 545 (d) 549

Ans. (b) 550

Q.7 If an Adjournment Motion is passed in the Lok Sabha .... **(ICSE 2025)**

(a) the Lok Sabha will be dissolved.
(b) the House will discuss a matter of urgent public importance.
(c) the President ends the session.
(d) the Government will fall.

Ans. (b) the House will discuss a matter of urgent public importance.

Q.8 Identify the odd exclusive powers of the Rajya Sabha. **(ICSE Specimen 2025)**

P : Can introduce a new All India Service
Q : Can impeach the President
R : Can never be dissolved as a whole.
S : Can introduce a Money Bill

Codes

(a) P and Q (b) R and S
(c) P and R (d) Q and S

Ans. (c) P and R

Q.9 Complete the given analogy. **(ICSE Semester I 2021)**

Election of Lok Sabha members : Citizen of India
Election of Rajya Sabha member : ?

(a) Members of the Legislative Assembly
(b) Members of the Legislative Council
(c) Members of the Lok Sabha
(d) Members of the Cabinet

Ans. (a) Members of the Legislative Assembly

Q.10 A major natural calamity has taken place and the opposition wants the house to lay aside all other business and take up this matter of urgent importance. Which motion should the House move to allow this? **(ICSE 2023)**

(a) Adjournment motion
(b) No-confidence motion
(c) Confidence motion
(d) Censure motion

Ans. (a) Adjournment motion

Exp. An adjournment motion is a motion introduced in the Lok Sabha or Rajya Sabha to temporarily suspend the proceedings of the house and discuss a specific urgent matter of public importance. It requires the approval of the Speaker or Chairman, and if accepted, the discussion usually takes precedence over other scheduled business.

Q.11 Identify the motion which is used for the fall of wafer-thin majority government by the opposition party

(a) No-confidence (b) Adjournment
(c) Censure (d) Prorogation

Ans. (a) No-confidence

Exp. A wafer-thin majority refers to a situation where a political party or government holds a very narrow majority in a legislative body, often by just a few votes.

Q.12 On 23rd March, 2024, a Constitutional Amendment Bill was introduced in the Parliament to amend certain provisions related to the distribution of powers between the Centre and the States. *The Hindu 24th March, 2024*

What can we infer about the Constitutional Amendment Bill from the above passage?

(a) The bill requires approval by a simple majority in both Houses.
(b) It must be ratified by at least half of the State Legislatures.
(c) The bill can be passed by the Lok Sabha alone without the Rajya Sabha.
(d) It can be passed only if the President gives his assent immediately after the vote

Ans. (b) It must be ratified by at least half of the State Legislatures.

Exp. A Constitution Amendment Act is a law passed by the Parliament of India to modify or change the provisions of the Indian Constitution. If the amendment affects the powers or responsibilities of the states, it must be approved by at least half of the state legislatures in addition to being passed by both houses of Parliament.

Q.13 What does the cartoon criticize about the perception of politics?

(a) The lack of interest among youth in politics.
(b) The absence of work culture in legislative bodies like the Parliament and Assemblies.
(c) The overwhelming workload of politicians.
(d) The difficulty in becoming a politician in India.

Ans. (b) The absence of work culture in legislative bodies like the Parliament and Assemblies.

Exp. The absence of work culture in legislative bodies like Parliament and state legislature is seen due to frequent disruptions like low attendance and limited focus on important issues. This hinders the productivity of the sessions in legislative assemblies.

Q.14 Observe the given picture. In case of a similar unruly situation in the Lok Sabha, choose the action that may be taken by the Speaker. **(ICSE 2025)**

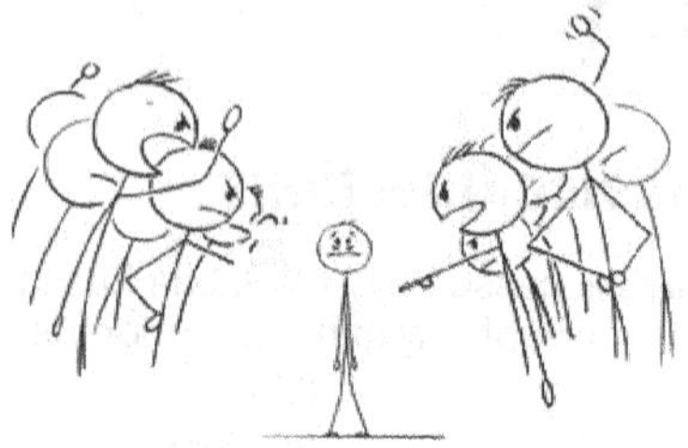

(a) Adjourn the House for lack of quorum.
(b) Dissolve the Lok Sabha.
(c) Adjourn the House for lack of discipline.
(d) Disqualify the members under Anti-defection law.

Ans. (c) Adjourn the House for lack of discipline.

Q.15 In case of a conflict between the centre and the state law on subject of the concurrent list, which law will prevail?

(a) Each follow their own law
(b) The state law will prevail
(c) The president is overpowered to decide
(d) The union law will prevail

Ans. (d) The union law will prevail

Q.16 Which of the following procedures authorises the Executive to draw funds from the Consolidated Fund until the budget is passed by the Parliament? **(ICSE Specimen Semester I 2021)**

(a) Vote on Account (b) Prorogation
(c) Veto (d) Appropriation Bill

Ans. (a) Vote on Account

Q.17 Read the description and identify the person.
He is the ex-officio chairman of the Rajya Sabha and presides over its meetings.

(a) Speaker of Lok Sabha (b) President of India
(c) Prime Minister of India (d) Vice President of India

Ans. (d) Vice President of India

Q.18 Your school has organised a poster making competition on the topic – The role of the Prime Minister in Union Legislature of India. Which of the following leaders would most likely be featured in the poster?

(a) Rajendra Prasad (b) Lala Lajpat Rai
(c) V.P. Menon (d) Jawaharlal Nehru

Ans. (d) Jawaharlal Nehru

Exp. Nehru was India's first Prime Minister and played a key role in leading the Union Legislature, shaping policies, and guiding India's early governance after independence.

Q.19 Given below are details of a few Indian Citizens.

Person	Age (In Years)	Description
W	25	Is a famous journalist
X	45	Is an industrialist
Y	35	Has declared insolvency
Z	50	Has taken citizenship of another country

Select the one who is eligible to be a member of the Rajya Sabha. **(ICSE 2025)**

(a) X (b) W (c) Y (d) Z

Ans. (a) X

Q.20 Look at the table given below and select the person who fulfills the eligibility criteria to become the members of Lok Sabha in India.

Person	Age	Description
W	27	Have criminal record
X	22	Citizen of India
Z	26	Does not hold any office of profit under the government

(a) W (b) X
(c) Z (d) All of these

Ans. (c) Z

Q.21 On 5th December, 2023, the Speaker of the Lok Sabha announced that a special session of Parliament would be held to discuss the upcoming bills. The Prime Minister of India, during his speech, emphasised the importance of passing crucial reforms in the coming session. *The Hindu, 6th December, 2023*

What information about the Union Legislature can we obtain from the above passage?

(a) The Speaker of the Lok Sabha has the authority to call a special session.
(b) The Prime Minister is responsible for calling Parliament sessions.
(c) Only the Speaker can discuss bills in Parliament.
(d) The Prime Minister does not play a role in Parliament sessions.

Ans. (a) The Speaker of the Lok Sabha has the authority to call a special session.

Q.22 Which of the following statements is correct about the salaries and allowances of the ministers in India?

(a) The salaries and allowances of ministers are decided by the Parliament.
(b) The Finance Minister alone decides the salaries and allowances of ministers.
(c) The President determines the salaries and allowances of the ministers.
(d) The Prime Minister has the authority to decide the salaries and allowances of ministers.

Ans. (a) The salaries and allowances of ministers are decided by the Parliament.

Q.23 In the image given below, members of the Rajya Sabha are discussing an issue. How many members of the Rajya Sabha retire every year?

(a) 2/8 (b) 2/3
(c) 1/3 (d) 1/2

Ans. (c) 1/3

Q.24 When can the Parliament not legislate on subject included in the state list? **(ICSE Specimen 2021)**

(a) When the state is ruled by a coalition.
(b) During the proclamation of an emergency.
(c) When the Rajya Sabha passes a resolution by two third majority.
(d) When two or more states are of opinion that the Parliament should legislate on the subject.

Ans. (c) When the Rajya Sabha passes a resolution by two third majority.

Q.25 Who made the amendment which resulted in the below headline? **(ICSE Specimen 2025)**

THE TIMES OF INDIA

In Historic Move Within 100 Days Of Modi-2, Govt Bifurcates State Into 2 UTs, Defangs Article 370 & Scraps 35A

KASHMIR IS NOW UNION'S TERRITORY

J&K To Lose Special Status, Centre To Directly Rule Ladakh

INDIA'S NORTH POLE SHIFTS TO CENTRE

Why now? PM, Shah felt political tide and timing favoured action

(a) The Supreme Court (b) The President
(c) The Parliament (d) The Prime Minister

Ans. (c) The Parliament

TYPE - 2
1 Mark

Assertion-Reason Questions

Q.1 Read the two statements given below about the Union Legislature and select the option that shows the correct relationship between (A) and (R).

Assertion (A) The Union Legislature includes the President, Lok Sabha and Rajya Sabha.

Reason (R) The President is part of the Parliament.

(a) R Contradicts A
(b) R is the reason for A
(c) A is true but R is false
(d) A and R are independent of each other

Ans. (b) R is the reason for A

Q.2 Read the two statements given below about the adjournment motion and select the option that shows the correct relationship between (A) and (R).

Assertion (A) An adjournment motion allows the House to take up a definite matter of urgent importance.

Reason (R) An adjournment motion is a formal motion used in Parliament to suspend the normal proceedings and discuss an urgent issue that requires immediate attention.

(a) R contradicts A
(b) R is the reason for A
(c) A is true, but R is false
(d) A and R are independent of each other

Ans. (b) R is the reason for A

Q.3 Read the two statement given below about the exclusive powers of the Lok Sabha and select the option that shows correct relationship between (A) and (R)

Assertion (A) The Lok Sabha has exclusive powers to introduce and approve money bills.

Reason (R) The Rajya Sabha can reject a money bill introduced in the Lok Sabha.

(a) R contradicts A
(b) R is the reason for A
(c) A is true, but R is false
(d) A and R are independent of each other

Ans. (c) A is true, but R is false

Q.4 Read the two statements given below about the Speaker of the Lok Sabha and select the option that shows the correct relationship between (A) and (B).

Assertion (A) The Speaker of the Lok Sabha maintains order and discipline during parliamentary debates.

Reason (R) The Speaker has no authority to suspend a member for unruly behavior.

(a) R contradicts A
(b) R is the reason for A
(c) A is true, but R is false
(d) A and R are independent of each other.

Ans. (c) A is true, but R is false

Q.5 Read the two statements given below about the Speaker of the Lok Sabha and select the option that shows the correct relationship between (A) and (B).

Assertion (A) The Speaker of the Lok Sabha does not vote in the initial stages of a debate.

Reason (R) The Speaker has the right to cast vote in case of a tie.

(a) R contradicts A
(b) R is the reason for A
(c) A is true, but R is false
(d) A and R are independent of each other

Ans. (b) R is the reason for A

TYPE - 3
2 Marks

Very Short Answer Type Questions

Q.1 Explain any two electoral functions of the Union Parliament.

Ans. Two functions of the Union Parliament are as follows

(i) It along with the state legislatures elects the President of India.

(ii) The Vice President of India is also elected by the Parliament.

Q.2 State any two federal features of the Indian Constitution.

Ans. The two federal features of the Indian Constitution are as follows

(i) Constitution of India has made provisions for the distribution of revenues between the Centre and the States, ensuring financial autonomy for both.

(ii) The Constitution of India has divided matters into three lists-Union List, State List and Concurrent List under the Seventh Schedule which ensures federal structure in india.

Q.3 Mention any two primary functions of the Union Legislature in India?

Ans. The primary functions of the Union Legislature in India are as follows

(i) It makes laws for the country, including on subjects mentioned in the Union and Concurrent List

(ii) The Union Legislature has the power to amend the Constitution of india through Constitutional Amendment Bill.

Q.4 Explain the concept of "bicameralism" in the Union Legislature.

Ans. Bicameralism refers to a legislature having two Houses. In India, the Union Legislature consists of the Lok Sabha (Lower House) and the Rajya Sabha (Upper House), each with different powers and responsibilities.

Q.5 Analyse the role of Parliament in a democracy like India.

Ans. Parliament in India is responsible for making laws, holding the government accountable and representation of citizens choice into the House.

It ensures transparency through debates and scrutiny of policies, reflects the people's interests, and upholds the Constitution, maintaining checks and balances in governance.

Q.6 Mention two provisions of the Constitution, which clearly establish the supremacy of the Lok Sabha with regard to the Money Bill. (ICSE 2017)

Ans. Two provisions of the Constitution are as follows

(i) The ultimate authority to either pass or reject the money bill, lies with the Lok Sabha. The Rajya Sabha does not have the power to reject the Money Bill, nor the power to amend it.

(ii) The Lok Sabha can accept or reject any recommendations made by Rajya Sabha.

Q.7 How does the casting vote of the Speaker of the Lok Sabha impact the decision-making process?

Ans. The casting vote of the speaker of the Lok Sabha is used to break ties, ensuring smooth decision making. It also plays a crucial role in maintaining the flow of Parliamentary proceeding.

Q.8 Which category of power is being exercised by the Lok Sabha in the following

(i) Introduction of Money bill

(ii) Removal of High Court Judge

Ans. (i) Exclusive Legislative power of the Lok Sabha.

(ii) Judicial Power of the Lok Sabha.

Q.9 Explain the procedure to elect the members of Rajya Sabha in India?

Ans. The members of the Rajya Sabha are elected by the Members of Legislative Assemblies on the basis of proportional representation with a single transferable vote.

Q.10 Explain the procedure for the removal of the Speaker of the Lok Sabha in parliamentary structure of India.

Ans. The Speaker of the Lok Sabha can be removed through a resolution passed by the Lok Sabha only. The resolution must have a majority of the entire House (more than 50% of members) to succeed.

Q.11 Imagine you are living in rural areas, mention any two ways in which the Union Executive helps improve the living conditions of people in rural areas.

Ans. Two ways by which the Union Executive helps improve the living conditions of people in rural areas are as follows

(i) The Union Executive implements schemes like the "Pradhan Mantri Awas Yojana" (PMAY), which provides affordable housing for rural families.

(ii) It promotes rural development through programmes like Pradhan Mantri Kisan Samman Nidhi (PM-KISAN), which offers financial support to farmers in rural areas.

Q.12 Mention any one subject wherein the Lok Sabha and the Rajya Sabha enjoy co-equal powers in legislation of laws.

Ans. Introduction and passage of a Constitutional Amendment Bill is the subject wherein the Lok Sabha and the Rajya Sabha enjoy co-equal powers in legislation of laws.

Q.13 Analyse the effect of a no-confidence motion on the government in India.

Ans. No-confidence motion is a formal motion moved in the Lok Sabha to express lack of confidence in the ruling government. If the motion is passed by a majority vote, it leads to the resignation of the Prime Minister and the entire Council of Ministers. This signifies the collapse of the current government, compelling the formation of a new government or calling for general elections.

Q.14 Mention about the procedure for the dissolution of the Lok Sabha.

Ans. The Lok Sabha is dissolved by the President of India, usually after the completion of its five-year term. After dissolution, new elections are held to form a new Lok Sabha.

Q.15 With reference to the Union Parliament, highlight any two subjects over which both the Houses of Parliament in India enjoy co-equal powers.

Ans. The two Houses of Parliament enjoy co-equal powers in the following subjects

(i) Emergencies proclaimed by the President, have to be approved by both the Houses of Parliament.

(ii) Impeachment of the President.

Q.16 A Legislative Assembly has 230 members. How many members need to be present in order to enable the House to maintain quorum of the house?

Ans. The minimum number of members required to be present in order to enable the House to transact its business is termed as 'quorum', which is 1/10th of the total strength. There should be 23 members present in the house to maintain quorum.

Q.17 Imagine you are a member of the Rajya Sabha, and you are discussing a bill related to environmental protection. What two things would you do to make sure the bill is passed effectively?

Ans. To ensure the passing of the bill, I would actively participate in the debate, presenting compelling facts and data to highlight the urgency of addressing environmental issues. Additionally, I would consult experts to propose well-informed amendments, making the bill more robust and comprehensive in tackling environmental challenges.

Q.18 Who appoints the nominated members in the Rajya Sabha? Mention the criteria on which they are appointed.

Ans. The President of India appoints the nominated members of the Rajya Sabha. They are appointed based on their outstanding contributions in areas such as literature, science, arts, social services, or public life, ensuring a diverse representation of expertise and experience in the House.

Q.19 Discuss the relationship between the two Houses of the Parliament with reference to the Money Bill. (ICSE 2013)

Ans. A Money Bill can originate in the Lok Sabha only. After the bill gets passed by the Lok Sabha, it is then sent to Rajya Sabha for recommendations, which it must send back within 14 days.

The bill then comes to the Lok Sabha again, which is upon them to either accept or reject any of the recommendations. In financial matters, the Rajya Sabha has only an advisory role.

Q.20 Discuss two ways in which the Rajya Sabha differs from the Lok Sabha.

Ans. Rajya Sabha is different from Lok Sabha in the following ways

(i) The Rajya Sabha represents the states, while the Lok Sabha represents the people of India.

(ii) The Rajya Sabha is a permanent House and is not dissolved, unlike the Lok Sabha.

Q.21 Mention two powers of the Lok Sabha used in the legislative process.

Ans. The two powers of the Lok Sabha used in the legislative process are

(i) The Lok Sabha has the power to introduce and pass Money Bills.

(ii) The Lok Sabha can pass or reject bills introduced by members of both Houses of Parliament.

Q.22 Which type of power is being exercised by the Parliament in the following cases?

(i) Amending the Constitution

(ii) Formation of All India Judiciary Services

Ans. (i) Amendment power of the Parliament

(ii) Legislative powers of the Parliament

Q.23 Explain the meaning of the term Universal Adult Franchise.

Ans. Universal Adult Franchise grants the right to vote to all citizens aged 18 years or above, ensuring equal participation in the electoral process.It prohibits discrimination in voting rights based on caste, creed, religion, sex, or gender and fostering equality in democracy.

Q.24 Highlight the difference between a Money Bill and a non-Money Bill in context to the Indian Parliament.

Ans. A Money Bill deals with matters such as taxes, government spending, and loans, and can only be introduced in the Lok Sabha. A non-Money Bill deals with other legislative matters and can be introduced in either House of Parliament.

Q.25 Name two responsibilities of the Speaker of the Lok Sabha.

Ans. Two responsibilities of the Speaker of the Lok Sabha are

(i) The Speaker maintains order during debates in the Lok Sabha.

(ii) The Speaker decides on the admissibility of questions and motions.

Q.26 Name the types of Bills that can be introduced only in the Lok Sabha and Rajya Sabha

Ans. Money Bill can be introduced in the Lok Sabha only. New All India Service Bill can be initiated in the Rajya Sabha only.

Q.27 Read the extract given below and answer the question which follows (ICSE Specimen 2025)

Congress member's adjournment motion disallowed. The notice, along with another moved demanding a discussion on China, was disallowed in the Lok Sabha *The Times of India, 10th Feb, 2023*

Who can allow or disallow the above motion? What does this motion mean?

Ans. The Speaker of the Lok Sabha has the authority to allow or disallow motions such as the adjournment motion.

An adjournment motion is a motion moved by a member to seek the suspension of the normal business of the House to discuss an urgent issue. It is usually raised when there is an important matter that needs immediate attention. If the Speaker disallows it, the motion cannot be discussed further in the House.

Q.28 Read the given news carefully and answer the question that follows. (ICSE 2024)

Government's power to promulgate, repromulgate Ordinances - why and how An Ordinance "shall have the same force and effect as an Act of Parliament". But the government is required to bring an Ordinance before Parliament for ratification - and failure to do so will lead to its lapsing "at the expiration of six weeks from the reassembly of Parliament".

The Indian Express 25th May, 2023

Mention any two points regarding an ordinance that can be deduced from the above news.

Ans. From the given news, the following two points regarding an ordinance can be deduced

(i) An ordinance has the same force and effect as an Act of Parliament, meaning it holds the same legal authority until it is ratified or rejected by the Parliament.

(ii) The government is required to present the ordinance before Parliament for ratification. If it is not ratified within six weeks from the reassembly of Parliament, the ordinance will lapse and no longer remain in effect.

TYPE - 4 — 3 Marks

Short Answer Type Questions

Q.1 Explain the power sharing relationship between the Lok Sabha and Rajya Sabha

Ans. The power sharing relationship between the Lok Sabha and Rajya Sabha can be understood through the following points

- **Money Bills** Money bills can only be introduced in the Lok Sabha, and the Rajya Sabha can only suggest amendments. The Rajya Sabha cannot
- reject or delay money bills, thus giving the Lok Sabha more control over financial matters.
- **Resolution of Deadlocks** In case of a deadlock between the two Houses on a bill, a joint session can be called by the President, where the Lok Sabha's larger strength often ensures its dominance in decision-making.
- **Creation of New All India Services** The Rajya Sabha holds exclusive power to initiate a bill for creating new All India Services granting it a unique authority that surpasses the Lok Sabha in this specific area.

Q.2 Highlight the significance of the Rajya Sabha in protecting the interests of the States.

Ans. The Rajya Sabha is designed to represent the states of India at the national level. Members of the Rajya Sabha are elected by the Legislative Assemblies of states, ensuring that the interests of different states are represented in Parliament. This safeguards federalism by allowing states to have a voice in national legislation.

The Rajya Sabha can debate and recommend amendments to bills passed by the Lok Sabha, thus ensuring that state-level concerns are taken into account before national laws are passed.

Q.3 The Rajya Sabha is called a Permanent House. Explain this statement. **(ICSE 2024)**

Ans. The Rajya Sabha is called a Permanent House because it cannot be dissolved, unlike the Lok Sabha.

It is a continuous body, with one-third of its members retiring every two years, ensuring its uninterrupted functioning.

Elections for the Rajya Sabha are held, and new members are elected while the House remains in operation. As a result, the Rajya Sabha operates without needing to be reconstituted, maintaining its permanence.

Q.4 The Lok Sabha is more powerful than the Rajya Sabha. Justify this by mentioning any three points. **(ICSE Specimen 2025)**

Ans. The Lok Sabha is more powerful than the Rajya Sabha due to the following reasons

(i) **Power Over Money Bills** The Lok Sabha exclusively introduces and passes Money Bills, while the Rajya Sabha can only suggest amendments.

(ii) **No-Confidence Motion** The Lok Sabha has the power to introduce no-confidence motion.

(iii) **Greater Legislative Power** In case of a deadlock, the Lok Sabha's larger membership gives it the decisive role in passing Bills.

TYPE - 5 — 4 Marks

Long Answer Type Questions

Q.1 Explain the concept of 'Question Hour' in the Parliament and mention its significance in the legislative process.

Ans. Question Hour is the first hour on every working day of the Parliament, during which members can ask questions to the government on matters of public interest.

The questions can be of three types: Starred, Unstarred, and Short Notice questions. Starred questions require an oral answer, whereas unstarred questions receive written responses. Short Notice questions can be asked without prior notice.

Significance

- It holds the government accountable by allowing members to seek information about government policies, actions and decisions.
- It promotes transparency and ensures the executive remains answerable to the legislature.
- It provides a platform for members to highlight public issues and seek government intervention.

Q.2 Explain the judicial powers of the Parliament of India, with some examples.

Ans. The Parliament of India holds significant judicial powers which is the judicial part of the legislation of india.

For example,

- **Removal of Judges** Parliament can remove judges of both the Supreme Court and High Court through the process of impeachment for misconduct or incapacity, ensuring accountability in the judiciary.
- **Impeachment of the President** Parliament has the authority to impeach the President of India for violating the Constitution. The process involves a detailed procedure, including a special majority in both Houses.
- **Punishment for Contempt** Parliament can punish individuals who obstruct its functioning or show disrespect to its members, ensuring the integrity and smooth functioning of the legislative process.

Q.3 Explain the qualifications required for a person to be a member of the Indian Parliament.

Ans. There are some conditions for becoming the member of Parliament in india, those are as follows

(i) The person must be a citizen of India.

(ii) The person must be at least 25 years old for the Lok Sabha and 30 years old for the Rajya Sabha.

(iii) The person should not be of unsound mind.

(iv) The person should not be holding an office of profit under the government.

(v) He/She should not be proven guilty in any court of law.

Q.4 Why is it crucial for the Speaker of the Lok Sabha to be impartial, and how does the election process ensure this impartiality?

Ans. The Speaker must be impartial to uphold the democratic principles and ensure fair proceedings in the House.

The election process involves voting by all members of the Lok Sabha, ensuring that the Speaker is not just a representative of the ruling party but of the entire House. This democratic method fosters accountability and impartiality.

TYPE - 6 — 10 Marks

Structured Questions

Q.1 Look at the picture given below and answer the following questions. **(ICSE 2024)**

(i) The Rajya Sabha is called a Permanent House. Explain this statement. (3)

(ii) Explain the composition of the Rajya Sabha. (3)

(iii) Mention any two exclusive powers of the Lok Sabha and two powers exclusive to the Rajya Sabha. (4)

Ans. (i) For answer refer to Q. 3 of Short Answer Type Questions.

(ii) The Rajya Sabha consists of a total of 250 members. Of these, 238 members are directly elected by the members of State Legislative Assemblies and by the members of the Legislative Assemblies of Delhi and Puducherry through a system of proportional representation.

The remaining 12 members are nominated by the President of India from individuals who have made distinguished contributions in fields such as literature, science, art, and social services. Members of the Rajya Sabha serve for a term of six years.

(iii) **Exclusive Powers of the Lok Sabha**

- **Power over Money Bills** The Lok Sabha has the exclusive authority to introduce and approve Money Bills, which deal with government finances, including taxation and public spending.
- **Initiation of No-confidence** The no-confidence motion against government can be introduced in the Lok Sabha only.

Exclusive Powers of the Rajya Sabha

- **Power to Approve Certain Laws** The Rajya Sabha has the exclusive power to approve laws regarding the extension of the Union List and the enactment of laws that apply to states.
- **Nominations and Representation of States** The Rajya Sabha plays a unique role in representing the states and union territories in the Parliament. It is responsible for nominating members from the states to form part of the Upper House.

Q.2 The Union Legislature of India is not only the law-making body, but the center of all democratic political process. With reference to the Parliament, answer the following questions.

(i) The Lok Sabha is referred to as the 'House of the People'. Justify the statement by mentioning any three points. **(3)**

(ii) Rajya Sabha adjourned sine die, overall productivity at 79 percent. **(3)**

THE ABC NEWS, 21st December, 2023

Who can adjourn the above session? Explain the composition of this House.

(iii) Highlight any four legislative powers of the Parliament. **(4)**

Ans. (i) The Lok Sabha is referred to as the 'House of the People' because of the following reasons

(a) **Direct Elections** Members of the Lok Sabha are directly elected by the people of India through general elections. This democratic process ensures that the representatives are chosen by the citizens themselves.

(b) **Representation of the People** The Lok Sabha is meant to represent the interests, views, and concerns of the Indian population. It is a platform where elected representatives debate and discuss issues that affect the citizens, making it a true reflection of the people's voice.

(c) **Legislative Authority** The Lok Sabha plays a crucial role in the legislative process, including the passage of laws and the approval of government budgets. Its decisions directly impact the lives of the people, reinforcing its identity as the House of the People.

(ii) The Chairman of the Rajya Sabha, who is the Vice President of India, has the authority to adjourn the Rajya Sabha. The Chairman can adjourn the session either sine die (without a fixed date for resumption) or for a specific time.

The Rajya Sabha is the Council of States, and its composition consists of 245 members. In Rajya Sabha 233 members are elected from the states and union territories, and 12 members are nominated by the President for their expertise in fields like literature,

(iii) Four legislative powers of the Parliament are

(a) **Law-making** The Parliament can make laws on matters listed in the Union List, Concurrent List, and also amend the Constitution.

(b) **Budget and Finance** The Parliament approves the annual budget and has the power to raise funds, taxes, and allocate government expenditure.

(c) **Impeachment of the President** Parliament has the power to impeach the President of India if they violate the Constitution.

(d) **Approval of Treaties and Agreements** The Parliament approves international treaties and agreements signed by the government, especially those that involve significant national interest or expenditure.

Q.3. The Parliament of India comprises the President and the two Houses. With reference to the Indian Parliament, answer the following questions. **(ICSE 2025)**

(i) Mention any three circumstances under which the Parliament can make laws.

(ii) Explain the following terms

(a) Question Hour (b) Quorum

(c) No-confidence Motion

(iii) When can the term of Lok Sabha be extended?

Mention any three powers of the Lok Sabha which show its superiority over the Rajya Sabha.

Ans. (i) Three circumstances under which Parliament can make laws on subjects in the State List are

- **During a National Emergency** Under Article 249, Parliament can legislate on State List subjects when an emergency is declared.
- **When Rajya Sabha Passes a Resolution** If the Rajya Sabha declares, by a two-thirds majority, that a subject in the State List is of national importance, Parliament can legislate on it.
- **When States Request Parliament** If two or more states pass resolutions requesting Parliament to make a law on a State List subject, Parliament can legislate on it.

(ii) (a) **Question Hour** The first hour of a parliamentary sitting, where members ask questions to ministers regarding government policies and decisions.

(b) **Quorum** The minimum number of members required to be present in either House for proceedings to take place. In Lok Sabha, it is 1/10th of total number of members.

(c) **No-confidence Motion** A motion moved in Lok Sabha to test if the government still has majority support. If passed, the government must resign.

(iii) The term of the Lok Sabha can be extended by one year at a time during a National Emergency under Article 352.

Three powers of Lok Sabha that Show its superiority over Rajya Sabha are

- **Control Over the Executive** The Council of Ministers is responsible to the Lok Sabha, and it can be removed through a No-confidence Motion.
- **Financial Supremacy** Money Bills can only be introduced in the Lok Sabha and the Rajya Sabha cannot amend or reject them.
- **Final Decision in Case of Disagreements** In case of a disagreement over an Ordinary Bill, a joint session is held where the Lok Sabha's larger strength ensures its dominance.

THE UNION EXECUTIVE

The Union Executive is the executive branch of the Indian government responsible for implementing and enforcing laws, policies, and decisions at the national level. It consists of the President and council of ministers.

The President

The President is the executive head of the Union of India. He is assisted by the council of ministers which is headed by the Prime minister who helps in the execution of powers and duties of the President.

Qualifications

- He must be a citizen of India.
- He must have completed 35 years of age.
- He must be qualified to be elected as a member of the Lok Sabha.
- He must not hold any office of profit under the Government of India or State.

Election of The President

- The manner and procedure of election of the President is mentioned in Article 55 of the Indian Constitution.
- The election is based on the principle of proportional representation.
- The President is elected by the members of the electoral college.

Composition of Electoral College

- The elected members of both Houses of Parliament (Lok Sabha and Rajya Sabha).
- The elected members of the Legislative Assemblies of the States and union territories with assemblies (Delhi, Puducherry, Jammu & Kashmir)

Reason for Indirect Election

- If elected directly, the President could become a rival centre of Powers to the Council of Ministers.
- An indirect election protects the president from becoming the nominee of the ruling party.

Term of Office

- The President holds office for a period of 5 years.

Powers of The President

Executive Powers of The President

- The President is the executive head of the country & all executive actions are taken in his name
- He appoints the Prime Minister, Council of Ministers, Governor of States, CJI and other key officials.
- He can appoint an inter-state council to promote centre-state and inter-state cooperation.

Legislative Powers of The President

- The President can summon and prorogue Parliament sessions and dissolve the Lok Sabha.
- The President can promulgate ordinances (Article 123) when Parliament is not in session.
- A bill related to formation of a new state must be moved only after the prior approval of the President.
- The president addresses a joint session at the beginning of the Parliament every year.

Financial Powers of The President

- The President appoints financial commission after every 5 years.
- The President can withdraw money from the Contingency fund of India for emergency needs.
- A Money Bill can be introduced after the President's recommendations.

Judicial Powers of The President

- The President has the power to grant pardons , respites, reprieves or remission to remit or commute the sentence of any person convicted for an offence.
- He is protected from criminal proceedings while performing his official duties.

Discretionary Powers of The President

- The President uses discretionary powers in case no party gains a majority.
- After a no-confidence motion and dissolution of the ruling government, the President can ask the other government to prove his majority.

Emergency Powers of The President

- **National Emergency** ***(Article 352)*** The President can declare a National Emergency in case of war, external aggression, or armed rebellion.
- **State Emergency** ***(President's Rule) (Article 356)*** The President can impose a State Emergency if there is a constitutional breakdown of state machinery.
- **Financial Emergency** ***(Article 360)*** The President can declare a Financial Emergency if the financial stability or credit of the nation is threatened.

Procedure for Impeachment of the President

- The President can be impeached in case of violation of the Constitution.
- The procedure for impeachment of the President of India begins with a 14-day notice of the charges signed by at least one-fourth of the total members of the House who initiated charges.
- The motion is then investigated, and if approved by a two-thirds majority in both Houses, the President is removed from office.

Vice President

The Vice President of India is the second-highest constitutional office in the country.

Qualifications

The Vice President of India should be

- A citizen of India.
- At least 35 years of age.
- Eligible to be elected to the Rajya Sabha.
- Not holding any office of profit under the government or a local authority.

Term of Office

- The term of the Vice President of India is five years from the date he assumes office.

Powers of the Office of the Vice President

- The Vice President is the ex-officio Chairman of the Rajya Sabha. He acts as the President of India if the President is unable to perform duties due to illness, absence, or vacancy.
- He nominates members to the committees of the Rajya Sabha's committees.
- He can suspend or expel members of the House for their misbehaviour.

EXAM ORIENTED QUESTIONS

TYPE - 1 1 Mark

Multiple Choice Questions

Q.1 Identify the odd one out who is not a part of Union executive.

(a) President (b) Prime Minister
(c) Vice President (d) Chief Justice of India

Ans. (d) Chief Justice of India

Q.2 On 19th May, 2023, the President of India exercised legislative power under Article 123 of the Constitution, during the period Parliament was in recess, to promulgate.

The Government of National Capital Territory of Delhi Ordinance, 2023. *The Hindu, 26th May, 2023*

(ICSE Specimen 2025)

What information about an ordinance can we obtain from the above passage?

(a) The ordinance must be approved within six weeks.
(b) Only the Cabinet can prepare an ordinance.
(c) It is issued when the Parliament is not functioning.
(d) If the Parliament does not approve it within six weeks it becomes inoperative.

Ans. (c) It is issued when the Parliament is not functioning.

Exp. Ordinances are temporary laws issued by the President of India under Article 123 of the Constitution when Parliament is not in session and immediate legislative action is required.

Q.3 Given below are details of few Indian Citizens.

Person	Article	Description
W	34	Is a Professor in the Government College
X	35	Has taken up the citizenship of the United states of America
Y	27	Is a reputed sportsperson
Z	36	Is a scientist

Select the person who fulfills the eligibility criteria to become the President of India. **(ICSE specimen 2025)**

(a) W (b) X
(c) Y (d) Z

Ans. (d) Z

Q.4 Which of the following statements regarding the term of office of the President of India is correct?

(a) The President holds office for a term of 6 years, with no provision for re-election.
(b) The President's term of office can be extended under special circumstances by the Parliament.
(c) The President of India is elected for a term of 5 years, with the possibility of re-election.
(d) The President's term of office is fixed at 4 years, subject to renewal by the Parliament.

Ans. (c) The President of India is elected for a term of 5 years, with the possibility of re-election.

Q.5 Identify the correct statement which is related to the composition of electoral college of the President

(a) Only the members of Rajya Sabha
(b) Only the members of Lok Sabha
(c) Members of Legislative Assembly
(d) The elected members of Rajya Sabha, Lok Sabha and State Legislative Assembly

Ans. (d) The elected members of Rajya Sabha, Lok Sabha and State Legislative Assembly

Q.6 During a hung assembly when no party gets the majority, the President appoints the Prime Minister. What power is the President exercising? **(ICSE 2024)**

(a) Legislative (b) Executive
(c) Discretionary (d) Judicial

Ans. (c) Discretionary

Exp. Discretionary power allows the President to make a decision based on the situation, such as appointing the leader of the largest party or coalition, or someone who is likely to command a majority in the House.

Q.7 Which of the following statements about the President of India's nomination powers is correct?

(a) The President can nominate members to both the Lok Sabha and Rajya Sabha without any restrictions.
(b) The President can nominate 12 members to the Rajya Sabha, including experts in various fields.
(c) The President can nominate 10 members to the Lok Sabha for representing specific communities.
(d) The President can only nominate members to the Rajya Sabha from the ruling party.

Ans. (b) The President can nominate 12 members to the Rajya Sabha, including experts in various fields.

Q.8 Complete the given analogy.
Control over States : Executive Power : : Address to the Parliament:?
(a) Legislative Power (b) Administrative Power
(c) Judicial Power (d) Financial Power

Ans. (a) Legislative Power

Q.9. Identify who among the following advises the President on the matters of execution of his official duties.
P : Prime Minister Q : Council of Ministers
R : Vice-President S : Speaker
Codes
(a) P and Q (b) P and R (c) R and Q (d) Q and S

Ans. (a) P and Q

Exp. The advice of the Council headed by Prime Minister is binding on the President, except in cases where the President may exercise discretion.

Q.10 An ordinance is called a temporary law. Which of the following statements correctly describes the same?
(a) Only the Prime Minister can prepare an ordinance.
(b) It is issued when the Parliament is in session.
(c) If the Parliament does not approve it within six weeks it becomes inoperative.
(d) Only the President can promulgate an ordinance.

Ans. (d) Only the President can promulgate an ordinance.

Q.11 With reference to the image given below, how many numbers of electors are required for the nomination of a candidate's name for Presidential election.

(a) 20 (b) 30 (c) 40 (d) 50

Ans. (d) 50

Q.12 The President of India has the power to appoint judges to the Supreme Court and High Court.
Based on this information, what can we infer about the President's judicial powers?
(a) The President has the authority to directly intervene in court rulings.
(b) The President plays a significant role in the appointment of judicial officers.
(c) The President has the power to review and modify judicial decisions.
(d) The President can remove judges from the judiciary at any time.

Ans. (b) The President plays a significant role in the appointment of judicial officers.

Q.13 Imagine the President of India 'Mr. X' is advised by the Council of Ministers to dissolve the Lok Sabha, but the President has doubts about the government's stability. What can the President do?
(a) The President can refuse to dissolve the Lok Sabha and ask the Prime Minister to prove the majority.
(b) The President must dissolve the Lok Sabha immediately.
(c) The President can dissolve the Lok Sabha only after consulting the Speaker.
(d) The President can call a special session to discuss the dissolution.

Ans. (a) The President can refuse to dissolve the Lok Sabha and ask the Prime Minister to prove the majority.

Q.14 Read the description and identify the person.
He is the Supreme Commander of the Indian Armed Forces.
(a) Prime Minister (b) Chief Justice of India
(c) President of India (d) Vice-president of India

Ans. (c) President of India

Q.15 Which emergency will be declared by the President if the security of the Nation is under threat? **(ICSE 2025)**
(a) General Emergency
(b) Financial Emergency
(c) Constitutional Emergency
(d) President's Rule

Ans. (a) General Emergency

Q.16 The Vice President of India can only be removed from office under the provisions of the Constitution. Which of the following conditions is correct regarding his removal?
(a) The Vice President can be removed by a resolution passed by a simple majority in the Rajya Sabha.
(b) The Vice President can be removed by a resolution passed by a two-thirds majority in both Houses of Parliament.
(c) The Vice President can be removed by the President without any involvement of Parliament.
(d) The Vice President can be removed only by the President's discretion after consultation with the Prime Minister.

Ans. (b) The Vice President can be removed by a resolution passed by a two-thirds majority in both Houses of Parliament.

Q.17 Imagine the Vice President of India is unable to fulfill his duties due to a sudden health crisis, and the President is abroad for an official visit. Who would temporarily assume the responsibilities of the Vice President in such a situation?
(a) The Speaker of the Lok Sabha
(b) A member of the Rajya Sabha, appointed by the President
(c) The Prime Minister of India
(d) The President of India

Ans. (a) The Speaker of the Lok Sabha

Q.18 Imagine the Vice President of India presides over a session of the Rajya Sabha. During the session, a motion is introduced to amend the Constitution. As the Chairman, what would be the role of the Vice President in this situation?

(a) The Vice President can vote on the amendment if the motion is related to a financial matter.

(b) The Vice President has no role other than ensuring the smooth conduct of the session and maintaining order.

(c) The Vice President can propose the amendment to the Parliament.

(d) The Vice President can approve or reject the amendment directly.

Ans. (b) The Vice President has no role other than ensuring the smooth conduct of the session and maintaining order.

Q.19 Read the description and identify the constitutional office.

He can assume the role of the President for a maximum of six months.

(a) Attorney General (b) Vice President of India
(c) Prime Minister of India (d) Governor of a state

Ans. (b) Vice President of India

TYPE - 2 — 1 Mark

Assertion-Reason Questions

Q.1 Read the two statements given below about election of the Presdient and select the option that shows the correct relationship between (A) and (B).

Assertion (A) The President of India is elected by an electoral college.

Reason (R) The election is conducted through a proportional representation system.

(a) R contradicts A
(b) R is the reason for A
(c) A is true, but R is false.
(d) A and R are independent of each other

Ans. (b) R is the reason for A

Q.2 Read the two statements given below about the financial powers of the President and select the option that shows the correct relationship between (A) and (R).

Assertion (A) The President of India has the power to approve the budget presented by the government.

Reason (R) Money Bills can be introduced only on the recommendation of the President.

(a) R Contradicts A
(b) R is the reason for A
(c) A is true but R is false
(d) A and R are independent of each other

Ans. (d) A and R are independent of each other

Q.3 Read the two statements given below about powers of the President and select the option that shows the correct relationship between (A) and (B).

Assertion (A) The President of India has the power to dissolve the Lok Sabha.

Reason (R) The President can dissolve the Lok Sabha only on the advice of the Prime Minister.

(a) R contradicts A
(b) R is the reason for A
(c) A is true, but R is false
(d) A and R are independent of each other

Ans. (b) R is the reason for A

4. Read the two statements given below and select the option that shows the correct relationship between (A) and (R)

Assertion (A) The President holds office for a period of 5 years.

Reason (R) The Vice President of India cannot perform any other role in the Rajya Sabha other than presiding over its sessions.

(a) R contradicts A (b) R is the reason for A
(c) A is true, but R is false
(d) A and R are independent of each other

Ans. (c) A is true, but R is false

Q.5 Read the two statements given below about the power of the President and select the option that shows the correct relationship between (A) and (B).

Assertion (A) The President of India appoints the Council of Ministers.

Reason (R) The Council of Ministers is appointed by the President based on the recommendations of the Speaker.

(a) R contradicts A (b) R is the reason for A
(c) A is true, but R is false
(d) A and R are independent of each other

Ans. (c) A is true, but R is false

TYPE - 3 — 2 Marks

Very Short Answer Type Questions

Q.1 Explain how the President of India acts as the symbol of unity, integrity and solidarity of the nation.

Ans. The President of India symbolises the unity, integrity, and solidarity of the nation by serving as the Head of State and the first citizen of India.

As the constitutional authority, the President represents all sections of the country, transcending political and regional divides. This role ensures that the democratic processes function smoothly while safeguarding the values enshrined in the Constitution.

Q.2 **Which part of the Constitution describes the oath of office to the President of India? Who administers the President's oath of office?**

Ans. The oath of the President is described in Article 60 of the Constitution. The Chief Justice of India is responsible for administering the oath of office to the President.

Q.3 **Mention any two financial powers of the President of India.**

Ans. Financial powers of the President include

(i) The president appoints a Finance Commission after every five years to recommend on financial matters.

(ii) Money bill can be introduced in the Loksabha on the recommendations of the President.

Q.4 **Which category of power is being exercised by the President in the following.** **(ICSE Specimen 2025)**

(a) Approval of Bills

(b) Appointment of the Supreme Court judges

Ans. (a) **Approval of Bills** This falls under the Legislative Powers of the President.

(b) **Appointment of the Supreme Court judges** This falls under the Executive Powers of the President.

Q.5 **When was the 39th Constitutional Amendment Act introduced? What did it change regarding the President's election disputes?**

Ans. The 39th Constitutional Amendment was introduced during the 1975-77 Internal Emergency. This Act has taken away the power of the Supreme Court to settle disputes in connection with the election of the President of India.

Q.6 **Explain the meaning of the term 'Single Transferable Vote'?**

Ans. The Single Transferable Vote (STV) is an electoral system of proportional representation in which a person's vote can be transferred to the second or further competing candidate.

Q.7 **Analyse any two reasons for the indirect election of the President in india.**

Ans. The President of India is indirectly elected to maintain balance and stability in the democratic system. Two reasons for the Indirect election of the President in india are

(i) **Federal Representation** Indirect election ensures equal representation of both the Union and States in choosing the President.

(ii) **Neutrality** It maintains the President's neutrality, preventing party dominance and ensuring stability.

Q.8 **Under which Article can the President's rule be of extended beyond one year? Who approves the continuance of President's rule beyond one year?**

Ans. The President's rule can be extended beyond one year under Article 352. The Parliament approves the continuance of President's rule beyond one year.

Q.9 **Which Article is being used by the president in the following cases.**

(i) Declaring emergency on armed rebellion.

(ii) Declaring financial emergency.

Ans. (i) Article 352 is used in case of Armed Rebellion.

(ii) Article 360 is used by the president in case of the financial emergency.

Q.10 **With reference to the executive powers of the Union, explain two key executive powers vested in the President of India under the Constitution.**

Ans. The President of India exercises key executive powers, including

(i) **Appointment Power** The President appoints key officials like the Prime Minister, Council of Ministers, on the advice of prime minister, Governors, and Attorney General, ensuring proper governance.

(ii) **Power to Issue Ordinances** The President can issue ordinances when Parliament is not in session, making temporary laws in urgent situations.

Q.11 **The executive power of the Indian Union is vested in the President of India. In this context, give any two reasons for the indirect election of the President.** **(ICSE Specimen 2022)**

Ans. Reasons for the indirect election of the President are

(i) **Representation of the States** Indirect election ensures that both the Union and States are represented in the election process, fostering a sense of balance between the Centre and the States.

(ii) **Neutrality and Independence** Indirect election helps preserve the President's neutrality by preventing direct political influence, ensuring the President acts impartially without being tied to any political party.

Q.12 **Mention two executive powers of the President of India in relation to the appointment of key officials in India.**

Ans. The President of India has significant executive powers in relation to the appointment of key officials

(i) **Appointment of the Prime Minister and Council of Ministers** The President appoints the Prime Minister and, on his advice, he appoints other ministers who form the government.

(ii) **Appointment of Judges** The President appoints judges to the Supreme Court and High Court based on recommendations from the collegium of judges. These executive powers ensure proper functioning of the government and judiciary.

Q.13 How does the President exercise legislative powers during a joint sitting of both Houses of Parliament?

Ans. The President can call for a joint sitting of both Houses of Parliament to resolve deadlocks between the Lok Sabha and Rajya Sabha on a bill. In such cases, the President ensures that the legislation is passed by both Houses, fostering the legislative process.

Q.14 Imagine Sameer is the President of India. What power does he exercise when he gives assent to a bill passed by Parliament?

Ans. Sameer is exercising Legislative power. As a President, he must give his assent to a bill passed by both Houses of Parliament for it to become law. This power is essential in the legislative process, ensuring that bills are formally enacted after passing through Parliament.

Q.15 Who heads the Council of Ministers that advises the President? Which Constitutional Amendment Act made the President's decisions subject to ministerial advice?

Ans. The Prime Minister heads the Council of Ministers that advises the President. 42nd Amendment Act, 1976 made the President's decisions subject to ministerial advice.

Q.16 Discuss the following different scenarios which are related to the use of discretionary powers of the President.

(i) When does the President of India exercise discretion in appointing the Prime Minister?

(ii) What happens if the Prime Minister dies suddenly while in office?

Ans. (i) The President exercises discretion in appointing the Prime Minister when no party has a clear majority in the Lok Sabha, resulting in a hung Parliament.

(ii) If the Prime Minister dies suddenly, the President uses discretion to appoint a suitable successor to ensure the government continues to function.

Q.17 Explain about the two significant judicial powers of the President of India.

Ans. The President of India exercises two significant judicial powers which are

(i) **Granting Pardons** The President has the power to grant pardons, reprieves, respites, remissions, or commute sentences of convicted individuals.

(ii) **Appointment of Judges** The President appoints judges to the Supreme Court and High Courts based on collegium recommendations.

Q.18 Name the official procedure by which the President can be removed. **(ISCE 2016)**

Ans. The official procedure of removing President is the process of impeachment which can be initiated by either House of the Parliament for violation of the Constitution.

Q.19 Highlight the impact of National Emergency over the State Legislature?

Ans. When National Emergency is proclaimed, then the State Legislature will not be suspended, but the distribution of legislative powers between Union and State gets suspended.

Q.20 Government power to promulgate, repromulgate Ordinances - why and how An Ordinance "shall have the same force and effect as an Act of Parliament". But the government is required to bring an Ordinance before Parliament for ratification - and failure to do so will lead to its lapsing "at the expiration of six weeks from the reassembly of Parliament".

The Indian Express 25th May 2023

Mention any two points regarding an ordinance that can be deduced from the above news **(ICSE 2024)**

Ans. Two points regarding an ordinance that can be deduced from the above news are

(i) **Ordinance has the same force as an Act of Parliament** The ordinance issued by the government has the same power and effect as an Act of Parliament, meaning it can enforce laws on the same level until the legislature decides otherwise.

(ii) **Ordinance lapses if not ratified by Parliament** The government must present the ordinance to Parliament for approval within six weeks of its reassembly. If not ratified, the ordinance will lapse and cease to have legal effect after this period.

Q.21 Analyse two qualifications required for a person to be eligible for the office of the Vice-President of India.

Ans. To qualify for the office of the Vice-President of India, a candidate must meet the following criteria

(i) The candidate must be a citizen of India, ensuring that only individuals with a direct connection to the nation can hold the office.

(ii) The candidate must be at least 35 years old, which ensures that the individual has attained a certain level of maturity and experience to assume the responsibilities of the office.

Q.22 Jagdeep Dhankhar takes oath as 14th Vice-President of India, succeeds Naidu.

Business Standard, 12th August, 2022

(i) Which part of the Indian Constitution describes the oath of office for the Vice President of India?

(ii) Who administers the oath of office to the Vice President of India?

Ans. (i) The oath of office for the Vice President of India is described in Article 69 of the Indian Constitution.

(ii) The President of India administers the oath of office to the Vice President.

Q.23 State the members who participates in the election process of the following.

(i) President

(ii) Vice President

Ans. (i) **President** Elected by both Parliament and State Legislatures.

(ii) **Vice President** Elected by members of both Houses of Parliament only.

Q.24 Mr. Konar was not found eligible for the election as the Vice President of India even though he had the qualifications of being a citizen of India and not being a member of the Parliament and the State Legislature. On what grounds was he disqualified? Give two reason.

Ans. Mr. Konar was disqualified from the Vice President election due to the following reasons

(i) **Age Requirement** He did not meet the minimum age of 35 years.

(ii) **Eligibility for Rajya Sabha** He was not eligible to be a member of the Rajya Sabha.

Q.25 Name the authority which decides the following.

(i) Election Dispute of the President

(ii) Ineligibility of a member of Rajya Sabha.

Ans. (i) Supreme Court of India

(ii) Chairman of Rajya Sabha

Q.26 Who holds the authority to administer the oath of office to the Prime Minister of India, and under what circumstances can this responsibility be delegated?

Ans. The President of India has the authority to administer the oath of office to the Prime Minister. However, if the President is unable to perform this duty, the responsibility can be delegated to a person appointed by the President for this purpose.

Q.27 Mention two powers of the Vice President of India and explain their significance.

Ans. Powers of Vice President of India are as follows

(i) **Presiding over Rajya Sabha** The Vice President is the ex-officio Chairman of the Rajya Sabha and oversees its proceedings, maintaining order during debates.

(ii) **Casting Vote** The Vice President has the power to cast a vote in the event of a tie in the Rajya Sabha which help to resolve deadlocks.

Q.28 Imagine you are the Vice President of India, and the President has resigned unexpectedly. What steps would you take to ensure the continuity of the office of the President?

Ans. As the Vice President of India, I would immediately assume the role of acting President as per the Constitution, since the Vice President is the next in line to hold the office in such a scenario. I would discharge the duties of the President until a new President is elected.

Q.29 Discuss these two different scenarios which are related to the Vice President of India.

(i) When can the Vice President assume the role of the President of India?

(ii) What is the role of the Vice President when some members in Rajya Sabha do misbehaviour?

Ans. (i) If the President is unable to discharge their duties due to illness, absence, or other temporary reasons, the Vice President acts as the President until the President resumes office.

(ii) The Vice President can suspend members of the Rajya Sabha for their misbehaviour.

Q.30 Read the following passage and mention any two points regarding the impeachment of the Vice President of India that can be deduced.

The Vice President of India can be removed from office through impeachment. The process requires a resolution to be passed by a majority of the members in both Houses of Parliament. The grounds for impeachment include violation of the Constitution. If the Vice President is removed, the office becomes vacant and a new election is held.

Ans. **Impeachment Process for Vice President**

The Vice President of India can be impeached if a resolution is passed by a majority of members in both Houses of Parliament.

Grounds for Impeachment

The Vice President can be impeached on the grounds of violating the Constitution. If impeached, the office of the Vice President becomes vacant, and a new election is conducted.

TYPE - 4

3 Marks

Short Answer Type Questions

Q.1 The President and the Vice President are part of the Union Executive. In this context, answer the question. **(ICSE 2018)**

(i) Mention the role of the President in the appointment of the Prime Minister of India.

(ii) Explain the circumstances under which the Vice-President of India can act as the President.

Ans: (i) The President of India appoints the Prime Minister, usually the leader of the majority party in the Lok Sabha. However, if no party has a clear majority, the President may use discretion to appoint the person most likely to command a majority in the Lok Sabha.

(ii) The Vice President of India can act as the President in cases of resignation, death, or impeachment of the President. In such situations, the Vice-President temporarily assumes the duties of the President until a new President is elected.

Q.2 Mention three differences between the President and the Vice President of India in terms of their roles and functions.

Ans. The differences between the President and the Vice President of India in terms of roles and functions are

Aspect	President of India	Vice President of India
Role in Government	Head of the State with executive, legislative and judicial powers	Ceremonial figure and Chairman of the Rajya Sabha
Executive Functions	Holds significant executive powers (e.g., appointing Prime Minister, issuing ordinances)	Limited executive functions, mainly in Rajya Sabha.
Presiding over Parliament	Formal head of Parliament, summons and prorogues sessions	Presides over Rajya Sabha sessions, maintains order and discipline

Q.3 The executive power of the country is vested in the President. Mention any three executive powers of the President.

Ans. Three executive powers of the President are as follows

(i) The President is the head of the executive branch of the Union Government.

(ii) He/She appoints the Prime Minister and on the advice of Prime Minister, he/she appoints the Council of Ministers.

(iii) He/She exercises control over the Union's administration through the Council of Ministers headed by the Prime Minister.

Q.4 "Discretionary Power of the President is crucial in the functioning of the Indian political system". Justify your answer. **(ICSE 2020)**

Ans. The discretionary power of the President is crucial because it allows the President to take decisions in situations where no clear majority exists or during political instability.

For example, when no party has a clear mandate, the President can use discretion to appoint a Prime Minister who can command the confidence of the Lok Sabha. This power ensures that the functioning of the government is not disrupted and that the democratic process continues, even in complex political scenarios.

Q.5 Do you agree with the statement that the President of India is just a 'rubber stamp'? Justify your answer.

Ans. The statement that the President of India is just a 'rubber stamp' is not entirely accurate. While the President's role is largely ceremonial, they do possess significant powers in situations of constitutional crisis or when exercising discretion, such as appointing the Prime Minister in a hung Parliament or sending a bill for reconsideration.

The President's decisions is not always automatic and can influence critical moments in the political process, making their role more than just a 'rubber stamp'.

Q.6 Explain the circumstances under which the Vice President of India can be disqualified from office, considering both constitutional provisions and ethical standards.

Ans. The Vice President of India may be disqualified under the following circumstances

- **Violation of Constitutional Provisions** If the Vice President is found guilty of violating any provisions of the Constitution, they can be disqualified. This includes actions that undermine the integrity of the office.
- **Holding an Office of Profit** The Vice President must not hold any office of profit under the Union or State Government. If the Vice President is found to be occupying such an office, it could lead to disqualification, as it conflicts with the principle of impartiality expected from the position.

TYPE - 5

4 Marks

Long Answer Type Questions

Q.1 Discuss four key powers of the President of India in the functioning of the Union Executive.

Ans. Key powers of the President of India in the functioning of the Union Executive are

(i) **Executive Powers** The President holds executive powers, which include the appointment of key officials such as the Prime Minister, Cabinet Ministers, Governors, and judges of the Supreme Court and High Court. These powers ensure the effective administration of the Union Government.

(ii) **Legislative Powers** The President plays a critical role in the legislative process. The President summons, prorogues and dissolves Parliament.

They also give assent to bills, without which a bill cannot become a law. Additionally, the President addresses joint sessions of Parliament.

(iii) **Judicial Powers** The President exercises judicial powers, including the power to grant pardons, reprieves, respites, or remissions of punishment. They also have the authority to appoint judges to the Supreme Court and High Courts, influencing the judicial system of the country.

(iv) **Emergency Powers** The President has the authority to declare three types of emergencies-National, State and Financial-under certain conditions. These powers allow the President to address situations that threaten the security or stability of the country and its institutions.

Q.2 Analyse the role of the President's pardoning powers in the Indian legal system and its significance.

Ans. The role of the President's pardoning powers in the Indian legal system is as follows

- **Constitutional Role in Justice** The President's pardoning powers are outlined under Article 72 of the Indian Constitution. The President can grant pardons, reprieves, respites, or remissions of punishment, and suspend, remit, or commute sentences. This power ensures that justice is tempered with mercy, allowing for a compassionate review of cases where harsh punishment may not be warranted.
- **Correcting Judicial Errors** The pardoning powers provide an important check on the judicial system by offering a mechanism to correct potential judicial errors or excesses. If a person is convicted unjustly or if the sentence is excessively harsh, the President has the authority to review and mitigate the punishment.
- **National Interest and Security** The President may also use their pardoning powers in situations that align with national interest or security. For example, in cases involving political prisoners, the President can exercise discretion to ease tensions or promote national reconciliation.
- **Independent Discretion** The President's power is independent, though it is often exercised based on recommendations from the Union Cabinet. The power to grant clemency is significant as it reflects the President's role in the balance of justice, fairness and political considerations.

Q.3 Explain the role of the President's legislative powers in the functioning of Parliament.

Ans. The role of the President's legislative powers in the functioning of Parliament are as follows

- **Summoning and Proroguing Parliament** The President plays a critical role in the functioning of Parliament by summoning the sessions and proroguing them. The President also has the power to dissolve the Lok Sabha, triggering general elections. This ensures the timely and orderly conduct of legislative business.
- **Addressing Parliament** The President addresses both Houses of Parliament at the beginning of the first session after each general election and the first session of each year. This address outlines the government's policies, priorities, and legislative agenda, providing a roadmap for Parliament's legislative activities.
- **Assent to Bills** No bill passed by Parliament can become a law without the President's assent. The President can either assent to a bill, withhold
- assent, or return it (except money bills) to Parliament for reconsideration. This ensures that legislation is in compliance with the Constitution and reflects national interests.
- **Promulgating Ordinances** In situations where immediate action is required, the President has the power to promulgate ordinances when Parliament is not in session. These ordinances have the same effect as laws passed by Parliament but must be ratified within six weeks of Parliament reassembling, ensuring the continuous functioning of the legislative process.

Q.4 Mention four reasons why emergency powers given to the President are significant for the governance of India?

Ans. Emergency powers given to the President are significant for the governance of India because of the following reasons

(i) **Ensuring National Security** The President's emergency powers are crucial in situations where the country faces external aggression or internal disturbances. In such cases, the President can declare a National Emergency to safeguard the sovereignty, integrity, and security of the nation. This power allows the government to take swift action during critical times.

(ii) **Addressing Internal Disruptions** The President can declare a State Emergency (also called President's Rule) if the government in a state is unable to function according to the provisions of the Constitution. This ensures the stability of governance at the state level and prevents breakdowns in law and order.

(iii) **Maintaining Financial Stability** In times of financial crisis, the President has the power to declare a Financial Emergency. This power allows the Union Government to take control of the financial resources of the country to restore economic stability and ensure the smooth functioning of the nation's economy.

(iv) **Centralisation of Powers in Times of Crisis** Emergency powers enable the Central government to assume greater control over the functioning of state governments or other organs of governance. This centralisation is essential for maintaining unity and continuity in the administration during national or state crises.

Q.5 Describe the conditions under which a 'National Emergency' can be declared in India.

Ans. The conditions for declaring a 'National Emergency' in India are

- **External Aggression or War** The President of India can declare a National Emergency if there is a threat of external aggression or war. This situation arises when the country faces a direct military threat or is involved in a war with a foreign country. In such cases, the central government gains the authority to take necessary actions to protect national security.
- **Armed Rebellion** It is declared if there is an armed rebellion or large-scale internal violence posing a threat to India's sovereignty or security as per the 44th Amendment Act, 1978.
- **Proclamation by the President** The President of India can declare a National Emergency through a formal proclamation if there is a grave threat to India's security. This decision is made based on the advice of the Union Cabinet.
- **Approval by Parliament** Once a National Emergency is declared, it must be approved by both Houses of Parliament within one month. If Parliament does not approve the declaration within this time, the emergency ceases to be valid. This ensures that the President's declaration is subject to parliamentary scrutiny and approval.

Q.6 Highlight the significance of the Vice President of India in the functioning of the Indian political system.

Ans. The significance of the Vice President of India in the functioning of the Indian political system is as follows

- **Chairman of the Rajya Sabha** The Vice President serves as the ex-officio Chairman of the Rajya Sabha, playing a crucial role in maintaining order, decorum, and impartiality during its proceedings. This position enables the Vice President to have a direct impact on legislative processes.
- **Acting President in Certain Circumstances** In the event of the President's resignation, death, or temporary incapacity, the Vice President assumes the role of the acting President. This ensures continuity in governance and prevents any power vacuum at the top of the executive.
- **Promotes Constitutional Balance** The Vice President holds a constitutional office that supports the functioning of the Union Executive by performing duties of significant importance, such as overseeing the Rajya Sabha and performing presidential duties when necessary, thus maintaining stability in the political system.

TYPE - 6 — 10 Marks

Structured Questions

Q.1 The President is the nominal head of the executive, the first citizen of the country, as well as the commander-in-chief of the Indian Armed Forces. With reference to this, answer the following questions. **(ICSE Specimen 2025)**

(i) Mention any three qualifications required for a person to be nominated to the post of the President. **(3)**

(ii) Mention any three discretionary powers of the President. **(3)**

(iii) Describe the procedure of impeachment of the President. **(4)**

Ans. (i) Qualifications required for a person to be nominated to the post of the President of India are

(a) The person must be a citizen of India.

(b) The person must have completed the age of 35 years.

(c) The person must be qualified to be elected as a member of the Lok Sabha (i.e., they should not be disqualified for membership of the Parliament).

(ii) **The three discretionary powers of the President are**

(a) **Appointment of the Prime Minister** If no party has a clear majority in the Lok Sabha after elections, the President has the discretion to appoint the Prime Minister, usually the leader of the largest party or coalition, but can also make the decision based on their judgment of who can command the majority support in the House.

(b) **Dissolution of the Lok Sabha** The President can dissolve the Lok Sabha and call for fresh elections, typically done on the advice of the Prime Minister, but they can exercise this power if the government loses the confidence of the House.

(c) **Promulgation of Ordinances** When Parliament is not in session, the President can promulgate ordinances to make laws on matters that require urgent attention.

However, these ordinances must be approved by Parliament within six weeks of its reassembly.

(iii) **The procedure of impeachment of the President of India involves the following steps**

- **Initiation of Impeachment** The impeachment process starts when a motion is introduced in either the Lok Sabha or the Rajya Sabha. The motion must be signed by at least one-fourth of the total members of the House in which it is introduced.
- **Adoption of the Motion** The motion must be passed by a two-thirds majority in the House where it is introduced. After passing in one House, the motion is sent to the other House.
- **Investigation and Findings** The second House (where the motion is sent) investigates the charges, and the President is given an opportunity to defend themselves. The second House must also pass the motion with a two-thirds majority.
- **Final Decision** If the motion is passed in both Houses, the President is considered to have been impeached, and the impeachment is completed. The President is then removed from office.

Q.2 With reference to the post of Vice President, answer the following questions.

(i) The Vice President of India holds an important position in the functioning of the Indian Parliament. Justify the statement. **(3)**

(ii) Describe the process of election of the Vice President of India. **(3)**

(iii) In Rajya Sabha opposition will initiate impeachment notice against Vice-President Dhankhar.

The Hindu 19th December, 2024

Discuss the process of impeachment of the Vice-President. **(4)**

Ans. (i) For answer, refer to Q. 6 of Long Answer Type Questions.

(ii) The Vice President of India is elected indirectly by members of both Houses of Parliament (Rajya Sabha and Lok Sabha) through a single transferable vote system.

The eligibility conditions are the essential part of the Vice President elections, which are as follows

- The candidate must be an Indian citizen, 35 years old and qualified to be a member of the Rajya Sabha.
- The candidate needs nominations from at least 20 members.
- The candidate securing the majority of votes is declared elected.

(iii) **The Process of Impeachment of the Vice-President includes**

- **Initiation of the Motion** An impeachment motion against the Vice President can be introduced in the Rajya Sabha, as the Vice President is the Chairman of this House. The motion needs to be supported by at least one-fourth of the total members of the Rajya Sabha.
- **Approval by Majority** The motion must then be approved by a majority of the total members of the Rajya Sabha. This requires a simple majority, meaning more than half of the members present and voting in the Rajya Sabha must support the motion.
- **Transmission to Lok Sabha** Once the motion is approved in the Rajya Sabha, it is sent to the Lok Sabha (the lower house of Parliament) for its consideration. In the Lok Sabha, the motion must be supported by a majority of the members as well.
- **Final Decision by the President** If both Houses of Parliament-Rajya Sabha and Lok Sabha-approve the motion by a two-thirds majority of the members present and voting, it is then sent to the President of India for final approval. The President can then remove the Vice President from office.

Q.3 The Executive Power of the country is vested in the President and Vice President. With reference to this answer the following questions. **(ICSE Board Paper 2025)**

(i) Explain the impeachment process through which the Parliament can remove the President from power.

(ii) Mention any three powers of the Vice President in her/his role as the Chairman of the Rajya Sabha.

(iii) With reference to the powers of President, mention

(a) any two financial powers

(b) any two executive powers

Ans. (i) The President of India can be removed through impeachment under Article 61 for violating the Constitution. The process involves:

(a) **A Charge** is initiated in either House of Parliament with one-fourth of the members signing a notice.

(b) **Investigation** The charges are investigated and the President is given an opportunity to defend.

(c) **Two-thirds Majority Required** If both Houses pass the resolution with a two-thirds majority, the President is removed from office.

(ii) Three powers of the Vice President as Chairman of the Rajya Sabha are

(a) **Presiding Over Sessions** The Vice President conducts and maintains order in the Rajya Sabha.

(b) **Deciding on Points of Order** The Vice President interprets rules of procedure and ensures smooth functioning of debates.

(c) **Casting Vote in Case of a Tie** If there is a tie in voting, the Vice President (as Chairman) casts the deciding vote.

(iii) (a) Two financial powers of the President are

- **Money Bills Require Presidential Recommendation** No Money Bill can be introduced in Parliament without the President's approval.
- **Control Over the Contingency Fund** The President authorises emergency expenditures from the Contingency Fund of India.

(b) Two executive powers of the President are

- **Appointment Powers** The President appoints the Prime Minister, Governors, Chief Justice, Judges and other key officials.
- **Administration of Union Territories** The President directly administers Union Territories through Lieutenant Governors or Administrators.

3

PRIME MINISTER AND COUNCIL OF MINISTERS

The Prime Minister and the Council of Ministers together form the executive branch of the Indian government. Article 74 of the Indian Constitution states that there shall be a Council of Ministers, headed by the Prime Minister, to assist and advise the President.

The Prime Minister

- The Prime Minister is the real executive authority (de facto executive).
- The Prime Minister, as the head of the government, leads the Council of Ministers and plays a central role in policy-making and governance.

Appointment and Oath

- Article 75 states that the President appoints the Prime Minister.
- The President must appoint the leader of the majority party in the Lok Sabha as the Prime Minister.
- Before entering upon the office of Prime Minister, the President administers the oath of office and secrecy to the Prime Minister.

Term The term of the Prime Minister is 5 years.

Position and Powers of the Prime Minister

In Relation to the Council of Ministers

- The Prime Minister is the Head of the Cabinet.
- He recommends the persons to be appointed as ministers to the President.
- He allocates and reshuffles ministeries among ministers.
- He dissolves the Council of Ministers by resigning from his office.

In Relation to the President

- The Prime Minister communicates all decisions of the Council of Ministers regarding administration of union to the President.
- He advises the President with regard to the appointment of important officials, such as Comptroller and Auditor General, members of UPSC, etc.

In Relation to the Parliament

- He is the leader of the Lok Sabha in the Parliament and the chief spokesperson of the government.
- The Prime Minister can recommend dissolution of the Lok Sabha to the President at any time.

As the Leader of the Nation

- The Prime Minister represents the nation, both domestically and internationally.
- He decides the kind of relation India would have with other countries.
- He is the ex-officio Chairman of the NITI and Atomic Energy Commission.

Council of Ministers

The Union Council of Ministers exercises executive authority in India which are collectively responsible to the Lok Sabha.

Oath Before entering to the office, the President administers the oath and secrecy of office to the Council of Ministers.

Formation The 91st Amendment Act of 2003 limits the size of the Council of Ministers to 15% of the total strength of the Lok Sabha or State Legislatures.

Tenure

- The maximum term of the Council of Ministers is 5 years.
- The Prime Minister can demand a resignation from any minister or recommend to the President to do so.

Composition

The council of ministers consists of three types of ministers which are as follows

(i) **Cabinet Ministers** They are senior leaders in charge of departments like Finance, Defence, and Home Affairs. They make key decisions and advise the President on important matters.

(ii) **Ministers of State** They are junior ministers who may be given independent charge of specific department or may assist cabinet ministers.

(iii) **Deputy Ministers** They usually assist both cabinet minister and minister of state. They are placed under the guidance of senior minister to assist them in their work.

Responsibilities of the Members of the Cabinet

(i) Collective Responsibility

- Article 75 of the Constitution clearly states that the Council of Ministers is collectively responsible to the Lok Sabha. This means that all the ministers are jointly responsible to the Lok Sabha for all their acts of omission and commission.
- When the Lok Sabha passes a no-confidence motion against the Council of Ministers, all the ministers have to resign including those ministers who are from the Rajya Sabha.

(ii) Individual Responsibility

- Article 75 of the Constitution also contains the principle of individual responsibility. It states that the ministers hold the office during the pleasure of the President.

Functions of the Cabinet

- The Union Cabinet is the smaller, supreme decision-making body in India.
- It is responsible for making important government policies.
- The Cabinet, led by the Prime Minister, ensures effective policy implementation. It advises the President on critical matters.

Policy Making Functions

- The Cabinet formulates and decides on key policies affecting the nation's governance, including economic, social and international matters.

Legislative Functions

- The Cabinet drafts bills, introduces legislation in Parliament, and ensures their passage.
- It also advises the President on summoning and dissolution of the Lok Sabha.

Financial Functions

- The cabinet prepares the annual budget, approves financial policies, manages government expenditures and revenues.
- The Money Bill is introduced only after the consensus among the Cabinet.

Emergency Powers

- Under Article 352, the Cabinet advises the President to declare a National Emergency during war, external aggression or armed rebellion.
- Under Article 356, the Cabinet can recommend President's rule in a state if there is a failure of the constitutional machinery.
- Under Article 360, the Cabinet advises the President for proclamation of the Financial Emergency in case of a severe financial crisis.

Distinction Between the Council of Ministers and the Cabinet

Basis	Council of Ministers	Cabinet
Members	It includes three categories of ministers i.e. Cabinet Ministers, Ministers of State and Deputy Ministers.	It is a smaller body consisting of senior ministers who holds important portfolios such as Finance, Defence, etc.
Collective Function	It has no collective function, so that it does not meet as a body to transact government.	It has collective function so that it meets as a body to transact government business.
Supremacy of the Cabinet	Its functions are determined by the Cabinet.	It directs the Council of Ministers by taking policy decisions which are binding on all the ministers.
Implementation	It implements the decisions taken by the Cabinet	It supervises the implementation of its decisions by the Council of Ministers.
Responsibility	It is collectively responsible to the Lower House (Lok Sabha of the Parliament.)	It enforces the collective responsibility of the Council of Ministers to the Lok Sabha.

EXAM ORIENTED QUESTIONS

TYPE - 1 — 1 Mark

Multiple Choice Questions

Q.1 Identify the odd one out among the following statements related to the Prime Minister of India.
(a) The Prime Minister is the leader of the majority party in the Lok Sabha.
(b) The Prime Minister appoints the Chief Justice of India.
(c) The Prime Minister is the head of the Council of Ministers.
(d) The Prime Minister plays a key role in foreign policy decisions.

Ans. (c) The Prime Minister is the head of the Council of Ministers.

Q.2 Complete the given analogy
President : Appoints Chief Justice of India :: Prime Minister : ?
Options
(a) Presides over Rajya Sabha
(b) Appoints Governors of States
(c) Advises on the appointment of Council of Ministers
(d) Declares Financial Emergency

Ans. (c) Advises on the appointment of Council of Ministers
Exp. The President appoints the Chief Justice of India on advise of the government and collegium whereas the Prime Minister advises the President on the appointment of Council of Ministers.

Q.3 Which of the following statements are correct in the Prime Minister's role in relation to the President?
P : He is the principal advisor to the President.
Q : He can directly appoint ministers without the President's approval.
R : He advises the President regarding the appointment of important officials like the CAG and members of UPSC.
S : He plays no role in communicating the decisions of the Council of Ministers to the President.
(a) P and R are correct
(b) P and Q are correct
(c) P and S are correct
(d) P and S are correct

Ans. (a) P and R are correct

Q.4 On 15th November, 2024, the Prime Minister of India addressed the nation, explaining the government's latest policy decisions aimed at improving the economy. The Prime Minister also emphasized the role of clean energies in reducing the challenges of global warming etc. *The Hindu, 17th November, 2024*

What can be inferred about the Prime Minister's role from the above passage?
(a) The Prime Minister focuses only on economic development.
(b) The Prime Minister only addresses domestic policies, not global issues.
(c) The Prime Minister plays a role in addressing both economic and environmental challenges.
(d) The Prime Minister is not involved in shaping policies related to clean energy.

Ans. (c) The Prime Minister plays a role in addressing both economic and environmental challenges.

Q.5 With reference to the image below, who administered the oath to the Prime Minister?

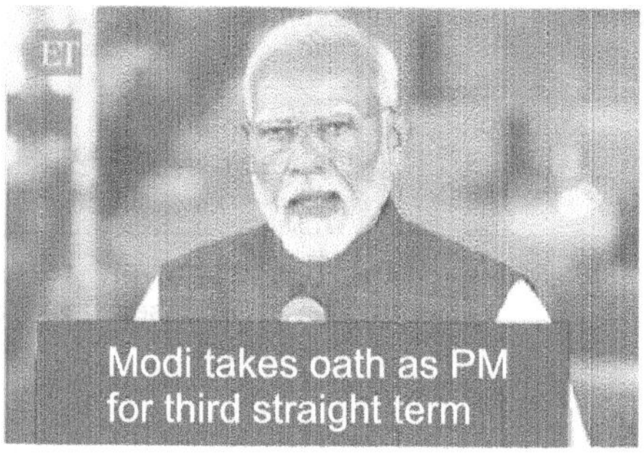

(a) The President
(b) Chief Justice of India
(c) Speaker of the Lok Sabha
(d) Vice-President of India

Ans. (a) The President

Q.6 Which of the following is true about the collective responsibility of the Council of Ministers?
(a) The Council of Ministers is responsible to the President of India for all its actions.
(b) The Council of Ministers is responsible to the Lok Sabha, and if it loses the confidence of the Lok Sabha, all members must resign.
(c) The Council of Ministers is responsible to the Rajya Sabha for all its actions.
(d) The Prime Minister is solely responsible for the actions of the Council of Ministers.

Ans. (b) The Council of Ministers is responsible to the Lok Sabha, and if it loses the confidence of the Lok Sabha, all members must resign.
Exp. Collective responsibility refers to the principle where all members of the Cabinet are collectively accountable for government decisions. If any policy fails or criticised, the entire Cabinet faces it together.

Q.7 Given below are details of few Indian citizens

Candidate	Age	Description
X	22	Citizen of China
Y	25	Citizen of India
Z	21	Member of the Rajya Sabha

Select the person who is eligible to be appointed as a member of the Cabinet from Lok Sabha in india?

(a) X (b) Y
(c) Z (d) All of these

Ans. (b) Y

Q.8 The government is facing a situation where it has lost the confidence of the majority in the Lok Sabha, and the opposition is asking to prove majority in the house. Which motion should the house move to address this situation?

(a) Adjournment Motion (b) No-confidence Motion
(c) Confidence Motion (d) Censure Motion

Ans. (b) No-confidence Motion

Exp. A no-confidence motion is used to challenge the government's authority reflecting a loss of trust in its leadership. The opposition demands this motion to hold the government accountable and force it to prove its majority or face resignation.

Q.9 Which of the following statements about the composition of the Council of Ministers is correct as amended by the 91st Amendment Act, 2003?

(a) The total number of ministers in the Council of Ministers cannot exceed 15% of the total strength of the Lok Sabha, including the Prime Minister.
(b) The Council of Ministers consist of only elected and nominated members from the Rajya Sabha.
(c) Ministers of State with independent charge have no authority as Cabinet Ministers but attend all Cabinet meetings.
(d) The number of ministers in the Council of Ministers is decided solely by the President of India, without any constraints.

Ans. (a) The total number of ministers in the Council of Ministers cannot exceed 15% of the total strength of the Lok Sabha, including the Prime Minister.

Q.10 The junior category of ministers who assist senior ministers are **(ICSE 2023)**

(a) Cabinet Ministers (b) Ministers of State
(c) Deputy Ministers (d) Council of Ministers

Ans. (c) Deputy Ministers

Exp. The junior category of ministers who assist senior ministers are known as deputy ministers. They are appointed to support and handle specific tasks under the direction of a senior ministers.

Q.11 Read the description and identify the person.
He is the head of the government and the leader of the Lok Sabha.

(a) Chief Justice of India
(b) Prime Minister of India
(c) Speaker of Lok Sabha
(d) Attorney General of India

Ans. (b) Prime Minister of India

Q.12 Which of the following is not correct about the composition of the Council of Ministers seen in the image below?

(a) It includes Cabinet Ministers, Ministers of State and Deputy Ministers.
(b) The Prime Minister is the head of the Council of Ministers.
(c) The President is a part of the Council of Ministers.
(d) Ministers of state may have independent charge or assist Cabinet Ministers.

Ans. (c) The President is a part of the Council of Ministers.

Q.13 The Council of Ministers is collectively responsible to the......... **(ICSE 2025, ICSE Specimen 2023)**

(a) Lok Sabha (b) Rajya Sabha
(c) Prime Minister (d) President

Ans. (a) Lok Sabha

TYPE - 2 1 Mark

Assertion-Reason Question

1. Read the two statements given below about the Prime Minister of India and select the option that shows the correct relationship between (A) and (R).

Assertion (A) The Prime Minister of India is the head of the government and holds significant executive powers.

Reason (R) The Prime Minister's role is primarily ceremonial, with no significant decision-making authority.

(a) R contradicts A
(b) R is the reason for A
(c) A is true but R is false
(d) A and R are independent of each other.

Ans. (c) A is true but R is false

Q.2 Read the two statements given below about powers of the Council of Ministers and select the option that shows the correct relationship between (A) and (R).

Assertion (A) The Prime Minister is the head of the Council of Ministers.

Reason (R) The Prime Minister represents the government in the states and leads the decision-making process.

(a) R contradicts A (b) R is the reason for A
(c) A is true, but R is false
(d) A and R are independent of each other

Ans. (c) A is true, but R is false

Q.3 Read the two statements given below about the Council of Ministers and select the option that shows the correct relationship between (A) and (R).

Assertion (A) The President of India appoints the Council of Ministers.

Reason (R) Article 23 states that the President appoints the Prime Minister.

(a) R contradicts A (b) R is the reason for A
(c) A is true, but R is false
(d) A and R are independent of each other

Ans. (c) A is true, but R is false

TYPE - 3

2 Marks

Very Short Answer Quetions

Q.1 Mention the procedure for the appointment of the Prime Minister of India.

Ans. The procedure for the appointment of the Prime Minister of India is as follows

(i) The President of India appoints the Prime Minister, usually the leader of the majority party or coalition in the Lok Sabha.

(ii) After the appointment, the Prime Minister takes the oath of office and secrecy.

Q.2 What is the term of office of the Prime Minister? Under what condition can it end before the completion of the term?

Ans. The term of office of the Prime Minister is 5 years. However, the President may dismiss the Prime Minister before the completion of the term if the Prime Minister loses the majority support of the Lok Sabha.

Q.3 Mention any two ways by which the authority of the Prime Minister can be checked. **(ICSE 2014)**

Ans. The authority of the Prime Minister can be checked in the following ways

(i) The Council of Ministers can check the authority of the Prime Minister by resigning collectively, forcing the Prime Minister to step down.

(ii) The Parliament can check the authority of the Prime Minister through motions like a no-confidence motion, which can lead to the removal of the Prime Minister.

Q.4 Name the authority which chairs the following institutions in India.

(i) Heads the NITI Aayog
(ii) Heads the GST Council in India

Ans. (i) Prime Minister (ii) Union Finance Minister

Q.5 Analyse the position of the Prime Minister as the leader of the majority party in the Lok Sabha.

Ans. As the leader of the majority party in the Lok Sabha, the Prime Minister holds significant influence in the legislative process. This position enables the Prime Minister to ensure the passage of key government policies and bills, as they command the support of the majority in the House.

The Prime Minister also plays a central role in setting the legislative agenda, directing discussions and coordinating efforts among ministers.

Q.6 Discuss the terms de jure and de facto executive used in the Constitution of India.

Ans. The de jure executive refers to the legal or constitutional authority vested in the President of India.

The de facto executive, on the other hand, refers to the actual power holder like which is exercised by the Prime Minister and the Council of Ministers.

Q.7 How does Article 356 allow the Cabinet to intervene in state governance?

Ans. Article 356 allow the Cabinet to intervene in state governance. Under Article 356, the Cabinet can recommend the imposition of President's Rule in a state if there is a breakdown of constitutional machinery. This allows the Cabinet to assume control of the state's administration through President.

Q.8 Identify the type of powers used in the given statements by the Prime minister.

(i) The Prime Minister is the principal advisor to the President and communicates all decisions of the Council of Ministers to the President.
(ii) Advising the President on summoning and proroguing the Parliament.

Ans. (i) Advisory Power (ii) Legislative Powers

9. Who recommends for appointment to the Council of Ministers and who administers their oath of office in India?

Ans. The Prime Minister of India recommends for the Appointment of ministers to the President. The President administers the oath of office to the Council of Ministers.

10. Explain the term collective responsibility which is used in the context of the Council of Minister.

Ans. The collective responsibility of the Cabinet means that all the ministers own collective responsibility to the Lok Sabha for all their acts of omission and commission. They work as a team together and sink together.

11. Read the given news carefully and answer the question that follow

Prime Minister's Role in Managing National Crisis
In recent months, the Prime Minister has been instrumental in steering the country through various crises, from economic challenges to international tensions. He has taken proactive measures to ensure policy continuity and has frequently addressed the nation to provide clear directives and maintain public confidence. *The Hindu - 10th January, 2025*

Mention any two roles of the Prime Minister that can be deduced from the above news.

Ans. Two roles of the Prime Minister that can be deduced from the above news are as follows

(i) **Leadership in Crisis Management** The Prime Minister plays a central role in managing national crises by taking proactive measures to address challenges, ensuring policy continuity during difficult times.

(ii) **Direct Communication with the Public** The Prime Minister frequently addresses the nation to provide clear directives, help to maintain public confidence and providing reassurance during critical situations.

Q.12 What happens if a vote of no-confidence is passed against a minister in the Lok Sabha?

Ans. When the Lok Sabha passes a no-confidence motion against minister, then all ministers have to resign including those ministers who are from the Rajya Sabha.

Q.13 Mention the different categories of ministers in the Union Council of Ministers.

Ans. The different categories of ministers in the Union Council of Ministers are

- The Cabinet Ministers
- The Ministers of State
- The Deputy Ministers

Q.14 Highlight any two legislative powers of the Cabinet. **(ICSE 2023)**

Ans. The two legislative powers of the Cabinet are as follows

(i) All major policies, decisions or amendments are moved by the Cabinet in the Parliament.

(ii) The ministers of the concerned departments answer the questions of the members of the Parliament.

Q.15 Imagine yourself as being the head of the Cabinet. You have to manage your ministers. How would you handle a situation where two key ministers are in disagreement over a major policy decision?

Ans. As the head of the Cabinet, I would handle a disagreement between two key ministers by first assessing the issue and understanding both viewpoints. I would encourage open dialogue between the ministers to reach a compromise. If needed, I would consult experts for advice and make the final decision in the best interest of the government. Finally, I would ensure unity within the Cabinet and ensure that both ministers publicly support the decision.

Q.16 Mention any two powers of the cabinet in terms of financial matters.

Ans. The two powers of the cabinet in financial matters are as follows

(i) **Preparation of the Budget** The Cabinet is responsible for preparing and presenting the Union Budget to the Parliament for the financial year.

(ii) **Approval of Financial Bills** The Cabinet approves financial bills and money bills before they are introduced in the Lok Sabha for the discussion.

Q.17 State two points of difference between the Cabinet and the Council of Ministers with reference to their responsibility to the government.

Ans. Differences between the Cabinet and the Council of Ministers are

Aspect	Cabinet	Council of Ministers
Scope of Responsibility	Responsible for key decision-making and policy formulation.	Includes all ministers; responsible for implementing policies.
Collective Responsibility	Collectively responsible to the Parliament.	Entirely accountable to the Prime Minister and Cabinet decisions.

Q.18 Mention any two powers of the Prime Minister with reference to the Cabinet.

Ans. Two powers of the Prime Minister with reference to the Cabinet are

- **Appointment and Allocation of Portfolios** The Prime Minister selects ministers and assigns them specific departments.
- **Presiding over Cabinet Meetings** The Prime Minister leads discussions and ensures decisions align with government policies.

TYPE - 4 — 3 Marks

Short Answer Type Questions

1. The head of the Council of Ministers in the country is the Prime Minister, who is the real executive head of the government.

In this context, explain the significance of the Prime Minister's role in the decision-making process.

Ans. The Prime Minister is the head of the Council of Ministers and the real executive head of the government in India. He is appointed by the President based on the majority support in the Lok Sabha.

As a leader of the majority party, the Prime Minister forms the Cabinet, oversees decision-making and ensures the implementation of policies. The Prime Minister acts as a key link between the President and the Cabinet, influencing both domestic and foreign policy.

2. Differentiate between the roles of the Prime Minister in domestic and international policymaking.

Ans. The differences between the roles of the Prime Minister in domestic and international policymaking are

Aspect	Role in Domestic Policymaking	Role in International Policymaking
Focus Area	Addresses national issues like economic growth, social welfare, law and order.	Deals with foreign relations, trade agreements and global diplomacy.
Key Responsibilities	Formulating and implementing policies for internal development and governance.	Representing India in international forums, fostering diplomatic ties.
Decision-Making	Works closely with the Cabinet and Parliament.	Collaborates with the Ministry of External Affairs and foreign diplomats.
Outcome Impact	Aims at improving the lives of Indian citizens and ensuring national stability.	Enhances India's global image and protects its international interests.

Q.3 "The resignation of the Prime Minister leads to the dissolution of the entire Council of Ministers". Justify the statement.

Ans. The Prime Minister is the head of the Council of Ministers and the central figure of the executive branch where ministers collectively holds office only on Prime Ministers' will.

When the Prime Minister resigns, the entire Council of Ministers must also resign. This is because the Prime Minister is the leader of the Council, and without their leadership, the Council cannot function.

Q.4 'Under Article 75, the Council of Ministers is collectively responsible to the Lok Sabha'. Justify this statement with any three points.

Ans. Under Article 75, the Council of Ministers is collectively responsible to the Lok Sabha.

This statement can be justified with the following points

(i) The Council of Ministers, as a team, is accountable to the Lok Sabha for all its decisions and actions. If a policy or decision fails, the entire Council must take responsibility, not just an individual minister.

(ii) If the Lok Sabha passes a vote of no-confidence against the Council of Ministers, the entire Council, including the Prime Minister, must resign. This ensures that the government reflects the will of the majority in the Lok Sabha.

(iii) The principle ensures unity in governance. Ministers cannot publicly criticise Cabinet decisions, maintaining collective solidarity and accountability to the Lok Sabha as a unified body.

Q.5 PM meets Council of Ministers; stresses on good governance, public service

Business Standard, 10th October, 2024

Who is the head of the Council of Ministers in India? Explain the composition of the Council of Ministers.

Ans. The Prime Minister is the head of the Council of Ministers in India.

The Council of Ministers consists of three categories: Cabinet Ministers, Ministers of State, and Deputy Ministers. The Cabinet is the core decision-making body, while Ministers of State may assist Cabinet Ministers or hold independent portfolios. Deputy Ministers support the work of Cabinet and State Ministers in specific areas.

TYPE - 5 — 4 Marks

Long Answer Type Questions

Q.1 The Prime Minister represents the country both in domestic and international affairs. Mention any four points highlighting the Prime Minister's role in representing the country in domestic and international affairs.

Ans. Four points highlighting the Prime Minister's role in representing the country in domestic and international affairs are as follows

(i) The Prime Minister represents the government domestically by leading discussions in the Parliament, addressing public concerns, and shaping public opinion. He act as the face of the government, making key decisions on national policies and ensuring the effective functioning of the Cabinet.

(ii) The Prime Minister plays a pivotal role in formulating and guiding national policies. He leads discussions within the Cabinet, direct the implementation of government programmess, and ensure the government's decisions align with the interests of the people.

(iii) On the global stage, the Prime Minister represents India at international forums, bilateral meetings, and summits. He gets engaged in diplomatic relations, promote India's foreign policy, and work on strengthening bilateral ties with other countries.

(iv) The Prime Minister advocates for India's interests in matters of global security, economy, and international cooperation. He engage in trade negotiations, support India's position on key global issues, and play a vital role in shaping the country's global image.

Q.2 The Prime Minister can only recommends about persons who can be appointed as ministers by the President. Justify the statement with suitable reasons.

Ans. Four reasons that justify the above statement are

(i) The Prime Minister is the leader of the majority party in the Lok Sabha and has the responsibility of forming a government. As the head of the government, the Prime Minister is in the best position to recommend individuals who are suitable for various ministerial roles.

(ii) The Prime Minister has a clear understanding of the government's needs and the required expertise in different sectors. By recommending suitable candidates, the Prime Minister ensures effective coordination between various ministries and the smooth functioning of the government.

(iii) The Prime Minister has the authority to allocate specific portfolios to the ministers. Based on the needs of the government, the Prime Minister selects individuals who have the knowledge and capability to handle those specific responsibilities.

(iv) The Prime Minister's recommendations help ensure the stability and cohesion of the government. By selecting ministers who are trusted and capable, the Prime Minister ensures that the government can function efficiently and maintain its majority support in the Lok Sabha.

Q.3 With reference to the Council of Minister, explain the following

(i) Collective Responsibility

(ii) Individual Responsibility

Ans. (i) Article 75 of the Constitution clearly states that the Council of Ministers is collectively responsible to the Lok Sabha. This means that all the ministers are jointly responsible to the Lok Sabha for all their acts of omission and commission. When the Lok Sabha passes a no-confidence motion against the Council of Ministers, all the ministers have to resign including those ministers who are from the Rajya Sabha.

(ii) Article 75 of the Constitution also contains the principle of individual responsibility. It states that the ministers hold the office during the pleasure of the President.

Q.4 Highlight the role of the Prime Minister in the functioning of the Council of Ministers.

Ans. The role of the Prime Minister in the functioning of the Council of Ministers is as follows

- As the head of the government, the Prime Minister leads the Council and is responsible for ensuring that the government's policies and decisions are effectively implemented.
- The Prime Minister is responsible for recommending individuals for ministerial positions to the President and allocating portfolios to ministers.
- The Prime Minister is also responsible for coordinating the work of various ministries and resolving any conflicts between them.
- Additionally, the Prime Minister represents the Council of Ministers in the Lok Sabha and is the chief spokesperson of the government.

TYPE - 6 — 10 Marks

Structured Questions

Q.1 **The Council of Ministers headed by the Prime Minister, is the most powerful institution in the Indian Polity. In this context, answer the following.**

(i) State briefly the position of the Prime Minister in the Parliamentary system of Government. State any two powers of the Prime Minister as a leader of the nation. (3)

(ii) PM Modi tasks entire Council of Ministers to develop resources for further improving governance. *16th Nov., 2024, The Hindu*

"The Council of Ministers is the real power holder in India's parliamentary system". Justify this statement. (3)

(iii) Mention any four functions of the Cabinet. (4)

Ans. (i) The Prime Minister, with the backing of the majority party or groups in the Parliament, is the real executive head of the nation (i.e. de-facto head). The powers of the Prime Minister as a leader of the nation are

(a) The Prime Minister decides the kind of relation India would have with other countries.

(b) PM protects the interest of the country in international forums.

(ii) The Council of Ministers is the real power holder in India's Parliamentary system due to its pivotal role in governance and decision-making because of the following reasons

(a) **Executive Authority** The Council of Ministers, led by the Prime Minister, exercises executive powers in the name of the President. They formulate and implement policies, manage national administration, and make decisions on critical issues.

(b) **Collective Responsibility** The Council of Ministers is collectively responsible to the Lok Sabha. This means the government's survival depends on the confidence of the majority in the lower house, ensuring that real authority rests with the council only.

(c) **Policy Formulation and Legislation** The Council drafts and introduces bills in Parliament, controls legislative business, and advises the President on ordinances making when Parliament is not in session.

(iii) The Council of Ministers holds the real power in India's parliamentary system becauses of the following reasons.

(a) All major appointments to various key posts are made by the President are advised by the Cabinet.

(b) The Cabinet/ministers' co-ordinates the functioning of various ministries for smooth implementation of government policies.

(c) All major policies, decisions or amendments are moved by the Cabinet in the Parliament.

(d) The ministers of the concerned departments answer the questions of the Members of the Parliament.

Q.2 There is no Council of Ministers without the Prime Minister. With reference to the Prime Minister and council of ministers, answer the following questions.

(i) "The Prime Minister serves as the key link between the President and the Council of Ministers". Justify this statement. (3)

(ii) How does the Prime Minister of India ensure coordination and unity within the Council of Ministers? (3)

(iii) "Prime Minister calls for a Cabinet meeting to address national security concerns amidst rising tensions". *The Daily Times, January 2025.*

Based on the Prime Minister's role, explain his responsibilities in times of crisis. (4)

Ans. (i) The Prime Minister acts as the key link between the President and the Council of Ministers, ensuring that the President is kept informed about Cabinet decisions.

This role is critical in a parliamentary democracy where the President functions as the nominal head, while the Council of Ministers exercises real power.

The Prime Minister advises the President on crucial appointments, such as those of ministers and high-ranking officials, and ensures that the government's policies and administrative affairs are taken properly. This connection enables smooth governance and the effective functioning of the executive branch.

(ii) The Prime Minister plays a pivotal role in ensuring coordination and unity within the Council of Ministers by acting as the head of the executive branch. By presiding over meetings of the Council, the Prime Minister sets the agenda, resolves conflicts between ministries and provides a unified direction on governance.

As the leader of the ruling party, the Prime Minister ensures that the ministers adhere to collective responsibility and align with the government's policy priorities, fostering collaboration and coherence in decision-making.

(iii) The responsiblities of the Prime Minister in times of crisis are

- During a national crisis, the Prime Minister assumes the role of the chief crisis manager and decision-maker.
- As the leader of the Cabinet, the Prime Minister coordinates with key ministries such as Home, Defense, and External Affairs to formulate strategies and implement measures.
- The Prime Minister ensures that resources are mobilised effectively, maintains communication with the President to Parliament and addresses the nation to instill confidence.
- By exercising leadership and providing a clear vision, the Prime Minister safeguards national interests and ensures stability during challenging times

THE SUPREME COURT

- India's judicial system is made up of courts that interpret the law. It also provides a mechanism for the resolution of disputes.
- The Indian Constitution provides a single, integrated judicial system for both the Union and the States, where all courts (High Courts and Lower Courts) operate under one framework.

The Supreme Court

- It is the supreme Judicial body of India and the highest court of the Republic of India under Indian Constitution.
- It was inaugurated on 28th January, 1950. The seat of the Supreme Court is in Delhi.

Composition The Supreme Court consists of 34 Judges in which there is 1 Chief Justice and 33 other Judges.

Qualifications of Judges

A person to be appointed as a Judge of the Supreme Court should

- Be a citizen of India.
- Have been the Judge of a High Court for at least five years.
- Have been an advocate of a High Court for at least ten years.
- Be a distinguished jurist in the opinion of the President.

Appointment

Chief Justice and Other Judges The President of India appoints the Chief Justice and Judges of the Supreme Court, after consulting with the Chief Justice and other relevant judges.

Acting Chief Justice Article 126 states that the President can appoint a Judge of the Supreme Court as an acting Chief Justice of India when the office of Chief Justice is vacant.

Ad hoc Judges

- Under Article 127, if there is lack of permanent judges to hold or continue a session of the Supreme Court, the Chief Justice can appoint a High Court Judge as an Ad hoc Judge for a temporary period.
- This appointment is made with the prior consent of the President.
- The Chief Justice of the concerned High Court must also be consulted before the appointment.

Term of Office Judges of the Supreme Court hold office upto the age of 65 years.

Removal of Judges

- A Supreme Court Judge can be removed for misbehavior or incapacity.
- An impeachment motion for removal must be signed by 100 Lok Sabha or 50 Rajya Sabha members and approved by a two-thirds majority.
- After both Houses approve, the President of India formally removes the Judge from office.

Independence of Judiciary from the Control of Executive and Legislature

The Constitution of India has made some provisions to safeguard and ensure the independence of judiciary which are as follows

- **Appointment of Judges** The Judges of the Supreme Court are appointed by the President after consulting the other Judges of the Supreme Court and the High Court. This process reduces the interference of Executive and Political considerations.
- **Security of Tenure** The Judges of the Supreme Court are removed by the President only in the manner and the grounds mentioned in the Indian Constitution.
- **Salaries and Emoluments** The salaries and other emoluments of the Judges cannot be changed except in case of Financial Emergency.
- **Conduct of Judges** The Constitution of India provides that the conduct of the Judges of the Supreme Court cannot be discussed in the Parliament or in the State Legislature.

Jurisdictions and Functions of the Supreme Court

- **Original Jurisdiction** Original jurisdiction means the power of the Supreme Court to hear and determine a dispute in the first instance. These cases include centre-state or inter-state disputes.
- **Appellate Jurisdiction**
  - The Supreme Court is primarily a court of appeal.
  - The appellate jurisdiction of the Supreme Court allows it to hear appeals against decisions made by lower courts, such as High Courts.
  - The appellate jurisdiction of the Supreme Court extends to the cases involving constitutional issues, civil disputes, criminal matters or other significant legal questions.
- **Advisory Jurisdiction** Under Article 143, the Constitution of India authorises the President to seek the opinion of the Supreme Court on the following matters
  - Any question of law or fact of public importance which has arisen or which is likely to arise.
  - Any dispute arising out of any pre-constitution treaty, agreement, engagement, etc.
- **Revisory Jurisdiction** According to Article 137, the Supreme Court has power to review its own judgement to remove any mistake or error.
- **Court of Record** The judgements, proceedings and acts of the Supreme Court are recorded for perpetual memory and testimony. These records cannot be questioned when produced before any court.
- **Judicial Review** The Supreme Court is the sole interpreter of the Constitution, it has the power to review any laws or ordinance passed by the Union or State Legislature.

Enforcement of Fundamental Rights and Writs

Fundamental Rights, guaranteed under Part III of the Indian Constitution, can be enforced by the Supreme Court according to Article 32. If they are violated, individuals can approach the judiciary for remedy and writs. There are 5 types of writs, these are

- **Habeas Corpus** A writ issued to produce a person who has been unlawfully detained before the court.
- **Mandamus** A writ commanding a public authority to perform a duty that it has failed to perform.
- **Prohibition** A writ issued by a higher court to a lower court or tribunal to prevent it from exceeding its jurisdiction.
- **Quo Warranto** A writ issued to inquire if someone has the legal right to hold a public office.
- **Certiorari** A writ issued by a higher court to cancel the order, decision of a lower court or tribunal acting beyond its authority.

EXAM ORIENTED QUESTIONS

TYPE - 1   1 Mark

Multiple Choice Questions

Q.1 Identify the correct statement about the Supreme Court of India:
(a) The Supreme Court of India is not the highest court of appeal under the Constitution of India.
(b) The Supreme Court was inaugurated on 28th January, 1950.
(c) The Supreme Court is located in Mumbai.
(d) Supreme court is subordinate to the High Court.

Ans. (b) The Supreme Court was inaugurated on 28th January, 1950.

Q.2 Which of the following is the highest judicial authority in India whose decisions are binding on all Courts?
(a) Supreme Court (b) Law Minister
(c) Parliament (d) Lok Sabha

Ans. (a) Supreme Court

Q.3 The composition of the Supreme court is ....
(a) 33 Judges +1 Chief Justice
(b) 32 Judges +1 Chief Justice
(c) 31 Judges +1 Chief Justice
(d) 30 Judges +1 Chief Justice

Ans. (a) 33 Judges +1 Chief Justice

Q.4 Complete the given analogy.
High Court Judge : 62 years : Supreme Court Judge : ?
(a) 65 year (b) 64 years (c) 63 years (d) 66 years

Ans. (a) 65 year

Q.5 Identify the incorrect option from the following which is not the part of Higher judiciary in India
(a) High Court Judge
(b) District Judge
(c) Supreme Court Judge
(d) Chief Justice of the High Court

Ans. (b) District Judge

Q.6 Which among the following is not a criteria for being eligible to be a Judge of the Supreme Court?
(a) Judge of one High Court or more (continuously), for at least five years.
(b) An advocate of the High Court for at least ten years.
(c) A distinguished jurist in the opinion of the President.
(d) Above 40 years of age.

Ans. (d) Above 40 years of age.

Q.7 Given below are details of a few individuals

Person	Age	Description
W	40	Is a High Court Judge for 4 years
X	48	Is an advocate of a High Court for 7 years
Y	50	Is a distinguished jurist
Z	38	Is a foreign citizen

Select the one who is eligible to be appointed as a Judge of the Supreme Court.
(a) W (b) X
(c) Y (d) Z

Ans. (b) X

Q.8 Your school is conducting a poster-making competition on the topic – 'The Independence of the Judiciary in India'.
Which of the following would most likely be featured in the poster as an idol for the independence of the judiciary?
(a) Lal Bahadur Shastri (b) Mahatma Gandhi
(c) CJI D.Y. Chandrachud (d) Sardar Vallabhbhai Patel

Ans. (c) CJI D.Y. Chandrachud

Exp. Chief Justice of India D.Y. Chandrachud emphasised the independence of the judiciary as vital for democracy. He advocated that impartiality, free decision-making, and safeguarding constitutional values is core motive of the Judiciary.

Q.9 Look at the picture given below and answer the question.

When Supreme Court checks the legitimacy of Parliamentary laws, that power is known as
(a) Judicial review (b) Original jurisdiction
(c) Appellate jurisdiction (d) Advisory jurisdiction

Ans. (a) Judicial review

Q.10 When the Supreme Court reviews any judgement made by it to remove an error, it falls under .... jurisdiction. **(ICSE 2023)**

(a) Advisory (b) Revisory
(c) Original (d) Appellate

Ans. (b) Revisory

Q.11 14th December, 2024, CJI said, the Supreme Court of India holds the distinction of being the highest judicial authority in the country. It is the guardian of the Constitution and ensures that the laws are interpreted and applied in the most effective manner. The court has the power to take up cases that involve disputes between the Union and states, as well as inter-state conflicts. *The Hindu*

Which of the following can be inferred from the passage regarding the role of the Supreme Court of India?

(a) It only handles constitutional matters and has no role in ordinary cases.
(b) It is essential for maintaining the balance between the Union and states, as well as protecting citizens' rights.
(c) Its role is limited to issuing writs for fundamental rights enforcement.
(d) Its decisions are not considered important in shaping India's legal system.

Ans. (b) It is essential for maintaining the balance between the Union and states, as well as protecting citizens' rights.

Q.12 Identify the statements that are correct about the powers of the Supreme Court.

P : The Supreme Court has the power of judicial review over laws passed by Parliament.
Q : The Supreme Court can dissolve the Lok Sabha if it fails to function properly.
R : The Supreme Court can issue writs to enforce Fundamental Rights under Article 32.
S : The Supreme Court can't act as an advisory body to the President in legal matters.

Codes

(a) P and R (b) Q and S (c) R and S (d) P and Q

Ans. (a) P and R

Q.13 In case of a dispute between two or more states regarding their legal rights, who has the authority to resolve the issue?

(a) The concerned states must resolve the dispute themselves.
(b) The President of India will resolve the dispute.
(c) The Supreme Court has the original jurisdiction to resolve such disputes.
(d) The High Court of the state where the dispute originated will resolve it.

Ans. (c) The Supreme Court has the original jurisdiction to resolve such disputes.

Q.14 Imagine you are a judge in the Supreme Court of India, looking at a case where a law that limits free speech is being challenged. The person filing the case argues that this law goes against their fundamental rights. under Article 19(1) (a).

Which factor would most likely guide your decision on the constitutionality of the law?

(a) Whether the law imposes a threat to article 19 or not
(b) The popularity of the law among the public.
(c) The political affiliation of lawmakers.
(d) The number of previous challenges to the law.

Ans. (a) Whether the law imposes a threat to article 19 or not.

Q.15 Identify the person who is associated with the quote, 'Justice delayed is Justice denied'?

(a) Mahatma Gandhi (b) A.V. Dicey
(c) William E. Gladstone (d) None of these

Ans. (c) William E. Gladstone

Exp. The phrase 'Justice delayed is justice denied' highlights that delaying justice amounts to denying it, as prolonged resolutions can harm victims and undermine trust in the legal system.

Q.16 With reference to the news headline below, which body plays a key role in recommending the appointment of judges to the Supreme Court?

SC flags delay in appointment of judges

Bench seeks details on 213 names pending with government and Collegium

Empty chairs

38% of all sanctioned posts for judges in High Courts are lying vacant as of December 1, 2019. The six HCs with most vacancies

Name of High Court	Sanctioned strength	Working strength	Vacancies	% of vacancies
A.P.	37	15	22	59.46
Rajasthan	50	21	29	58
J&K	17	8	9	52.94
Patna	53	27	26	49.06
Odisha	27	14	13	48.15
Gujarat	52	28	24	46.15

(a) Lok Sabha (b) Rajya Sabha
(c) Collegium System (d) State Legislative Assemblies

Ans. (c) Collegium System

Q.17 With reference to the Supreme Court of India, complete the following

Advisory Jurisdiction: Advice the President:: Judicial Review .... **(ICSE 2025)**

(a) Review its own judgements.
(b) Review the judgements of the High Cout.
(c) Review the laws passed by the Parliament.
(d) Review the administration of the Government.

Ans. (c) Review the laws passed by the Parliament.

Q.18 Complete the given analogy.

Mandamus : We command : : Prohibition : ?

(a) Quo Warranto (b) To be certified
(c) Forbid (d) Shall have the body

Ans. (c) Forbid

TYPE - 2 1 Mark

Assertion-Reason Questions

Q.1 Read the two statements given below about the writ jurisdiction powers of Supreme Court and select the option that shows the correct relationship between (A) and (R).

Assertion (A) The Supreme Court of India has the authority to issue writs for the enforcement of Fundamental Rights.

Reason (R) Writ jurisdiction of the Supreme Court is exercised under Article 32 of the Constitution.

(a) R Contradicts A
(b) R is the reason for A
(c) A is true but R is false
(d) A and R are independent of each other

Ans. (b) R is the reason for A

Q.2 Read the two statements given below about the Court of Record and select the option that shows the correct relationship between (A) and (R).

Assertion (A) The Supreme Court of India is a Court of Record, meaning its decisions are considered authoritative and binding.

Reason (R) A Court of Record's decisions are not only binding within its jurisdiction but can also be cited as precedents in other courts.

(a) R Contradicts A
(b) R is the reason for A
(c) A is true but R is false
(d) A and R are independent of each other

Ans. (b) R is the reason for A

Q.3 Read the two statements given below about the Powers of the Supreme Court and select the option that shows the correct relationship between (A) and (R).

Assertion (A) The Supreme Court of India has the power to strike down any law that is inconsistent with the Constitution.

Reason (R) The power of judicial review allows the Supreme Court to examine the constitutionality of laws and executive actions.

(a) R contradicts A (b) R is the reason for A
(c) A is true but R is false
(d) A and R are independent of each other

Ans. (b) R is the reason for A

Q.4 Read the two statements given below about the Powers of the Supreme Court and select the option that shows the correct relationship between (A) and (R)

Assertion (A) The power of judicial review in India is vested in the Supreme Court and High Courts.

Reason (R) Judicial review allows courts to declare laws unconstitutional if they violate fundamental rights or other provisions of the Constitution.

(a) R contradicts A
(b) R is the reason for A
(c) A is true but R is false
(d) A and R are independent of each other

Ans. (b) R is the reason for A

Q.5 Read the two statements given below about the Powers of the Supreme Court and select the option that shows the correct relationship between (A) and (R).

Assertion (A) The Supreme Court has the power to review its jurisdiction, which allows it to correct any errors or mistakes.

Reason (R) The Supreme Court consists of 20 judges.

(a) R contradicts A
(b) R is the reason for A
(c) A is true but R is false
(d) A and R are independent of each other

Ans. (c) A is true but R is false

TYPE - 3 2 Marks

Very Short Answer Type Questions

1. Analyse the meaning of the term 'single integrated judiciary'.

Ans. A single integrated judiciary refers to a court system where all courts (local, high and supreme court) are well interconnected and operate as part of one unified structure. It contributes to a more efficient and accessible justice system by maintaining harmony in legal decisions across different levels of the judiciary.

Q.2 Mention any two ways in which the Constitution ensures the independence of the Judiciary from the Executive. **(ICSE 2023)**

Ans. The independence of the Judiciary is ensured through the following

(i) The salaries and other emoluments of the Judges cannot be changed to their disadvantage during their term of office, except in case of financial emergency.

(ii) The judges are appointed by President only after the consultation with CJI and other judges of the Supreme or High Courts.

Q.3 **Who appoints the Chief Justice of the Supreme Court and under what circumstances the salaries and allowances of the Supreme Court Judges can be reduced?**

Ans. The President of India appoints the Chief Justice of the Supreme Court.The allowances can be reduced only at the times of Financial emergency.

Q.4 **"In a recent ruling, the Supreme Court of India emphasised the importance of judicial independence, stating that the judiciary must be free from any external pressure to uphold the rule of law and protect citizens' rights. The court emphasised that any attempts to interfere with the judicial appointments process would undermine the foundational principles of the Constitution."** *The Hindu*

Why does the independence of the judiciary important?

Ans. The independence of the judiciary is important for the following reasons

- It allows judges to make decisions based on the law and facts, free from external influences like political pressure or public opinion.
- An independent judiciary protects individuals' fundamental rights by checking any arbitrary actions, laws of the government or of any other authority.

Q.5 **Imagine you are a legal advisor in the Ministry of Law and Justice, and a report emerges accusing a Supreme Court judge of misconduct. How would you ensure that the conduct of the judge is examined while maintaining the independence of the judiciary?**

Ans. To maintain the integrity of the judicial system while ensuring fairness, the following steps should be taken

- **Initiate Constitutional Process** Follow the impeachment process and ensures the action is in line with constitutional provisions.
- **Form an In-House Committee** Set up an independent committee of senior judges to investigate the allegations impartially and to preserve judicial autonomy.

Q.6 **What is the process for the impeachment of a Judge of the Supreme Court of India?**

Ans. The process for the impeachment of a Judge of the Supreme Court of India is as follows

- An impeachment motion must be introduced in either the Lok Sabha or the Rajya Sabha. It requires the support of at least 100 members in the Lok Sabha or 50 members in the Rajya Sabha.
- Then it is to be approved by Parliament with two-thirds majority, and sent to the President of India, who has the authority to remove the Judge from office.

Q.7 **Under what conditions, a Judge of the Supreme Court of India can leave his office?**

Ans. A Judge can leave his office before reaching the retirement age in two conditions

(i) **Resignation** A judge can voluntarily resign from their position at any time before reaching 65.

(ii) **Impeachment** A judge can be removed from office through a formal impeachment process if they are found guilty of misconduct or incapacity.

Q.8 **When a judicial system is correctly calibrated, the law is applied by judges fearlessly, without favour or fear and with respect. That is why judicial security of tenure is so fundamental. It is also why judges must be properly paid without any interference from the Executive or Legislature.**

(The Need for Independent Judiciary) UNODC

From the passage, deduce and mention any two ways in which the Constitution ensures the independence of the Judiciary. **(ICSE 2025)**

Ans. Two ways in which the Constitution ensures the independence of the Judiciary are

- **Security of Tenure** Judges cannot be removed arbitrarily; they can only be removed through impeachment on grounds of proven misconduct.
- **Financial Independence** Judges' salaries and allowances are charged on the Consolidated Fund of India, ensuring they are not controlled by the Executive or Legislature.

Q.9 **Analyse the meaning of the term 'appellate jurisdiction'.**

Ans. Appellate jurisdiction refers to the authority of a higher court to review and potentially change the decision of a lower court. In this type of jurisdiction, the higher court does not conduct a new trial but reviews the case based on the record and legal arguments presented in the lower court.

Q.10 **Explain the meaning of the term 'judicial review'.**

Ans. Judicial review is the power of the Supreme Court to examine whether laws and ordinances passed by the legislature or executive are consistent with the Constitution of India. If a law or ordinance violates the principles or provisions of the Constitution, the Supreme Court can declare it invalid or unconstitutional.

Q.11 **Mention the Articles which empowers the Supreme court in the following cases.**

(i) Judicial Review (ii) Original Jurisdiction

Ans. (i) Article 13, 32, 131-136 and 226 empowers Supreme Court for judicial review in India.

(ii) Article 131 is related to original jurisdiction powers of the Supreme Court.

Q.12 Name two courts that are empowered to issue writs for enforcement of Fundamental Rights? **(ICSE 2020)**

Ans. Two courts that are empowered to issue writs for enforcement of Fundamental Rights are Supreme Court (under Article 32) and High Court (under Article 226).

Q.13 Name any two writs issued by the Supreme Court of India.

Ans. Two writs issued by the Supreme Court are

(i) Mandamus (ii) Quo warranto

Q.14 Mention any two matters that are outside the original jurisdiction of the Supreme Court.

Ans. Two matters that are outside the original jurisdiction of the Supreme Court are

(i) A dispute arising out of any pre-constitution treaty, agreement other similar instrument.

(ii) Matters related to the disputes between a state and its citizens.

Q.15 "On 24th November, 2024, the Supreme Court of India has ordered the government to take decisive action on the increasing air pollution in Delhi, including the implementation of a 'graded response action plan'. The court highlighted the urgent need for both the Union and State governments to work together to address this growing environmental issue". *XYZ Express*

How can the Supreme Court's directive on air pollution influence the role of both Union and State governments in environmental management?

Ans. The Supreme Court's directive can influence the role of the Union and State governments by emphasising the need for a unified approach to environmental management. This cooperative model ensures a more effective and streamlined response to the crisis.

Q.16 Imagine you are the Chief Justice of India, and a major case, involving the rights of workers in hazardous industries is brought before the Supreme Court. How would you ensure that the decision taken by the court balances both workers' safety and the economic interests of industries?

Ans. As the Chief Justice of India, I would ensure that the decision protects workers' safety by enforcing strict regulations, while also considering the economic interests of industries. The ruling would aim to create a balance, encouraging industries to adopt safer practices without hindering growth.

TYPE - 4

3 Marks

Short Answer Type Questions

Q.1 The Supreme Court is the apex court of our country. In this context, explain the following.

The evolution of composition in the Supreme Court of India.

Ans. The evolution of composition of the Supreme Court of India is as follows

- Originally, the strength of the Supreme Court was fixed at 8 (1 Chief Justice and 7 other Judges).
- The Parliament has increased the number of other Judges progressively to 10 in 1956, 13 in 1960, 17 in 1977 and 25 in 1986.
- In February 2009, the Judges were increased to 31 and in 2019, it increased to 33 excluding 1 Chief Justice.

Q.2 'The Collegium system influences the appointment process of Judges to the Supreme Court.' Mention any three of its key features.

Ans. Collegium system is a method of appointing and transferring judges that was developed by the Supreme Court rulings. Its key features are as follows

(i) **Composition and Role** The Collegium, consist of the Chief Justice of India (CJI) and the four senior-most judges, who recommends for appointments to the Supreme Court on merit and integrity basis.

(ii) **Judicial Independence** It ensures independence by reducing executive influence over judicial appointments and maintaining the integrity of the judiciary.

(iii) **Approval Process** The recommendations are sent to the President of India for approval, with limited scope for objections from the government.

Q.3. Analyse the term of office and the process for removing a judge from the Supreme Court of India.

Ans. A Supreme Court judge holds office until the age of 65. To remove a judge, there must be a motion for impeachment due to misbehaviour or incapacity. This motion needs to be signed by 100 Lok Sabha or 50 Rajya Sabha members.

After the motion is passed by a two-thirds majority in both Houses of Parliament, the President formally removes the judge from office. This process ensures that judges are only removed through a constitutional procedure, maintaining their independence and security during their tenure.

Q.4 Analyse the meaning of 'the independent judiciary' and 'the need to do so'.

Ans. The meaning of independent of judiciary is that the Judiciary is free to work without the influence of other forms of government like executive and legislature.

The need for an independent judiciary because

- In a representative democracy, the independence of the judiciary is essential to protect any violation of the rights of people.
- In a federal set-up, there is a constitutional division of powers between the government. Thus, an independent and impartial judiciary is essential for proper check and balance.

Q.5. 'Security of tenure is important in preserving the independence of the judiciary'. Justify this by mentioning any three points.

Ans. Security of tenure is important in preserving the independence of the judiciary for several reasons

(i) **Protection from External Influence** Judges can make decisions without fear as they cannot be removed easily by the government or legislature.

(ii) **Impartiality and Fairness** Knowing their position is secure, judges can deliver impartial judgments based solely on law and free from outside pressure.

(iiii) **Stability in Legal System** Security of tenure ensures consistency in judicial rulings, promoting a stable and predictable legal system.

Q.6 Highlight the role of the Supreme Court in resolving disputes between the Union and States and how does it exercise its original jurisdiction in such cases?

Ans. The Supreme Court of India plays a key role in resolving disputes between the Union and States by interpreting the Constitution and ensuring the balance of power in India's federal system.

Under its original jurisdiction, the court directly hears such disputes, by passing lower courts. This includes conflicts over issues like resource distribution and legislative powers, etc. The Supreme Court's rulings clarify the roles and powers of the Union and States, ensuring that the Constitutional framework is upheld and the federal balance is maintained.

Q.7 Discuss the concept of Judicial Review in India. How does the Supreme Court use its power of judicial review to ensure the constitutionality of laws passed by the Union or State Legislature?

Ans. Judicial Review in India means the power of the Supreme Court to examine and decide whether laws passed by the Union or State Legislatures are in line with the Constitution.

If a law violates the Constitution, the Supreme Court can declare it unconstitutional and invalid. This ensures that the laws do not harm citizens' fundamental rights and uphold the Constitution's principles. Through Judicial Review, the Supreme Court acts as a guardian of the Constitution, ensuring that legislative actions remain within the boundaries set by it.

Q.8 Analyse the role of the Supreme Court in enforcing Fundamental Rights in India. How does the judiciary provide remedies to individuals whose rights are violated?

Ans. The Supreme Court of India plays a crucial role in protecting Fundamental Rights guaranteed by the Constitution. If someone's rights are violated, the Supreme Court provides a remedy under Article 32. People can directly approach the Court for justice.

The Court can issue writs like Habeas Corpus (to free someone unlawfully detained), Mandamus (to force authorities to act), and others to ensure rights are protected. This power makes the judiciary an essential guardian of individual freedoms in India, ensuring that laws and actions respect Constitutional rights.

TYPE - 5 — 4 Marks

Long Answer Type Questions

Q.1 Justify the importance of the composition of the Supreme Court of India in maintaining judicial independence and impartiality.

Ans. The composition of the Supreme Court of India is crucial in maintaining judicial independence and impartiality because of the following reasons

- **Diverse Representation** The court includes Judges from various legal backgrounds and experiences, ensuring that decisions are well-rounded, fair and represent all perspectives of law.

- **Leadership of the Chief Justice** The Chief Justice of India (CJI), (as the highest-ranking judge), provides strong leadership, guides the Court and ensures its independence from the executive and legislature.
- **Independence from Political Influence** The Collegium system for judicial appointments minimises executive influence, ensuring judges are appointed based on merit and legal expertise, not on political considerations.
- **Ensuring Fairness and Impartiality** With a diverse bench and structured leadership, the composition guarantees that the Supreme Court can make impartial decisions, uphold the Constitution and protect citizens' rights.

Q.2 "Article 32 is the spirit and soul of the Indian Constitution", said B.R. Ambedkar. Justify this statement.

Ans. Dr. B.R. Ambedkar described Article 32 as the 'spirit and soul' of the Indian Constitution because of its various provisions which are as follows

- **Right to Constitutional Remedies** Article 32 allows citizens to directly approach the Supreme Court if their Fundamental Rights are violated.
- **Judicial Safeguard for Rights** It ensures that Fundamental Rights are meaningful by providing an effective remedy through the courts.
- **Writ Powers** The Supreme Court has the authority to issue writs under Article 32 to enforce fundamental rights, reinforcing its role as a guardian of justice.
- **Role of the Supreme Court** It emphasises the Supreme Court's role as the ultimate protector of the Constitution and citizens' rights.

Q.3 The appellate jurisdiction of the Supreme Court is wider than its writ jurisdiction. Analyse this statement by stating any four differences between appellate jurisdiction and writ jurisdiction of the Supreme Court of India.

Ans. Appellate jurisdiction and writ Jurisdiction are two distinct types of powers exercised by the Supreme Court and High Courts of India. While both are crucial in ensuring justice, they differ in their purpose, scope, and type of relief provided.

The differences between appellate jurisdiction and writ jurisdiction are as follows

Aspect	Appellate Jurisdiction	Writ Jurisdiction
Nature of Jurisdiction	Deals with appeals against decisions made by lower courts.	Deals with the enforcement of Fundamental Rights and checks government actions.
Purpose	Aims to correct errors or review decisions made by lower courts.	Aims to provide immediate relief against violations of Fundamental Rights.
Scope	Limited to cases that have already been decided by lower courts.	Can be invoked in cases of rights violation, even if the case hasn't gone through lower courts.
Type of Relief	Provides relief by modifying, reversing, or affirming lower court decisions.	Provides immediate relief through writs like Habeas Corpus, Mandamus, etc.

Q.4 The Supreme Court recognises Fundamental Rights against climate change, linking it to Articles 21 and 14. Mention any four contributions of the Supreme Court of India in protecting Fundamental Rights.

Ans. The contributions of the Supreme Court of India in protecting Fundamental Rights are as follows

(i) The Supreme Court review laws and executive actions to ensure that they do not violate the Fundamental Rights guaranteed by the Constitution. If a law or action is found to be unconstitutional, it can be struck down by the Court.

(ii) Under Article 32, the Supreme Court can issue writs like Habeas Corpus, Mandamus, Prohibition, Certiorari, and Quo Warranto to enforce Fundamental Rights. This allows individuals to seek judicial intervention when their rights are violated.

(iii) The Supreme Court has interpreted Fundamental Rights broadly. For example, it has expanded the scope of the Right to Life under Article 21 to include various rights like the Right to a Clean Environment, the Right to Privacy, etc.

(iv) The Supreme Court has been instrumental in ensuring that laws and government actions do not discriminate on the basis of caste, gender, religion, or other unjust grounds, thereby safeguarding the Right to Equality under Article 14.

5. Explain the following terms.
(i) Original jurisdiction
(ii) Appellate jurisdiction

Ans. (i) **Original Jurisdiction**

The original jurisdiction of the Supreme Court of India refers to the cases that can be directly filed in the Supreme Court, without the need of going through hierarchy of lower to higher courts. It primarily deals with disputes between the government of India and states, or between two or more states.

This power allows the Supreme Court to address certain cases directly, ensuring the timely resolution of significant legal issues.

(ii) **Appellate Jurisdiction**

The appellate jurisdiction of the Supreme Court of India allows it to hear appeals against the judgments and orders passed by lower courts, including High Courts. Under this jurisdiction, the Supreme Court reviews cases on matters of law, fact, or both, specially when an individual or party believes that a lower court has made an error in its decision.

The Supreme Court has the power to modify, reverse, or affirm the lower court's decision. This jurisdiction ensures uniformity in the interpretation of the law and plays a vital role in maintaining legal consistency across the country.

TYPE - 6 — 10 Marks

Structured Questions

Q.1 The Supreme Court of India is the supreme judicial authority and the highest court of the Republic of India. It is the final court of appeal for all civil and criminal cases. **(ICSE Specimen 2025)**

With reference to the Supreme Court, answer the following questions.

(i) Who appoints the Judges of the Supreme Court? Mention any two qualifications required for a person to be appointed as a judge of the Supreme Court. **(3)**

(ii) 'Under Article 129, the Supreme Court of India is called a Court of Record'. Justify this statement with any three points. **(3)**

(iii) Explain the following terms. **(4)**
(a) Revisory jurisdiction
(b) Advisory jurisdiction

Ans. (i) The President of India appoints the Judges of the Supreme Court. Two qualifications required for a person to be appointed as a judge of the Supreme Court are as follows

- The person must be a citizen of India.
- The person must have been either a judge of a High Court or two or more High Courts for at least five years, or an eminent lawyer who has practiced law in the High Court or a Court of equivalent jurisdiction for at least ten years.

(ii) The Supreme Court of India is called a Court of Record, because of the following reasons

(a) As a Court of Record, the Supreme Court's judgements and orders are maintained permanently.

(b) The case records are kept for future reference and can be used as precedents in future legal cases.

(c) The decisions made by the Supreme Court serve as binding precedents for all other courts in India. All Courts including Supreme Court itself must follow these decisions unless they are overturned by a larger bench.

(iii) (a) **Revisory Jurisdiction**

Revisory jurisdiction of the Supreme Court allows it to review and correct decisions made by lower courts, such as High Courts or subordinate courts. Under this jurisdiction, the Supreme Court can call for the record of a case, examine it, and take corrective action if necessary. It ensures that justice is properly administered and errors made by lower courts do not result in an unjust outcome. This power is part of the Court's role in overseeing the entire judicial system to ensure fairness and accuracy.

(b) **Advisory Jurisdiction**

The advisory jurisdiction of the Supreme Court, under Article 143 of the Indian Constitution, allows the President of India to seek the court's opinion on important legal or constitutional matters. The President may refer any question of law or fact which is of public importance, to the Supreme Court for its advice. While the opinion given by the court is not binding, it holds significant legal and constitutional value. This provision helps the government in making laws on complex issues.

Q.2 Look at the image given below and answer the following questions.

(i) Where does this court was inaugurated? Explain its compositions and qualifications for its Judges. **(3)**

(ii) Mention any three differences between the Ad hoc Judge and Acting Chief Justice. **(3)**

(iii) Under which jurisdiction can the Supreme Court of India give its opinion to the President on constitutional matters? What is the significance of the advisory jurisdiction of the Supreme Court in India? **(4)**

Ans. (i) The above picutre depicts the Supreme Court of India which was inaugurated on 28th January, 1950.

Composition The Supreme Court consists of 34 Judges in which there is 1 Chief Justice and 33 other Judges.

Qualifications of Judges

- A person to be appointed as a Judge of the Supreme Court should
- Be a citizen of India
- Have been the Judge of a High Court for at least five years.
- Have been an advocate of a High Court for at least ten years.
- Be a distinguished jurist in the opinion of the President.

(ii) The differences between Ad hoc Judges and Acting Chief Justice are as follows

Aspect	Ad hoc Judges	Acting Chief Justice
Appointment	Temporarily appointed to handle cases, often to reduce backlog.	Temporarily appointed to perform the duties of the Chief Justice during their absence.
Role and Function	Assist in hearing cases and managing the workload of the court.	Takes over the full responsibilities of the Chief Justice, including administrative and judicial duties.
Duration	Appointed for a specific period or until a permanent appointment is made.	Serves for the duration of the regular Chief Justice's absence.

(iii) Under its advisory jurisdiction, the Supreme Court can give its opinion to the President on legal or constitutional matters.

The significance of the advisory jurisdiction of the Supreme Court in India is as follows

- It provides legal and constitutional clarity on complex issues referred by the President.
- It helps the President and the government in making informed decisions on constitutional matters.
- It plays a role in maintaining the checks and balances between the executive and judiciary by providing expert advice.

5

THE HIGH COURT AND SUBORDINATE COURTS

The High Court

- The High Court is the highest judicial court in a state.
- The Constitution of India mandates the establishment of a High Court for each state, but the 7th Constitutional Amendment Act of 1956 allowed Parliament to create a common High Court for multiple states and Union Territories.
- Currently, there are 25 High Courts across India.

Composition

- Every High Court consists of a Chief Justice and other Judges which are appointed by the President of India.
- The President of India also determines the number of Judges of High Court which is based upon the workload of these courts.

Qualifications of Judges

According to the Constitution, to be qualified for appointment as a Judge of a High Court, a person should be

- a citizen of India.
- should have held a judicial office in the territory of India for 10 years.
- should have been an advocate of a High Court for 10 years.

Appointment of Judges

- The President of India appoints the Judges of the High Court.
- The Chief Justice is appointed after consulting the Chief Justice of India and the Governor of the state. For the appointment of other Judges, the Chief Justice of the concerned High Court is consulted.

Term of Office Judges of High Court hold office upto the age of 62 years.

Removal of Judges

- A High Court Judge can be removed for misbehavior or incapacity.
- A motion for removal must be signed by 100 Lok Sabha or 50 Rajya Sabha members and approved by a two-thirds majority.
- After approval from both Houses, the President of India formally removes the Judge from office.

Jurisdiction and Functions of High Court

Original Jurisdiction

It means the power of the High Court to hear disputes in the first instance, not by way of appeal. It include the following matters

- Matters of admiralty, will, marriage, divorce, company laws and contempt of court.
- Disputes relating to the election of the members of Parliament and state legislatures.
- Revenue matters or an act ordered or done in revenue collection.

Appellate Jurisdiction

- The High Court is primarily a court of appeal. It hears appeals against the judgements of subordinate courts functioning in its territorial jurisdiction.
- It has appellate jurisdiction in both civil and criminal matters.

Revisory Jurisdiction

- It allows the High Court to review a case decided by a lower court.
- If there is an error in judgment or procedure, the High Court can take appropriate action.

Power of Judicial Review

- The High Court examines the constitutionality of legislative enactment and executive orders of both the centre and the state governments.
- The enactments and executive orders can be challenged in a High Court on the following grounds
  (i) If it violates the Fundamental Rights.
  (ii) If it is outside the competence of the authority which has framed it.
  (iii) If it is against the constitutional provisions.

Court of Record The judgements, proceedings and acts of the High Court are recorded for perpetual memory and testimony.

Enforcement of Fundamental Rights and Writs

The Constitution of India empowers High Court under Article 226 to issue writs for the enforcement of any legal and Fundamental Right unlike Supreme Court. These writs are

- **Habeas Corpus** A writ issued to produce a person before the court who has been unlawfully detained.
- **Mandamus** A writ commanding a public authority to perform his duty which it failed to perform.
- **Prohibition** A writ issued by a higher court to a lower court or tribunal to prevent it from exceeding its jurisdiction.
- **Quo Warranto** A writ issued to inquire if someone has the legal right to hold a public office or not.
- **Certiorari** A writ issued by a higher court to review the order or decision of a lower court or tribunal and directing them to transfer the record of a particular case.

Subordinate Courts

- In every state, besides the High Court there are a number of judicial courts to administer justice. These courts are known as Subordinate Courts.
- They function under the complete control and supervision of the High Court.

Structure and Composition

For judicial administration purposes, every state is divided into a number of districts, each under the jurisdiction of a District Judge.

Qualifications of District Judge

For the appointment of a person as a District Judge he

- should have been an advocate or a pleader for 7 years.
- should be recommended by the High Court for appointment.

Types of Subordinate Courts

There are three types of subordinate courts in every district: Civil Courts, and Criminal Courts and court of revenue.

Distinction Between Court of District Judge and Session Court Judge

Sessions Judge	District Judge
A Sessions Judge is appointed to handle serious criminal cases, and has power to impose death or life imprisonment penalties.	A District Judge is in charge of the administration of the district court and handles civil cases only.
Sessions Judges have authority to hear and decide criminal appeals, from Subordinate Court like of Judicial magistrate etc.	District Judges mainly handle civil matters and appeals from subordinate courts like Munsif Court etc.
Sessions Judges and Additional Sessions Judges are appointed by the Governor after consultation with the High Court of the state.	District Judges and Additional District Judges are appointed by the Governor after consultation with the High Court of the state.
The role of a Sessions Judge is often seen as a specialised judicial position focused on criminal law.	The role of District judge is often seen as a specialised judicial position focused on civil law.

Lok Adalats

- It is a system of Alternative Dispute Resolution (ADR) in India, initiated by the efforts of P.N. Bhagwati (Former CJI).
- The first Lok Adalat was held at Junagarh, in Gujarat, on 14th March, 1982.

Types of Lok Adalats

Lok Adalats provide an effective alternative dispute resolution mechanism, aiming to settle disputes in a more accessible and speedy manner. The different types of Lok Adalats are

- National Lok Adalat
- Permanent Lok Adalat
- Mobile Lok Adalat

Advantages of Lok Adalat

- It delivers fast and inexpensive justice.
- It reduces the workload of other courts enabling them to deal with more serious matters.
- It promotes social justice by providing legal aid to weaker sections of the society.

EXAM ORIENTED QUESTIONS

TYPE - 1 — 1 Mark

Multiple Choice Questions

Q.1 Who is empowered to establish the High Court for a state or for some collective states?
(a) President (b) Governor
(c) State Legislature (d) Parliament

Ans. (d) Parliament

Q.2 Which of the following Union Territories has a High Court of its own?
(a) Andaman and Nicobar
(b) Delhi
(c) Puducherry
(d) Lakshadweep

Ans. (b) Delhi

Q.3 Look at the picture showing the Punjab and Haryana High Court. Identify the act which authorised the Parliament to establish a common High Court.

(a) 7th Amendment Act, 1956
(b) 6th Amendment Act, 1956
(c) 8th Amendment Act, 1960
(d) 9th Amendment Act, 196

Ans. (a) 7th Amendment Act, 1956

Exp. 7th Amendment Act, 1956 allowed the Parliament to set up a single High Court for two or more states or Union Territories for better efficiency.

Q.4 Complete the given analogy.
High Court : Judiciary at State Level :: District Court : ??
(a) Judiciary at Local Level
(b) Judiciary at National Level
(c) Parliament
(d) Judiciary at Central Level

Ans. (a) Judiciary at Local Level

Q.5 Read the details carefully and answer the question.

Judge	Court	Age
X	District Judge having 11 years experience.	61 years
Y	Additional Sessions Judge having 14 years of experience	63 years
Z	District Judge having 12 Years of Experience.	64 years

Which one is eligible to hold the post of High Court Judge in India?
(a) X (b) Y
(c) Z (d) All of these

Ans. (a) X

Q.6 The High Court Judge can remain in office till he attains the age of........ **(ICSE Semester II 2022)**
(a) 60 years (b) 62 years
(c) 63 years (d) 65 years

Ans. (b) 62 years

Q.7 Which of the following is correct about the appointment of Chief Justice in High Courts?
(a) The Chief Justice of India appoints all the Judges in a High Court.
(b) The President of India appoints High Court Chief Justice only after consultation with the Governor of the state and the Chief Justice of India.
(c) The number of Judges in a High Court is decided by the Prime Minister.
(d) High Court Judges are appointed by the Governor of the respective state only.

Ans. (b) The President of India appoints High Court Chief Justice only after consultation with the Governor of the state and the Chief Justice of India.

Q.8 Which of the following was the High Court Judge against whom an impeachment motion was initiated?
(a) Justice Soumitra Sen (b) M.K. Basu
(c) H. Benerjee Biswas (d) Pradeep Kumar

Ans. (a) Justice Soumitra Sen

Exp. Justice Soumitra Sen was a High Court judge from the Calcutta High Court against whom an impeachment motion was initiated in 2011. He was accused of misappropriating public funds, making him the first judge to face such proceedings.

Q.9 When a case comes from a Subordinate Court, the High Court deals with it under.... **(ICSE Specimen 2023)**

(a) Revisory jurisdiction
(b) Advisory jurisdiction
(c) Original jurisdiction
(d) Appellate jurisdiction

Ans. (d) Appellate jurisdiction

Exp. When a case is appealed from a Subordinate Court, the High Court reviews and decides it under its appellate jurisdiction. This allows the High Court to correct errors made by lower courts.

Q.10 "A businessman from Delhi has been convicted by the Sessions Court for financial fraud. His lawyer has confirmed that they will approach a higher court for an appeal against the conviction." *THE XYZ Express*

Identify the statements which is correct about appellate jurisdiction of High Court?

(a) The High Court has appellate jurisdiction over decisions made by the Sessions Court.
(b) The Supreme Court must hear all appeals from the Sessions Court.
(c) The High Court has appellate jurisdiction only for civil cases.
(d) The District Court has appellate jurisdiction over Sessions Court decisions.

Ans. (a) The High Court has appellate jurisdiction over decisions made by the Sessions Court.

Q.11 "In a recent ruling on 25th October,2024. The Delhi High Court quashed a government order that restricted the rights of individuals under certain circumstances, citing that it violated Fundamental Rights guaranteed by the Constitution".

27th Oct, 2024, The XYZ EXPRESS

What can be inferred about the judicial review power of the High Court from the above passage?

(a) The High Court can only review legislative actions, not executive orders.
(b) The High Court cannot challenge government decisions.
(c) The High Court has the power to review government actions that violate constitutional values.
(d) The High Court's judicial review power is limited to criminal cases only.

Ans. (c) The High Court has the power to review government actions that violate constitutional values.

Q.12 Which of the following statements best describes the revisory jurisdiction of the High Court?

(a) The High Court has the power to revise its own judgments in any case.
(b) The High Court can only review decisions made by the Supreme Court.
(c) The High Court has the power to examine and modify its earlier decisions in criminal cases only.
(d) The High Court can issue writs for revising laws passed by the Parliament.

Ans. (a) The High Court has the power to revise its own judgments in any case.

Q.13 Complete the given analogy.

High Court Verdicts : Appeal in Supreme Court :: District Court Verdicts : ?

(a) Appeal in Nyay Adalat
(b) Appeal in Lok Adalat
(c) Appeal in High Court
(d) Appeal in Supreme Court

Ans. (c) Appeal in High Court

Q.14 Imagine you are facing a legal issue related to the violation of your Fundamental Rights. Which of the following statements best describes the role of the High Court in this context?

(a) You must approach the District Court for violation of Fundamental Rights.
(b) You can directly approach the High Court under Article 226 for enforcement of your Fundamental Rights.
(c) The High Court has no authority over Fundamental Rights, and only the Supreme Court can handle such cases.
(d) The High Court can only hear criminal cases, not cases related to Fundamental Rights.

Ans. (b) You can directly approach the High Court under Article 226 for enforcement of your Fundamental Rights.

Q.15 Identify the incorrect statement about the writ jurisdiction of the High Court.

(a) The High Court can issue writs for the enforcement of Fundamental Rights.
(b) The High Court has the power to issue writs for the enforcement of legal rights, even beyond Fundamental Rights.
(c) The High Court can issue writs under Article 226 of the Constitution.
(d) The High Court has the power to issue writs under Article 226 of the Constitution.

Ans. (c) The High Court can issue writs under Article 226 of the Constitution.

Exp. High Courts issue writs under Article 226, covering both Fundamental and Legal Rights.

Q.16 Complete the given analogy.

Court of District Judge : Civil Cases: : Sessions Court : .... Cases **(ICSE Specimen 2025, 2023)**

(a) Advisory
(b) Criminal
(c) Constitutional
(d) Appellate

Ans. (b) Criminal

Q.17 "The District Judge presides over the District Court and is responsible for managing the court's docket, hearing serious criminal cases, and handling civil disputes within the district. They also play a key role in supervising lower courts".

Which of the following provides the correct inference regarding the position of a District Judge?

(a) The District Judge only handles minor criminal cases.
(b) The District Judge has the authority to supervise lower courts and hear serious cases.
(c) The District Judge is not involved in supervising lower courts.
(d) The District Judge is only responsible to civil disputes of Munsif Court.

Ans. (b) The District Judge has the authority to supervise lower courts and hear serious cases.

Q.18 Identify the pair which is related to the power of subordinate courts.

P : Can issue orders of bail in criminal cases.
Q : Can introduce new laws.
R : Can hear cases related to civil matters within the district.
S : Can interpret Constitution.

Codes

(a) P and Q (b) R and S (c) P and R (d) Q and S

Ans. (c) P and R

Q.19 Which of the following statements is true about Lok Adalats in India?

(a) Lok Adalats are conducted by government-appointed officials.
(b) Only criminal cases can be referred to Lok Adalats.
(c) Lok Adalats aim to provide quick and amicable settlements of disputes outside the formal court system.
(d) Lok Adalats are limited to family-related disputes only.

Ans. (c) Lok Adalats aim to provide quick and amicable settlements of disputes outside the formal court system.

Q.20 Read the description and identify the person.

He advocated the idea of Lok Adalats in India and played a key role in promoting legal aid for the weaker section of society.

(a) Justice Deepak Mishra
(b) Justice M.N. Venkatachaliah
(c) Justice P.N. Bhagwati
(d) Chief Justice K.G. Balakrishnan

Ans. (c) Justice P.N. Bhagwati

Q.21 PIL plays a crucial role in resolving the problem of masses. What does the word PIL stand for?

(a) Public Interest Litigation
(b) Public Important Litigation
(c) Public Involved Litigation
(d) Public Issue Litigation

Ans. (a) Public Interest Litigation

Q.22 Which of the following statement does not apply to the Lok Adalat. **(ICSE Specimen Semester II 2022)**

(a) It reduces the burden on High Courts
(b) Works on the spirit of compromise
(c) The cases takes a long time to get resolved
(d) It involves very less expenses

Ans. (c) The cases takes a long time to get resolved

Exp. Lok Adalats are known for quickly resolving cases through compromise and mutual agreement. They reduce the burden on courts and involve minimal expenses, making them efficient.

Q.23 Residents of Jodhpur, X and Y got married in the year 2014 and after 4 months of wedlock, petty family issues and arguments resulted in their separation for 6 years. The matter was placed before the Bench of Lok Adalat Family Court, Jodhpur wherein all efforts were made to reunite the family again. With constant efforts of counselling, parties agreed to live together and withdraw their divorce petition.

Case Study, Lok Adalat,District - Jodhpur

(ICSE Specimen 2025)

Which advantage of the Lok Adalat is highlighted in the above case?

(a) Saves money (b) Speedy justice
(c) Works on the spirit of compromise
(d) Reduces the burden on High Courts

Ans. (c) Works on the spirit of compromise

TYPE - 2 — 1 Mark

Assertion-Reason Questions

Q.1 Read the two statements given below about the High Court and select the option that shows the correct relationship between (A) and (R).

Assertion (A) The High Court is the highest judicial authority in the state.

Reason (R) The High Court has the power to supervise and control all subordinate courts within its jurisdiction.

(a) R contradicts A
(b) R is the reason for A
(c) A is true but R is false
(d) A and R are independent of each other

Ans. (b) R is the reason for A

Q. 2 Read the two statements given below about the High Court and subordinate court and select the option that shows the correct relationship between (A) and (R).

Assertion (A) Subordinate courts are bound by the decisions and guidelines issued by the High Court.

Reason (R) The High Court has no power to issue directions to subordinate courts, ensuring consistency in legal proceedings across its jurisdiction.

(a) R contradicts A
(b) R is the reason for A
(c) A is true but R is false
(d) A and R are independent of each other

Ans. (c) A is true but R is false

TYPE - 3 — 2 Marks

Very Short Answer Type Questions

Q.1 State any two qualifications required for becoming a High Court Judge in India.

Ans. Two qualifications required for becoming a High Court Judge in India are as follows

(i) The candidate must be a citizen of India.

(ii) The candidate must have practiced as an advocate in a High Court for at least 10 years or must held a judicial office in India for at least 10 years.

Q.2 Explain how security of tenure for High Court Judges brings independence in the judiciary?

Ans. Security of tenure of High Court Judges ensures Independence in the judiciary in the following ways

- **Protection from Removal** High Court Judges can only be removed through a rigorous impeachment process, which ensures their freedom from external influence.
- **Impartiality** The fixed tenure allows Judges to make decisions without fear of retaliation, ensuring fairness and independence in their judgments.

Q.3 Name the two types of Jurisdiction of High Court by reading the statements which are given below.
(i) Power to hear cases directly, such as writ petitions and election disputes.
(ii) Power to hear appeals from lower courts, including district courts and subordinate courts in civil and criminal matters.

Ans. (i) Original jurisdiction

(ii) Appellate jurisdiction

Q.4 Mention the names of any two High Courts whose jurisdiction extends to more than one state.

Ans. Two High Courts whose jurisdiction extends to more than one state are

(i) **Bombay High Court** Its jurisdiction extends to the states of Maharashtra, Goa and the Union Territories of Dadra and Nagar Haveli and Daman and Diu.

(ii) **Punjab and Haryana High Court** Its jurisdiction covers the states of Punjab, Haryana and the Union Territory of Chandigarh.

Q.5 Read the questions and answer the following.
(i) Who administers the oath of office to the High Court Judges?
(ii) Who is responsible for the appointment of Judges in High Court?

Ans. (i) The Governor administers the oath of office to the High Court Judges.

(ii) President is responsible for the appointment of Judges in High Court.

Q.6 Imagine you are a Judge in a High Court and a case is brought before you where the decision of a lower court is challenged. The decision seems to have some legal errors but is not part of an appeal. What two things would you do to exercise your power effectively?

Ans. As a judge of the particular case, I will do the following things

(i) Review the case thoroughly to ensure that the decision is in line with principles of justice.

(ii) Rectify the errors in the lower court's decision if necessary and ensure justice is served without any need for further appeal.

Q.7 Analyse the meaning of the term 'appellate jurisdiction' of the High Court.

Ans. The appellate jurisdiction of the High Court refers to the power of the High Court to hear appeals against the judgments of Subordinate Courts.

Q.8 Mention any two grounds of judicial review power where the enactments and executive orders can be challenged.

Ans. The enactments and executive orders can be challenged in a High Court on the following grounds

(i) **Violation of Fundamental Rights** When an enactment or executive order infringes upon the Fundamental Rights guaranteed by the Constitution.

(ii) **Excess of Legislative or Executive Power** When an enactment or executive order exceeds the authority granted to the legislature or the executive under the Constitution.

Q.9 On 12th February, 2024 'The High Court of Punjab and Haryana said that it has the authority to issue writs to safeguard the Fundamental Rights of citizens. These writs can be issued against the government, its agencies, and private individuals if they violate citizens rights'.
Highlight any two points regarding the powers of the High Court that can be deduced from the above news.

Ans. The High Court plays a key role in safeguarding citizens' rights through its judicial powers in the following ways

(i) **Power to Issue Writs** The High Court has the authority to issue writs for the protection of Fundamental Rights.

(ii) **Jurisdiction Over Government and Individuals** The High Court can issue writs against both government agencies and private individuals for violations of citizens' rights.

Q.10 **Name the two courts that are empowered to issue writs for the enforcement of Fundamental Rights.** **(ICSE 2020)**

Ans. The Supreme Court and the High Court are empowered to issue writs for the enforcement of Fundamental Rights.

Q.11 **Name the writ issued by the High Court in the following cases.**

(i) **Which provides a remedy to the person who has been unlawfully detained in prison.**

(ii) **When the High Court prohibits the lower court.**

Ans. (i) The writ of Habeas Corpus is issued by the High Court which provides a remedy to the person who has been unlawfully detained in prison.

(ii) A writ of prohibition is issued by the High Court to prevent a lower court from acting outside its jurisdiction or exceeding its legal authority.

Q.12 **Mention the types of Court that a district usually has.**

Ans. A district has three types of courts, which are

(i) Civil Courts (ii) Criminal Courts

(iii) Courts of Revenue.

Q.13 **Briefly explain the composition of district and Subordinate Courts in India.**

Ans. District and Subordinate Courts form the lower judiciary in India which deals with a wide range of legal matters. Their composition are as follows

- **District Courts** The highest court at the district level, is headed by a District Judge, who oversees civil and criminal cases.
- **Subordinate Courts** These include Civil Courts, Criminal Courts, and Magistrate Courts, headed by Judicial Magistrates or Civil Judges, who handle specific types of cases within their jurisdiction.

Q.14 **Mention any two conditions for the appointment of a District Judge in India.**

Ans. The conditions for the appointment of a District Judge in India are as follows

(i) **Appointment by Governor** A District Judge is appointed by the Governor of the respective state on the recommendation of the High Court.

(ii) **Eligibility Criteria** A candidate must have at least seven years of experience as an advocate or judicial officer to be eligible for the position of District Judge.

Q.15 **Briefly explain any two powers of the Sessions Judge.**

Ans. The two powers of the Sessions Judge are as follows

(i) The Sessions Judge has the power to impose any sentence, including life imprisonment and capital punishment.

(ii) The Sessions Judge can hear appeals against decisions of Magistrate Courts in criminal matters.

Q.16 **State two advantages of a Lok Adalat.**

Or **Mention two reasons to state that the Lok Adalat has its own advantage.**

Ans. Two advantages of Lok Adalat are as follows

(i) **Speedy Resolution** Lok Adalats provide quick settlements to disputes which, help parties to avoid the lengthy court procedures.

(ii) **Cost-Effective** The process is free of cost, making it an affordable method for individuals to resolve their conflicts without incurring high legal fees.

Q.17 **Imagine you are a Sessions Judge in a district court. You are hearing a case of a serious criminal offense. What two key actions would you take to ensure the fair and just trial of the case?**

Ans. As a District judge I will ensure the following things

(i) **Ensure Proper Legal Procedures** I would carefully examine the evidence, ensure that all legal procedures are followed and grant the accused a fair opportunity for defense.

(ii) **Deliver an Impartial Judgment** After hearing the arguments, I would ensure that my judgment is based on the law and facts by remaining impartial to both the prosecution and defense.

TYPE - 4 (3 Marks)

Short Answer Type Questions

Q.1 **Justify the importance of the High Court's Original jurisdiction in the Indian legal system.**

Ans. The original jurisdiction of the High Court plays a crucial role in delivering justice at the state level, particularly in matters that are of significant legal importance.

Its importance is as follows

- **Disputes Between State and Citizens** The High Court has the authority to directly deal with cases where the state government or its actions are challenged by citizens which ensures quick resolution of legal conflicts within the state.
- **Constitutional Interpretation at State Level** It ensures that the laws and actions of state governments are in line with the Constitution values.

- **Direct Access to High Court** The Original Jurisdiction provides citizens and organisations direct access to the High Court, bypassing lower Courts which enhances the speed and efficiency of the legal process.

Q.2 Differentiate between appellate and judicial review powers of the High Court.

Ans. The differences between appellate and judicial review powers of the High Court are

Appellate Power	Judicial Review Power
Appellate power refers to the authority to hear appeals from lower courts and tribunals.	Judicial review power refers to the authority to review the constitutionality of laws and executive actions.
It reviews decisions made by lower courts to ensure justice is delivered correctly.	It examines the legality and constitutionality of laws, executive actions and legislative decisions.
Appellate power is focused on decisions made in individual cases.	Judicial review focuses on the constitutionality and legality of the actions and decisions of the legislature and executive.

Q.3 Analyse three main differences between powers of District Judge and Sessions Judge.

Ans. The differences between powers of District Judge and Sessions Judge are as follows

District Judge	Sessions Judge
The District Judge is responsible for handling of civil cases within a district.	The Sessions Judge deals primarily with criminal cases, including serious offenses.
The District Judge has the authority to pass judgments in civil matters and can impose civil penalties.	The Sessions Judge has the authority to hear and pass judgments on serious criminal cases, including life imprisonment and capital punishment.
The District Judge has appellate powers over decisions made by lower courts in civil matters.	The Sessions Judge hears appeals from the decisions of Magistrate Courts in criminal matters.

Q.4 Lok Adalats play an important role in the resolution of disputes through amicable settlement. In this context, answer the following questions.

(i) What is the role of Lok Adalats in the settlement of disputes?

(ii) Under what circumstances can a case be referred to a Lok Adalat for resolution?

Ans. (i) Lok Adalats provide an alternative dispute resolution mechanism where disputes are settled through mutual consent between the parties involved, without the need for lengthy litigation. It promotes a quicker, cost-effective and amicable resolution of cases.

(ii) A case can be referred to a Lok Adalat either by the courts (if both parties agree) or by the parties themselves at any stage of the litigation process. Additionally, cases involving compoundable offenses and disputes like civil, matrimonial, or labour issues are commonly referred to Lok Adalats for quicker resolution.

Q.5 How does the High Court ensure the enforcement of Fundamental Rights and Legal Rights through its writ jurisdiction?

Ans. The High Court ensures the enforcement of Fundamental Rights and Legal Rights through its writ jurisdiction under Article 226 of the Constitution. It can issue five types of writs: Habeas Corpus, Mandamus, Prohibition, Quo Warranto, and Certiorari.

These writs help to protect individual rights and ensure that authorities act within the law, providing justice and safeguarding citizens' rights.

TYPE - 5 — 4 Marks

Long Answer Type Questions

Q.1 Highlight the significance of High Court writs in protection of Fundamental Rights in India.

Ans. The High Court's power to issue writs plays a crucial role in the protection of Fundamental Rights in India in the following ways

- **Enforcement of Fundamental Rights** The High Court can issue writs to enforce the Fundamental Rights of individuals being violated by the government or its agencies. Citizens can directly approach to the High Court for timely remedies.
- **Types of Writs** The High Court can issue five types of writs-Habeas Corpus, Mandamus, Prohibition, Certiorari and Quo Warranto for protection of citizen against different forms of legal or Constitutional violations.
- **Judicial Review** The High Court has the authority to review executive actions and legislation through its writ jurisdiction to ensure that they align with the Constitution values.

- **Protection of Individual Liberties** The writ jurisdiction of the High Court acts as an essential tool for the protection and enforcement of Fundamental Rights and ensure that governmental actions do not infringe upon the liberties and freedoms of individuals.

Q.2 **"Hierarchy of Courts is important to protect the civil rights". Justify this statement.**

Ans. The hierarchical structure of courts in India plays a pivotal role in ensuring the protection of civil rights by creating a well-defined and effective judicial framework. It is important due to the following reasons

- **Access to Justice** The presence of lower courts at the district level ensures that justice is accessible to the common people. Cases involving civil rights violations can be addressed locally, ensuring timely resolution.
- **Appeals and Review Mechanism** The hierarchy provides a structured avenue for appeals, allowing individuals to challenge decisions of lower courts in higher courts. This ensures that errors or injustices can be corrected to safeguard the civil rights.
- **Judicial Oversight** Higher courts, including High Court and the Supreme Court, exercise supervisory jurisdiction over lower courts. This oversight ensures accountability and consistency in decisions related to civil rights.
- **Constitutional Remedies** High Court and the Supreme Court are at the apex levels of the hierarchy, which are empowered to issue writs for the enforcement of Fundamental Rights under Articles 226 and 32. Thus provides a robust safeguard for civil liberties.

Q.3 **India has a single integrated judicial system that is independent and supreme. With reference to judiciary, answer the following.**

List any four types of cases that are dealt by the High Court which are exclusively part of it

Ans. The four types of cases which are exclusively dealt by the High Court are as follows

(i) **Writ Petitions under Article 226** The High Court has the exclusive power to issue writs for enforcing Fundamental Rights and other legal rights.

(ii) **Appeals** High Court hear petition against the verdict of the lower courts.

(iii) **Election Petitions for State Legislatures** The High Court handles disputes exclusively related to elections for state legislative assemblies.

(iv) **Death Sentence Confirmation** The High Court must confirm death sentences passed by sessions courts before execution.

Q.4 **Discuss about the writ jurisdiction power of the High Court mentioned under the Article 226.**

Ans. Article 226 of the Indian Constitution grants the High Court the authority to issue writs for the enforcement of Fundamental Rights and other legal remedies. This jurisdiction is a crucial aspect of the Indian judicial system.

Different types of writs are

Type of Writ	Purpose	Example
Habeas Corpus	To secure the release of a person unlawfully detained or imprisoned.	A person detained without a valid reason can be released through this writ.
Mandamus	To command a public authority or government to perform a duty that has been neglected.	Compelling a government official to take an action as required by law.
Prohibition	To prevent a lower court or tribunal from acting outside its jurisdiction or unlawfully.	Preventing a court from taking up a case that it has no jurisdiction over.
Certiorari	To quash the order or decision of a lower court, tribunal, or authority acting beyond its jurisdiction.	Quashing a decision made by a tribunal without the authority to do so.
Quo Warranto	To question the legality of a person's claim to a public office.	Challenging an individual's right to hold a public office due to lack of qualifications.

Q.5 In context to Indian judiciary, explain the following.
(i) Importance of PIL
(ii) Importance of Lok Adalats

Ans. (i) **Importance of Public Interest Litigation (PIL)**
- Public Interest Litigation (PIL) enables individuals or organisations to approach the courts for the protection of public rights, social justice and the welfare of vulnerable groups.
- It addresses issues which affect society at large, such as environmental concerns or human rights violations.

(ii) **Importance of Lok Adalats in Judiciary**
- Lok Adalats provide an informal platform for the peaceful settlement of disputes hence reduces the burden on the judiciary.
- They offer quicker, cost-effective, and accessible resolutions, especially for minor cases, thus help to decrease case backlogs in law courts.

TYPE - 6

10 Marks

Structured Questions

Q.1 With reference to the jurisdiction of the High Court, answer the following questions.
(i) 'The High Court's supervisory power contributes to maintaining consistency and fairness in the judicial system'. Justify this statement. **(3)**
(ii) Which Article of the Indian Constitution defines the jurisdiction of High Court over states? Give any two reasons why a High Court in India only has jurisdiction over a particular state? **(3)**
(iii) Mark any four differences between National Lok Adalat, Permanent and Mobile Lok Adalat. **(4)**

Ans. (i) The High Court's supervisory power is essential for ensuring the proper functioning of the judicial system. It enables the High Court to oversee the actions of lower courts and tribunals to maintain fairness and legal consistency. The above statement can be justified in the following ways
- **Error Correction** The High Court can review and correct mistakes in decision made by Subordinate Courts.
- **Guidance for Lower Courts** It provides directions to ensure uniformity in legal interpretation.
- **Protection of Legal Rights** The High Court safeguards individuals' rights by intervening in cases of injustice.

(ii) Article 214 of the Indian Constitution defines the jurisdiction of High Court over individual states or union territories.

Two reasons why a High Court in India only has jurisdiction over a particular state are as follows
- The Constitution of India establishes a High Court for each state or union territory under Article 214. This ensures that each state has its own judicial body to handle matters locally and effectively.
- Limiting the jurisdiction to a specific state allows the High Court to deal with state laws, regional issues, and local matters in a more focused and efficient manner, ensuring quicker and more relevant resolutions for the people of that state.

(iii) Differences between National Lok Adalat, Permanent and Mobile Lok Adalat are given below

National Lok Adalat	Permanent Lok Adalat	Mobile Lok Adalat
A one-day nationwide event held for the settlement of disputes.	A permanent forum for dispute resolution set up for a specific region.	A Lok Adalat that travels to different locations to settle disputes.
From February 2015, it is being held on a specific subject matter every month.	It is held throughout the year in a designated area.	It is held periodically at various locations based on demand.
It covers cases of a general nature across the country.	It covers cases related to public utility services	It covers local disputes within the jurisdiction of the mobile unit.
It aims to reduce the backlog of cases and provide quick resolutions.	It aims to provide a long-term solution for disputes, especially in public services.	It aims to bring justice to remote or rural areas by reaching people in different regions.

Q.2 With reference to the lower courts under the jurisdiction of the High Court, answer the following questions.
(i) At the level of a district, which court hear the civil and criminal matters? **(3)**
(ii) SC transfers pleas on anti-trust probe against Amazon, Flipkart to Karnataka HC. *Hindustan Times*
Which Article of the Indian Constitution allows the Supreme Court to transfer cases to High Courts? Mention main purposes of transferring a case to a High Court. **(3)**

iii) The powers of Chief Justice of the High Court is more powerful than the High Court Judge. In reference to powers and control. Justify this statement. **(4)**

Ans. (i) At the district level in India, the following courts hear civil and criminal matters

(a) Civil Matters

- **District Judge Court** The District Judge Court is the principal court that hears civil matters, including disputes related to property, contracts, family law, and other civil issues in a district. It also has appellate jurisdiction over cases decided by subordinate courts like munsif etc. in the district.

(b) Criminal Matters

- **Sessions Court** The Sessions Court handles serious criminal cases such as murder, rape, and other offenses punishable by death or life imprisonment. It also hears appeals from lower criminal courts.
- **Judicial Magistrate's Court** The Magistrate's Court handles minor criminal offenses, such as theft, assault and traffic violations. Judicial Magistrates are divided into first class and second class, based on the severity of the offenses they can deal with.

(ii) Article 139A of the Indian Constitution allows the Supreme Court to transfer cases from one High Court to another or from lower court to a High Court, under specific circumstances.

Main purposes of transferring a case to a High Court are as follows

- To ensure faith for High Court in people that the case is heard impartially.
- For the speedy resolution of the case and all the facts of case are checked by High Court before the case comes to Supreme Court.

(iii) The High Court Judge and the Chief Justice of the High Court both play crucial roles in the judicial system, but their powers and functions differ significantly as mentioned below

- **Administrative Authority** High Court Judge focuses only on adjudicating cases with no administrative responsibilities. On the other hand, Chief Justice of the High Court manages the court's administrative duties, such as allocating cases and overseeing court functions.
- **Supervision and Leadership High Court Judge** Does not have supervisory control over other judges. On the other hand, Chief Justice of the High Court supervises the work of other judges, assigns cases, and ensures the court's effective operation.
- **Influence in Judicial Decisions** High Court Judge influences the judicial system through individual judgments but has no control over the court's overall operations.
- Chief Justice of the High Court holds significant influence in decision-making, case assignments, and guiding the overall judicial structure.

Q.3 **With reference to the powers and functions of the High Court, answer the following questions.**

(i) Explain the writ jurisdiction power of the High Court under Article 226 of the Indian Constitution.

(ii) Explain why is the High Court recognised as a Court of Record?

(iii) Highlight any four cases in which High Court enjoys Original jurisdictions.

Ans. (i) For answer, refer to Q.4 of Long Answer Type Questions.

(ii) The High Court is recognised as a Court of Record because of the following reasons

- It has the power to enforce its orders and ensure compliance.
- Its judgments and records are of legal authority and can be referred to in other courts.
- It can penalise individuals for contempt.

(iii) The High Court enjoys the power of Original jurisdiction in following cases

(a) **Writ Petitions** (Article 226) High Courts can directly hear cases related to the enforcement of Fundamental Rights and other legal matters.

(b) **Disputes Related to Elections** (Article 226/227) High Courts have Original jurisdiction in election disputes concerning the validity of elections to the State Legislature.

(c) **Divorce and Family Matters** High Courts sometimes exercise Original jurisdiction in divorce cases, especially in situations where one of the parties is from outside the jurisdiction of a District Court or when complex legal issues arise.

(d) **Admiralty and Maritime Cases** High Courts have exclusive Original jurisdiction over disputes related to shipping, contracts, and maritime laws.

Q.4 The High Courts of India are the highest courts of appeal in each state. With reference to the High Courts of India, answer the following questions. **(ICSE 2025)**

(i) What is meant by the term Original Jurisdiction of the High Court? Mention any two cases which fall under this jurisdiction. **(3)**

(ii) Mention any two advantages of the Lok Adalat. Mention any one difference between the Sessions Court and the Court of the District Judge. **(3)**

(iii) Explain the following with reference to the High Court. **(4)**

(a) Revisory Jurisdiction (b) Court of Record

Ans. (i) The Original Jurisdiction of a High Court refers to cases that can be directly filed in the High Court, rather than coming through an appeal from lower courts.

Two cases under this jurisdiction are

- **Disputes involving Fundamental Rights** The High Court can issue writs under Article 226 to protect citizens' rights.
- **Cases involving State Government and Individuals** The High Court can hear cases between the state government and private parties.

(ii) Two advantages of Lok Adalat are

- **Speedy and Low-Cost Justice** Cases are resolved quickly without expensive court procedures.
- **Binding Decisions with No Appeal** The decision of Lok Adalat is final, preventing unnecessary delays.

The difference between Sessions Court and the Court of the District Judge can be seen as

Session Court	Court of the District Judge
It deals with criminal cases like murder, robbery and serious offenses.	It handles civil cases like property disputes and contracts.

(iii) **(a) Revisory Jurisdiction** The High Court has the power of Revisory Jurisdiction, which allows it to review and correct decisions made by lower courts if they contain legal errors. If a subordinate court exceeds its authority or fails to follow proper legal procedures, the High Court can call for records, examine the case and make necessary corrections. This ensures that justice is administered fairly and that lower courts function within their prescribed limits. However, the High Court does not re-examine evidence but only checks for procedural and legal correctness.

(b) Court of Record The High Court is a Court of Record, meaning its judgements, decisions and legal proceedings are permanently recorded and can be used as legal precedents in future cases. These records hold binding authority over lower courts. Additionally, as a Court of Record, the High Court has the power to punish for contempt of court if someone disrespects or disobeys its rulings, ensuring the dignity of the judiciary.

History

THE FIRST WAR OF INDEPENDENCE

The Indian Rebellion of 1857-58 was a significant uprising against the British East India Company's rule in India. The Revolt is also considered as the First War of Independence.

Political Causes of the Revolt

- Disrespect towards famous leaders like Rani Laxmi Bai and Bahadur Shah Zafar angered Indians and increased resistance to British rule.
- The corrupt and inefficient administration of the East India Company also caused resentment.
- Policies like the Subsidiary Alliance and Doctrine of Lapse weakened the power of Indian rulers, which led to the Revolt of 1857.

Lord Wellesley

Subsidiary Alliance

- It was introduced by Lord Wellesley in 1798 as a strategy to expand British control in India.
- Indian rulers were required to maintain a British army within their territory at their own expense.
- They had to forbid foreign powers (like the French) from entering their territory.
- In return, the British promised military protection and political support to the rulers.

Doctrine of Lapse

- It was introduced by Lord Dalhousie in the 1840s.
- It stated that if a ruler died without a natural heir, their state would be annexed by the British Company.
- Several states like Satara (1848), Jhansi(1854), and Nagpur (1854) were annexed under this policy.

Socio-Religious Causes of the Revolt

- **Ban on Sati (1829)** The British made the practice of sati (widow burning) illegal and punishable.
- **Ban on Infanticide and Polygamy** The British stopped practices like killing infant girls and having multiple wives.
- **Introduction of Western Education** In the 19th century, the British started teaching Western ideas and education in India.

Economic Causes of the Revolt

- The British imposed high taxes on Indian farmers, causing economic hardship.
- British trade policies and monopolies destroyed local industries, leading to unemployment.
- The drain of wealth sent profits from India to Britain, and worsening of the local population.

Military Causes of the Revolt

- Indian soldiers suffered from low pay and harsh working conditions.
- The introduction of greased cartridges offended religious sentiments of Hindu and Muslim, also led to anger among sepoys.
- Discrimination in the army, with limited promotions and lower pay compared to British soldiers, caused resentment.

Events of the Revolt of 1857

Mangal Pandey

- **Barrackpore (29th March, 1857)** Mangal Pandey attacked a British officer, leading to his arrest and execution.
- **Meerut (10th May, 1857)** Sepoys rebel after being punished for refusing to use greased cartridges and it become spark for the revolt.
- **Delhi (11th May, 1857)** The sepoys marched to Delhi and declared Bahadur Shah Zafar the leader of the rebellion.
- **Kanpur (June 1857)** Nana Saheb led the revolt in Kanpur, he played significant role in battle against British forces in 1857.
- **Lucknow (June 1857)** Begum Hazrat Mahal takes charge of the revolt in Lucknow, resisting British forces.
- **Jhansi (June 1857)** Rani Lakshmibai defended Jhansi against the British attacks and become a symbol of resistance.
- **Fall of Delhi (September 1857)** British forces recaptured Delhi and ended the Mughal-led resistance.
- **Final Suppression (1858)** The British suppressed the remaining resistance by 1858 and officially ended the revolt.

Consequences of the Revolt of 1857

- **Changes in Military Organisation** The number of European soldiers was increased, and they were kept in key geographical and military positions. To prevent soldiers from developing nationalistic feelings, regiments were formed based on caste, community, and region.
- **End of Company's Rule** The power to govern India passed from the East India Company to the British Crown through an Act of 1858. A Secretary of State for India aided by a Council was now in charge of India's governance. Previously, the Company's Directors held this authority.
- **Divide and Rule Policy** Muslims were severely punished and discrimination was made against them in public appointments. Policies were made to make rift between Hindus and Muslims in India.
- **New Policy towards the Princely** The earlier policy of annexation was now abandoned, and the rulers of these states were now authorised to adopt heirs.
- **Abolition of Peshwaship & Mughal Rule** The Peshwa was removed and Bahadur Shah Zafar was sent to jail in Rangoon which ended the Mughal dynasty in India.
- **Economic Exploitation** Indian economy suffered due to Drain of Wealth from India to England.
- **Rise of Nationalism** The revolt sparked Indian nationalism and inspired future independence movements.

EXAM ORIENTED QUESTIONS

TYPE - 1 1 Mark

Multiple Choice Questions

Q.1 Complete the given analogy.

1757 : The Battle of Plassey : : ? : Battle of Buxar

(a) 1750 (b) 1764 (c) 1857 (d) 1855

Ans. (b) 1764

Exp. The Battle of Buxar (1764) was fought between the British East India Company and the combined forces of Mir Qasim, Shuja-ud-Daula, and Shah Alam II. The British victory established their dominance in India and secured revenue rights.

Q.2 Consider the following statements.

I. The First Anglo-Sikh War was fought between the British East India Company and the Sikh Empire.

II. The Third Anglo-Mysore War ended with the defeat of Tipu Sultan.

Which of the following is/are correct?

(a) Only I is correct
(b) Only II is correct
(c) Both I and II are correct
(d) Neither I nor II is correct

Ans. (c) Both I and II are correct

Q.3 In 1856, the British East India Company justified the annexation of Awadh, a princely state in Northern India, on what grounds? **(ICSE Specimen 2024)**

(a) Acquire more land for British colonies.
(b) Stop the rebellion against the British.
(c) Punish the Nawab of Awadh for opposing British rule.
(d) Due to alleged misgovernance by the Nawab of Awadh.

Ans. (d) Due to alleged misgovernance by the Nawab of Awadh.

Q.4 .... announced that the successors of Bahadur Shah could not use imperial titles. **(ICSE Specimen 2023)**

(a) Lord Canning (b) Lord Wellesley
(c) Lord Dalhousie (d) Lord Ripon

Ans. (a) Lord Canning

Q.5 Complete the given analogy.

Begum Hazrat Mahal : Awadh : : Tatya Tope : ....

(a) Delhi (b) Kanpur
(c) Lucknow (d) Meerut

Ans. (b) Kanpur

Q.6 Complete the given analogy.

Bahadur Shah Zafar : Symbol of the Revolt
Rani Lakshmibai : ....

(a) Commander-in-Chief (b) Leader of the British Forces
(c) Symbol of Resistance (d) Last Mughal Emperor

Ans. (c) Symbol of Resistance

Exp. Rani Lakshmibai opposed British annexation of Jhansi under the Doctrine of Lapse. During the 1857 Revolt she fiercely defended Jhansi against British forces and symbolised resistance and sacrifice.

Q.7 Who amongst the following was refused from grant of pension under Company Rule?

(a) Peshwa Baji Rao II (b) Nana Saheb
(c) Peshwa Baji Rao I (d) Tatya Tope

Ans. (b) Nana Saheb

Exp. Nana Saheb, a prominent leader during the 1857 rebellion, was denied a pension under the British Company rule. The British refused to honor the pension promised to his family after his father's death.

Q.8 Which statements does not apply to the Doctrine of Subsidiary Alliance? **(ICSE Specimen 2021)**

(a) The kings virtually lost their powers.
(b) It was introduced by Lord Dalhousie.
(c) The kings had to maintain the British army at their cost.
(d) They had a British resident in their court.

Ans. (b) It was introduced by Lord Dalhousie.

Q.9 Read the description and identify the person.

He introduced the Subsidiary Alliance to expand the British control over India. **(ICSE 2025)**

(a) Lord Dalhousie (b) Lord Canning
(c) Lord Wellesley (d) Lord Curzon

Ans. (c) Lord Wellesley

Q.10 The British administration's attempts to reform Indian society included the abolition of Sati, which was seen by many Hindus as an attack on their traditional customs. These reforms were met with resistance from conservative elements of society who viewed them as foreign impositions.

Based upon the information given above, what was the primary reason for the resistance to the abolition of Sati?

(a) It improved the status of women in society.
(b) It was perceived as an attack on religious beliefs.
(c) It was a step towards modernising India.
(d) It led to social equality for women.

Ans. (b) It was perceived as an attack on religious beliefs.

Q.11 Identify the pair which is related to the socio-religious causes of the 1857 revolt.

P : The abolition of Sati by the British in 1829.

Q : British policies on religious tolerance, including the promotion of Christianity.

R : The introduction of the Newer Agricultural Revenue Law in india.

S : The annexation of states under the policy of Doctrine of Lapse .

(a) P and Q (b) R and S
(c) P and R (d) Q and S

Ans. (a) P and Q

Q.12 Identify the odd one out related to 1857 Revolt?

(a) High taxes on land
(b) Economic exploitation through railways construction
(c) Discriminatory tariff policies
(d) Establishment of the Indian National Congress

Ans. (d) Establishment of the Indian National Congress

Q.13 Which of the following issues did not contributed in spread of revolt?

(a) Issue of Cartridges
(b) Conversion of Indians to Christianity
(c) Mixing of bone dust in flour
(d) Dishonouring Hindu Women

Ans. (d) Dishonouring Hindu Women

Q.14 Which of the following leaders was associated with the state of Bihar during the Indian Rebellion of 1857?

(a) Rani Laxmi Bai (b) Mangal Pandey
(c) Kunwar Singh (d) Tantya Tope

Ans. (c) Kunwar Singh

Q.15 In a recent turn of events, Indian sepoys in the British East India Company's army have expressed widespread discontent over the introduction of new policies. Reports indicate that the soldiers are particularly upset over the decision to issue new rifle cartridges, rumored to be greased with animal fat, which violates their religious beliefs. *The London Times*

What can be inferred from the passage above?

(a) Indian soldiers were treated with great respect and fairness in the British army.
(b) The sepoys had no reason to object to the new rifle cartridges.
(c) The sepoys' frustration stemmed from both economic inequality and religious disrespect.
(d) The sepoys were upset only because of the low wages, not their religious concerns.

Ans. (c) The sepoys' frustration stemmed from both, economic inequality and religious disrespect.

Q.16 Read the details carefully and answer the question.

Cause	Event
X	The introduction of railways by the British
Y	Execution of the Mangal Pandey
Z	Queen Victoria assumed the title of the 'Empress of India'.

Which of the following causes directly triggered the outbreak of the 1857 revolt?

(a) X and Y (b) Y
(c) X and Z (d) X

Ans. (b) Y

Q.17 Arrange the following events of the 1857 revolt in chronological order.

(i) The rebellion breaks out in Meerut.
(ii) Mangal Pandey's execution at Barrackpore.
(iii) The British forces capture Delhi and Bahadur Shah Zafar is exiled.
(iv) Rani Lakshmibai defends Jhansi.

Select the correct chronological order:

(a) (i), (ii), (iv), (iii) (b) (ii), (i), (iv), (iii)
(c) (i), (iii), (ii), (iv) (d) (ii), (iv), (i), (iii)

Ans. (b) (ii), (i), (iv), (iii)

Q.18 Look at the picture and answer the question

What was the result of Bahadur Shah Zafar's involvement in the 1857 Revolt?

(a) The Mughal Empire was reinstated and flourished under his leadership.
(b) The British authorities removed all Mughal emperors from India.
(c) Bahadur Shah Zafar was captured, it marked the end of the Mughal Empire.
(d) Bahadur Shah Zafar led to the establishment of an independent India.

Ans. (c) Bahadur Shah Zafar was captured, it marked the end of the Mughal Empire.

Q.19 Who among the following captured Delhi when Bahadur Shah Zafar led the rebels during 1857?
(a) Sir John Nicholson
(b) Sir Henry Lawrence
(c) Lord William Bentinck
(d) Sir Colin Campbell

Ans. (a) Sir John Nicholson

Exp. Sir John Nicholson was a British officer who played a key role in the capture of Delhi during the 1857 rebellion. He led the British forces and helped defeat Bahadur Shah Zafar's rebels.

Q.20 In which year 'Queen Victoria's proclamation' was announced?
(a) 1899 (b) 1858
(c) 1845 (d) 1865

Ans. (b) 1858

TYPE - 2 — 1 Mark

Assertion-Reason Questions

Q.1 Read the two statements given below about the consequences of the 1857 Revolt and select the option that shows the correct relationship between (A) and (R).

Assertion (A) The British government took direct control of India, ending the rule of the East India Company after the 1857 Revolt.

Reason (R) The British wanted to avoid further rebellions and believed that a direct governmental rule would stabilise India and strengthen their control.
(a) R contradicts A
(b) R is the reason for A
(c) A is true but R is false
(d) A and R are independent of each other

Ans. (b) R is the reason for A

Q.2 Read the two statements given below about the consequences of the 1857 Revolt and select the option that shows the correct relationship between (A) and (R).

Assertion (A) After the 1857 Revolt, the British introduced significant military reforms in India.

Reason (R) The British were confident that their existing military structure was effective, so no major reforms were necessary after the revolt.
(a) R contradicts A
(b) R is the reason for A
(c) A is true but R is false
(d) A and R are independent of each other

Ans. (a) R contradicts A

Q.3 Read the two statements given below About the Revolt of 1857 and select the option that shows the correct relationship between (A) and (R).

Assertion (A) The 1857 Revolt led to a fundamental shift in British policies towards Indian princely states.

Reason (R) The British didn't abandon the Doctrine of Lapse and adopted a policy of intervention in princely affairs after revolt.
(a) R contradicts A
(b) R is the reason for A
(c) A is true, but R is false
(d) A and R are independent of each other

Ans. (c) A is true, but R is false

Q.4 Read the two statements given below About the Powers of the Revolt of 1857 and select the option that shows the correct relationship between (A) and (R)

Assertion (A) The Revolt of 1857 was both a military uprising and a civil rebellion.

Reason (R) Peasants, artisans and zamindars supported the revolt because of British economic policies, which disrupted their livelihoods.
(a) R contradicts A
(b) R is the reason for A
(c) A is true, but R is false
(d) A and R are independent of each other

Ans. (b) R is the reason for A

Q.5 Read the two statements given below About the Powers of the Revolt of 1857 and select the option that shows the correct relationship between (A) and (R).

Assertion (A) The failure of the 1857 Revolt solidified British control over India.

Reason (R) The revolt resulted in widespread destruction, weakening of Indian rulers and increasing British reliance on Indian soldiers.
(a) R contradicts A
(b) R is the reason for A
(c) A is true, but R is false
(d) A and R are independent of each other

Ans. (b) (R) is the reason for (A)

Q.6 Read the two statements given below About the Powers of the Revolt of 1857 and select the option that shows the correct relationship between (A) and (R).

Assertion (A) The Revolt of 1857 saw limited participation from the educated middle class.

Reason (R) Society believed that British rule would bring modern education, reforms and economic benefits to India.
(a) R contradicts A
(b) R is the reason for A
(c) A is true, but R is false
(d) A and R are independent of each other

Ans. (a) R contradicts A

TYPE - 3 — 2 Marks

Very Short Answer Type Questions

Q.1 Analyse the impact of the defeat of the British in the First Afghan War on the Indian soldiers?

Ans. The major effects of defeat of Britishers in Afghan wars were as follows

(i) The defeat in the First Afghan War exposed British vulnerabilities, leading to disillusionment among Indian soldiers and a loss of faith in British invincibility.

(ii) The heavy casualties suffered by Indian soldiers during the war caused resentment against British leadership, contributed to the growing discontent which led to the Indian Rebellion of 1857.

Q.2 Name any two states annexed by the British using the Doctrine of Lapse.

Ans. The two states annexed by the British using the Doctrine of Lapse were Jhansi and Satara. This policy was resented by the local rulers and people.

Q.3 Read the questions and answer the following.

(i) Who was the British Governor-General of India during the 1857 Revolt?

(ii) Which policy of Lord Dalhousie was a significant cause for the 1857 Revolt?

Ans. (i) Lord Canning

(ii) Doctrine of Lapse

Q.4 Read the questions and answer

(i) Which Indian king's kingdom was annexed under the Doctrine of Lapse, sparking widespread resentment and contributing to the uprising of 1857?

(ii) What was the primary cause of the discontent among sepoys before the 1857 Revolt?

Ans. (i) Raja of Satara

(ii) Use of greased cartridges (made from cow and pig fat)

Q.5 Imagine you are an Indian ruler in the 1850s, and your state has been annexed by the British under the Doctrine of Lapse, as you have no direct male heir. You are deeply agitated by the loss of sovereignty and the British interference in your kingdom.

How might this annexation affect your relationship with the British and influence your actions during the 1857 Revolt?

Ans. The annexation of my state under the Doctrine of Lapse would lead to a deep sense of anger and betrayal. It would motivate me to resist British control, fueling my participation in the 1857 Revolt as a fight for Indian sovereignty and justice.

Q.6 What was Nana Saheb's grievance against the British?

Ans. Nana Sahib was the adopted son of the last Peshwa Baji Rao II. His grievance against the British was that they refused to grant him pension, which they were paying to Peshwa Baji Rao II.

Q.7 Highlight any two provisions of the General Service Enlistment Act?

Ans. The British Parliament passed the General Service Enlistment Act in 1856. Two provisions of this act were

(i) According to this Act, the Indian Soldiers in the East India Company could be sent overseas on duty.

(ii) Indian soldiers feared sea voyage and considered it against their religious customs.

Q.8 Mention any two reasons which encouraged the Indian soldiers to revolt.

Ans. The two reasons which encouraged the Indian soldiers to revolt were

(i) Numerical strength of Indian soldiers was approximately 2 lakhs against the 40,000 British soldiers.

(ii) The defeat of the British army in the Afghan War, Punjab War and the Crimean War inspired the Indian soldiers that they could also win against the mighty Britishers.

Q.9 Analyse the immediate impact of the Revolt of 1857 on the East India Company?

Ans. The immediate impact of the Revolt of 1857 on the East India Company was the end of the Company's rule and India was put directly under the British Crown. This was done by the Government of India Act of 1858.

Q.10 Read the question and answer

(i) When and where was Queen Victoria's proclamation made public in India?

(ii) Who made Queen Victoria's proclamation public in India?

Ans. (i) Queen Victoria's proclamation was made public on 1st November, 1858 at Allahabad currently Prayagraj.

(ii) Lord Canning, the first Viceroy of India, made the proclamation public in India.

Q.11 Explain any two assurances that were given to the Indian people by Queen Victoria in her proclamation of 1858.

Ans. The assurances given to Indian people by Queen Victoria's proclamation of 1858 were

(i) The British Government would follow a policy of non-intervention in social and religious matters of Indians.

(ii) The Government would treat all subjects i.e. Indians and Europeans equal. Education and ability would be the base of all appointments.

Q.12 The war of 1857 was much more than just a sepoy mutiny or a peasant revolt.

The first war of independence, often termed as a mutiny by the Marxist and the British historians, had started on 10th May, 1857. 162 years on, it is important to revisit what happened during those days as Bharat continues to bear the consequences of fault lines created by the British government in the post-1857 era. *3rd Jan,2019 The Hindustan Times*

What does the article suggest about the 1857 revolt and its long-term consequences?

Ans. The article emphasises the significance of the 1857 revolt, often misunderstood as merely a mutiny or peasant uprising.

The article also highlights that post-1857, the British government created fault lines through their policy of divide and rule, which is still impacting the society at large.

Q.13 Imagine you were an artisan, in the year 1856. Mention any two ways in which the economic policies of the British would have affected you.

Ans. As an artisan in 1856 under British rule, the economic policies of the British would have significantly affected me in the following ways

(i) **Competition from British Goods** The influx of inexpensive, machine-made British products overwhelmed the market and diminish the demand for my handcrafted goods and endanger my livelihood.

(ii) **High Taxes** Excessive taxation and exploitative revenue systems compel artisans to abandon their crafts and make it difficult for me to sustain.

TYPE - 4 3 Marks

Short Answer Type Questions

Q.1 Indian rulers were alienated as the British interfered in their internal affairs and denied their sovereignty. Mention any three ways how British interference in the internal affairs of Indian princely states contribute to the revolt.

Ans. British interference in the internal affairs of Indian princely states contributed to the revolt in the following ways

(i) **Doctrine of Lapse** The British annexed states without a direct male heir, such as Jhansi and Satara, denying Indian rulers their right to adopt heirs. This created anger and alienation among the rulers.

(ii) **Annexation of Awadh** Awadh was annexed in 1856 under the pretext of misgovernance. This move not only displaced the ruling family but also caused resentment among the local nobility and common people.

(iii) **Abolition of Titles and Privileges** Many Indian rulers and nobles were stripped of their titles, pensions, and privileges. For example, the Mughal emperor Bahadur Shah was denied from his symbolic authority, which deeply hurt the sentiments of his followers.

Q.2 Explain the effect of expansion policies like Subsidiary alliance on sovereignty of the Indian kingdoms?

Ans. The Subsidiary Alliance, introduced by Lord Wellesley in 1798, significantly affected the sovereignty of Indian kingdoms. It was a strategic policy that allowed the British East India Company to exert influence over Indian rulers without direct conquest. The three key effects on sovereignty were as follows

(i) **Loss of Political Autonomy** The policy required Indian rulers to maintain British troops and accept British control over their foreign relations, hence reducing their political independence. Rulers were no longer free to make decisions regarding alliances or military actions without British approval.

(ii) **Economic Drain** Indian rulers had to bear the cost of maintaining British forces within their states. This financial burden drained their resources, weakening their ability to govern effectively and leaving them economically dependent on the British.

(iii) **Fragmentation of Indian Kingdoms** The Subsidiary Alliance led to divisions among Indian states, as rulers either accepted or resisted British demands. These rivalries made it easier for the British to divide and conquer, preventing the formation of a united resistance against British expansion.

Q.3 The British introduced the Permanent Settlement system, where landlords were made responsible for collecting revenue, often exploiting peasants. Justify the statement by mentioning any three points.

Ans. The above statement can be justified as follows

(i) Under the Permanent Settlement system, landlords were required to pay a fixed revenue to the British government. To meet these demands and maximise their profits, landlords often imposed exorbitant taxes on the peasants, exploiting them mercilessly.

(ii) Peasants who were unable to pay the high taxes were frequently evicted from their lands, leading to widespread displacement and economic insecurity. Therefore, Land became concentrated in the hands of landlords, and peasants became mere tenants or labourers.

(iii) The fixed revenue system discouraged landlords from investing in agricultural improvements. This lack of investment deteriorated the condition of land and frequent famines.

Q.4 **Mention any three economic causes responsible for the beginning of Sepoy revolt In india.**

Ans. Three economic causes responsible for the beginning of sepoy revolt in india were as follows

(i) **High Land Revenue** Excessive taxes on peasants through systems like Zamindari and Ryotwari led to widespread poverty, affected sepoys who were from agrarian backgrounds.

(ii) **Decline of Local Industries** British policies destroyed traditional industries, causing economic hardship and unemployment among Indians, including the sepoys.

(iii) **Inflation and Rising Costs** Increased prices of goods due to British economic policies led to a reduced standard of living, heightening dissatisfaction among the sepoys.

Q.5 **Describe the aspirations and objectives of the rebels during the Indian Rebellion of 1857, as reflected in their proclamations and actions.**

Ans. The aspirations and objectives of the rebels during the Indian Rebellion of 1857, as reflected in their proclamations and actions are given below

- **Opposition to Annexations** Rebels condemned British annexations and broken treaties, seeking to restore sovereignty to dethroned rulers and reinstate traditional governance structures.
- **Rejection of Revenue Policies** They criticised British land revenue settlements, which they felt exploited local farmers and disrupted traditional agricultural practices.
- **Defense of Tradition** The rebels attacked various aspects of British rule, accusing the British of undermining cherished cultural and social norms, and aiming to preserve their familiar way of life.

Q.6 **List any three major consequences of the Revolt of 1857 that led to significant changes in the British administration of India.**

Ans. Major consequences of the Revolt of 1857 that led to significant changes in the British administration of India are as follows

(i) **End of the East India Company's Rule** The British government dissolved the East India Company after the revolt, ending its direct control over India. India was brought under direct British rule, marking the beginning of the British Raj.

(ii) **Reorganisation of the British Army** After the revolt, the British reorganised the Indian army, reducing the number of Indian sepoys and increasing the proportion of British soldiers. This was done to prevent further uprisings and ensure loyalty to the British Crown.

(iii) **Increased British Control over Indian Affairs** The British Crown took more direct control over the administration of India. The Government of India Act of 1858 was enacted, which allowed the British monarch to govern India directly, with a viceroy as the representative.

Q.7 **Mention any two strategies that were adopted by the British to suppress the revolt in the Ganegtic Plain.**

Ans. To suppress the revolt in the Ganegtic plain, the British adopted the following strategies

(i) The British tried to conquer the area village by village. The area was brought under control only in March 1858 after endless fighting. The British used military power on a gigantic scale.

(ii) Rebel landholders were dispossessed and the loyal rewarded. Many landholders died fighting the British, or they escaped into Nepal, where they died of illness or starvation.

Q.8 **The 1857 revolt, also known as the First War of Indian Independence, witnessed large-scale uprisings across various parts of India.**

The British East India Company's policies, including the introduction of the Enfield rifle cartridges, heavy taxation, and annexation of territories, were seen as acts of subjugation.

(i) Name two prominent leaders of the Revolt of 1857 from Meerut.

(ii) How did the introduction of the Doctrine of Lapse contribute to the discontent leading to this revolt?

(iii) Which major Indian region witnessed the initial flare-up of the rebellion?

Ans. (i) The two prominent leaders of the Revolt of 1857 are

(a) Bakht Khan

(b) Mangal Pandey

(ii) The Doctrine of Lapse was introduced by Lord Dalhousie, which stated that if an Indian ruler died without a male heir, their kingdom would be annexed by the British. This policy led to widespread resentment among Indian rulers.

(iii) The initial flare-up of the rebellion occurred in Meerut, where the sepoys of the British East India Company's army rebelled on 10th May, 1857.

TYPE - 5 4 Marks

Long Answer Type Questions

Q.1 Highlight the differences between policies of the colonial empire before and after the 1857 revolt in India.

Ans. The major differences between the policies of the colonial empire before and after the 1857 Revolt in India were as follows

Basis	Before the 1857 Revolt	After the 1857 Revolt
Governance	Controlled by the British East India Company.	Direct control by the British Crown, with a Viceroy.
Military Structure	Relied on a mix of Indian sepoys and British soldiers.	Increased reliance on British soldiers and reduced Indian sepoy presence.
Control over Indian Rulers	Indian rulers retained some autonomy, but were controlled by policies like the Doctrine of Lapse.	Policies like Doctrine of Lapse and Subsidiary Alliance were discontinued.
Economic Control	The East India Company controlled trade and revenues.	The British Crown took full economic control, with more direct exploitation of resources.

Q.2 How did the Doctrine of Lapse challenge Indian traditions regarding the adoption of heirs?

Ans. The Doctrine of Lapse challenged Indian traditions regarding the adoption of heirs in the following ways

(i) The Doctrine of Lapse disallowed Indian rulers without a biological male heir from adopting an heir to inherit the throne. This went against the long-standing Indian tradition, where adoption was a legitimate way to continue the family lineage and maintain sovereignty.

(ii) According to Indian customs, an adopted heir had the same rights as a biological heir. By denying this, the British disregarded Indian cultural and legal practices, leading to the annexation of princely states and undermining their autonomy.

(iii) Adoption was deeply rooted in Indian society as a means to preserve family legacy and perform religious duties. The Doctrine of Lapse ignored these cultural values, causing resentment and alienation among Indian rulers and the masses.

(iv) Many Indian rulers had adopted heirs to ensure the stability and continuity of their kingdoms. The British enforcement of the Doctrine of Lapse disrupted these succession plans, leading to political instability and resentment among the ruling families, as their legitimate heirs were not recognised by the British authorities.

Q.3 Analyse the role of British social reforms in shaping the discontent that led to the Revolt of 1857.

Ans. The British social reforms played a significant role in shaping the discontent that ultimately led to the Revolt of 1857.

Some of the major reforms were as follows

(i) **Abolition of Sati (1829)** The British abolition of the Sati system was viewed by many as an attack on Hindu religious practices, leading to resistance from traditionalists.

(ii) **Widow Remarriage Act (1856)** This law was enacted to legalise the widow remarriage but it went against the customs of the traditional Indian society.

(iii) **Western Education and Missionary Activities** The promotion of Western education and the spread of Christianity alienated many Indians, who felt their culture and religion were being undermined.

(iv) **General Services Enlistment Act (1856)** The requirement for Indian sepoys to serve overseas violated their religious beliefs, especially among Hindus.

Q.4 'Rumours and prophecies played a part in moving people to action'. Explain the statement in the context of the Revolt of 1857.

Ans. Rumours and prophecies played a part in moving people to action. There was a rumour among sepoys that bullets are coated with the fat of cows and pigs. They believed that biting those bullets would corrupt their caste and religion.

There was another rumour that the British government had hatched a massive conspiracy to destroy the caste and religion of Hindus and Muslims.

The British had mixed the bone dust of cows and pigs into the flour that was sold in the market. These fears inspired men to action.

The response to the call for action was reinforced by the prophecy that British rule would come to an end on the centenary of the Battle of Plassey, on 23rd June, 1857.

Q.5 The Government of India Act, 1858, ended the direct rule of the East India Company and made India a part of the British Empire. What change did the Government of India Act, 1858, bring in terms of the governance of India?

Ans. The Government of India Act, 1858 brought significant changes to the governance of India in the following ways

(i) The Act marked the end of the direct rule of the East India Company, which had governed India since the 18th century. The British Crown took over control, making India a part of the British Empire.

(ii) The British Crown assumed direct control over India through the appointment of a Viceroy, who would act as the Crown's representative in India. This replaced the position of the Governor-General of India, who had previously been appointed by the East India Company.

(iii) The Act created a new office called the Secretary of State for India, who would oversee all matters concerning India from Britain. This position was supported by a Council of India, which advised the Secretary of State.

(iv) With the British Crown taking over, the governance became more centralised, with the ultimate decision-making power resting in the hands of the British government in London. The act aimed to maintain tighter control over Indian affairs and avoid the administrative challenges faced during the rule of the East India Company.

Q.6 Describe the contribution of the following leaders to the Revolt of 1857.

(i) Rani Lakshmibai of Jhansi

(ii) Kunwar Singh of Bihar

Ans. (i) Rani Lakshmibai was the Queen of Jhansi. After the annexation of Jhansi, under Doctrine of Lapse she became a rebel and joined in the uprising of 1857. Her contribution in the Revolt of 1857 were as follows

(a) She was considered the bravest and best military leader of the rebels and with the help of Tantia-Tope, she occupied Gwalior.

(b) Sir Hugh Rose advanced towards Gwalior and defeated the Indian troops. Rani fought like a real hero and died on the battlefield.

(c) Her courage and military skill inspired her countrymen. She is still remembered by Indians for her great sacrifice.

(ii) Kunwar Singh was a prominent leader during the 1857 Revolt and played a significant role in the uprising in Bihar. His contribution in the Revolt of 1857 were

(a) He used guerrilla warfare effectively, inflicting significant losses on the British army.

(b) He became a symbol of Indian resistance, inspiring local communities to rise against British rule.

(c) Although unsuccessful, his efforts delayed British control and left a lasting legacy as a freedom fighter.

TYPE - 6 — 10 Marks

Structured Questions

Q.1 "Numerous causes were at work in causing the great upsurge of 1857" with reference to this, explain the following **(ICSE 2018)**

(i) Apprehension about Modern Innovations **(3)**

(ii) The introduction of the Enfield rifles **(3)**

(iii) The laws that interfered with the religious customs of the people and racial discrimination policy **(4)**

Ans. (i) The apprehension about modern innovations were

(a) The rapid spread of modern civilisation made people afraid and suspicious.

(b) People spread the rumours that the telegraph poles were erected for the purpose of hanging people, who opposed the British rule in India.

(c) The orthodox Indians felt humiliated to know that in the railway compartments, Brahmins and people from the backward classes were made to sit side by side.

(ii) The introduction of Enfield rifles was the immediate cause of the revolt. In 1856, the British authorities decided to replace the old fashioned musket by the new 'Enfield rifles'. There was a rumour that the cartridges of these rifles were greased with the fat of cows and pigs.

The loading process of the Enfield rifles involved bringing the cartridge to the mouth and biting off the top greased paper with the mouth. Both the Hindu and Muslim sepoys refused to use the cartridges, as they felt that the English were defiling their religion.

(iii) The British introduced several laws that interfered with the religious customs of the people in India, leading to widespread discontent and resentment. Some of the key laws included

(a) **The General Services Enlistment Act (1856)** This law required Indian soldiers to serve overseas if needed, which was against the religious beliefs of many Hindu and Muslim soldiers.

(b) **The Widow Remarriage Act (1856)** The British passed this law to allow the remarriage of widows, which was a practice that went against traditional Hindu customs, particularly in conservative sections of society.

(c) **The Religious Disabilities Act (1856)** This law was seen as an attempt to interfere in religious matters, as it allowed Christians to inherit property regardless of religious differences.

(d) **Abolition of Sati** Sati system was banned in 1829, which was seen as a direct attack on religious traditions of India.

Q.2 **Answer the following questions based on the picture given below.**

(i) **Describe the incident in the above image.** **(3)**

(ii) **Lack of unity and coordination among Indian leaders was the major cause behind failure of the revolt of 1857. Justify the statement.** **(3)**

(iii) **Bahadur Shah Zafar, as the last Mughal Emperor, was seen as a symbol of unity and legitimacy by the Indian rebels. How did his position influence his selection as the leader of the revolt?** **(4)**

Ans. (i) The image shows the fight between British forces and Indian sepoys during the Revolt of 1857, also known as the First War of Indian Independence. The British soldiers, supported by loyal Indian forces, used superior weaponry and tactics to suppress the rebellion.

The British response was harsh, involving massacres, heavy artillery, and the destruction of towns supporting the rebels. Despite its defeat, the revolt weakened British control over India and laid the foundation for the future independence struggle, which culminated in 1947.

(ii) The lack of unity and coordination among Indian leaders was a major cause behind the failure of the 1857 Revolt due to the following reasons

(a) **Fragmented Leadership** Indian leaders like Bahadur Shah Zafar, Rani Lakshmibai, and Tatya Tope had differing regional interests and lacked a unified strategy, that caused poor coordination in the revolt.

(b) **Regional and Religious Divides** The revolt was largely regional, with leaders from different areas having separate priorities. This lack of a national vision weakened the overall unity and effectiveness of the uprising.

(c) **British Exploitation of Divisions** The British capitalised on India's social, religious, and caste divisions, using divide and rule tactics to create distrust and further fragment the efforts of the rebels.

(iii) Bahadur Shah Zafar, as the last Mughal Emperor, was chosen as the leader of the Revolt of 1857 due to his symbolic status and the legitimacy his position provided. His selection was influenced by several factors which were as follows

(a) Despite being largely powerless under British rule, Bahadur Shah Zafar represented the continuity of the Mughal dynasty and was seen as a unifying figure for diverse groups across India.

(b) As the Mughal Emperor, Zafar's position carried historical and cultural significance. His leadership was seen as legitimate by the rebels, who hoped that by rallying under his banner, they could restore India's sovereignty and challenge British authority.

(c) Zafar's position as the Mughal Emperor also gave him importance in both Hindu and Muslim communities. While his personal influence was limited, the rebellion sought to restore a sense of Indian pride and identity, with Zafar's leadership representing the glory of India's past.

(d) As the Emperor of Delhi, Zafar provided moral support and inspired the rebels to rise against British rule. His selection was not based on his administrative power but rather on the emotional and cultural appeal of his position as a symbol of resistance against foreign domination.

Q.3 **Although the First War of Independence of 1857 failed, it had major consequences for India. In this context, answer the following questions.**

(i) **How did the revolt give rise to nationalism in India?** **(3)**

(ii) **Explain how the end of the East India Company's rule brought grave economic perils in India?** **(3)**

(iii) **State how the British Government tried to pacify the feelings of Indians with regard to** **(4)**

(a) **their religion and practices**

(b) **the princely states**

Ans. (i) The 1857 Uprising, though ultimately unsuccessful, played a pivotal role in the rise of nationalism in India. The rebellion brought together people from diverse backgrounds-peasants, artisans, soldiers, and royalty-against a common colonial enemy, the British.

This unity sowed the seeds of a shared Indian identity. The struggle fostered a sense of national consciousness, showing that Indians, regardless of caste, religion, or region, could unite against foreign rule. The uprising also gave rise to early Indian leaders who began to advocate for Indian rights and self-rule, paving the way for later nationalist movements, like the formation of the Indian National Congress in 1885.

(ii) After the British Crown took control of India following the 1857 uprising, India became a direct colony of Britain. This shift worsened India's economic conditions, with increased exploitation. The British government imposed heavy taxes on agricultural products and extracted more resources to support Britain's Industrial Revolution.

India's economy was focused on producing cash crops like cotton and indigo for Britain, while food crops were neglected, making India prone to famines. Local industries, like textiles, were destroyed, leaving India dependent on Britain for goods.

(iii) (a) To calm religious tensions, especially after the fear caused by the introduction of new cartridges rumored to be greased with cow and pig fat, the British Government assured Indians that their religious beliefs and practices would be respected.

The British also made efforts to create a buffer between their policies and religious sentiments, promising to protect Hindu and Muslim traditions.

(b) After the rebellion, the British sought to maintain stability in the princely states by assuring the rulers that their titles and territories would be protected as long as they remained loyal to the British Crown.

The British offered security and autonomy in return for allegiance which helped pacify many princely states that had previously supported the revolt or were at risk of joining it.

Q.4 **The Indian Rebellion of 1857 was a major uprising against the rule of the British East India Company, which functioned as a sovereign power on behalf of the British Crown. With reference to this, answer the following questions.** **(ICSE Specimen 2025)**

(i) The British used many policies of expansion. Mention any three such policies. **(3)**

(ii) How did the failure of this revolt impact the Mughals and the Peshwas? **(3)**

(iii) The Indian army was reorganised after 1858, to prevent the reoccurrence of another uprising. Analyse this statement by stating any four changes made in the army after the revolt. **(4)**

Ans. (i) The British used several policies of expansion in India to extend their control over the region.

Three major policies of expansion were

(a) **Doctrine of Lapse** Introduced by Lord Dalhousie, this policy allowed the British to annex Indian states where the ruler died without a direct male heir. The annexation was justified on the grounds that the rulers had no legitimate successor, leading to the annexation of several princely states such as Jhansi, Satara, and Nagpur.

(b) **Subsidiary Alliance** This policy, introduced by Lord Wellesley, required Indian rulers to maintain British troops in their territories and pay for their upkeep. The rulers also had to agree not to employ any other foreign forces. This policy effectively made Indian rulers dependent on the British for military support and led to the expansion of British influence over Indian states.

(c) **Annexation under the Pretext of Misrule** The British annexed various states on the grounds that the rulers were mismanaging their territories or were unable to maintain law and order. For instance, the annexation of Awadh (Oudh) in 1856 was justified by the British on the pretext that the Nawab was misgoverning the region, even though the real reason was to strengthen British control over the region.

(ii) The failure of the Revolt of 1857 had significant consequences for both the Mughals and the Peshwas

Impact on the Mughals

The failure of the revolt led to the formal end of the Mughal Empire. The British deposed the last Mughal emperor Bahadur Shah Zafar and exiled him to 'Rangoon' in Burma. His sovereignty, which had already been symbolic was completely eradicated after the revolt. With Bahadur Shah Zafar's exile, the Mughal dynasty came to an official end and the British formally established direct control over India, marking the beginning of the British Raj in 1858.

Impact on the Peshwas

The failure of the revolt also had lasting consequences for the Maratha community. Baji Rao II, the last Peshwa, had already been deposed by the British in 1808, following the defeat of the Marathas in the Third Anglo-Maratha War (1817-1818).

Although the Peshwas were no longer in power by 1857, the failure of the revolt further consolidated British authority over the Marathas and their territories. The British solidified their dominance over the Maratha region and ensured that no leader from the Maratha family could challenge their rule.

(iii) After the Revolt of 1857, the British made the following changes to the Indian army

(a) The British restructured the Indian army to reduce the proportion of Indian soldiers in key positions. The army was now divided into British and Indian sections. British soldiers were given the majority of important and higher-ranking positions, while Indian soldiers were mostly restricted to lower ranks.

(b) The number of British soldiers stationed in India increased after 1858. The British believed that by having more of their own troops in the country, they could prevent any large-scale rebellion.

(c) The recruitment of Indian soldiers was based on a more strategic approach. The British began to recruit soldiers from specific communities or regions that were seen as more loyal or less likely to revolt.

(d) The British shifted the composition of the Indian army by increasing the number of artillery units and making sure that these units were manned by British soldiers only.

Q.5. **With reference to the 1857 revolt answer the following questions.**

(i) "The annexation of Awadh displaced not just the Nawab, but also dispossessed the taluqdars of the region, causing breakdown of an entire social order". Justify the statement. (3)

(ii) Examine the repressive measures adopted by British to subdue the rebels of 1857. (3)

(iii) How did the rumors play a role in moving the people to revolt against the British during 1857? Explain. (4)

Ans. (i) The annexation of Awadh on 13th February, 1856 by Lord Dalhousie also dispossessed the taluqdars of the region with the displacing of the Nawab in the following ways

- With the dissolution of the royal administration, large number of courtiers, officials and taluqdars became jobless.
- With the removal of nawab, all taluqdars of the Awadh were dispossessed, disarmed and their forts were destroyed.
- With a new revenue system i.e. Summary Settlement, taluqdars lost their very large share of revenue from land.
- Wherever possible, taluqdars were removed and settlement was done directly with peasant.

(ii) The measures taken by the British to subdue the rebels of 1857 were

- **Passing of Laws to help the Troops** The British passed new laws to punish Indian rebels quickly without following normal trials. They also brought more troops from Britain and started retaking North India. In June 1857, they attacked Delhi from two sides to suppress the revolt.
- **Resorting to Diplomacy** The British used clever strategies to divide the rebels. They promised zamindars their land back, keeping them away from the rebels.
- **Use of Military Power** The British used a strong army. They controlled railways and could send troops quickly to fight rebels in different areas.
- **Communication System** The telegraph system helped the British to get timely information about the incidents occurring in different parts of the country.

(iii) For answer, refer to Q. 4 of Long Answer Type Question.

Q.6. **The Revolt of 1857 was conscious beginning of the independence struggle against the British. With reference to this, answer the following questions.** **(ICSE 2025)**

(i) What was the Doctrine of Lapse? Who introduced it? (3)

(ii) British Government interfered in the social and religious matters of the Indians. Mention any three socio religious causes to justify this statement. (3)

(iii) Mention any four military causes which led to this revolt. (4)

Ans. (i) The Doctrine of Lapse was a policy introduced by Lord Dalhousie, the Governor-General of India.

According to this doctrine, if a ruling king died without a biological heir, his kingdom would automatically be annexed by the British East India Company. Adopted sons were not recognised as legitimate heirs. Using this policy, the British annexed several princely states, including Satara, Jhansi, Nagpur and Awadh. This caused widespread resentment among Indian rulers and was one of the major political causes of the Revolt of 1857.

(ii) The British government interfered in the social and religious matters of Indians, which led to widespread dissatisfaction. The three socio-religious causes to justify this statement are

(a) **Interference in Religious Practices** The British banned Sati (1829) and discouraged child marriage, which was seen as an attack on Hindu customs and traditions.

(b) **Promotion of Christian Missionaries** The British encouraged Christian conversions, making Indians fear that their religion and cultural practices were under threat.

(c) **Social Discrimination** Indians were treated as inferior to the British, facing racial discrimination in jobs and administration, which created resentment among the people.

(iii) Four military causes which led to this revolt were

(a) **Discontent Among Sepoys** Indian soldiers (sepoys) were paid less, treated unfairly, and had fewer promotion opportunities compared to British soldiers.

(b) **General Service Enlistment Act** (1856) This act forced sepoys to serve overseas, which was against Hindu religious beliefs, as crossing the sea (Kala Pani) was considered impure.

(c) **Greased Cartridge Incident** The new Enfield rifle cartridges were rumoured to be greased with cow and pig fat, offending both Hindus and Muslims. Sepoys who refused to use them were punished, increasing their anger.

(d) **Annexation of Awadh** Many sepoys were from Awadh, which was annexed under the Doctrine of Lapse, leading to resentment among soldiers who had family ties to the region.

2

THE RISE OF NATIONALISM & THE INDIAN NATIONAL CONGRESS

- Nationalism is a strong sentiment, a feeling of love and pride for one's own country. It is fundamental for a nation's progress and unity.
- Nationalism in India emerged in the late 19th and early 20th centuries and it was driven by the desire for self-rule, social reform, and economic developments.

Factors Leading to the Growth of Nationalism in India

British Policy of Economic Exploitation

- British goods were sold at low prices in Indian markets, making it difficult for traditional Indian handicrafts and cottage industries to survive.
- India was turned to a supplier of raw materials (such as cotton, jute, indigo) for British industries and a market for British manufactured goods.
- The British imposed high land taxes on Indian farmers, which drained the rural economy and left peasants impoverished.
- British policies forced farmers to grow cash crops like opium, indigo, and cotton for export, which resulted in the negligence towards food crops needed to sustain the local population.

Lord Lytton

Repressive Colonial Policies

- The Vernacular Press Act, also known as the Gagging Act, was passed in 1878 by Lord Lytton to suppress the freedom of native press.
- The Indian Arms Act, 1878 was introduced by Lord Lytton. It forced Indians to acquire a licence to keep, sell or purchase arms.
- The Ilbert Bill of 1883 was passed to abolish judicial disqualification on the basis of racial distinction but it did not succeed in its objective properly.

Socio-Religious Reform Movements

The second half of the 19th century witnessed the rise of many religious and social reformers in India like Raja Ram Mohan Roy and Jyotiba Phule.

Raja Ram Mohan Roy

He was the first great socio-religious reformer of the 19th century also known as the Father of Indian Renaissance. His contributions include

Raja Ram Mohan Roy

- Raja Ram Mohan Roy led the fight against Sati, resulting in its ban in 1829 by the British government.
- He founded Brahmo Samaj in 1828 to promote monotheism, social equality, and rational reform in Hinduism.
- Roy advocated for widow remarriage and better status for women, influencing the Widow Remarriage Act of 1856.
- He promoted modern, scientific education and established the first English-medium school in India.
- He started a Bengali weekly called *Samvad Kaumudi* and a paper in Persian called *Mirat-ul-Akbar*.

Jyotiba Phule

Jyotiba Phule

He was an activist, thinker, social reformer who belonged to a low caste family from Maharashtra. He fought a long-struggled life against caste discrimination and Brahmanical supremacy. His contributions include

- Phule and his wife established the first girls school at Poona in 1848.
- In 1854, he started a private orphanage for the widows and established a school for untouchables.
- In 1873, he founded the Satya Shodhak Samaj to fight against the caste system.
- He wrote the famous book 'Gulamgiri' in which he described the poor conditions of lower castes.

Role of the Press

- Many newspapers like, The Amrita Bazar Patrika, The Hindu, The Patriot criticised the unjust policies of the colonial government.
- Indian Press became the primary medium of popular public education.
- The Indian Press played an important role in exchanging views among different social groups from different parts of the country.

East India Association

- The 'East India Association' was founded by Dadabhai Naroji (also called 'The Grand Old Man of India') in London in 1866.
- Through this association, Dadabhai wanted to inform the British about the grievances of Indian people and suggested remedial measures.
- The association demanded the withdrawal of the Vernacular Press Act and abolition of cotton duties.

The Indian National Association

- The Indian National Association was founded in 1876 by Surendranath Banerjee.
- The main objectives of this association were to create public opinion on political matters.
- This association tried to evolve a common political programme.
- It demanded changes in the Indian Civil Service Examination, cancellation of the Arms Act, the Vernacular Press Act, etc.

Indian National Congress (INC)

A.O. Hume

- The Indian National Congress was founded on 28th December, 1885 after a meeting held in Bombay (now Mumbai).
- The formation was initiated by A.O. Hume, a retired British Civil Servant, who sought to provide a peaceful platform for Indians to express their concerns under British rule.
- The first President of the Congress was W.C. Bonnerjee.

Immediate Objectives of the Indian National Congress

The first session of congress was held at Bombay in 1885. Its President was W.C. Bonnerjee. Its objectives were

- Promotion of close relations between nationalist workers from different parts of the country.
- Development and consolidation of a feeling of national unity, irrespective of caste, religion or province.
- Formulation of popular demands and their presentation before the government.

The second session of the Congress was held at Calcutta in 1886. Its President was Dadabhai Naoroji. The objectives of the session were

- The Congress called for an increase in the number of Indians in legislative bodies and for Indianisation of the civil services.
- A major focus was on the economic policies of the British, demanding that India's resources should be used for the benefit of Indians.
- Thereafter, the national congress gathered every year in December, changing locations around the country.

EXAM ORIENTED QUESTIONS

TYPE - 1

1 Mark

Multiple Choice Questions

Q.1 Identify the odd one out from the following statements related to the British economic exploitation in India.

(a) India was turned into a supplier of raw materials like cotton, jute, and indigo for British industries.

(b) British policies imposed high land taxes on Indian farmers, which drained the rural economy.

(c) British policies encouraged the growth of food crops for local consumption.

(d) Farmers were forced to grow cash crops like opium and cotton for export, neglecting food crops.

Ans. (c) British policies encouraged the growth of food crops for local consumption.

Q.2 Who among the following Governor-Generals repealed the Vernacular Press Act, 1878?

(a) Lord Lytton (b) Lord Dufferin

(c) William Bentinck (d) Lord Ripon

Ans. (d) Lord Ripon

Exp. The Vernacular Press Act of 1878 suppressed Indian language newspapers that were critical of British rule, and allowed the government to seise press and shut publications.

Q.3 Identify the correct statements about the British colonial policies

P : Vernacular Press Act suppressed the freedom of the native press.

Q : The Indian Arms Act, 1878 allowed Indians to freely purchase arms.

R : The Ilbert Bill, 1883 ended racial disqualification in the judiciary.

S : Lord Curzon's policies encouraged Indian self-rule and empowerment.

(a) P and Q (b) P and R

(c) R and S (d) S and Q

Ans. (b) P and R

Q.4 The law passed by Lytton reduced the age limit for appearing for Civil Service Examination from 21 to how many years?

(a) 20 years (b) 18 years

(c) 17 years (d) 19 years

Ans. (d) 19 years

Q.5 Which of the following is incorrect about the contribution of Raja Ram Mohan Roy to the Indian reform movement?

(a) He promoted the abolition of Sati.

(b) He supported the introduction of English education in India.

(c) He was the founder of the Indian National Congress.

(d) He advocated for the reform of social practices in India.

Ans. (c) He was the founder of the Indian National Congress.

Q.6 Complete the given analogy.

Jyotiba Phule: Satya Shodhak Samaj :: Raja Ram Mohan Roy : ?

(a) Arya Samaj (b) Brahmo Samaj

(c) Prarthna Samaj (d) Servants of Indian Society

Ans. (b) Brahmo Samaj

Q.7 Which of the following actions was not part of Phule's efforts to promote social reform?

(a) Establishing the first girls' school in Poona in 1851.

(b) Founding the Satya Shodhak Samaj in 1873.

(c) Writing the book Gulamgiri to describe the hardships of lower castes.

(d) Promote the caste system through his writings and social initiatives.

Ans. (d) Promote the caste system through his writings and social initiatives.

Q.8 Jyotiba Phule, a social reformer from Maharashtra, fought against the caste system and worked to improve the lives of lower castes. He and his wife established the first girls' school in Pune in 1851 and later founded the Satya Shodhak Samaj to challenge social inequalities. *The Hindu 11th April, 2023*

What can be inferred from the passage above about Jyotirao Phule?

(a) Phule focused only on education for upper-caste children.

(b) Phule worked towards social equality, particularly for women and lower castes.

(c) Phule supported the caste system and Brahmanical supremacy.

(d) Phule's efforts were only limited to the establishment of schools.

Ans. (b) Phule worked towards social equality, particularly for women and lower castes.

Exp. Jyotiba Phule belonged to a low caste family from Maharashtra. He established the first girls school at Poona in 1848.

Q.9 Read the description and identify the person.
He was associated with the Slogan of 'Ishwar Keval Ek Hai. Uska Koi Aant Nahin'.
(a) Keshav Chandra Sen (b) Raja Ram Mohan Roy
(c) Dada Bhai Naoroji (d) Rabindranath Tagore

Ans. (b) Raja Ram Mohan Roy

Q.10 Identify the person in the image below who was associated with Satya Shodak Samaj.

(a) Keshav Chandra Sen (b) Lord Rippon
(c) Swami Dayanand Saraswat (d) Jyotiba Phule

Ans. (d) Jyotiba Phule

Q.11 Who among the following is most associated with this picture? **(ICSE 2025)**

(a) Jyotiba Phule (b) Raja Ram Mohan Roy
(c) Swami Dayanand Saraswati (d) Aurobindo Ghosh

Q.12 Tahir is preparing to give a speech about the Sati system in India. Which of the following Indian leader's contributions regarding he must mention in his speech? **(ICSE 2024)**
(a) Raja Ram Mohan Roy (b) W. C. Bonnerjee
(c) Bipin Chandra Pal (d) Jyotiba Phule

Ans. (a) Raja Ram Mohan Roy

Exp. Raja Ram Mohan Roy, a social reformer campaigned against the inhumane practice of sati where widows were forced to self-immolate. His efforts led to the British banning Sati through Regulation XVII in 1829.

Q.13 Complete the given analogy.
Indian Association of Calcutta :?? ::Dadabhai Naoroji : East India Association.
(a) Womesh Chandra Bonnerjee
(b) Bankim Chandra Chatterjee
(c) Dwarkanath Tagore
(d) Surendranath Banerjee

Ans. (d) Surendranath Banerjee

Q.14 Who was the founder of the Indian National Congress? **(ICSE Semester-I 2022)**
(a) A.O. Hume (b) W.C. Bonnerjee
(c) Dadabhai Naoroji (d) Gopal Krishna Gokhale

Ans. (a) A.O. Hume

Q.15 The year in which Congress was established **(ICSE Specimen 2021)**
(a) 1880 (b) 1885
(c) 1889 (d) 1890

Ans. (b) 1885

Q.16 Which of these was not an aim of the Indian National Congress? **(ICSE Specimen 2023)**
(a) To train and organise public opinion in the country.
(b) To promote friendly relations between nationalists and political workers.
(c) To make the world aware of the true nature of the British.
(d) To formulate popular demands and present them before the government.

Ans. (c) To make the world aware of the true nature of the British.

Q.17 Which of the following is the correct statement about the Indian National Congress (INC)?
(i) INC was formed in the year 1885.
(ii) The viceroy during the formation of INC was Lord Ripon.
(iii) It was a political association since its formation.
(iv) The Second Session of INC was presided by Dadabhai Naoroji.

Codes
(a) All are correct (b) Only (i)
(c) Both (i) and (iv) (d) Both (ii) and (iii)

Ans. (c) Both (i) and (iv)

18. Identify the person in the image below who was associated with formation of a major party in India

(a) A.O. Hume (b) William Wordsworth
(c) Keshav Chandra Sen (d) Lord Rippon

Ans. (a) A.O. Hume

Exp. A.O. Hume was a British civil servant who played a key role in forming the Indian National Congress in 1885, a major political party that led India's freedom struggle.

TYPE - 2 1 Mark

Assertion-Reason Questions

Q.1 Read the two statements given below about the Indian National Congress and select the option that shows the correct relationship between (A) and (R).

Assertion (A) The Indian National Congress (INC) played a pivotal role in mobilising Indian public opinion and promoting nationalist movements against British colonial rule.

Reason (R) It was founded in 1885 with the primary aim of representing Indian interests and seeking reforms within the British colonial system.

(a) R contradicts A

(b) R is the reason for A

(c) A is true but R is false

(d) A and R are independent of each other

Ans. (b) R is the reason for A

Q.2 Read the two statements given below about the rise of nationalism in India and select the option that shows the correct relationship between (A) and (R).

Assertion (A) The rise of nationalism in India during the late 19th century was largely influenced by the social reforms and the spread of education.

Reason (R) The introduction of Western education by the British led to the emergence of a new educated middle class that began questioning colonial rule and advocating for Indian rights.

(a) R contradicts A

(b) R is the reason for A

(c) A is true but R is false

(d) A and R are independent of each other

Ans. (b) R is the reason for A

Q.3 Read the two statements given below about the Indian National Congress and select the option that shows the correct relationship between (A) and (R).

Assertion (A) The rise of nationalism in India was influenced by Western education and ideas of liberty and equality.

Reason (R) The first session of Indian National Congress held in Delhi in November.

(a) R contradicts A

(b) R is the reason for A

(c) A is true but R is false

(d) A and R are independent of each other

Ans. (c) A is true but R is false

Q.4 Read the two statements given below about the Indian National Congress and select the option that shows the correct relationship between (A) and (R).

Assertion (A) The formation of the Indian National Congress played a crucial role in the Indian independence movement.

Reason (R) Assertive Indians also expressed their political and social grievances against British rule.

(a) R contradicts A

(b) R is the reason for A

(c) A is true but R false

(d) A and R are independent of each other

Ans. (d) A and R are independent of each other

Q.5 Read the two statements given below about the Indian National Congress and select the option that shows the correct relationship between (A) and (R).

Assertion (A) The formation of the Indian National Congress was initially intended to seek reforms within the British framework.

Reason (R) The Congress initially focused on petitioning the British government for improvements in administrative and social policies for Indians.

(a) R contradicts A

(b) R is the reason for A

(c) A is true but R is false

(d) A and R are independent of each other

Ans. (b) R is the reason for A

TYPE - 3 2 Marks

Very Short Answer Type Questions

Q.1 There were various factors that promoted the growth of nationalism in India in the 19th century. Give the meaning of 'nationalism' in this context.

Ans. In the context of 19th-century India, nationalism refers to the sense of unity and collective identity among the people of India in their struggle against British colonial rule. It was the growing awareness of a shared national identity, culture, and history that transcended regional and communal divisions.

Q.2 Discuss any two reasons for industrial stagnation in British India.

Ans. Industrial stagnation in British India refers to the slow or limited growth of industries due to various reasons which are as follows

(i) **Colonial Exploitation** British policies prioritised raw material extraction from India, limiting the growth of local industries.

(ii) **Lack of Investment** The British focused on using India as a market for British goods, resulting in limited investment in industrial development.

Q.3 **Mention any two objectives of the Ilbert Bill.**

Ans. The Ilbert Bill was introduced in 1883, aimed to address judicial inequalities in British-ruled India. Two key objectives of the Ilbert Bill were as follows

(i) One of the primary objectives of the Ilbert Bill was to give Indian judges the authority to try European offenders in criminal cases.

(ii) The Ilbert Bill sought to promote equality in the judicial system by removing the racial discrimination that existed in the courts.

Q.4 **Explain the purpose of the Vernacular Press Act of 1878 and its impact on the Indian press.**

Ans. The Vernacular Press Act of 1878 was aimed at controlling and censoring Indian newspapers published in local languages that were critical of British rule.

It allowed the government to seize newspapers and prosecute their editors for publishing seditious content. This severely restricted press freedom and led to protests, thus raised nationalist sentiments among Indians.

Q.5 **Mention any two repressive policies of Lord Lytton.** **(ICSE 2023)**

Ans. Two repressive policies of Lord Lytton were

(i) **The Vernacular Press Act (1878)** This law aimed to suppress Indian-language newspapers critical of British rule by allowing the government to confiscate press materials and shut down publications without trial.

(ii) **The Indian Arms Act (1878)** This act prohibited Indians from possessing arms or ammunition without a license, further limiting their ability to resist British authority and control.

Q.6 **Mention any two economic factors responsible for the growth of nationalism in India.**

Ans. Two economic factors responsible for the growth of nationalism in India were

(i) Educated Indians were not appointed to high posts. High posts in civil and military services were only reserved for the British. As a result the Indian began to feel alienated by the British.

(ii) The government levied high taxes on land. Revenues were generally not reduced even during droughts, floods, etc. This led to growth of nationalism among Indian peasantry.

Q.7 **How did the English language play a leading role in the growth of nationalism in India?**

Ans. The English language played a key role in India's nationalism in following ways

(i) **Access to Western Ideas** English exposed Indians to democratic and nationalist ideas from the West.

(ii) **Unified Communication** It allowed communication among educated Indians from diverse regions.

Q.8 **Mention any two social reforms suggested to the British by Raja Ram Mohan Roy.**

Ans. The two social reforms suggested to the British by Raja Ram Mohan Roy were

(i) Banning Sati, the practice of burning widows

(ii) Promoting women's education to uplift their status and give them equal rights in society.

Q.9 **Mention any two contributions of Jyotiba Phule in preparing the ground for the national movement.** **(ICSE 2015)**

Ans. The two great contribution of Jyotiba Phule in preparing the ground for the national movement were follows

(i) In 1873, Jyotiba Phule founded Satya Shodhak Samaj to fight against the caste system.

(ii) He pioneered the widow remarriage movement in Maharashtra and worked for the education of women.

Q.10 **Imagine you are a devoted member of the Brahmo Samaj in the early 19th century, deeply disturbed by the horrors of the Sati system. You have just returned from witnessing a scene where a young widow, barely in her twenties, is forced onto her husband's funeral pyre. The flames consumed not just her body but your hope in the justice of traditional customs.**

What steps would you take to end such types of traditional superstitious practices in society?

Ans. To get rid of such harmful traditions, I would focus on spreading education, especially among women and marginalised groups, to challenge superstitions and encourage logical thinking.

I would push for fair laws and make sure they are followed while promoting simple and ethical religious practices. I would also work with other reform movements to strengthen our efforts and create communities that practice equality and justice for all.

Q.11 **Which were the two papers published by Raja Ram Mohan Roy?**

Ans. The two papers published by Raja Ram Mohan Roy were

(i) 'Sambad Kaumudi' in Bengali

(ii) 'Mirat-ul-Akbar' in Persian

Q.12 **Name the two main associations that were the precursors of the Indian National Congress?** **(ICSE 2017)**

Ans. East India Association (1866) founded by Dadabhai Naoroji and Indian Association of Calcutta (1876) founded by Surendranath Banerjee, were two precursors or forerunners of the Indian National Congress.

Q.13 **Mention two acts against which Surendranath Banerjee protested.** **(ICSE 2008)**

Ans. Surendranath Banerjee protested against the following acts

(i) The Indian Arms Act (ii) The Vernacular Press Act

Q.14 **Mention the regional association that Surendranath Banerjee was associated with.**

Ans. Surendranath Banerjee was associated with the Indian Association of Calcutta. He founded the Association in 1876. This was the first organised political party to express people's disillusionment with British administration.

Q.15 **Mention any two main objectives of the Indian National Association.**

Ans. Two main objectives of the Indian National Association were as follows

(i) **Promoting Political Awareness** The association was aimed to create political awareness among Indians and encourage them to actively participate in the political process.

(ii) **Advocating for Reforms** It sought to push for social, economic, and administrative reforms. It also demanded greater representation for Indians in the government.

Q.16 **Analyse the importance of predecessor organisations before Indian National Congress in the growth of Nationalism in India.**

Ans. Predecessor organisations before the Indian National Congress played a vital role in the growth of nationalism in India. They spread political awareness and encouraged the idea of self-rule.

Organisations like the Indian Association and Poona Sarvajanik Sabha promoted discussions on social reforms and Indian rights. These groups helped in developing leadership and connected various regions which created a foundation for national unity.

Q.17 **Indian National Congress Formation: Birth of a Nationalist Movement that shaped India's future. This movement went on for several decades, involving countless leaders, numerous debates, and various political struggles.** ***The Birth of a Nation, The National Archives***

How did the formation of the Indian National Congress in 1885 contribute to the development of Indian nationalism?

Ans. The formation of the Indian National Congress in 1885 contributed to Indian nationalism in the following ways

(i) **Fostering Unity** It brought together people from diverse regions and communities, creating a sense of collective identity.

(ii) **Political Awareness** It educated Indians about their political rights and gradually shifted its demands towards self-rule and strengthening of the nationalist movement.

TYPE - 4 — 3 Marks

Short Answer Type Questions

Q.1 **In the context of the rise of national consciousness in India, explain the significance of the development in communication and transportation systems.**

Ans. The significance of the development in communication and transportation systems into National Consciousness was as follows

- **Better Connectivity** Railways and telegraphs linked distant regions and connected leaders to far flung areas.
- **Spread of Ideas** Enhanced communication allowed quicker spread of nationalist ideas.
- **Coordination of Movements** Improved transportation helped organise protests and political activities across India.

Q.2 **The Vernacular Press Act of 1878 was a major setback for native press in India. Justify this statement.**

Ans. The Vernacular Press Act of 1878 was a major setback for native press in India because of following reasons

(i) **Suppression of Native Press** The Vernacular Press Act targeted Indian-language newspapers and allowing the British government to confiscate press and publications without trial to restrict free expression.

(ii) **Censorship** The Act imposed severe censorship on Indian newspapers, preventing criticism of the British government and limiting the press's role in political discourse.

(iii) **Strengthening Nationalism** Instead of silencing dissent, the Act fueled protests and strengthened nationalist sentiments, leading to greater resistance against British rule.

Q.3 **Mention any three ways in which the Indian press played a role in uniting Indians in the freedom struggle.**

Ans. The Indian press played a significant role in uniting Indians during the freedom struggle through the following ways

(i) Newspapers and journals like Kesari, Amrita Bazar Patrika, and The Hindu published articles and editorials that inspired patriotic sentiments as well as promoted the idea of self-rule, and encouraged Indians to join the independence movement.

(ii) The press acted as a watchdog by exposing the oppressive policies and exploitative practices of the British government, such as the economic drain of India, unfair taxation, and social injustices. This created awareness and unity among Indians against colonial rule.

(iii) Through articles and reports, the press informed the public about major events, protests, and campaigns like the Swadeshi Movement and Non-Cooperation Movement, encouraging people from different regions and communities to participate in the struggle for independence.

Q.4 Analyse the importance of the Socio Religious reform movements in the growth of nationalism in India.

Ans. The importance of the Socio Religious reform movements in the growth of nationalism in India were as follows

(i) **Promoting Social Equality** Reformers like Raja Ram Mohan Roy and Swami Vivekananda challenged social injustices and fostered unity among different communities.

(ii) **Encouraging Education** These movements promoted education, especially for women and marginalised groups, empowering people to engage in political and social change.

(iii) **Instilling National Pride** They emphasised Indian culture and heritage, awakening a sense of national identity that fueled the nationalist movement.

Q.5 The Rise of Indian Nationalism: A Struggle for Unity and Self-Rule.

The second half of the 19th century witnessed the growing tide of Indian nationalism, as various movements and political organisations sought to challenge British colonial rule and demand self-governance. *The National Archive*

What were the three key events that shaped India's political landscape in the 19th century?

Ans. Three key events that shaped India's political landscape in the 19th century were

(i) **The Revolt of 1857** Often referred to as the First War of Independence, as it was the first large-scale uprising against British rule. It marked the beginning of political awakening and highlighted the discontent among various sections of Indian society with British policies.

(ii) **Formation of the Indian National Congress (1885)** The establishment of the Indian National Congress provided a platform for educated Indians to voice their grievances and demand political reforms. It played a central role in organising the nationalist movement.

(iii) **Emergence of Socio-Religious Reform Movements** Movements like the Brahmo Samaj, Arya Samaj, and Aligarh Movement addressed social issues and promoted education, equality, and political awareness. These reforms contributed to the rise of political consciousness among Indians.

Q.6 The Indian National Congress played a key role in uniting people from different regions, religions, and communities to build a collective national identity. Justify the statement.

Ans. The above statement can be justified through the following points

(i) The INC provided a common platform to leaders and citizens from various regions, religions, and linguistic backgrounds to come together and discuss issues affecting the nation.

(ii) The INC worked to represent the interests of all sections of society, including Hindus, Muslims and all other communities. Leaders like Dadabhai Naoroji, Gopal Krishna Gokhale, and later Mahatma Gandhi emphasised the importance of secularism and collective action.

(iii) Through movements like the Swadeshi Movement, Non-Cooperation Movement, and Civil Disobedience Movement, the INC united people across India to fight against British rule. These movements involved widespread participation from farmers, workers, students, and women, breaking old social and regional barriers.

Q.7 Discuss any three objectives of the Congress as enumerated by W.C. Bonnerjee.

Ans. Three objectives of the Congress as enumerated by W.C. Bonnerjee were

(i) **Promote National Unity** Unite people of different regions and communities for a common cause.

(ii) **Represent Indian Interests** Present Indian grievances to the British government.

(iii) **Seek Constitutional Reforms** Demand gradual political reforms and increased Indian participation in governance.

TYPE - 5 — 4 Marks

Long Answer Type Questions

Q.1. After 1858, various factors led to the rise of Indian nationalism. In this context, describe the impact of the following

(i) Ilbert Bill Controversy (ii) Indian Literature

Ans (i) The Ilbert Bill was a measure to put Indian judges on the same footing as Europeans in dealing with all cases in the Bengal Presidency. It suggested the trials of Europeans by Indian Judges for criminal offences. This provoked strong criticism among the Britishers.

A systematic campaign to criticise Indian character and culture was launched by Britishers through press and public meetings.

(ii) Literature became an important instrument for promoting social reforms, awareness of social problems and patriotism and nationalism. During this period, prose writing became important and new forms of literary writings such as novel, short story, drama and essay began to develop.

Writers like Bankim Chandra Chattopadhyay, Rabindranath Tagore, Bharatendu Harishchandra etc, played an important role in promoting consciousness among people.

Q.2 Mention any four conditions responsible for the rise of consciousness against Britishers in the later half of the 19th century in India.

Ans. Four conditions responsible for the rise of consciousness against the British in the later half of the 19th century in India were

(i) **Economic Exploitation** British policies drained India's resources leading to poverty, high taxes, and economic stagnation ultimately which created widespread resentment among Indians.

(ii) **Social Reforms and Awareness** The socio-religious reform movements, like those led by Raja Ram Mohan Roy and Swami Vivekananda, raised awareness about social inequality and injustice, which also contributed to anti-British sentiments.

(iii) **Spread of Education** The spread of Western education among Indians led to the emergence of a new educated class that began questioning to British rule and start demanding political reforms.

(iv) **Influence of Nationalist Leaders** Leaders like Bal Gangadhar Tilak, Dadabhai Naoroji, and Bipin Chandra Pal inspired Indians through their speeches and writings. They created a strong sense of unity and resistance against British rule.

Q.3 Explain the influence of Western education on the minds of the educated Indians in the 19th century.

Ans. The major influence of Western education on educated Indians in the 19th Century were

(i) **Exposure to Progressive Ideas** Western education introduced ideas like democracy, equality, and human rights, inspiring reformist thinking.

(ii) **Social Reform Movements** Educated Indians like Raja Ram Mohan Roy used Western ideas to advocate for social changes, such as the abolition of Sati and child marriage.

(iii) **Growth of Nationalism** The exposure to Western political concepts led to the rise of Indian nationalism and the formation of political groups like the Indian National Congress.

(iv) **Critique of British Rule** Western education encouraged Indians to challenge the injustices of British colonial rule and demand reforms.

Q.4 Raja Ram Mohan Roy was a strong proponent of modern education. Justify the statement by mentioning any four points.

Ans. Raja Ram Mohan Roy was indeed a strong proponent of modern education, which can be justified by the following points

(i) Raja Ram Mohan Roy recognised the importance of Western education in modernising Indian society. He advocated for the introduction of English education in India to bridge the gap between traditional Indian knowledge and modern scientific and rational thought.

(ii) In 1822, Roy established the first English-medium school in India, the Hindu College (later known as Presidency College), in Kolkata. This institution played a key role in providing a modern and Western-style education to Indians.

(iii) Raja Ram Mohan Roy also advocated for reforms in the traditional educational system. He supported the study of subjects like Science, Mathematics, and Social Studies, which were neglected in traditional education.

(iv) The Atmiya Sabha was founded by Roy in 1815, which aimed to encourage intellectual debates and discussions.

Q.5 The Indian National Association of Calcutta focused on uniting Indians of all communities. Justify the statement.

Ans. The Indian National Association was focused on uniting Indians of all communities under one political banner, irrespective of religion or region, through the following ways

(i) The INA encouraged participation from people across various regions, communities, and religions. It aimed to create a united front of educated Indians against British rule.

(ii) The INA's primary focus was on issues that affected all Indians, such as demands for Indian representation in the civil services, reforms in laws like the Arms Act and Vernacular Press Act, and greater political autonomy.

(iii) Surendranath Banerjee, the founder of the INA, travelled across India, encouraging participation from both urban and rural areas. This helped in breaking regional barriers and creating a sense of solidarity among people from different parts of the country.

(iv) The INA emphasised secularism and a non-sectarian approach, focusing on national rather than religious or regional identities. By advocating for a collective Indian identity, it aimed to build a broad-based political movement that transcended religious and regional divisions.

Q.6. **Who presided over the second session of the Indian National Congress? Mention any three objectives of the Congress.** **(ICSE 2025)**

Ans. The second session of the Indian National Congress (INC) was presided over by Dadabhai Naoroji in 1886 in Calcutta.

The Indian National Congress (INC) was formed in 1885 by A.O. Hume with the goal of achieving political rights and self-governance for Indians. Its three key objectives were

- **Promoting National Unity** The INC aimed to bring together Indians from different regions, religions and communities to develop a common national identity.
- **Political Awareness and Representation** It worked to educate Indians about their rights and demanded greater representation in government through constitutional means.
- **Social and Economic Reforms** The Congress sought to address issues like poverty, taxation and economic exploitation caused by British rule while promoting Indian industries and education.

TYPE - 6 — 10 Marks

Structured Questions

Q.1 **The Second half of the 19th century witnessed the growth of a strong feeling of nationalism. With reference to the statement, answer the following**

(i) Jyotiba Phule was the pioneer of equality in India. Explain. **(3)**

(ii) Mention any three ways in which Brahmo Samaj helped in breaking the barriers of the traditional superstitious beliefs in India. **(3)**

(iii) In what ways did Raja Ram Mohan Roy and Jyotiba Phule contribute to the overall rise of social and political consciousness about women's rights and education in India? **(4)**

Ans.

(i) Jyotiba Phule is known as pioneer of the equality because of several reasons

(a) **Fight Against Caste Discrimination** Phule strongly opposed the caste system and worked to uplift lower castes, challenging Brahmanical supremacy in society.

(b) **Promotion of Education** He advocated for education for all, especially for girls and marginalised communities. He and his wife opened the first school for girls in Pune in 1851.

(c) **Founding Satya Shodhak Samaj** In 1873, he established the Satya Shodhak Samaj, aiming to eliminate caste discrimination and promote social equality and justice.

(ii) Three ways in which the Brahmo Samaj helped in breaking the barriers of traditional superstitious beliefs in India are

(a) **Promotion of Monotheism** It rejected idol worship and promoted belief in one formless God.

(b) **Abolition of Social Inequality** It advocated for equality and opposed caste discrimination.

(c) **Rejection of Superstitions** It criticised traditional rituals, superstitions and encouraged rational thinking.

(iii) Raja Ram Mohan Roy and Jyotiba Phule played key roles in raising social and political consciousness about women's rights and education in India in the following ways

(a) **Advocacy for Women's Rights** Roy fought against practices like Sati and promoted widow remarriage, while Phule was focused on educating girls and untouchables.

(b) **Challenging Social Norms** They both challenged rigid caste and gender norms in India. Raja Ram Mohan Roy advocated for rational thinking through the Brahmo Samaj and Phule promoted equality through the Satya Shodhak Samaj.

(c) **Influence on Future Reforms** Their efforts laid the groundwork for later reforms, including legal changes and the promotion of women's rights and education.

(d) **Empowerment Through Education** Both saw education as crucial for women empowerment and development of society.

Q.2. **Nationalism refers to the feeling of oneness that emerges when people consider themselves as one nation. With reference to the growth of nationalism, answer the following.** **(ICSE Specimen 2025)**

(i) Name the first President of the Congress. Mention any two of its objectives. **(3)**

(ii) The press played an important role in the growth of Indian Nationalism. Thus, the British saw the need for curbs on the press. Mention any three points to analyse the role of the press in the growth of nationalism. **(3)**

Or Mention any three ways in which the press promoted nationalism. **(ICSE 2025)**

(iii) Lord Lytton's repressive policies led to the growth of Nationalism. Mention any four policies enforced by him. **(4)**

Or The repressive policies of Lord Lytton became a catalyst to the growth of nationalism. Mention any three of his repressive policies to justify this statement. **(ICSE 2025)**

Ans. (i) Womesh Chandra Bonnerjee was the first President of the Indian National Congress (INC) in 1885.

Two objectives of the INC were

(a) To promote the welfare and interests of the people of India.

(b) To secure a greater share in government for educated Indians and to work towards constitutional reforms.

(ii) The role of the press in the growth of nationalism is as follows

(a) **Spread of Nationalist Ideas** Newspapers and journals played a key role in spreading nationalist ideas and raising awareness about the need for political and social reforms in India.

(b) **Mobilising Public Opinion** The press was crucial in organising protests, educating the masses, and creating public opinion against British rule, especially through the writings of leaders like Raja Ram Mohan Roy, Bal Gangadhar Tilak, etc.

(c) **Voice of Resistance** It acted as a medium for expressing dissent against British policies, making it a significant tool in the resistance movement, as seen in the role of publications like The Hindu, The Amrit Bazar Patrika, and The Kesari.

(iii) Lord Lytton, the British Viceroy of India from 1876 to 1880, enforced several repressive policies that contributed to the rise of nationalism in India. These policies were seen as unjust and led to widespread discontent among Indians. Some of his major policies were as follows

(a) **Vernacular Press Act (1878)** This act was aimed at curbing the influence of nationalist newspapers. It gave the government the power to confiscate and censor publications critical of British rule, particularly targeting the vernacular press.

(b) **Arms Act (1878)** The Arms Act prohibited Indians from possessing arms, making it harder for them to defend themselves or organise resistance against British colonial rule.

(c) **The Ilbert Bill Controversy (1883)** The Ilbert Bill proposed that Indian judges would be allowed to try European criminals. The backlash from the British community led to the modification of the bill, causing anger and resentment among Indians, who viewed it as a sign of racial inequality.

(d) **Indifference during the 1878-79 Famine** Lord Lytton's hard response to the devastating famine in India, resulted in the deaths of millions. The British government's inability to address the suffering of the masses encouraged nationalist sentiments and criticism of colonial rule.

Q.3 **Look at the picture given below and answer the questions that follow.**

(i) **Identify the personality in the given picture.**

(ii) **Explain, how Vernacular Press Act of 1878 was a major setback for native press in India.**

(iii) **Write about his policies which heightened the resentment against the British rule.**

Ans. (i) The above picture belongs to Viceroy Lord Lytton (1876-80). During his tenure the suppressive policies of the British encouraged the growth of nationalist movement in India.

(ii) For answer, refer Q.2 of Short Answer Type Questions.

(iii) Lord Lytton's policies which heightened the resentment against the British rule were as follows

- He abolished import duties which crippled the local textile industry. It created a wave of anger throughout India.
- He organised a Grand Delhi Durbar in 1877 to proclaim Queen Victoria as the Empress of India. Lakhs of rupees were spent on the event but nothing was done for the people of South India who were suffering from the effects of a severe famine.
- In order to suppress public opinion, Lytton passed the Vernacular Press Act in 1878.

FIRST PHASE OF INDIAN NATIONAL MOVEMENT (1885-1907)

- The First Phase of Indian Nationalism refers to the initial phase of the Indian freedom struggle that occurred between 1885 to 1907.
- This phase was characterised by the rise of moderate nationalism and efforts to seek reforms through constitutional means, rather than demanding immediate independence from British rule.

Early Nationalists

- From 1885 to 1907, the Congress was led by early nationalists or moderates, mainly educated middle-class professionals like lawyers, teachers and officials.
- It included members like Womesh Chandra Bonnerjee, Rash Behari Ghosh and Surendranath Banerjee, etc.

Objectives and Methods of the Early Nationalists

First Objective The first objective of the early nationalist was to educate people, arouse political consciousness and create public opinions which could change the destiny of the Indians. To achieve this, they used the following methods

(i) Arranging meetings and organising annual sessions of the Congress.

(ii) Using the print media (e.g. press) to criticise the British policies.

(iii) Sending memorandums and petitions to British Government officials and the British Parliament.

Second Objective The second objective of the early nationalists was to influence the British Government and the British public.
To achieve this, they used the following methods

(i) They used three P's–Petitions, prayers and protests. They sent requests and protest letters to the British Government to address Indian Problems.

(ii) Sending delegation for the fulfilment of its programme and to divert the attention of the British Government towards Indians.

(iii) Formation of a British Committee of the Indian National Congress in London in 1889.

Contributions of the Early Nationalists

Some of the prominent leaders were Dadabhai Naoroji, Surendranath Banerjee and Gopal Krishna Gokhale.

Dadabhai Naoroji

He was born on 4th September, 1825 in a Parsi family of Bombay. He was a Parsi intellectual and educator. He is popularly known as the Grand Old Man of India. He made significant contributions to early Indian nationalism. Some of them are as follows

- He Introduced the Drain of Wealth Theory in his book 'Poverty and Un-British Rule in India'. In his theory, he highlighted how British policies were draining India's wealth to Britain.This became a cornerstone of economic nationalism.

Dadabhai Naoroji

REVISION NOTES

- He founded the East India Association (1866) in London to educate the British public and Parliament about socio-economic issues and gather support for Indian welfare.
- He was the first Indian who was elected to the British House of Common in 1892 as Liberal Party candidate.
- Due to his efforts, a resolution was passed by the House of Commons in 1893 to hold the Imperial Civil Service (ICS) examination in England and India simultaneously.

Surendranath Banerjee

He was born on 10th November, 1848 in Bengal in a Brahmin family. He is popularly known as the Father of the Nationalist Movement in India. He contributed to the Indian National Movement in the following ways

Surendranath Banerjee

- He founded the Indian Association in 1876 to fight against the wrong policies of the British.
- He founded the Indian National Conference in 1883, which merged with the Indian National Congress in 1886 due to shared objectives.
- Banerjee was the editor of the newspaper, *Bengalee* and served as a powerful medium for mobilising public opinion. His book, Nation in the Making, gives an account of his political concern and his views about self-government.
- Banerjee started agitation against the Licence Act, Vernacular Press Act and protested against the age limit for candidates for Indian Civil Service exam in 1877.
- He opposed the Morley-Minto Reforms of 1909 which introduced separate electorates for the Hindus and the Muslims.
- He also opposed the division of Bengal by Lord Curzon in 1905.

Gopal Krishna Gokhale

He was born at Kolhapur in Maharashtra on 9th May, 1866. He was greatly influenced by the ideals of Justice MG Ranade. Some major contributions of Gopal Krishna Gokhale were as follows

Gopal Krishna Gokhale

- He founded the Servants of India Society in 1905 to train individuals dedicated to serving the nation and promate education and public welfare in India.
- He served as Congress President in 1905. He advocated for constitutional methods to demand gradual reforms and self-governance.
- He believed education as a key to national progress and worked to expand access to quality education, he also served as a member of the Imperial Legislative Council and push for education reforms.
- He mentored leaders like Mahatma Gandhi in shaping of their political philosophy of non-violence and truth, which later became central to India's freedom movement.
- As a member of the Imperial Legislative Council he campaigned for reduced taxation, improving lives of Indian labourers, and greater Indian representation in governance.

EXAM ORIENTED QUESTIONS

TYPE - 1 — 1 Mark

Multiple Choice Questions

Q.1 Which of the following was the prevailing social evil in the Indian Society during the times of early nationalists?

(a) Sati system (b) Untouchability
(c) Child marriage (d) All of these

Ans. (d) All of the above

Q.2 Which of the following was the main aim of the Early Nationalists?

(a) Eradication of British rule in India.
(b) Promotion of equality among the workers in India.
(c) Collection of popular demands which has to be presented before the government.
(d) Organisation of a violent struggle for the political independence of India.

Ans. (c) Collection of popular demands which has be presented before the government.

Exp. The main aim of the Early Nationalists was to collect the people's demands and present them to the British government, hoping for reforms rather than seeking complete independence through violence.

Q.3 Identify the early nationalist leader. **(ICSE 2023)**

(a) Gopal Krishna Gokhale
(b) Bipin Chandra Pal
(c) Jyotiba Phule
(d) Bal Gangadhar Tilak

Ans. (a) Gopal Krishna Gokhale

Q.4 Which of the following statements about Early Nationalists is false? **(ICSE 2021)**

(a) Their leaders were Dadabhai Naoroji and Gopal Krishna Gokhale.
(b) They believed in Constitutional means of Protests.
(c) They wanted self-government under British rule.
(d) They wanted to launch violent agitations against the British.

Ans. (d) They wanted to launch violent agitations against the British.

Exp. They wanted to launch violent agitations against the British.

Early Nationalists believed in peaceful, constitutional methods of protest, not violence, to achieve self-government under British rule.

Q.5 The area in which Anand stays has had no water supply for three days in spite of repeated complaints. The residents have a meeting and discuss a few methods to resolve this problem. Being a follower of the beliefs and methods of the early nationalists, which of the following methods is Anand not likely to approve? **(ICSE Specimen 2025)**

(a) Peaceful procession by the residents
(b) Follow the method of boycott
(c) Write a petition to the government
(d) Write an article in the newspaper highlighting the problem.

Ans. (b) Follow the method of boycott

Q.6 The first phase of Indian National Congress was called the phase of ....

(a) Revolutions (b) Militants (c) Moderates (d) Extremists

Ans. (c) Moderates

Exp. Moderates in the Indian freedom movement were early leaders who believed in gradual political reforms through peaceful methods, like petitions and negotiations with the British.

Q.7 Complete the given analogy.
1885 : First Indian National Congress Session : : ? : Second Indian National Congress

(a) 1885 (b) 1886 (c) 1887 (d) 1888

Ans. (b) 1886

Q.8 Identify the incorrect statement related to the moderate phase in India.

(a) The moderates believed in working within the British system to achieve reforms.
(b) The moderates were focused upon mass agitations and protests against the British rule.
(c) The moderates emphasised on constitutional methods of petitions and prayers to demand reforms.
(d) The moderates advocated for gradual political and social reforms through dialogue with the British.

Ans. (b) The moderates were focused upon mass agitations and protests against the British rule.

Q.9 The prominent members of the moderates were....... .

(a) Lala Lajpat Rai, Bipin Chandra Pal, Subhash Chandra Bose
(b) Bipin Chandra Pal, Chandra Shekar Azad, Dadabhai Naoroji
(c) Chandra Shekar Azad, Gopal Krishna Gokhale, Feroz Shah Mehta
(d) Surendranath Banerjee, Gopal Krishna Gokhale, Dadabhai Naoroji

Ans. (d) Surendranath Banerjee, Gopal Krishna Gokhale, Dadabhai Naoroji

Q.10 Which of the pairs do not align with the beliefs and objectives of the early nationalists.

P. Dadabhai Naoroji	- Known for his violent agitation and Protest against British Government.
Q. Gopal Krishna Gokhale	- Belief in gradual social reforms like the abolition of child marriage and untouchability.
R. Lala Lajpat Rai	- Focus on indirect confrontation with British authorities.
S. Surendranath Banerjee	- Demand for constitutional reforms and self-government within the British Empire.

Codes

(a) P and Q (b) P and R (c) Q and S (d) S and P

Ans. (b) P and R

Q.11 Identify the below leader who was associated with 'Drain of Wealth' theory.

(a) Gopal Krishna Gokhale (b) Digambar Bishvas
(c) Dadabhai Naoroji (d) Surendranath Banerjee

Ans. (c) Dadabhai Naoroji

Q.12 The early nationalists in the first phase of the Indian national movement demanded constitutional reforms, better representation of Indians in the legislative bodies, and social reforms. However, these demands were met with resistance from certain sections of society. *The Hindu*

Based on the information above, what was the primary reason for the resistance to these early nationalist demands?

(a) Fear of losing traditional social structures
(b) Concern over the economic impact of reforms
(c) Rejection of all forms of colonial rule
(d) Desire for immediate independence from British rule

Ans. (a) Fear of losing traditional social structures

Q.13. Read the description and identify the person.

He was associated with the foundation of 'Servants of Indian Society'

(a) Gopal Krishna Gokhale (b) Dadabhai Naoroji
(c) Surendranath Banerjee (d) M.G. Ranade

Ans. (a) Gopal Krishna Gokhale

Exp. Gopal Krishna Gokhale was a prominent moderate leader, reformer, and mentor to Gandhi. He also demanded for social and political reforms in India.

Q.14 This individual is widely recognised for founding the Indian National Association in 1876, which was one of the precursors to the Indian National Congress.

Which of the following is the individual referred to in the statement?

(a) Surendranath Banerjee (b) Madan Mohan Malviya
(c) Dadabhai Naoroji (d) Gopal Krishna Gokhale

Ans. (a) Surendranath Banerjee

TYPE - 2 — 1 Mark

Assertion-Reason Questions

Q.1 Read the two statements given below about the Early Nationalism and select the option that shows the correct relationship between (A) and (R).

Assertion (A) The early nationalists demanded Swaraj (self-rule) for India.

Reason (R) The early nationalist wanted a larger share in the government of their country.

(a) R contradicts A
(b) R is the reason for A
(c) A is true, but R is false
(d) A and R are independent of each other

Ans. (d) A and R are independent of each other

Q.2 Read the two statements given below about the Early Nationalism and select the option that shows the correct relationship between (A) and (R).

Assertion (A) The early nationalists stressed the importance of economic development in India.

Reason (R) They advocated for modern industries and infrastructure to reduce poverty.

(a) R contradicts A
(b) R is the reason for A
(c) A is true, but R is not relevant
(d) A and R are independent of each other

Ans. (b) R is the reason for A

Q.3 Read the two statements given below about the Early Nationalism and select the option that shows the correct relationship between (A) and (R).

Assertion (A) The early nationalists focused on Constitutional reforms in India.

Reason (R) They believed that using petitions and resolutions would bring no change.

(a) R contradicts A
(b) R is the reason for A
(c) A is true, but R is not false
(d) A and R are independent of each other

Ans. (c) A is true, but R is false

Q.4 Read the two statements given below about the phase of Indian nationalism and select the option that shows the correct relationship between (A) and (R).

Assertion (A) The early nationalists adopted a moderate approach towards British rule, aiming for gradual reforms within the existing framework.

Reason (R) They believed that by working within the British system and presenting their demands peacefully, they could gain self-governance without conflict.

(a) R contradicts A
(b) R is the reason for A
(c) A is true, but R is false
(d) A and R are independent of each other

Ans. (b) R is the reason for A

Q.5 Read the two statements given below about the early nationalists and select the option that shows the correct relationship between (A) and (R).

Assertion (A) The early nationalists were not in favour of mass agitation or direct confrontation with the British Government.

Reason (R) The early nationalists believed that gradual reforms through dialogue with the British would lead to political improvements for India.

(a) R contradicts A
(b) R is the reason for A
(c) A is true, but R is false
(d) A and R are independent of each other

Ans. (b) R is the reason for A

Q.6 Read the two statements given below about the early nationalists and select the option that shows the correct relationship between (A) and (R).

Assertion (A) The early nationalists supported the idea of self-governance within the British Empire.

Reason (R) Early nationalists demanded sovereign economic rights and reforms which could be obtained by the help of other colonial empires.

(a) R contradicts A
(b) R is the reason for A
(c) A is true, but R is false
(d) A and R are independent of each other

Ans. (d) A and R are independent of each other

TYPE - 3 — 2 Marks

Very Short Answer Type Questions

Q.1 Name any two leaders of the Congress who are known as early nationalists.

Ans. Two leaders of the Congress who are known as early nationalists were

(i) W.C. Bonnerjee (ii) Dadabhai Naoroji

Q.2 What according to the early nationalists was an obstacle in India's progress? What kind of self government did the early nationalists demand?

Ans. According to the early nationalists, the main obstacle in India's progress was social and economic backwardness of Indians not only the British colonial rule.

The early nationalists demanded self-government or swaraj within the British empire.

Q.3 Mention any two demands of the early nationalists that aimed at improving the conditions of the peasants.

Ans. Two demands of the early nationalists that aimed to improve the conditions of the peasants were

(i) Reduction in land revenue and protection of ryots or peasants against unjust demand of the zamindars.

(ii) Reduction in expenditure on the army and the money that saved to be spent on welfare activities such as health and education.

Q.4 Analyse the period of India's freedom struggle, which is known as moderate phase.

Ans. The period between 1885 to 1907 is known as moderate phase of India's freedom struggle days. This period was dominated by the early nationalists or moderates. W.C. Bonnerjee, Gopal K Gokhale and Dadabhai Naoroji, etc were some of the moderate leaders.

Q.5 Why were the early Congressmen called moderates?

Ans. Early Congressmen were called moderates because they believed in Constitutional methods like petitions, resolutions, and dialogues to achieve political reforms. They had faith in British justice and aimed to bring about change through peaceful and gradual means.

Q.6 Mention two reasons for the faith of the moderates in the British sense of justice.

Ans. Two reasons for the faith of the moderates in the British sense of justice were

(i) The moderates believed that the Englishmen thinks about progressing India and putting it on the path of democracy and self-governance.

(ii) The moderates thought that English rule had conferred benefits upon them, especially the English language and the modern means of communication and transport.

Q.7 Imagine you are a member of the Indian National Association (INA) in the late 19th century. You have just returned from a meeting where you discussed the growing dissatisfaction among Indians under British rule. What steps would you take to address these concerns and rally support for the cause?

Ans. As a member of the Indian National Association (INA), I would focus on educating the masses about their rights, organising public meetings, and advocating for constitutional reforms. I would also promote the boycott of British goods and encourage unity among nationalist leaders.

Mobilising youth and fostering national pride through cultural revival would be a key to gain support for India's freedom movement.

Q.8 State any two methods adopted by the early nationalists in the National Movement. (ICSE 2020)

Ans. Two methods adopted by the early nationalists in the National Movement were

(i) Passing Resolution (ii) Sending Petitions

Q.9 Discuss about the regional association that each nationalist was associated with.

(i) Surendranath Banerjee

(ii) Dadabhai Naoroji

Ans. (i) Surendranath Banerjee was associated with the Indian Association of Calcutta (1876).

(ii) Dadabhai Naoroji was associated with the East India Association (1866).

Q.10 Name the two books that Dadabhai Naoroji authored explaining the Drain of India's Wealth.

Ans. Two books of Dadabhai Naoroji explaining the Drain of India's Wealth are

(i) Poverty of India

(ii) Poverty and Un-British Rule in India.

Q.11 Imagine you are an Early Nationalist leader. Mention any two methods you would follow to fight against the British. (ICSE 2025)

Ans. I would follow the following methods to fight against British

(i) **Petitions and Appeals** I submit petitions and requests to the British government to demand reforms and justice.

(ii) **Public Meetings and Speeches** I organise meetings to raise awareness and encourage Indians to demand their rights peacefully.

TYPE - 4 3 Marks

Short Answer Type Questions

Q.1 With reference to the growth of nationalism, mention three associations which served as the forerunners (precursors) of the Indian National Congress. Who were the founders of the Three Associations?

Ans. Before the formation of the Indian National Congress in 1885, several associations laid the groundwork for the rise of Indian nationalism, which were as follows

East India Association

- It was founded by Dadabhai Naoroji in 1866.
- It aimed to raise awareness about Indian issues among the British public and gather their support for Indian reforms.

Poona Sarvajanik Sabha

- It was founded by M.G Ranade in 1870.
- This association focused upon social reforms, political rights, and Indian self-governance thus, laying the foundation for future nationalist activities.

Indian National Association (INA)

- It was founded by Surendranath Banerjee in 1876.
- This was one of the earliest political associations in India that worked to unite Indians and promote their rights. It later merged with the Indian National Congress.

Q.2 The Moderates of the Indian National Congress (1885-1905) adopted a reformist and cooperative approach towards British rule.Their demands included increased Indian representation, administrative reforms and economic justice. However, their faith in the British waned as their demands were ignored, paving the way for more radical nationalists.

The New Times, 10th March, 2023

What can you infer about the moderates' approach to achieving self-governance in India?

Ans. The moderates' approach to achieving self-governance in India was rooted in trust and optimism toward British fairness. They believed in gradual reforms and sought change through peaceful and Constitutional means by avoiding confrontation.

Their reliance on dialogue and persuasion indicates that they hoped to work within the colonial framework rather than overthrow it outright.

Q.3 Highlight any three contributions of Dadabhai Naoroji in the Indian movement.

Ans. Three major contributions of Dadabhai Naoroji were as follows

(i) **East India Association (1866)** It was founded to educate the British about Indian issues and build support for India.

(ii) **Drain Theory** It explained that British policies were draining India's wealth. This theory was described by Naoroji in his book 'Poverty and Un-British Rule in India'.

(iii) **Role in Congress** Naoroji was a founding member of the Indian National Congress. He also served as its President three times, and advocated for self-rule.

Q.4 With reference to the phase of early nationalists, answer the following.

How did they expose the true nature of British rule in India?

Ans. The early nationalists exposed the true nature of British rule by highlighting its exploitative policies. They analysed issues like economic drain, high taxation, and the decline of Indian industries. Leaders like Dadabhai Naoroji explained how British governance drained India's wealth and depriving Indians of resources and opportunities.

They also criticised discriminatory practices, lack of political representation, and the neglect of Indian welfare thus exposing the real face of the British empire. Their efforts raised political awareness among the masses about colonial exploitation.

TYPE - 5

4 Marks

Long Answer Type Questions

Q.1 The first war of Independence was totally different from the methods of early nationalists. Justify this statement.

Ans. The first war of Independence was totally different from the methods of early nationalists in the following ways

Aspect	First War of Independence (1857)	Early Nationalists (1885-1905)
Nature of the Struggle	Military revolt and armed resistance against British rule.	Peaceful and constitutional methods to seek reforms.
Methods of Protest	Violent, with battles, sieges, and armed conflicts.	Petitions, speeches, resolutions and meetings.
Leadership	Local and military leaders like Mangal Pandey, Rani Lakshmibai, Nana Saheb were prominent.	Educated leaders like Dadabhai Naoroji, Gopal Krishna Gokhale, Surendranath Banerjee were prominent.
Objectives	Overthrow British rule and restored the Mughal Empire.	Demand for greater Indian representation and political reforms under British rule.
Impact	Failed, but sparked national awareness and future uprisings.	Led to the formation of the Indian National Congress and the foundation for future political movements.

Q.2 Analyse any four issues opposed by the early nationalists in the field of civil liberties.

Ans. The early nationalists strongly opposed several issues concerning civil liberties under British rule.

(i) **Restriction on Freedom of Speech and Press** The British government imposed strict censorship laws like the Vernacular Press Act (1878), which restricted Indian newspapers from criticising British policies. The early nationalists demanded freedom of the press and opposed its suppression.

(ii) **Preventive Detention and Arbitrary Arrests** The British enacted laws allowing the detention of Indians without trial. The nationalists protested against such unjust laws and demanded the repeal of the Preventive Detention Act to restore civil rights.

3. **Right to Assemble and Form Associations** The British restricted public meetings and the formation of political associations. Nationalists opposed these restrictions and demanded the right to organise meetings, protests and political movements.

4. **Discrimination in Public Services** Indians were denied high administrative positions due to racial bias. Early nationalists opposed this discrimination and demanded equal opportunities in government services through competitive exams.

Q.3 Analyse the major achievements of the early nationalists in building of the nationalism in india.

Ans. The early nationalists played a crucial role in shaping the foundation of Indian nationalism in the following ways

- **Formation of the Indian National Congress (INC)** The early nationalists played a pivotal role in founding the Indian National Congress in 1885, Congress later became the primary platform for India's freedom struggle and a unified voice for Indian demands.
- **Promotion of Political Awareness** Through petitions, speeches, and public meetings, the early nationalists created widespread political awareness among Indians by focusing on Constitutional reforms, civil rights, and self-governance within the British framework.
- **Demand for Reforms** They sought key political and social reforms like the inclusion of Indians in legislative bodies, reforms in the educational system, and the reduction of British economic exploitation, thus setting the stage for later demands of self-rule.
- **Social and Educational Upliftment** The early nationalists emphasised education and social reforms, thus helping to spread national consciousness among Indian masses about their rights and duties.

Q.4 **Highlight the major contributions of Gopal Krishna Gokhale in establishment of early nationalism in India.**

Ans. The major contributions of the Gopal Krishna Gokhale were as follows

- **Promotion of Education** Gokhale promoted modern education and helped in establishment of institutions like the Deccan Education Society etc. to inspire national consciousness.
- **Advocacy for Social Reforms** He advocated for reforms like the abolition of child marriage and the promotion of women's education, contributing to social progress.
- **Support for Political Reforms** Gokhale sought constitutional reforms and greater Indian representation in government, laying the foundation for future demands of self-rule.
- **Founding the Servants of India Society** He established the Servants of India Society in 1905 to promote public service and train young Indians for the nation's progress.

TYPE - 6 — 10 Marks

Structured Questions

Q.1 **With reference to the nationalism in India, Explain the following.**

(i) The objectives of the early nationalists were significant for achieving their goals.Justify this statement. **(3)**

(ii) Indian nationalism was the child of the 'British Raj' R. Coupland. Why does the foundation of early nationlists was challenged by some contemporary intellectuals? **(3)**

(iii) Mention any four contributions of the Surendranath Banerjee in the development of Nationalism in India. **(4)**

Ans. (i) Objectives of the early nationalists were significant for achieving their goals in the following ways

- **Demand for Political Reforms** The early nationalists aimed for greater Indian representation in the British Government. By seeking reforms such as Indian participation in decision-making processes. They laid the groundwork for self-governance and political empowerment.
- **Improvement of Economic Conditions** They focused on addressing economic exploitation under British rule, by analysing policies that drained India's wealth. This objective was vital in ensuring that India's resources were used for its development rather than for British interests.
- **Gradual Approach for Change** The early nationalists adopted a moderate and constitutional approach that focused on reforms within the existing framework of British rule

(ii) R. Coupland's statement suggests that Indian nationalism emerged as a response to British rule. While the early nationalists worked within the system and aimed for gradual reforms, their foundation was challenged by some contemporary intellectuals because

- **Limited Scope of Reforms** Critics argued that the early nationalists' demands for political reforms and better representation were insufficient to address the deep-rooted issues caused by British rule. Some felt that their moderate approach failed to challenge the colonial system fundamentally.
- **Failure to Address Masses** The early nationalists were primarily composed of educated elites and did not fully engage with the masses. Intellectuals like Bal Gangadhar Tilak criticised them for not involving the common people in the nationalist movement and focusing only on reforms for a small section of society.
- **Moderate Approach** Some thinkers, like Tilak, felt that the early nationalists were too moderate and overly reliant on British goodwill, which do not lead towards any significant change. They believed a more radical approach was necessary to achieve full independence.

These were the major reason which led to hesitation among Intellectuals against early nationalists.

(iii) Surendranath Banerjee is popularly known as 'Rashtraguru or the Father of the Nationalist Movement' in India. Surendranath Banerjee's contribution to India's freedom struggle is quite significant in following ways

- **Founding of the Indian National Association** (INA) Banerjee established the Indian National Association in 1876, which aimed to create awareness among Indians about their rights and mobilise them for political participation.
- **Role in the Formation of Indian National Congress (INC)** He was instrumental in the formation of the Indian National Congress in 1885 later it becomes a major platform for articulating Indian demands and leading the freedom struggle.
- **Advocacy for Civil Rights and Freedom of Expression** Banerjee worked for civil liberties and freedom of expression and opposed repressive laws like the Vernacular Press Act, which sought to reduce the freedom of press.
- **Educational Reforms and Public Awareness** He was a strong advocate for education through his leadership, he promoted the need for modern education to awaken national consciousness and unite Indians under the common cause of self-rule.

Q.2 Read the extract given below and answer the questions that follow. **(ICSE Specimen 2007)**

"....the Indians who actively worked for the creation of an All-India Political Organisation represented new social forces that were increasingly opposed to the exploitation of India for British interests. They needed an organisation that would fight for India's political and economic advancement. *From "Freedom Struggle"*

Picture -1

Picture -2

(i)(a) In the context of the above, identify the two individuals in pictures 1 & 2, who were the early leaders of the organisation to be formed. **(3)**

(b) How did the person in picture 2 explained the economic exploitation of India for British interest? **(3)**

(ii) Name the organisation which was to be formed. What were the objectives behind the formation of this political body? **(3)**

(iii) Explain the major ideological differences which emerged amongst the leaders within the first twenty years of the foundation of this organisation. **(4)**

Ans. (i) (a) The leaders shown in the Pictures are

Picture 1 Gopal Krishna Gokhale

Picture 2 Dadabhai Naoroji

(b) Dadabhai Naoroji exposed the economic exploitation of India by the Britishers, his views on the Indian economy are given in his book Poverty and Un British Rule in India. His famous Drain Theory explained about the economic exploitation based tendency of the Britishers.

(ii) The Indian National Congress was the organisation that was to be formed. The objectives of the Indian National Congress as follows

- To promote friendly relations between nationalist political workers from different parts of the country.
- To develop and consolidate the feelings of national unity irrespective of caste, religion or province.
- To formulate popular demands and present them before the government.
- To train and organise the public opinion in the country.

(iii) The major ideological differences emerged between moderates and extremists were as follows

Moderates Beliefs

- **Social base** Zamindars and upper middle classes living in towns.
- **Ideological inspiration** Influence of Western liberal thoughts and European history.
- They believed that political connections with Britain were infavour of India's social, political and cultural interests.

Extremists beliefs

- **Social base** Educated and lower middle classes living in towns.
- **Ideological inspiration** Indian history, cultural heritage and Hindu traditional symbols.
- They believed that political connections with Britain would increase exploitation of India.

Q.3 **With reference to the phase of early nationalism, Answer the following questions**

(i) **Who was Dadabhai Naoroji? What was his contribution to Indian nationalism? (3)**

(ii) **Analyse the major contribution of Dadabhai Naoroji in Indian movement. (3)**

(iii) **Dadabhai Naoroji propounded 'Drain of Wealth' to describe the exploitative nature of British rule in India. Justify the statement. (4)**

Ans. (i) Dadabhai Naoroji (1825-1917), known as the 'Grand Old Man of India', was a key leader in India's early nationalist movement. He co-founded the Indian National Congress (INC) and served as its President three times. Naoroji is best known for his Drain of Wealth Theory, which exposed how British policies impoverished India by transferring its wealth to Britain. His book, 'Poverty and Un-British Rule in India', highlighted the british exploitation. He was elected to the British Parliament in 1892, there he advocated for Indian rights and reforms.

(ii) For answer refer to Q. 3 of Short Answer Type Questions.

(iii) The given statement is justified as Dadabhai Naoroji's 'Drain of Wealth' theory explained the exploitative nature of British rule in India. He argued that a significant portion of India's wealth was drained to Britain without adequate returns. This included profits from British trade, salaries of British officials, pensions, and military expenses, which were funded by Indian revenues.

Naoroji highlighted that this economic drain caused widespread poverty, stunted industrial growth, and weakened India's economy. His analysis, particularly in his book 'Poverty and Un-British Rule in India', created political awareness about the economic exploitation under British rule.

4

SECOND PHASE OF INDIAN NATIONALISM

The Second Phase of the Indian National Movement (1907-1920), also known as the Extremist Phase, was focused on stronger and more aggressive actions, with new strategies, leaders and demands.

Partition of Bengal

The idea of Partition of Bengal was conveyed in 1903 and implemented on 16th October, 1905 after receiving Royal Assent. Lord Curzon divided Bengal into two provinces

(i) **West Bengal** It included the Western districts of Bengal, Bihar and Orissa. Calcutta was established as its capital.

(ii) **Eastern Bengal and Assam** It consisted of the Eastern districts of Bengal and Assam. Dacca was the capital of this province.

Lord Curzon

Causes of the Partition

According to the British administration, the main reason behind the Partition of Bengal was administrative necessity. However, there were additional reasons for partitioning of Bengal, which were

- **Divide and Rule Policy** The British aimed to weaken nationalist unity by dividing Bengal along religious lines and creating separate provinces for Hindus and Muslims.
- **Economic Reasons** The partition aimed to control Bengal's growing economic and political influence, which was seen as a threat to British rule.
- **Suppression of Nationalist Movements** The division sought to suppress the rising nationalist movements in Bengal, and the growing demand for self-rule.

Perspectives of Nationalists for Partition of Bengal

- Nationalist leaders realised that the Partition of Bengal was an attempt to divide the Bengalis that shared a common culture, language and tradition.
- The Indian National Congress, all national leaders, Zamindars and merchants protested against partition.
- Protests were organised by Surendranath Banerjee and Bipin Chandra Pal against Partition across Bengal.
- On 7th August, 1905, Anti-Partition Movement was started against Partition in the Town Hall of Calcutta.

Swadeshi Movement

- The Swadeshi Movement began in 1905 against Bengal's Partition of Lord Curzon. It was led by Extremist leaders Bal Gangadhar Tilak, Bipin Chandra Pal, Lala Lajpat Rai, and Aurobindo Ghosh.

Key Features of the Swadeshi Movement

- Indians rejected British goods and promoted local products.
- Emphasis on using locally made goods, spinning khadi and reviving traditional crafts.
- Establishment of national schools and colleges to promote Indian education.
- Involvement of students, women, and the general public in protests, picketing, and public bonfires of foreign goods.

People's Reaction against Partition

- The Partition of Bengal on 16th October, 1905 was observed as a Day of Mourning.
- There was a *hartal* in Kolkata. People fasted, walked bare-footed and bathed in Ganga.
- The Hindus and Muslims celebrated 'Raksha Bandhan' and tied rakhis on one another's wrist as a symbol of unity.
- People sang 'Vande Mataram' which became the theme song of the National Movement.
- The Partition was cancelled in 1911 through the efforts of leaders and civilians.

The Assertive Nationalists or Radicals

- In the second phase of the National Movement a new ideology emerged among young Congressman.
- They supported active resistance to British rule and were called assertive nationalists or radicals.

Objectives and Methods of the Radicals

- They asked the people to use only swadeshi goods, for example, goods produced in India.
- They called upon students to boycott schools and colleges run by the government.
- They engaged the masses through festivals, boycotts, Swadeshi and national education.

Surat Split of The INC

- The Surat Split was a major event in the history of the Indian National Congress (INC) that occurred during its annual session in Surat (Gujarat), in December 1907.
- It marked a division between the moderates and extremists wing of nationalist leaders within the Congress.

Causes of the Surat Split

- Moderates were led by Gokhale and Ghosh. They sought gradual reforms through petitions and talks with the British. However, extremists were led by Tilak, Lajpat Rai, and Pal. They demanded immediate Swaraj and supported mass agitation.
- The extremists wanted Tilak to be the Congress President, but the moderates opposed this and instead supported Rashbehari Ghosh.

Contributions of Extremist Leaders

Bal Gangadhar Tilak

Bal Gangadhar Tilak

He was born on 23rd July, 1856 in a Brahmin family of Maharashtra. He was also conferred with the title of Lokmanya. His main contributions were

- He was one of the first leaders who supported Swaraj ('Self-Rule').
- In 1880, he started the Poona New English School with a view to educate Indians with quality education by charging small fees.
- He started two newspapers i.e. the Mahratta (English) and Kesari (Marathi) to spread the idea of nationalism.
- He used events like Ganapati festival in 1893 and Shivaji festival in 1895 to promote national feeling among Indians.
- He set up Home Rule League in 1916 at Pune to attain self-government under the British.

Bipin Chandra Pal

Bipin Chandra Pal

He was born on 7th November, 1858 in Sylhet district of Assam. He joined the Brahmo Samaj in 1876. He is popularly known as the Father of Revolutionary Thought in India. His main contributions were

- He opposed the Arms Act and stressed on self-reliance and national pride.
- He advocated widow remarriage and opposed the existing caste system.
- He provided all his support to the Age of Consent Bill in 1891.
- He emphasised on the development of indigenous industries in the country and also promoted the use of swadeshi goods and boycott of foreign goods.

Lala Lajpat Rai

Lala Lajpat Rai

He was born in Jagraon in Ludhiana, Punjab on 28th January, 1865. He was popularly known as Sher-e-Punjab (The Lion of Punjab). He died on 17th November, 1928, a few weeks after being severely injured during a protest against the Simon Commission. His main contributions were

- He laid the foundation of DAV College at Lahore and also opened orphanages, hospitals and schools.
- He started various newspapers, like 'Punjabi', 'Vande Mataram' (Urdu Daily) and 'People' (English weekly).
- He wrote various books like, 'Young India', 'England's Debt to India', 'Political Future of India' and 'Unhappy India'.
- He became the First President of All India Trade Union Congress in 1920.

EXAM ORIENTED QUESTIONS

TYPE - 1

1 Mark

Multiple Choice Questions

Q.1 Read the statements given below and select the option that shows the correct relationship between (A) and (R). **(ICSE 2025)**

Assertion (A) Lord Curzon partitioned Bengal in 1905.

Reason (R) The Nationalists felt that the British wanted to divide the Hindus and the Muslims.

(a) A is true and R is false.
(b) R is true but A is false.
(c) Both A and R are independent of each other.
(d) A is the reason for R.

Ans. (d) A is the reason for R.

Q.2 Identify the odd one out of the following Assertive Nationalists Leaders. **(ICSE 2025)**

(a) Bipin Chandra Pal
(b) Lala Lajpat Rai
(c) Dadabhai Naoroji
(d) Bal Gangadhar Tilak

Ans. (c) Dadabhai Naoroji.

Q.3 The market of a small industrial town X has been dominated by many products of foreign companies. The local residents decide to save the Indian industries by helping them increase their sales.

Which method of the Assertive Nationalists must they follow to become self-reliant? **(ICSE 2025)**

(a) Passive Resistance
(b) National Education
(c) Swadeshi
(d) Revivalism

Ans. (c) Swadeshi

Q.4 Which of the following was a nationalist perspective of the Partition of Bengal?

(a) There were Hindus in West Bengal.
(b) To divide the Hindus and Muslims.
(c) There were many riots in Bengal.
(d) It was an administrative necessity as Bengal was a large territory.

Ans. (b) To divide the Hindus and Muslims.

Q.5 Identify the incorrect statement/statements with reference to the Bengal partition.

P : Lord Curzon wanted to divide Bengal into West and East Bengal.
Q : East Bengal was dominated by Bengali Hindus.
R : East Bengal consisted of Assam also.
S : Capital of East Bengal was declared to be Calcutta.

Options

(a) P and R
(b) Q and S
(c) R and S
(d) Q and P

Ans. (b) Q and S

Q.6 Identify the odd one out of the following objectives of the 'Partition of Bengal'.

(a) The partition was intended to weaken the growing nationalist movement in Bengal.
(b) The partition divided Bengal into two parts: Bengal and East Bengal.
(c) The partition was done to encourage economic development in the region.
(d) The partition was a strategy to divide the Hindu and Muslim communities.

Ans. (c) The partition was done to encourage economic development in the region.

Q.7 Complete the given analogy.

Bengal Divide Announcement : July 1905 :: Bengal Divide Executed: ??

(a) July, 1904
(b) October, 1903
(c) October, 1905
(d) October, 1906

Ans. (c) October, 1905

Q.8 Which of the following was the theme song of the Anti-Partition Movement?

(a) Amar Sonar Bangla
(b) Satyamev Jayate
(c) Jana Gana Mana
(d) None of these

Ans. (a) Amar Sonar Bangla

Q.9 The National Council of Education was established as a response to the dissatisfaction with the British educational policies and to provide an education system that was more aligned with Indian needs and aspirations. *The Hind Kesari*

The National Council of Education was set up in

(a) 1905 (b) 1908 (c) 1906 (d) 1907

Ans. (c) 1906

Exp. The National Council of Education (1906) was founded to promote nationalist education by focusing on Indian culture and technical training.

Q.10 Which festival was celebrated as a symbol of opposition against the Partition of Bengal?

(a) Diwali
(b) Holi
(c) Chhath
(d) Rakhi

Ans. (d) Rakhi

Exp. The Rakhi festival was used as a symbol of unity among Hindus and Muslims during Bengal division. Women tied Rakhi to men from the other community to promote harmony and protest against the British divide-and-rule strategy.

Q.11 Identify the correct statements.

P : The partition was intended to divide Bengal along religious lines, with the creation of East Bengal and West Bengal.

Q : The partition was aimed at weakening the growing nationalist movement in Bengal by dividing Hindus and Muslims.

R : The partition was a result of Lord Lytton's policy to promote administrative efficiency.

S : The Indian Council of Research was established as a response to the Partition of Bengal to promote nationalistic education.

Options

(a) P and Q (b) Q and R

(c) R and S (d) P and S

Ans. (a) P and Q

Q.12 Which of the following is true about assertive nationalists or radicals ?

(i) They wanted Swaraj, a form of self-government within the British Empire.

(ii) They were not loyal to the British Crown.

(iii) They wanted to protest within the Framework of Law.

(iv) They were supported by the educated middle class only.

Codes

(a) Only (ii) (b) Only (i)

(c) Both (iii) and (iv) (d) Both (i) and (iv)

Ans. (a) Only (ii)

Q.13 Look at the picture and identify the radical leader who played a key role in mobilising the public against the British during the Bengal Partition.

(a) Bal Gangadhar Tilak

(b) Surendranath Banerjee

(c) Gopal Krishna Gokhale

(d) M.G. Ranade

Ans. (a) Bal Gangadhar Tilak

Q.14 Which of the following leaders is associated with the Book 'The Story of My Deportation'?

(a) Bal Gangadhar Tilak (b) Bipin Chandra Pal

(c) Lala Lajpat Rai (d) Aurobindo Ghosh

Ans. (c) Lala Lajpat Rai

Exp. 'The Story of My Deportation' is an autobiography by Lala Lajpat Rai, where he talks about his arrest and being sent to Rangoon by the British because of his nationalist activities.

Q.15 Read the description and identify the person

A Radical Nationalist leader, who coined the slogan 'Swaraj is my birthright'.

(a) Bipin Chandra Pal (b) Lala Lajpat Rai

(c) Bal Gangadhar Tilak (d) Aurobindo Ghosh

Ans. (c) Bal Gangadhar Tilak

Exp. 'Swaraj is my birthright' is a famous slogan by Bal Gangadhar Tilak. He emphasised that self-rule and independence are the inherent rights of every Indian.

Q.16 Identify the main difference between the Early Nationalists and Radical Nationalists

(a) Early Nationalists were focused on social reforms, while Radical Nationalists were focused on political reforms only.

(b) Early Nationalists advocated for gradual change, while Radical Nationalists advocated for immediate and direct action.

(c) Early Nationalists favoured cooperation with the British, while Radical Nationalists promoted Petition method.

(d) Early Nationalists were in favour of social justice, while Radical Nationalists sought economic reforms.

Ans. (b) Early Nationalists advocated for gradual change, while Radical Nationalists advocated for immediate and direct action.

Q.17 The Surat Split of 1907 led to the division of the Indian National Congress into two groups.

The Surat Split of 1907 occurred during the presidency of which Indian National Congress leader?

(a) Gopal Krishna Gokhale (b) Dadabhai Naoroji

(c) Rashbehari Ghosh (d) Bal Gangadhar Tilak

Ans. (c) Rashbehari Ghosh

Q.18 The Surat Split of 1907 marked a significant turning point in the Indian National Congress. The Congress was divided into two factions: the moderates, who advocated for a peaceful approach to gaining rights, and the extremists, who demanded more direct and radical actions against British rule.

The ABC Express 28th Oct,2014

Which of the following was the primary reason for the Surat Split of 1907?

(a) Disagreement over the demand for complete independence.

(b) Differences in the approach to methods of protest and strategy.

(c) The influence of British policies in the Congress.
(d) The formation of a separate Muslim League.

Ans. (b) Differences in the approach to methods of protest and strategy.

Q.19 You have organised an essay writing competition on the rise of extremist nationalism in India. Which of the following leaders would most likely be a part of that essay?

(a) Dadabhai Naoroji (c) Bhagat Singh
(c) Annie Besant (d) Bal Gangadhar Tilak

Ans. (d) Bal Gangadhar Tilak

Q.20 Complete the given analogy about newspapers and its editor.

Punjabi : Lala Lajpat Rai : : Kesari : ?

(a) Bipin Chandra Pal (b) Aurobindo Ghosh
(c) Bal Gangadhar Tilak (d) Gopal Krishna Gokhale

Ans. (c) Bal Gangadhar Tilak

Q.21 Which leader was known as Punjab Kesari or Sher-e-Punjab in India?

(a) Lala Lajpat Rai (b) Lokmanya Tilak
(c) Bipin Chandra Pal (d) Lala Hardayal

Ans. (a) Lala Lajpat Rai

Q.22 Which leader is known as the Father of Revolutionary Thoughts in India?

(a) Lala Lajpat Rai (b) Lokmanya Tilak
(c) Bipin Chandra Pal (d) Lala Hardayal

Ans. (c) Bipin Chandra Pal

Q.23 Look at the picture given below and answer the question that follows.

Identify the correct chronology of leaders in the picture

(a) Surendranath Banerjee, Dadabhai Naoroji, Gopal Krishna Gokhale
(b) Dadabhai Naoroji, Lala Lajpat Rai, Bipin Chandra Pal
(c) Gopal Krishna Gokhale, Bal Gangadhar Tilak, Dadabhai Naoroji
(d) Lala Lajpat Rai, Bal Gangadhar Tilak, Bipin Chandra Pal

Ans. (d) Lala Lajpat Rai, Bal Gangadhar Tilak, Bipin Chandra Pal

Q.24 Which leader among the following was the founder of All India Trade Union Congress (AITUC) in Colonial India?

(a) Lala Hardayal (b) Madan Lal Dhingra
(c) Lokmanya Tilak (d) Lala Lajpat Rai

Ans. (d) Lala Lajpat Rai

TYPE - 2 — 1 Mark

Assertion- Reason Questions

Q.1 Read the two statements given below about the Surat Split of 1907 and select the option that shows the correct relationship between (A) and (R).

Assertion The 'Surat Split' significantly weakened the Indian National Congress and delayed the progress of the Indian Independence Movement.

Reason The split between the moderates and extremists strengthened the nationalist struggle.

(a) R contradicts A
(b) R is the reason for A
(c) A is true but R is false
(d) A and R are independent of each other

Ans. (a) R contradicts A

Q.2 Read the two statements given below about the Second phase of Indian Nationalism and select the option that shows the correct relationship between (A) and (R).

Assertion (A) The second phase of the Indian National Movement (1905-1916) was characterised by the rise of more extremists leadership under Bal Gangadhar Tilak.

Reason (R) The first phase of the movement, led by the extremists, had little success in convincing the British to make significant constitutional changes for India.

(a) R contradicts A (b) R is the reason for A
(c) A is true, but R is false
(d) A and R are independent of each other

Ans. (c) A is true, but R is false

Q.3 Read the two statements given below about the Surat Split of 1907 and select the option that shows the correct relationship between (A) and (R).

Assertion (A) The Surat Split was a significant event in the history of the Indian National Congress.

Reason (R) The split occurred due to differences between the moderates and the extremists over the methods of the freedom struggle, particularly the approach towards the British government.

(a) R contradicts A
(b) R is the reason for A
(c) A is true, but R is false
(d) A and R are independent of each other

Ans. (b) R is the reason for A

Q.4 Read the two statements given below about the Partition of Bengal and select the option that shows the correct relationship between (A) and (R).

Assertion (A) The Partition of Bengal in 1905 was carried out by the British to divide and rule in India.

Reason (R) The British believed that creating administrative divisions along religious lines would enhance national unity and prevent the growth of a unified nationalist movement.

(a) R contradicts A
(b) R is the reason for A
(c) A is true, but R is false
(d) A and R are independent of each other

Ans. (c) A is true, but R is false

TYPE - 3 — 2 Marks

Very Short Answer Type Questions

Q.1 Read the questions and answer the following.
(i) When was Bengal partitioned?
(ii) Name the Viceroy responsible for it.

Ans. (i) Bengal was partitioned on 16th October, 1905.

(ii) Viceroy Lord Curzon was responsible for the Bengal Partition.

Q.2 Mention any two leaders of the assertive nationalists. **(ICSE Specimen 2025)**

Ans. Two leaders of the assertive nationalists were
(i) Bal Gangadhar Tilak (ii) Lala Lajpat Rai

Q.3. Mention any two cause for the rise of assertive nationalism.

Ans. The two causes for the rise of assertive nationalism were as follows

(i) **Failure of Moderates** The ineffective results of petitions and reforms method of moderate leaders led to change in ideology of the leaders.

(ii) **Partition of Bengal** (1905) The unjust partition stirred anger and united Indians against British policies thus fueled assertive nationalism.

Q.4 Name two acts enacted by the government to suppress the Anti-Partition Movement.

Ans. The two acts enacted by the government to suppress the Anti-Partition Movement were
(i) Prevention of Seditious Meeting Act, 1907
(ii) Explosive Substances Act, 1908

Q.5 Mention two major official reasons given by Britishers for the Partition of Bengal In India.

Ans. Two major official reasons given by Britishers for the Partition of Bengal were

(i) **Administrative Efficiency** The British argued that Bengal was too large to manage effectively as a single province.

(ii) **Development of Eastern Bengal** They claimed partition would promote better governance and economic development in the eastern region.

Q.6 Briefly explain the term
(i) Swadeshi
(ii) Boycott

Ans. (i) **Swadeshi** was a movement to promote the use of Indian-made goods and boycott of foreign products, especially British goods.

(ii) **Boycott** was a strategy where people refused to buy British goods as a form of protest against colonial rule, aiming to weaken British economic control over India.

Q.7 State two impacts of the Swadeshi and Boycott Movements.

Ans. Two impacts of the Swadeshi and Boycott Movements were

(i) Indian industries received a great stimulus.

(ii) It enhanced the differences between the moderates and radicals.

Q.8 Name two leaders who were deported during the Swadeshi and Boycott Movements.

Ans. Two leaders who were deported during the Swadeshi and Boycott Movements were

(i) Bal Gangadhar Tilak

(ii) Lala Lajpat Rai

Q.9 Highlight the new lessons which were brought by the Swadeshi Movement.

Ans. The Swadeshi Movement gave some new lessons such as

- It taught the press to be fearless.
- It inspired Hindus and Muslims to cooperate. It also taught students to defy unjust authority and to make sacrifices even of their lives for the sake of their country.

Q.10 **What were the two methods adopted by the assertive nationalists in the freedom struggle?**

Ans. The two methods adopted by the assertive nationalists in the freedom struggle were

(i) **Swadeshi and Boycott** Economic boycott of British goods and use of swadeshi was designed to encourage Indian industries and provide the people with more opportunities for employment.

(ii) **National Education** The national leaders advocated national universities that were free from government control. A large number of national schools were established in East Bengal.

Q.11 **Mention any two contributions of Bipin Chandra Pal in promoting nationalism.**

Ans. Two key contributions of Bipin Chandra Pal in promoting nationalism were as follows

(i) He played a crucial role in the Swadeshi Movement by encouraging the boycott of British goods and supporting indigenous industries.

(ii) He strongly advocated for self-rule (Swaraj) and he was a key figure in the extremist faction of the Indian National Congress.

Q.12 **Imagine you are a leader during the Swadeshi Movement of 1905. You stand in front of a crowd, urging people to burn foreign cloth and embrace khadi as a symbol of self-reliance.**

As a leader of the Swadeshi Movement, what strategies would you adopt to strengthen the movement and inspire more people to join the cause?

Ans. As a leader, I would organise public meetings and rallies to spread awareness, encourage the establishment of Swadeshi industries and promote the use of khadi.

I will collaborate with schools and colleges to incorporate nationalist ideals in education. Additionally, I would emphasise the importance of unity and self-reliance to inspire widespread participation in the movement.

Q.13 **Mention two international events that influenced the radical groups of the Congress.**

Ans. Two International events that influenced the radical groups of the Congress were

(i) The Boer's War which was fought against the British Empire in South Africa (1879-1902).

(ii) The defeat of the Russians by the Japanese in 1905, thus shattered the myth of Western superiority.

Q.14 **In which year did the Surat Split happen? What was the result of this split?** **(ICSE 2024)**

Ans. Surat Spilt was happened in 1907. As a result of this split, the Indian National Congress was divided into two factions—the Moderates and the Extremists.

Q.15 **What were the two basic reasons responsible for the Surat Split in 1907 between the early nationalists and the assertive nationalists?**

Ans. The two major reasons for the Surat Split in 1907 were as follows

(i) **Differences in Methods** Moderates favoured constitutional methods for reform, while extremists, led by Tilak, advocated for direct action and protests.

(ii) **Leadership Struggle** Clashes between prominent leaders like Dadabhai Naoroji (Moderates) and Tilak (Extremists) over control and direction of the Congress.

Q.16. **In 1907, the Indian National Congress faced a major crisis when ideological differences between the Moderates and Extremists led to a split at the Surat Session.** *The Deccan times 23rd March, 2023*

What inference can be made from the news about the Surat Split of 1907?

Ans. The Surat Split of 1907 occurred due to differences between the moderates, (who favored gradual reforms and cooperation with the British), and the extremists, who demanded immediate self-rule and direct action.

This division weakened the Congress and delayed the progress of the Indian independence movement.

TYPE - 4 — 3 Marks

Short Answer Type Questions

Q.1 **What was the objective of the Assertive Nationalists? Mention any two contributions of Bal Gangadhar Tilak.** **(ICSE 2024)**

Ans. The objectives of the Assertive Nationalists were to achieve 'Swaraj' by self-reliant methods and sacrifices.

The major contributions of Bal Gangadhar Tilak were

(i) In 1880, he started the Poona New English School with a view to educate Indians by charging small fees.

(ii) He started two newspapers i.e. Mahratta (English) and Kesari (Marathi) in order to spread the idea of nationalism.

Q.2 **Who partitioned Bengal? Mention any two points to explain the perspective of the Nationalists regarding the actual motive behind the decision of partition.** **(ICSE 2024)**

Ans. Bengal was partitioned by the Viceroy Lord Curzon.

The two major points to explain the perspective of the Nationalists regarding the actual motive behind the decision of partition were as follows

(i) At that period, Bengal had become the main centre of the Indian politics and Indian nationalism. So, the British expected to regulate the rising tide of nationalism by the division of Bengal.

(ii) Another reason of the Partition of Bengal was to destroy the political influence of the educated middle class, among whom the Bengali intellectuals was the most prominent.

Q.3 **One of Lord Curzon's administrative measures that resulted in a strong resentment from the masses was the partition of Bengal in 1905. In this context, answer the following question.**

What was Lord Curzon's argument in favour of the partition of Bengal?

Ans. Curzon's arguments in favour of the partition of Bengal was that the area of Bengal was very large and it was also the most thickly populated province in British India.

It was difficult for the British to administer the same efficiently. Hence, according to Lord Curzon, partition of Bengal was administrative necessity.

Q.4 **Describe the impacts of division of Bengal upon the civilians of Bengal.**

Ans. The Bengal Partition of 1905 had the following impacts on the civilians of Bengal

- **Political Impact** It fueled nationalist movements like the Swadeshi Movement and united people against British rule.
- **Social Impact** It worsened religious tensions between Hindus and Muslims, leading to communal violence.
- **Economic Impact** It disrupted trade, particularly in Calcutta, and promoted boycotts of British goods.

Q.5 **Mention any three ways in which 'Divison of Bengal' weakened the nationalist movement in Bengal.**

Ans. The three ways in which divison of Bengal weakened the nationalist movement in Bengal are as follows

(i) The partition deepened religious divisions between Hindus and Muslims, thus weakend unity within Bengal's nationalist movement.

(ii) The division fragmented the strong political and intellectual unity among Bengali elites, hence reducing their collective opposition to British rule.

(iii) The creation of a Muslim-majority region aimed to foster loyalty to the British, which weakened the united opposition from both communities.

Q.6 **Mention any three points on the significance of the reaction of the Indian people to the partition of Bengal in 1905.**

Ans. The three significance of the reaction of the Indian people to the partition of Bengal were

(i) The day was observed as a 'day of mourning', with a hartal in Kolkata. People fasted, walked barefoot, and bathed in the Ganga as acts of protest.

(ii) Hindus and Muslims celebrated 'Raksha Bandhan', tying rakhis to each other's wrists as a symbol of unity, highlighting the cultural unity of the Bengali people.

(iii) This collective response united people across communities and regions, making the Anti-Partition Movement a strong force against British rule, eventually leading to the end of the partition in 1911.

Q.7 **How did the Swadeshi Movement influence the development of Indian education and cultural identity?**

Ans. The Swadeshi Movement influenced the development of Indian education and cultural identity in the following ways

- The movement led to the establishment of National schools and Colleges, which promoted an Indian-centered curriculum and created a sense of pride in Indian history, culture and traditions.
- Cultural activities like the promotion of traditional crafts and the use of khadi helped revival of India's cultural heritage and encouraged people to take pride in their own products and customs.

Q.8 **Explain about the changes initiated by radicals for attaining independence in the field of education?**

Ans. The radicals suggested numerous methods for attaining independence in the field of education. Some of them are as follows

- **Nationalist Education** Radicals promoted education that focused on Indian culture, history, and values to counter the British colonial curriculum.
- **Vocational Training** Radicals encouraged vocational and technical education to make Indians self-reliant and reduce dependence on British industries.
- **Indigenous Knowledge** Radicals emphasised teaching vernacular languages and Indian history to foster pride and resistance against British rule.

TYPE - 5

4 Marks

Long Answer Type Questions

Q.1 Discuss the reaction of the Indian National Congress, national leaders, zamindars and merchants to the Partition of Bengal.

Ans. The reactions of the Indian National Congress, national leaders, zamindars, and merchants to the Partition of Bengal are discussed below

- The Indian National Congress (INC) condemned the Partition as an attempt of the British to 'divide and rule' by creating communal divisions. It called for nationwide protests and supported movements like the Swadeshi and Boycott Movements to oppose the British government's decision.
- National leaders like Surendranath Banerjee and Bipin Chandra Pal led protests across Bengal, mobilising public opinion against the Partition. They highlighted the cultural and linguistic unity of Bengal and appealed to people to resist the British plan.
- Many zamindars, who were influential in rural Bengal, supported the movement as they saw the Partition as a threat to their regional influence and economic interests. They provided financial support to nationalist activities and encouraged tenant participation.
- Merchants protested by boycotting British goods and promoting indigenous products. They played a key role in the Swadeshi Movement, helping to establish and promote Indian industries as an economic response to British policies.

Q.2 How people reacted against the call of Swadeshi and Boycott movements?

Ans. People reacted against the call of Swadeshi and Boycott movements in the following ways

- Students actively took part in protests, stopped people from buying British goods, and encouraged the use of swadeshi (Indian-made) products. They also set up clubs and societies to spread the message of self-reliance and boycott.
- Women actively participated by spinning khadi, burning foreign goods, and spreading the swadeshi message within their communities. They played a vital role in inspiring and mobilising families and local groups.
- Rural peasants supported the movement by boycotting foreign goods and adopting locally made products.
- The movement also encouraged traditional crafts and industries, which involved artisans and labourers.

Q.3 How did the Moderates differ from the Assertive nationalists in realising their objectives?

Ans. Some of the major differences between Moderates and Assertive nationalists were as follows

Aspect	Moderates	Assertive Nationalists
Approach to British	Believed in gradual reforms through peaceful methods and cooperation with the British.	Advocated for more direct and confrontational methods, demanding immediate self-rule.
Methods of Protest	Focused on petitions, speeches, and debates in the British Parliament.	Emphasised mass agitation, protests, and boycotts (e.g., Swadeshi Movement).
Goal	Sought incremental constitutional reforms and self-governance within the British Empire.	Aimed for complete independence and self-rule (Purna Swaraj).
Leadership	Led by leaders like Dadabhai Naoroji, Gopal Krishna Gokhale, and Pherozeshah Mehta.	Led by leaders like Bal Gangadhar Tilak, Bipin Chandra Pal, and Lala Lajpat Rai.

Q.4 Read the questions and answer the following.
(i) Demand of Radicals before Surat session
(ii) Effects of Surat session on Britishers

Ans. (i) Demand of Radicals before the Surat Session

- **Immediate Self-rule** Radicals demanded full independence from British rule.
- **Aggressive Nationalism** They pushed for boycotts and direct protests against British policies.

(ii) Effects of Surat Session on Britishers

- **Weakened Nationalist Unity** The split between moderates and radicals temporarily weakened the Indian nationalist movement.
- **Increased British Control** The division made it easier for the British to continue their policies without unified opposition from the Congress.

Q.5 Analyse the importance of Lal, Bal, Pal in laying the foundation of Radical Nationalism in India.

Ans. The trio of Lal, Bal, Pal (Lala Lajpat Rai, Bal Gangadhar Tilak, and Bipin Chandra Pal) played a pivotal role in laying the foundation of Radical Nationalism in India in following ways

Lala Lajpat Rai

- He led the Swadeshi Movement in Punjab, encouraging boycott of British goods.
- He promoted national education and economic self-reliance.

Bal Gangadhar Tilak

- He advocated for immediate Swaraj with the slogan, 'Swaraj is my birthright.'
- He mobilised the masses through the Home Rule League and cultural movements like Ganesh Utsav.

Bipin Chandra Pal

- He provided intellectual support for self-reliance and direct action.
- He strongly backed Swadeshi and Boycott Movements, promoting economic independence.

Q.6 Tilak brought a new wave in Indian Politics that was distinct from the early Congressman. Analyse the statement by stating any four ways.

Ans. Bal Gangadhar Tilak brought a new wave in Indian politics that was distinct from the early Congress leaders in the following ways

(i) **Assertive Nationalism** Unlike the early moderates, Tilak was an advocate of 'Purna Swaraj' (complete independence) rather than limited self-rule. He believed in demanding full political freedom from the British.

(ii) **Mass Mobilisation** Tilak shifted focus from elite circles to the masses by using popular methods like the Ganesh and Shivaji festivals to mobilise people and promote nationalist sentiments across India.

(iii) **Radical Methods** Tilak adopted more confrontational tactics such as boycotts, protests, and non-cooperation with the British, as opposed to the moderate approach of petitions and appeals for reforms.

(iv) **Promotion of Hindu Identity** He emphasised Hindu cultural revival and unity, connecting nationalism with religious and cultural pride, which was different from the earlier Congress leaders who were focused more on universal and secular appeals.

TYPE - 6 — 10 Marks

Structured Questions

Q.1 With reference to the effect of the Swadeshi and Boycott Movements, describe the following.

(i) Involvement of the masses. (3)

(ii) Decline in import of foreign goods and the role of Cooperative organisations in extremist movements. (3)

(iii) Growth of national literature and culture. (4)

Ans. (i) For answer, refer Q.2 of Long Answer Type Questions.

(ii) Swadeshi and Boycott movements led to the decline of import of foreign goods in the following ways

- Though Manchester cloth was the chief target of attack, the movement was extended to other British manufacturers also, such as salt and sugar as well as luxury goods in general.
- Foreign cigarettes and clothes were bought and burnt on the streets. Traders were warned from importing foreign articles.
- The radicals encouraged co-operative organisations. Voluntary associations were set up for rural sanitation, preventives, police duties, regulation of fairs and pilgrim gatherings for providing relief during famines and other natural calamities.

(iii) Swadeshi and Boycott movements led to the growth of national literature and culture in the following ways

- Newspapers and journals such as Vande Mataram and Kesari published articles promoting the Swadeshi ideals and opposing British rule. These publications spread awareness and encouraged people to boycott foreign goods.
- The movement emphasised the revival of traditional crafts, such as handloom weaving, to promote Indian culture and economic self-reliance. Artists and artisans were encouraged to create works that reflected India's rich cultural heritage.
- Festivals and public gatherings became platforms to promote the Swadeshi spirit. For example, Raksha Bandhan was celebrated to foster unity between Hindus and Muslims.

Q.2. Look at the picture given below and answer the questions that follow.

(i) Identify the person given in the picture. To which section of the Congress did he belong and what was its ultimate objective? **(3)**

(ii) Mention any three contributions of the person in the freedom struggle. **(3)**

(iii) Surat split was one of the tragedies which divided the Congress. *The National Archives* **(4)**

Explain the impact of Surat Split on the pace of Indian Nationalism.

Ans. (i) The person given in the picture is Lala Lajpat Rai.

He belonged to the radical section of the Congress.

The main objective of this section was the immediate attainment of 'Swaraj'.

(ii) The contributions of Lala Lajpat Rai in the freedom struggle were

(a) He laid the foundation of DAV College at Lahore and also opened orphanages, hospitals and schools.

(b) He started various newspapers, like 'Punjabi', 'Vande Mataram' (Urdu Daily) and 'People' (English weekly).

(c) He supported the workers movement and became the first President of the All India Trade Union Congress in 1920.

(iii) The Surat Split of 1907 impacted the pace of Indian nationalism in the following ways

- **Weakened Unity** The split between moderates and radicals temporarily fragmented the Indian National Congress, slowing down the unified nationalist movement.
- **Rise of Aggressive Nationalism** The radical approach gained more support after the split, leading to more assertive movements like the Swadeshi Movement and greater calls for self-rule.
- **Shift in Strategies** The split led to a division in strategies, with moderates seeking reforms within the British system and radicals pushing for direct action and mass mobilisation.
- **Long-term Strengthening** Despite the setback, the split eventually led to a broader, more widespread nationalist sentiment, paving the way for major movements like Non-Cooperation and Civil Disobedience.

Q.3 To some extent, Lord Curzon was responsible for the transformation of the anti-partition agitation into a mass movement. In this context, answer the following questions.

(i) Explain about the reason given by Lord Curzon. Viceroy of India against the Bengal divide. **(3)**

(ii) The nationalists interpreted Lord Curzon's motives as an attempt to strengthen British control over India. Justify the statement. **(4)**

(iii) How did people react to the partition of Bengal in 1905. **(3)**

Ans. (i) For answer, refer Q.3 of Short Answer Type Questions.

(ii) Lord Curzon's motives were an attempt to strengthen British control over India in the following ways

- His most controversial move was the Partition of Bengal in 1905, which nationalists believed was aimed at dividing Hindus and Muslims to weaken the growing unity against British rule.
- Curzon implemented strict control over education, introducing the Universities Act of 1904 to limit nationalist influence in academic institutions.
- He also curbed Indian participation in governance, believing that Indians were unfit to rule themselves.
- His administrative measures, such as improving British infrastructure and military efficiency, were primarily designed to strengthen colonial control rather than benefit Indians.

These actions convinced nationalists that Curzon's true motive was to consolidate British power rather than promote Indian welfare.

(iii) For answer, refer Q.6 of Short Answer Type Questions.

5

THE MUSLIM LEAGUE AND LUCKNOW PACT

The Muslim League

The All-India Muslim League was founded in Dhaka under Nawab Salimullah Khan on 30th December, 1906, to protect Muslim interests in India.

Factors Leading to the Formation of the Muslim League

The British Policy of Divide and Rule

- The British tried to persuade Muslims that the partition of Bengal was intended to create a new Muslim-majority province where they could assert dominance over Hindus.
- They used foul words about both the communities, rulers and tried to create hatred among them.

Educational and Economic Backwardness of the Muslims

- There were very few Muslims who were educated in Western system of education.
- Muslims remained backward in the field of commerce and industry. They were not much involved in the growth of any organised industry.
- After 1858, a discrimination policy was adopted towards the Muslims by the British Government because they thought that the Muslims were responsible for the uprising of 1857.

Sir Syed Ahmad Khan

Role of Sir Syed Ahmad Khan

- Sir Syed Ahmad Khan was a renowned educationist and social reformer of India.
- He was one of the earliest advocates of the Two-Nation Theory which states that Hindus and Muslims should have separate nations.
- When the Indian National Congress was founded, Sir Syed Ahmad Khan opposed it.
- In 1888, Sir Syed founded the United Indian Patriotic Association which was a political organisation and aimed to oppose the Congress everywhere.
- In 1893, Sir Syed founded the Mohammedan Anglo-Oriental Defence Association to keep the Muslims away from the Congress.

The Aligarh Politics

- The Mohammedan Anglo-Oriental College was founded by Sir Syed Ahmad Khan at Aligarh in 1875.
- After the death of Sir Syed in 1898, Nawab Mohsin-ul- Mulk led the Aligarh Movement in India.
- The Aligarh Movement was started to make the Muslims loyal towards the British Government and to keep them away from the Indian political life.

The Hindi-Urdu Controversy

- In 1871, Lord Mayo's government adopted a resolution which made Urdu the medium of instruction for Muslims in primary and secondary schools.
- On 8th April, 1900, the government issued a decree granting equal status to both Hindi and Urdu languages.

Rise of Assertive Nationalism

- Assertive nationalism was a period when nationalism adopted a radical and militant approach to gain independence from the British Empire.
- Assertive nationalists made significant contributions to India's National Movement. However, some actions like celebrating Shivaji Mahotsav etc., were not accepted by all Indians. Certain Muslim leaders opposed such initiatives.

Muslim delegation to Lord Minto

- Lord Minto aimed to use Muslims against Hindus and invited Muslim delegations to present their demands.
- On 1st October 1906, Agha Khan led a delegation to meet the Viceroy, demanding separate constituencies for Muslims in legislative councils.
- The Viceroy agreed and introduced separate electorates for Muslims, as part of the Morley-Minto Reforms of 1909.

Lord Minto

Objectives of the Muslim League

- To protect and advance the political rights of Muslims in India.
- To maintain loyalty towards the British Crown as a means of securing political benefits.
- To promote unity and goodwill among Indian Muslims and address their socio-economic issues.

The Lucknow Pact

- The Lucknow Pact was signed in 1916 between the Indian National Congress and the Muslim League.
- It introduced the concept of communal electorates, leading to rise in communal tensions into the country.

Significance

- **Hindu-Muslim Unity** The Lucknow Pact symbolised Hindu-Muslim unity as both the Congress and the Muslim League worked together from 1916 to 1922.
- **Unity Within the Congress** The Lucknow Pact was a symbol of the unity between two sections of the Congress as extremists were welcomed back into the Congress.
- **Demand for Reforms** The British Government was pressured by the unity of the Congress and the Muslim League. It could not easily reject the demand for constitutional reforms.

Consequences

- The Lucknow Pact gave the impression of Hindu-Muslim unity in the national political scene but it was short-lived.
- The agreement between the parties on a separate communal electorate formally established communal politics in India.
- Through this pact, the INC indirectly accepted that India consisted of two different communities with different interests.
- The pact brought the previously less influential Muslim League to the forefront of Indian politics, alongside the Congress Party.

EXAM ORIENTED QUESTIONS

TYPE - 1   1 Mark

Multiple Choice Questions

Q.1 Identify the war, after when the British started to discriminate between Hindus and Muslims in India.
(a) Battle of Buxar
(b) Battle of Plassey
(c) First War of Independence in 1857
(d) None of the above

Ans. (c) First War of Independence in 1857

Exp. After the First War of Independence in 1857, the British blamed Muslims for initiating the rebellion due to their leadership roles. This led to widespread discrimination against Muslims, including exclusion from government jobs etc.

Q.2 Identify the incorrect reason for the educational and economic backwardness of Muslims during British rule?
(a) Lack of interest in the industrial sector.
(b) Opposition to Western education by upper-class Muslims.
(c) Over-representation of Muslims in government jobs.
(d) Discriminatory Policy of the Britishers against Muslims.

Ans. (c) Over-representation of Muslims in government jobs.

Q.3 Which government adopted a resolution in 1871 that made Urdu the medium of instruction for Muslims in primary and secondary schools?
(a) Lord Ripon's Government
(b) Lord Mayo's Government
(c) Lord Curzon's Government
(d) Lord Hastings' Government

Ans. (b) Lord Mayo's Government

Q.4 Identify the odd one one out of the following objectives of the Muslim League. **(ICSE Specimen 2025)**
(a) To promote among Muslims of India, support for the British.
(b) To promote cultural and socio-economic cooperation among Muslims.
(c) To protect and advance political rights and interests of the Muslims.
(d) To present the needs and demands of the Muslims to the government.

Ans. (b) To promote cultural and socio-economic cooperation among Muslims.

Exp. The Muslim League focused on political rights and interests, not on promoting cultural and socio-economic cooperation. The other options are political in nature.

Q.5 Where did the first session of the Muslim League was held?
(a) Calcutta
(b) Chittagong
(c) Dhaka
(d) Dispur

Ans. (c) Dhaka

Q.6 Complete the given analogy.

Muslim League : Salimullah Khan : : Mohammedan Anglo-Oriental Association : ?
(a) Laiquat Ali Khan (b) Maulana Abul Kalam Azad
(c) Sir Syed Ahmad Khan (d) Muhammad Ali Jinnah

Ans. (c) Sir Syed Ahmad Khan

Exp. The Mohammedan Anglo-Oriental Association was founded in 1870 by Sir Syed Ahmad Khan to promote modern education among Muslims in India.

Q.7 Identify the leader in the image below who was associated with the Muslim League.

(a) Sir Syed Ahmad Khan
(b) Maulana Muhammad Ali Jauhar
(c) Liaqat Ali Khan
(d) Muhammad Ali Jinnah

Ans. (d) Muhammad Ali Jinnah

Exp. Initially Muhammad Ali Jinnah was a Congress leader and later became the League's leader where he advocated for creation of Pakistan as a separate Muslim State.

Q.8 Read the description and identify the person.

He was a renowned educationist and social reformer in India. According to him, Hindus and Muslims were one Quam (Nation).

(a) Sir Aga Khan
(b) Muhammed Ali Jinnah
(c) Liaquat Ali Khan
(d) Sir Syed Ahmad Khan

Ans. (d) Sir Syed Ahmad Khan

Q.9 The Lucknow Pact was signed between the leaders of **(ICSE 2023)**

(a) Muslim League and Indian Nationalists
(b) Indian National Congress and Muslim League
(c) Muslim League and Theosophical Society
(d) None of the Above

Ans. (b) Indian National Congress and Muslim League

Q.10 Lucknow Pact was signed under which annual sessions of the INC?

(a) 1914 (b) 1915
(c) 1916 (d) 1917

Ans. (c) 1916

Exp. The Lucknow Pact was made during the 1916 session of the Indian National Congress (INC). It was an agreement between the INC and the Muslim League to work together for Constitutional reforms.

TYPE - 2 1 Mark

Assertion-Reason Questions

Q.1 Read the two statements given below about the Muslim League and select the option that shows the correct relationship between (A) and (R).

Assertion (A) The All India Muslim League was formed in 1906 to safeguard the political rights of Muslims in India.

Reason (R) The British supported the Muslim League to counterbalance the influence of the Indian National Congress.

(a) R contradicts A
(b) R is the reason for A
(c) A is true, but R is false
(d) A and R are independent of each other

Ans. (b) R is the reason for A

Q.2 Read the two statements given below about the Muslim League and select the option that shows the correct relationship between (A) and (R).

Assertion (A) The Muslim League was instrumental in pushing for a separate Muslim state.

Reason (R) The demand for a separate Muslim state was due to political marginalisation of Hindu in India.

(a) R contradicts A
(b) R is the reason for A
(c) A is true, but R is false
(d) A and R are independent of each other

Ans. (c) A is true, but R is false

Q.3 Read the two statements given below about the Muslim League and select the option that shows the correct relationship between (A) and (R).

Assertion (A) The Muslim League became more assertive in its demands after 1937.

Reason (R) The success of the Indian National Congress in the 1937 elections gave the Muslim League the opportunity to challenge the Congress's dominance and representation for Muslims.

(a) R contradicts A
(b) R is the reason for A
(c) A is true, but R is false
(d) A and R are independent of each other

Ans. (b) R is the reason for A

Q.4. Read the two statements given below about the All India Muslim League and select the option that shows the correct relationship between (A) and (R).

Assertion (A) The Muslim League initially participated in the Indian National Congress's struggle for independence.

Reason (R) The League never wanted to address Muslim concerns within a united India.

(a) R contradicts A
(b) R is the reason for A
(c) A is true, but R is false
(d) A and R are independent of each other

Ans. (c) A is true, but R is false

Q.5 Read the two statements given below about the All India Muslim League and select the option that shows the correct relationship between (A) and (R).

Assertion (A) The British wanted to prevent Muslims from participating in any political movement.

Reason (R) The British opposed the formation of the Mohammedan Anglo-Oriental (M.A.O) Defence Association in 1893.

(a) R contradicts A

(b) R is the reason for A

(c) A is true, but R is false

(d) A and R are independent of each other

Ans. (c) A is true, but R is false

TYPE - 3 (2 Marks)

Very Short Answer Type Questions

Q.1 Mention any two ways through which the Britishers encouraged separatist politics in India.

Ans. The two ways taken by the Britishers to encourage separatist politics in India were

(i) They started favouring Muslims against the Hindus.

(ii) They called the Congress as a Hindu organisation.

Q.2 Give two examples to show that the British encouraged communal and separatist attitude in Indian politics.

Ans. The British encouraged communal and separatist attitude in Indian politics. Some of the examples are as follows

(i) Lord Curzon partitioned Bengal to weaken the Hindu-Muslim unity.

(ii) Morley-Minto Reforms of 1909 provided for separate representation to the Muslim community in the Imperial Legislative Council.

Q.3 Mention any two leaders who were related to the Muslim League in India.

Ans. Sir Syed Ahmad Khan and Nawab Salimullah Khan were related to Muslim League in India.

Q.4 Read the question and answer the following.

(i) First President of All India Muslim League

(ii) Year of establishment of Mohammedan Anglo-Oriental Defence Association.

Ans. (i) Sir Agha Khan

(ii) It was established in 1893

Q.5 Write the name of any two associations founded by Sir Syed Ahmad Khan to safeguard the rights of the Muslims.

Ans. Sir Syed Ahmad Khan founded the following two associations to safeguard the rights of the Muslims which were as follows

(i) Mohammedan Anglo-Oriental Defence Association.

(ii) United Indian Patriotic Association

Q.6 Mention any two factors that led to the formation of the Muslim League. **(ICSE 2025)**

Ans. For answer, refer Q.2. (ii) of Structured Questions.

Q.7 State any two objectives of the Muslim League. **(ICSE Specimen 2023)**

Ans. Two objectives of Muslim League were as follows

(i) **Protecting Muslim Rights** Safeguarding the political and social rights of Muslims in India.

(ii) **Constitutional Reforms** Seeking reforms like separate electorates for Muslims.

Q.8 Mention any two demands forwarded by the delegation led by Agha Khan III.

Ans. Two demands forwarded by the delegation of the Agha Khan III were as follows

(i) Separate electoral constituency for the Muslims.

(ii) More State aids for promoting new Muslim Universities.

Q.9 Explain the meaning of term 'separate electorate'.

Ans. Separate electorate meant that elections will be held on the basis of communal representation. It meant that only Muslims could vote for a Muslim candidate.

Hence, it divides voters on the basis of religion, caste or occupation.

Q.10 Mention the significance of the Lucknow Pact of 1916.

Ans. The Lucknow Pact was significant due to the following reasons

- **Hindu-Muslim Unity** The Lucknow Pact symbolised unity between the Indian National Congress and the Muslim League, marking a significant step in bringing Hindus and Muslims together against British rule.
- **Common Demands** Both parties jointly demanded self-governance and increased Indian representation in legislative councils, strengthening the national movement.

TYPE - 4 (3 Marks)

Short Answer Type Questions

Q.1 The reasons for the formation of the Muslim League were many. In this context, explain the following questions.

(i) Any three demands made by the Muslim Deputation in 1906 to the Viceroy Lord Minto.

Ans. The demands of Muslim delegations to Viceroy Lord Minto were

(i) Fair representation of Muslim in civil and military services to address their under representation.

(ii) Separate electoral constituencies for the Muslims.

(iii) Special favours to the Muslims in appointment to government services and to the membership of Central and Provincial Councils.

Q.2 "The Congress is a body of Western-educated men who do not represent the masses of India." In the context of this statement, justify Syed Ahmad Khan's views on the Indian National Congress.

Ans. The views of Syed Ahmad Khan on the Indian National Congresss were as follows

- **Western Influence** Congress only led by Western-educated elites and disconnected from traditional Indian values.
- **Lack of Mass Representation** It mainly represented urban, educated elites, not the rural or Muslim populations.
- **Premature Demands** Syed Ahmad Khan believed Congress's push for self-rule was unrealistic and ignored India's readiness for change.

Q.3. Discuss the Hindi-Urdu controversy and its impact on Hindu and Muslims in colonial India.

Ans. In the United Provinces, Urdu served as the official court language, and petitions to courts and offices were traditionally submitted in Urdu. However, certain sections of society opposed this practice.

On 8th April, 1900, the government announced that people could now submit petitions in Hindi using the Devanagari script. It also decided that court notices and official announcements would be in both Hindi and Urdu.

This decision made many Muslims unhappy, causing a long-lasting argument. It led to increased tension between the communities and made their relationship even more difficult.

Q.4 In the context of the formation of the Muslim League,
(i) Explain its primary objectives.
(ii) Analyse its role in Indian politics.

Ans. (i) For answer, refer Q.3 of Long Answer Type Questions.

(ii) Role of the Muslim League in Indian Politics

- **Advocacy for Separate Electorate** The league played a key role in securing separate electorates for Muslims under the Morley-Minto Reforms (1909).
- **Alliances with the British** The League allied with the British to safeguard Muslim political rights and gain influence.

TYPE - 5   4 Marks

Long Answer Type Questions

Q.1 Analyse the reason behind the harsh treatment towards Muslims by Britishers immediately after the uprising of 1857.

Ans. After the 1857 uprising, the British viewed Muslims with suspicion because they had actively participated in the rebellion, especially after the fall of the Mughal Empire. The British believed that Muslims were a threat to their rule, as they had supported movements like the Wahabi Movement and played a significant role in the uprising. As a result, the British treated them harshly and blamed them for the revolt.

After the 1870s, the British changed their approach. They started favouring Muslims to weaken the unity of the Indian National Movement and created divisions between Hindus and Muslims to maintain control.

Q.2 Highlight the major differences between the Indian National Congress and Muslim League.

Ans. The ideologies and structures of the Indian National Congress (INC) and Muslim League were different in following ways

Basis	Indian National Congress (INC)	Muslim League
Ideology	Focused on a united and independent India.	Focused on separate Muslim identity and political rights.
Structure	Inclusive and open to all communities with branches across India.	Muslim-centric aimed at protecting Muslim interests.
Leadership	Led by leaders from various communities, including Hindus and Muslims.	Led by prominent Muslim leaders like Muhammad Ali Jinnah.
Approach to British	Moderate methods of prayer and petition were used for grievances	Initially loyal towards the Britishers, but later sought separate political rights for Muslims.

Q.3 **In which year was the Muslim League Formed? Mention any three objectives of the Muslim League.** **(ICSE 2024)**

Ans. Muslim League was formed in the year 1906.

(i) To protect and advance the political rights of the Muslims in India.

(ii) To maintain loyalty towards the British crown as a means of securing political benefits.

(iii) To promote unity and goodwill among Indian Muslims and address their socio-economic issues.

TYPE - 6

10 Marks

Structured Questions

Q.1 **Lucknow Pact of 1916 is considered as landmark in the history of Indian National Movement. Answer the following questions in this regard.**

(i) Changes in the relations between the Congress and Muslim League. **(3)**

(ii) The main significance of the Pact. **(3)**

(iii) Impact of the Pact on National Movement. **(4)**

Ans. (i) Following changes were seen in the relations between the Congress and Muslim League

- After Lucknow Pact Muslims began to support the Congress aim of self-government.
- Both the parties compromised with each other and the Pact symbolised Hindu-Muslim unity to both parties.
- The leaders of both the parties did not want to give the British Government an excuse for delaying political reforms.

(ii) The main significance of the pact were as follows

- **Hindu-Muslim Unity** The Lucknow Pact marked a rare cooperation between the Indian National Congress and the All India Muslim League and strengthening of inter-community collaboration for political reform.
- **Increased Muslim Representation** It provided Muslims greater political representation through separate electorates and ensured their voice in legislative bodies.
- **Pressure on British Government** The pact united Indian political forces, pressuring the British to implement constitutional reforms and grant greater self-governance.

(iii) Major impacts of the Pact on National Movement were as follows

- **Reunion of Moderates and Extremists** The session marked the reunion of the moderates and extremists within the Indian National Congress.
- **Prominence of Congress and Muslim League** The Lucknow Pact elevated the Congress Party and the Muslim League to prominent positions in Indian politics.
- **Influence on the Government of India Act, 1919** Many recommendations from the Lucknow Pact were incorporated into the Government of India Act of 1919.
- **Increased Communalism** The acceptance of separate electorates, seen as a major mistake by the Congress, led to increased communalism.

Q.2 **The Partition of Bengal and the formation of the Muslim League were two important events that had its impact on the national struggle for Independence.**

(i) Identify the leader and how he contributed in formation of Muslim League. **(3)**

(ii) Write any three factors leading to the formation of the Muslim League. **(3)**

(iii) 'At the time of its founding, in Dhaka, the Muslim League was mostly a collective of elite Muslim men'. Justify this statement. **(4)**

Ans. (i) The name of the leader is Sir Syed Ahmad Khan.

He later promoted separatist tendency among muslim under the influence of Mr. Beck (Principal of the Mohammedan Anglo-Oriental College). He started advising the Muslims to stay away from the Hindus and support the British Rule in India. Later this paved the way for the formation of the Muslim League.

(ii) Three factors leading to the formation of the Muslim League were

(a) **Fear of Hindu Dominance** Muslims felt that they would be politically marginalised in a Hindu-majority India, especially after the independence.

(b) **Sir Syed Ahmad Khan's Influence** Through Aligarh Movement, Sir Syed emphasised the need for Muslims to have their own political organisation to protect their rights and interests and foster the idea of a separate Muslim political identity.

(c) **British Support** The British encouraged the formation of the Muslim League to counterbalance the growing influence of the Indian National Congress and to maintain control over Indian politics by promoting communal divisions.

(iii) At the time of its founding in Dhaka in 1906, the Muslim League was predominantly a collective of elite Muslim men. The leadership and membership consisted primarily of aristocrats, landlords and educated professionals such as Nawab Salimullah, Sir Syed Ahemad Khan etc. These individuals represented the wealthiest and most influential segments of Muslim society.

The League's goals, such as securing separate electorates and maintaining loyalty to the British, reflected the interests of the elite class who wanted to protect their privileged status under colonial rule.

The broader Muslim population was mostly rural and economically disadvantaged which was excluded due to limited access to education and political platforms. Consequently, the Muslim League's early policies and activities emphasised primarily to the concerns of the Muslim upper class.

MAHATMA GANDHI AND THE NATIONAL MOVEMENT

- In India, the period from 1915 to 1947 is regarded as the Mass Phase of National Movement in which Mahatma Gandhi played a significant role.
- In this phase, various movements were organised against the British which include Non-Cooperation Movement, the Civil Disobedience Movement and the Quit India Movement.

Mahatma Gandhi

Mahatma Gandhi

- Mahatma Gandhi was born on 2nd October, 1869 in Porbandar, Gujarat. He studied law in London and practiced in Rajkot.
- He spent 21 years of his life in South Africa, where he led the Natal Indian Congress and developed Satyagraha, a method of non-violent resistance.
- Gandhi ji returned to India in 1915. Then he led three successful movements in Champaran, Kheda, and Ahmedabad between 1917-18.

Non-Cooperation Movement

- The Non-Cooperation Movement was the first mass based political movement under Mahatma Gandhi.
- The resolution of the Non-Cooperation Movement was adopted in the Calcutta session of the Congress in September, 1920.
- It was approved in the regular session of the Congress at Nagpur in December, 1920.

Causes of the Non-Cooperation Movement

- **Jallianwala Bagh Massacre (1919)** The Jallianwala Bagh massacre took place in Amritsar on (13th April, 1919). British troops opened fire on a peaceful gathering, killed hundreds of innocent people, and led to widespread resentment against British rule.
- **The Rowlatt Act (1919)** The Anarchical and Revolutionary Crimes Act of 1919, popularly known as The Rowlatt Act was introduced by the British to suppress the growing nationalist movement.

  It gave the government the power to arrest Indians without trial and extend detention without a judicial review, which led to widespread protests and anger across the country.
- **The Khilafat Movement** The Muslims protested against the British treatment to the Ottoman Caliph after World War I. It was led by Ali Brothers (Maulana Muhammad Ali and Maulana Shaukat Ali) and later supported by Gandhi ji.
- The Khilafat Committee demanded that the Ottoman Caliph should retain his empire and Arab lands must stay under Muslim control.

Programmes of the Non-Cooperation Movement

Boycott Programme

- Surrendering of titles and offices and resignation from nominated posts in the local bodies.
- Boycott of legislatures, law courts, schools, colleges and all institutions to industries having connection with the British.

Swadeshi Programmes

- Adoption of Swadeshi and Khadi by reviving hand-spinning and hand-weaving clothes in the country.
- Establishment of national schools, colleges, panchayats (private arbitration courts) all over the country and revival of the Hindu-Muslim unity.

Suspension of the Non-Cooperation Movement (Chauri Chaura Incident)

- In the Chauri Chaura incident, a procession of 3,000 peasants marched to the police station to protest against a police officer who had beaten some volunteers which were picketing a liquor shop.
- They were fired upon by the police, due to which some of the demonstrators set up nearby police station on fire and killed 23 policemen.
- Due to this violence, Gandhi ji withdrew movement on 12th February,1922.

Impact of the Non-Cooperation Movement

- Earlier the national movement had remained the concern of the middle class and intelligentsia but Gandhi ji added the plight of poor and weaker section into movement.
- By supporting the Khilafat Movement, Gandhiji was able to unite Hindu and Muslim community.
- The economic boycott during Non-Cooperation Movement affected British industries.
- The Congress became a continuous political organisation and its Constitution was amended in the Nagpur session of December, 1920.
- Provincial Congress Committees were established and reorganised on the basis of linguistic areas.
- Swaraj Party was formed by C.R. Das and Motilal Nehru to participate in Provincial Elections of 1923.

Protest against Simon Commission

Civil Disobedience Movement

- This movement was started by Gandhiji in 1930. It was an attempt to weaken the administration of British by breaking some specific rules and regulation.

Causes of the Civil Disobedience Movement

Reaction to the Simon Commission

- Simon Commission was constituted in November, 1927 under John Simon to review the functioning of the constitutional system in India.
- The National Congress in its Madras session in 1927, presided by Dr. Ansari, decided to boycott the Simon Commission because there were no Indian representatives in it.

Declaration of Purna Swaraj

- In Lahore session of December, 1929 under the presidency of Jawaharlal Nehru, the Congress formalised the demand of Purna Swaraj for India.
- For this, the Congress Working Committee met in January, 1930 and decided the following programmes
  - Preparation for Civil Disobedience Movement.
  - It was proposed that 26th January, 1930 would be celebrated as the Purna Swaraj Day or Independence Day all over the country.
  - Resignation by members of the legislature.

Dandi March and Beginning of the Civil Disobedience Movement

- On 31st January, 1930, Gandhiji sent a letter to Viceroy Irwin stating eleven demands, also called Eleven Points Ultimatum. The most strongest among all the demands was to abolish the salt tax.
- After getting no response from the British Government, Gandhiji started a March on 12th March, 1930 along with 78 followers from Sabarmati Ashram to Dandi (the coastal town of Gujarat).
- On 6th April, he reached Dandi and ceremonially violated the Salt Law, by manufacturing salt through sea water. This marked the beginning of the Civil Disobedience Movement.

Dandi March

Programmes of the Civil Disobedience Movement

- The Civil Disobedience Movement included violation of salt laws, non-payment of taxes and revenues, boycott of foreign cloth, British goods and liquor.
- This movement was followed by violation of forest laws in Maharashtra, Karnataka and the Central Provinces.
- People refused to pay the rural Chaukidari tax in Eastern India.
- The society of Khudai-Khidmatgars, known as Red Shirts was organised under the leadership of Khan Abdul Ghaffar Khan to continue struggle in North-West frontier province.

Gandhi-Irwin Pact

On 5th March, 1931, Viceroy Lord Irwin and Gandhiji signed an agreement. This agreement is known as Gandhi-Irwin Pact. This agreement led to the end of the Civil Disobedience Movement. Some of the major provisions of the pact were as follows

- The Viceroy agreed to release all political prisoners except those convicted of violence and killing.
- The government agreed to withdraw all ordinances and end prosecution.
- The Viceroy agreed to permit peaceful picketing of liquor as well as opium shops.
- The British Government agreed to restore the confiscated properties of the Satyagrahis.

Impact of the Civil-Disobedience Movement

- Civil Disobedience Movement created political consciousness and a deep sense of patriotism in the minds of the people.
- It brought women out of their homes and involved them in the freedom struggle.
- People adopted the idea of non-violence. People in towns and villages popularised the patriotic songs like 'Prabhat Pheris' etc.
- This movement improved the condition of depressed classes. They were now allowed to offer prayer in temples and could access to wells.

The Three Round Table Conferences

- The Round Table Conferences were a series of peace conferences organised by the British Government and Indian political leaders to discuss constitutional reforms in India.
- Three Round Table Conference were held from 1930 to 1932 as follows
  - (i) **First Round Table Conference** was held in 1930 in London. However, the Congress boycotted it.
  - (ii) **Second Round Table Conference** was held from 7th September to 1st December, 1931 in London. Mahatma Gandhi was appointed as the sole representative of the Congress to this conference. However, there was no substantial result due to disagreement among the groups.
  - (iii) **Third Round Table Conference** was held on 17th November, 1932 to 24th December, 1932 in London in which only 46 delegates were present. Dr. Bhimrao Ambedkar attended this conference and demanded separate electorate for the depressed classes. As a result, communal award was announced by the Prime Minister of Britain.

- 'Poona Pact' was signed between Dr. Bhimrao Ambedkar and the Congress (Mahatma Gandhi) on 25th September, 1932 to end the provisions of communal electorate.

Quit India Movement

- It was adopted by the Congress Working Committee at Wardha on 14th July, 1942.
- It proposed that the Congress would start a non-violent movement under the leadership of Gandhiji if its demand of complete independence was not accepted by the British.
- The Quit India Resolution was formally passed on 8th August, 1942 at the Bombay session of the Congress.

Causes of Quit India Movements

Cripps Mission

During World War II, as the Japanese Army approached India, the British Government tried to resolve political issues. Prime Minister Winston Churchill sent Sir Stafford Cripps, a seasoned diplomat with some proposals of constitutional reforms. This mission is known as Cripps Mission.

Sir Stafford Cripps

These constitutional reforms were

- Promise of dominion status after the Second World War.
- An elected Constituent Assembly for framing the Constitution of free India.
- Proposals of an interim government during the war.
- Indian leaders would invited to participate in the council of their country and the common wealth.
- There would be a federation of British India and Indian states.

However, the Cripps Mission failed due to the following reasons

- There was no clarity in the mission of the independence in the near future.
- The Hindu Mahasabha rejected the proposals because it feared the partition of the country.
- The Muslim League opposed the creation of a single nation.
- The mission did not provide sufficient safeguards for the interests of the Sikhs, the Anglo-Indians, the Indian Christians, etc.

Japanese Threat

- In 1942, the Japanese Army attacked Myanmar and marched towards India.
- This threat (of a Japanese invasion) convinced the Indian leaders of the need to eliminate the Britishers from India immediately. So, they decided to launch a movement that force the Britishers to Quit India.

Significance of the Quit India Movement

- It united people across all communities (Hindus, Muslims, Sikhs, Christians, Parsis), and showed the feeling of national sacrifice and deep patriotism.
- It gained global attention, with strong public opinion in the USA and Britain for India's independence.
- It weakened the British Raj's foundations, proving they could no longer rule against India's will.
- It awakened political consciousness among the masses and demonstrated strong anti-imperialist sentiments.
- It strengthened the Congress Socialist Party, which operated underground until 1944.

EXAM ORIENTED QUESTIONS

TYPE - 1 | 1 Mark

Multiple Choice Questions

Q.1 Complete the given analogy about birth of the leaders.

Jawaharlal Nehru : 14th November, 1889 : : Mahatma Gandhi : ?

(a) 15th August, 1870 (b) 2nd October, 1869
(c) 3rd October, 1869 (c) 5th September, 1869

Ans. (b) 2nd October, 1869

Q.2 Identify the odd one out regarding Mahatma Gandhi.

(a) Born in Porbandar, Gujarat, in 1869
(b) Studied law in England
(c) Headed sedition committee
(d) Experienced racial discrimination in South Africa

Ans. (c) He headed sedition committee

Q.3 Arrange the following movements led by Mahatma Gandhi in the correct chronological order.

1. Champaran 2. Kheda
3. Non-Cooperation Movement 4. Ahmedabad

Options

(a) 1, 3, 2, 4 (b) 1, 4, 2, 3
(c) 4, 1, 2, 3 (d) 2, 3, 1, 4

Ans. (b)

Exp. The correct chronological order of movements led by Mahatma Gandhi is

- **Champaran (1917)** First Satyagraha in India against indigo planters.
- **Ahmedabad Mill Strike (February, 1918)** Demand for better wages for textile workers.
- **Kheda Satyagraha (March, 1918)** Protest against tax collection during famine.
- **Non-Cooperation Movement (1920-22)** Mass movement against British rule.

Q.4 Which of these statements is not associated with the Jallianwala Bagh massacre? **(ICSE 2022)**

(a) It happened in the year 1919.
(b) General Dyer was responsible for this massacre.
(c) It became a cause for the Non-Cooperation Movement.
(d) It became a cause for the Civil Disobedience Movement.

Ans. (d) It became a cause for the Civil Disobedience Movement.

Exp. The Jallianwala Bagh massacre (1919) sparked nationwide outrage and this event led Mahatma Gandhi to launch the Non-Cooperation Movement in 1920 to resist British rule peacefully.

Q.5 Which of the following statements gives the proper explanation about the Non-Cooperation Movement?

(a) It was a movement to boycott foreign goods, promote the use of Swadeshi products and aim of complete independence.
(b) It was a violent struggle led by Mahatma Gandhi against British rule to achieve immediate independence.
(c) It was a non-violent movement launched by Mahatma Gandhi to withdraw cooperation from British institutions.
(d) It was a movement focused on industrial development and economic reforms in colonial India.

Ans. (c) It was a non-violent movement launched by Mahatma Gandhi to withdraw cooperation from British institutions.

Q.6 Identify the clauses of the Rowlatt Act. **(ICSE Specimen Semester-I 2022)**

(a) Proper trial and then punished.
(b) Arrest people without a warrant.
(c) Vernacular Press must not publish anything against the British.
(d) Compulsory license for arms.

Ans. (b) Arrest people without a warrant.

Q.7 The Khilafat Movement was started under the leadership of .... **(ICSE 2021)**

(a) Ali Brothers (b) Dr. Saifuddin Kitchulu
(c) Khan Abdul Ghaffar Khan (d) Sir Syed Ahmad Khan

Ans. (a) Ali Brothers

Exp. The Ali Brothers (Shaukat Ali and Mohammad Ali) were key leaders in the Khilafat Movement (1919-1924), which aimed to protect the Ottoman Caliphate after World War I.

Q.8 Which of the following activities took place during Khilafat Movement?

(a) People resigned from government services.
(b) Students boycotted schools and colleges.
(c) Shops selling foreign goods were picketed.
(d) All of the above

Ans. (d) All of the above

Q.9 Which of the following was the reason of Khilafat Movement?

(a) To unite Hindus and Muslims together through a mass struggle.

(b) Injustice done to Turkey and Caliph by the British.

(c) To end the First World War.

(d) Both (a) and (b)

Ans. (d) Both (a) and (b)

Q.10 The Non-Cooperation Movement was primarily launched as a reaction to specific British policies and incidents. The movement succeeded in achieving its immediate goal of Swaraj. Gandhi's principle of non-violence was central to the Non-Cooperation Movement. The suspension of the movement indicated a setback to Indian nationalism. *ABC News 2nd Oct,2024*

Which of the following statements can be inferred from the passage about the Non-Cooperation Movement?

(a) The Non-Cooperation Movement was primarily launched against British laws.

(b) The movement succeeded in trial of General Dyer.

(c) Gandhi's principle of violence was central to the Non-Cooperation Movement.

(d) The suspension of the movement was welcomed by all leaders.

Ans. (a) The Non-Cooperation Movement was primarily launched against British laws.

Q.11 Identify the leaders in the image given below who were associated with the beginning of Khilafat Movement.

(a) Ali Brothers (b) Biswas Brothers
(c) Kings of Patiala (d) None of these

Ans. (a) Ali Brothers

Q.12 During the Non-Cooperation Movement the Congress became a continuous political organisation and its Constitution was amended in the .... session in December, 1920.

(a) Nagpur (c) Madras
(b) Lahore (d) Kolkata

Ans. (a) Nagpur

Q.13. What was the cause for the sudden suspension of the Non-Cooperation Movement? **(ICSE 2021)**

(a) Repressive measures of the British

(b) The Chauri-Chaura incident

(c) The Gandhi-Irwin Pact

(d) The Jallianwala Bagh massacre

Ans. (b) The Chauri-Chaura incident

Q.14 Identify the year when the movement, given in the image given below, was launched by Gandhiji.

(a) 1929 (b) 1920 (c) 1930 (d) 1931

Ans. (c) 1930

Q.15 How did the Lahore Session of 1929 lead to the Civil Disobedience Movement? **(ICSE 2021)**

(a) The declaration of Purna Swaraj was passed.

(b) Subhash Bose was made the President of the Congress.

(c) Simon Commission recommendations were accepted.

(d) Congress passed a resolution to begin the Civil Disobedience Movement.

Ans. (a) The declaration of Purna Swaraj was passed.

Q.16 Identify which of the following was the primary reason behind opposition of the Simon Commission in India.

(a) The Simon Commission was formed in 1928.

(b) It included Indian members as part of the commission.

(c) It was rejected by Indian leaders due to the absence of Indian representation.

(d) The Simon Commission was created to address the Issue of Rowlatt act only.

Ans. (c) It was rejected by Indian leaders due to the absence of Indian representation.

Q.17 Which of the following was the feature of Ramsay MacDonald's Communal Award?

(a) Privy-purses to native princes.

(b) Communal representation to Anglo Indians.

(c) Reservations to Buddhists in election.

(d) Separate electorates for depressed classes.

Ans. (d) Separate electorates for depressed classes.

Q.18 Mahatma Gandhi signed a pact with .... to end the Civil Disobedience Movement. **(ICSE Specimen Semester-I 2022)**

(a) Lord Mountbatten (b) Lord Wavell
(c) Lord Irwin (d) Stafford Cripps

Ans. (c) Lord Irwin

Q.19 The Poona Pact which was signed between the Dr. Bhimrao Ambedkar and Mahatma Gandhi in 1934 provided for

(a) creation of dominion status for India

(b) separate electorates for the Muslims

(c) the separate electorate for the Harijans

(d) joint electorate with the reservation for Harijans

Ans. (d) joint electorate with the reservation for Harijans

Q.20 Which of the following statements about the Civil Disobedience Movement is incorrect?

(a) Gandhi led the Salt March to Dandi in 1930.

(b) The movement encouraged violent protests against the British.

(c) The Salt March was a key event that symbolised the movement.

(d) The movement spread across India and gained wide support.

Ans. (b) The movement encouraged violent protests against the British.

Q.21 Identify the odd one out of the following events related to the Civil Disobedience Movement.

(a) Dandi March

(b) Second Round Table Conference

(c) Chauri Chaura Incident

(d) Gandhi-Irwin Pact

Ans. (c) Chauri Chaura Incident

Q.22 Where did the call for purna Swaraj was made by the Congress?

(a) Bombay (b) Lahore (c) Pune (d) Nagpur

Ans. (b) Lahore

Exp. At Lahore session of 1929, the Indian National Congress led by Jawaharlal Nehru declared the goal of Poorna Swaraj (complete independence) from British rule.

Q.23 .... was the cause for the renewal of the Civil Disobedience Movement. **(ICSE Specimen 2024)**

(a) Failure of the Second Round Table Conference

(b) Rowlatt Act

(c) Mountbatten Plan

(d) Failure of the Cripps Mission

Ans. (a) Failure of the Second Round Table Conference

Exp. The Second Round Table Conference (1931) failed due to disagreements between the British government and Indian leaders.

Q.24 Which of the following statements about the Quit India Movement is correct?

(a) The movement was launched in 1942 under the leadership of Mahatma Gandhi.

(b) It was a peaceful movement aimed at achieving independence immediately.

(c) The British responded with politely with no arrests.

(d) It was not successful in forcing the British to grant immediate independence to India.

Ans. (a) The movement was launched in 1942 under the leadership of Mahatma Gandhi.

Q.25 Read the description and identify the person.
He was associated with the slogan of 'Do or Die'

(a) Subhash Chandra Bose

(b) Pt. Jawahar Lal Nehru

(c) Lal Bahadur Shastri

(d) Mohandas Karamchand Gandhi

Ans. (d) Mohandas Karamchand Gandhi

Exp. The 'Do or Die' slogan was coined by Mahatma Gandhi during the Quit India Movement in 1942. It urged Indians to either fight for independence or face death.

Q.26 .... was one of the causes of the Quit India Movement. **(ICSE 2023)**

(a) Failure of the Second Round Table Conference

(b) Rowlatt Act

(c) Mountbatten Plan

(d) Failure of the Cripps Mission

Ans. (d) Failure of the Cripps Mission

Q27. Look at the picture and identify the leader who was the political Guru of Mahatma Gandhi.

(a) Bal Gangadhar Tilak (b) Dadabhai Naoroji

(c) Gopal Krishna Gokhale (d) Surendranath Banerjee

Ans. (c) Gopal Krishna Gokhale

Q.28 Read the details given below and identify the correct statement?

P : In the First World War, Japan was defeated.

Q : On 9th August, 1942 the resolution for Civil Disobedience was passed.

R : Call for Purna Swaraj was made in Lahore.

S : M.K. Gandhi Led the Quit India Movement and was arrested immediately.

Options

(a) P and Q (b) R and S

(c) S and P (d) Q and S

Ans. (b) R and S

TYPE - 2   1 Mark

Assertion- Reason Questions

Q.1 Read the two statements given below about the Gandhian Movement and select the option that shows the correct relationship between (A) and (B).

Assertion (A) The Champaran Movement of 1917 was Gandhi's first major experiment with Satyagraha in India.

Reason (R) Gandhi used the Champaran Movement to fight against the oppressive plantation system imposed on peasants by the British colonialists in Haryana.

(a) R contradicts A
(b) R is the reason for A
(c) A is true, but R is false
(d) A and R are independent of each other

Ans. (c) A is true, but R is false

Q.2 Assertion (A) Gandhi's non-violent approach was central to the Indian independence movement.

Reason (R) Gandhi believed that violence would lead to division and long-term suffering, whereas non-violence would unite the people of India.

(a) R contradicts A
(b) R is the reason for A
(c) A is true, but R is false
(d) A and R are independent of each other

Ans. (b) R is the reason for A

Q.3 Read the two statements given below about the Civil Disobedience Movement and select the option that shows the correct relationship between (A) and (R).

(ICSE Specimen 2025)

Assertion (A) The Civil Disobedience Movement was renewed by Mahatma Gandhi.

Reason (R) The Second Round Table Conference was a failure.

(a) R contradicts A
(b) R is the reason for A
(c) A is true but R is false
(d) A and R are independent of each other

Ans. (b) R is the reason for A

Q.4 Read the two statements given below about the Civil Disobedience Movement and select the option that shows the correct relationship between (A) and (B).

(ICSE Specimen 2024)

Assertion (A) Gandhi's Civil Disobedience was based on engaging in dialogue and negotiation with the British.

Reason (R) Gandhi believed that violence and aggression are counterproductive to achieve any goal.

(a) R contradicts A
(b) R is the reason for A
(c) A is true but R is false
(d) A and R are independent of each other

Ans. (b) R is the reason for A

Q.5 Assertion (A) Failures of Cripps Mission led to disappointment and bitterness among Indians.

Reason (R) The Japanese Army's attack on Germany and threat of invasion convinced Indian leaders of the urgent need to eliminate British rule.

(a) R contradicts A
(b) R is the reason for A
(c) A is true but R is false
(d) A and R are independent of each other

Ans. (c) A is true but R is false

TYPE - 3   2 Marks

Very Short Answer Type Questions

Q.1 Name the two methods of political struggle evolved by Mahatma Gandhi as a part of the National Movement.

Ans. The two methods of political struggle evolved by Mahatma Gandhi were -Satyagraha and Non-Violence

Q.2 With reference to the life of Gandhiji, answer the following questions.

(i) When did Mahatma Gandhi returned from South Africa?

(ii) Which movements he started when he returned to India?

Ans. (i) Mahatma Gandhi returned from South Africa to India in 1915.

(ii) Mahatma Gandhi started three movements after returning to India : Champaran, Kheda and Ahmedabad movement.

Q.3 State any two causes for the Non-Cooperation Movement.

Ans. The two major causes that led to the beginning of Non-Cooperation Movement were as follows

(i) The Rowlatt Act that gave the British government the power to arrest and detain Indians without trial. It was seen as a tool for suppressing dissent and silencing the Indian freedom movement.

(ii) The Jallianwala Bagh Massacre that occurred as a direct consequence of the protests against the Rowlatt Act. General Dyer's harsh attack on unarmed civilians made many Indians very upset.

Q.4 State any two provisions of the Rowlatt Act passed by the government in 1919?

Ans. Following were the provisions of the Rowlatt Act

(i) The government could arrest any person without a warrant.

(ii) It gave the government enormous powers to repress any political activity.

Q.5 Explain about the Hunter Commission and its recommendations.

Ans. The Hunter Commission was appointed to enquire about the Jallianwala Bagh Massacre. The Commission criticised Dyer's action, but mentioned that legal prosecution against Dyer would not be possible due to political reasons.

Q.6 Name two leaders of the Khilafat Movement that was launched in India to champion the cause of the Caliph of Turkey.

Ans. Mohammed Ali and Shaukat Ali were the leaders of the Khilafat Movement.

Q.7 Mention any two methods of resistance which were adopted during the Non-Cooperation Movement.

Ans. Two methods of resistance adopted during the Non-Cooperation Movement were as follows

(i) Surrendering of titles and resignation from nominated posts in the local bodies.

(ii) Boycott of foreign goods and adoption of Swadeshi.

Q.8 Name two institutions which were setup during the Non-Cooperation Movement.

Ans. The two institutions setup during the non-cooperation Movement were

(i) Jamia Millia Islamia of Aligarh (ii) Kashi Vidyapeeth

Q.9 Highlight some important feature of the Non-Cooperation Movement.

Ans. Before the Non-Cooperation Movement, national movement had remained the concern of the middle class and intelligentsia only but the Non-Cooperation Movement became an All India Movement for the first time and Gandhiji became the symbol of the poor and downtrodden.

Q.10 Name the person who were associated with the following.

(i) Swaraj Party

(ii) Returning of Knighthood title

Ans. (i) Motilal Nehru and C.R. Das were two prominent leaders of the Swaraj Party.

(ii) Rabindranath Tagore returned his Knighthood title as a protest against massacre of Jallianwala Bagh.

Q.11 State any two causes which led to the Civil Disobedience Movement of 1930. **(ICSE 2018)**

Ans. The two causes which led to the Civil Disobedience Movement of 1930 were as follows

(i) A resolution was passed in the Lahore Session of Congress in 1929, which declared Poorna Swaraj to become the objective of the Congress.

(ii) An 'Eleven Points Ultimatum' was served by Gandhiji to the British Government. After the government's failure to negotiate, Gandhiji started the Civil Disobedience Movement.

Q.12 With reference to the Gandhi Irwin Pact, answer the following

(i) When did the Gandhi Irwin Pact was signed?

(ii) Mention any one provision of the Pact.

Ans. (i) The Gandhi-Irwin Pact was signed on 5th March,1931.

(ii) One of the provision of the Gandhi-Irwin Pact was the withdrawal of all the ordinances and prosecutions.

Q.13 Explain any two proposals which were given by Cripps Mission.

Ans. The two proposals given by Cripps Mission (1942) were

(i) Promise of dominion status after the Second World War.

(ii) Proposals of an interim government during the war.

Q.14 Imagine you are a young Indian living in 1942. Mahatma Gandhi has just launched the Quit India Movement with a call for immediate independence from British rule. The movement is gaining momentum, and protests are spreading throughout the country. You are part of a group of students who are eager to join the movement but are concerned about the consequences.

How would you motivate them to participate in this movement?

Ans. I would motivate individuals by appealing to their sense of national pride and duty by emphasising that this is a historic opportunity to free India from British rule and secure a brighter future for all.

I would also encourage them to participate through peaceful methods like boycotting British goods and institutions.

Q.15 Analyse the impact of the Quit India Movement on the British Government's stance towards India?

Ans. The British Government responded to the Quit India Movement with severe repression. They arrested key leaders, including Mahatma Gandhi, and banned the movement, which resulted in widespread protests, strikes, and unrest across the country. This harsh suppression demonstrated the British determination to maintain control, but also exposed the unsustainable nature of their rule.

Q.16 Mahatma Gandhi's leadership was defined by his deep commitment to non-violence (Ahimsa) and truth (Satya). His approach to leadership was rooted in simplicity, integrity, and moral authority, which set him apart from other leaders. *The Hindu 2nd Oct,2024*

What role did Satyagraha play in Gandhi's leadership during the Indian freedom movement?

Ans. Satyagraha, or non-violent resistance, was a core strategy of Gandhi's leadership. It empowered ordinary people to stand up against British oppression through peaceful protests, civil disobedience, and non-cooperation, making the freedom struggle a mass movement.

TYPE - 4 — 3 Marks

Short Answer Type Questions

Q.1 Mark the differences between the movements in India before and after arrival of Gandhiji in India.

Ans. The major differences between the movement in India before and after arrival of Gandhiji in India were as follows

	Before Arrival	After Arrival
Leadership	Led by moderate and radical leaders like Naoroji and Tilak.	Led by Mahatma Gandhi.
Methods of Protest	Petitions, speeches, and Constitutional reforms were methods.	Non-violence, non-cooperation, and civil disobedience were major tools.
Participation	Limited to the educated elite and professionals.	Widespread participation from all sections of society.
Key Movements	Swadeshi Movement, Home Rule League.	Non-Cooperation, Salt March, Quit India Movement.
Objective	Demand for Constitutional reforms and Indian representation into legislature.	Complete independence (Poorna Swaraj) and rejection of British rule.

Q.2 The advent of Mahatma Gandhi on the Indian political scene gave a new direction to the freedom struggle. In this context answer the following.

Why did Gandhi withdraw the Non-Cooperation Movement?

Ans. Gandhi withdrew the Non-Cooperation Movement in 1922 after the Chauri Chaura incident, where a violent mob set a police station on fire, that resulted in the death of 22 policemen. This act of violence went against Gandhi's principle of non-violence (Ahimsa), which was the foundation of the movement.

He believed that continuing the movement in a climate of violence would undermine its moral legitimacy and hamper the struggle for independence. Hence, he decided to call off the movement to maintain discipline and adhere to the principle of non-violence.

Q.3 Gandhiji introduced new ideas in politics and adopted new methods to give a new direction to the political movement. In this context, explain Gandhiji's Doctrine of Satyagraha.

Ans. Gandhiji introduced the Satyagraha, which was a method of agitation and protest based on truth and non-violence. It suggested that if the cause was true, if the struggle was against injustice, then physical force was not necessary.

A Satyagrahi could win the battle through non-violence. It was a passive resistance consisting of defiance of laws, non-payment of taxes, boycott of government institutions etc.

Gandhiji's Satyagraha Movement was directed against the British system of exploitation and not against the British people individually or collectively. These experiments in Satyagraha brought Gandhiji into a close touch with the masses, with both the peasants in the rural areas and the workers in the urban areas.

Q.4 Explain how Khilafat Movement helped in bringing unity among Hindu and Muslims during Non-Cooperation Movement in India?

Ans. The Khilafat Movement (1919-1924) played a significant role in fostering unity between Hindus and Muslims during the Non-Cooperation Movement in following ways

- **Shared Opposition to British Rule** The Khilafat and Non-Cooperation Movements united Hindus and Muslims against British policies, creating a common cause.
- **Gandhi's Support** Mahatma Gandhi strongly supported the Khilafat cause and integrated it with

the Non-Cooperation Movement. This alliance encouraged Muslims to join the freedom struggle under Gandhi's leadership.

- **Joint Protests** Both communities participated together in strikes, boycotts, and Swadeshi promotion. They also maintained the communal harmony during the movements.

Q.5 With reference to the Non-Cooperation Movement of Mahatma Gandhi analyse its impact on the Indian freedom struggle.

Ans. The Non-Cooperation Movement (1920-1922) had a profound impact on the Indian freedom struggle which were as follows

- **Mass Mobilisation** The movement united diverse groups, including peasants, workers, students, etc, and transformed the independence struggle into a mass movement.
- **Boycott of British Institutions** Indians widely boycotted British goods, schools, courts and titles etc. They weakened British authority by creating economic and administrative pressure.
- **Rise of Gandhian Leadership** Mahatma Gandhi emerged as the central figure of the freedom movement. He introduced the principles of non-violence and satyagraha in national independence movements.

Q.6 "The Non-Cooperation Movement marked the beginning of mass participation in India's freedom struggle". Justify this by mentioning any three points.

Ans. The statement, "The Non-Cooperation Movement marked the beginning of mass participation in India's freedom struggle", can be justified through the following three points

(i) **Mass Involvement** The Non-Cooperation Movement transformed the freedom struggle into a mass movement by involving people from all sections of society-peasants, workers, students, and women. This marked a shift from the earlier elitist phase of the freedom struggle, where participation was limited to a few educated leaders and urban elites.

(ii) **Nationwide Protests** The movement was not restricted to one region or group but was a pan-India effort. People across the country united to boycott British goods, schools, courts, and titles. This nationwide participation highlighted the collective opposition to British rule.

(iii) **Hindu-Muslim Unity** The inclusion of the Khilafat Movement within the Non-Cooperation Movement brought Hindus and Muslims together in their fight against the British. This unity expanded the base of the struggle and strengthened the spirit of mass participation.

Q.7 Explain the long-term effects of sudden recall of the Non-Cooperation Movement on India's freedom movement.

Ans. The sudden recall of the Non-Cooperation Movement by Gandhi in 1922 after the Chauri Chaura incident had significant long-term effects on India's freedom struggle, as follows

- **Disappointment Among Extremists** Many leaders, especially extremists, felt let down by the sudden end of the movement thus leading to a temporary slowdown in the freedom struggle.
- **Shift in Leadership** The withdrawal led to the emergence of new leadership, including younger leaders like Jawaharlal Nehru and Subhas Chandra Bose, who began advocating newer methods of struggles.
- **Renewed Focus on Reforms** Many leaders returned to Constitutional methods of struggle against the Britishers in India.
- **Foundation for Future Movements** The movement showcased the power of mass mobilisation and non-violent resistance, setting the stage for future movements like the Civil Disobedience Movement and Quit India Movement.
- **Communal Tensions** The break in unity after the movement's withdrawal weakened the Hindu-Muslim alliance, and communal tensions rise once again.

Q.8 "The Simon Commission was met with strong opposition in India". Justify the statement with suitable example.

Ans. The statement, "The Simon Commission was met with strong opposition in India", can be justified with the following points

- **Exclusion of Indian Leaders** The commission was entirely composed of British members without any Indian representation, which led to feelings of alienation and resentment among the Indian population.
- **Lack of Constitutional Reforms** The commission was seen as an attempt to delay meaningful political reforms in India, as it failed to address the demands for self-rule and greater Indian participation in governance.

- **Increased Nationalism** The arrival of the Simon Commission led to widespread protests, including the famous 'Simon Go Back' slogan, reflecting the growing discontent and unity among Indians in opposing British rule.

Q.9 "The declaration of Purna Swaraj was a significant turning point in the Indian independence movement". Justify the statement.

Ans. "The declaration of Purna Swaraj was a significant turning point in the Indian independence movement". This statement is justified as declaration of Poorna Swaraj in 1930 sparked a renewed sense of nationalist mobilisation across India.

It stimulated the masses thus, leading to widespread participation in movements such as the Civil Disobedience Movement.

Additionally, the declaration drew international attention to India's demand for independence, thus isolated British rule on the global stage.

Q.10 With reference to the mass phase of the national movement under the leadership of Gandhi, answer the following. **(ICSE 2020)**

Briefly explain the Dandi March of 1930.

Ans. The Dandi March, was led by Mahatma Gandhi in 1930. It was a protest against the British salt tax, in which Gandhi and his followers walked 240 miles to the coastal village of Dandi to make salt from seawater to defy British laws.

It marked the beginning of the Civil Disobedience Movement and gained national and international attention to India's fight against colonial laws.

The Dandi March led to the arrest of Gandhi and thousands of his followers, it increased pressure on the British government to reconsider its policies in India.

Q.11 The Civil Disobedience Movement was launched by Gandhiji with his famous Dandi March on 12th March, 1930. Mention the significance of this historic event.

Ans. The significance of Civil Disobedience Movement can be seen as follows

- **Highlighting Economic Exploitation** The movement directly targeted colonial economic policies by boycotting British goods, refusing to pay taxes, and breaching laws like the Salt Law, which symbolised British exploitation.
- **Integration of Non-Violent Resistance** Gandhi's strategy of non-violent satyagraha reached new heights during CDM. The Dandi March became an iconic symbol of peaceful defiance.
- **Setting the Stage for Future Movements** The movement was not a complete success in achieving its immediate goals, but it prepared Indians for greater sacrifices in the freedom struggle.

Q.12 With reference to the mass phase of the national movement from 1930 to 1947, answer the following.

What was the significance of the Second Round Table Conference held in 1931 ?

Ans. The Second Round Table Conference was held from 7th September to 1st December, 1931 in London. Mahatma Gandhi was appointed as the sole representative of the Congress to this conference. The significance of the conference was as follows

- The Second Round Table Conference gave various Indian communities a platform to present their demands and aspirations.
- The conference highlighted the difficulties of bringing diverse groups together and reaching a consensus on critical issues.
- Although the discussions and agreements did not result in immediate constitutional reforms, they laid the groundwork for future negotiations and paved the way for the eventual transfer of power from British rule to Indian self-rule.

TYPE - 5 — 4 Marks

Long Answer Type Questions

Q.1 On what assurances according to Gandhi Irwin Pact did Gandhiji withdraw the Civil Disobedience Movement?

Ans. Gandhiji withdrew the Civil Disobedience Movement based on the following assurances according to Gandhi Irwin Pact

- **Withdrawal of Ordinances** The British government agreed to withdraw all the ordinances imposed during the movement.
- **Termination of Prosecutions** All legal actions and prosecutions against individuals involved in the movement were to be discontinued.
- **Release of Political Prisoners** The government assured the release of political prisoners, except those accused of violence or killing.
- **Restoration of Civil Rights** The British Government promised to restore the civil rights of the people affected by the movement, thus creating a more peaceful atmosphere.

Q.2 **State any four features of the programme of the Civil Disobedience Movement launched in 1930.**

Ans. The three features of the programme of Civil Disobedience Movement were as follows

(i) It shattered people's faith in the British Government and received the will to fight the elections.

(ii) It laid the social roots for the freedom struggle and popularised the new methods of propaganda like the Prabhat pheris, pamphlets, etc.

(iii) Violation of the salt law was soon followed by the defiance of forest laws in Maharashtra, Karnataka etc.

(iv) People refused to pay the rural 'chaukidari tax' in Eastern India.

Q.3 **Highlight any four major clause which were produced by the Cabinet Mission Plan of India.**

Ans. The four main clauses of the Cabinet Mission Plan were as follows

(i) There will be a Federal Union of the British provinces and of the Princely States.

(ii) The Union Government would control Defence, Foreign Affairs and Communications.

(iii) The provinces would enjoy full autonomy for all subjects other than the union subjects.

(iv) The British provinces would be divided into three groups i.e. Group A, Group B and Group C on the basis of religion.

Q.4 **Differentiate between the Non-Cooperation and Civil Disobedience Movement.**

Ans. The differences between both movements were as follows

Basis	Non-Cooperation Movement (1920-1922)	Civil Disobedience Movement (1930-1934)
Objective	Aimed to achieve self governance through non-cooperation with British institutions.	Direct violation of British laws and demand for complete independence (Poorna Swaraj).
Nature of Protest	Passive resistance by boycotting British goods, schools, courts, and elections.	Active resistance, including breaking specific laws like the Salt Law, refusal to pay taxes, and picketing.
Leadership and Participation	All sections of society participated into it but Hindu-Muslim unity was at its zeneith.	Broader participation from section including peasants, women, and industrial workers.
Key Actions	Boycott of foreign goods, government schools, and resignation from titles.	Dandi March, refusal to pay land revenue, and breaking salt and forest laws.
End of Movement	Withdrawn after the Chauri Chaura incident due to Gandhi's commitment to non-violence.	Lost momentum after the Gandhi-Irwin Pact and renewed British repression.

Q.5 **The Congress Working Committee passed the famous Quit India Resolution at Wardha in July, 1942. With reference to this, answer the following questions.**

(i) What were the reasons for the passing of this resolution?

(ii) What was the British Government's reaction to the Quit India Movement?

Ans. (i) The reasons for the passing of the Quit India Resolution (1942) were as follows

- **Failure of the Cripps Mission (1942)** The British proposal for limited self-government was rejected by the Indians.
- **British Involvement in World War II** India was forced to join the war without its consent, which caused a lot of frustration among the people.

(ii) The reaction of the British government to the Quit India Movement were as follows

- The government resorted to severe measures to crush the Quit India Movement.
- The press was completely puzzled.
- The British military was deployed to disperse protestors. In some cases, airplanes were used to fire machine guns on crowds.

TYPE - 6 — 10 Marks

Structured Questions

Q.1 Read the excerpt given below and answer the questions that follow. **(ICSE Specimen 2025)**

"The March, which took place in India, was led by Mohandas Gandhi to protest British rule in India. During the march, thousands of Indians followed Gandhi from his religious retreat near Ahmedabad to the Arabian Sea coast, a distance of some 240 miles. The march resulted in the arrest of nearly 60,000 people, including Gandhi himself". *The Marion (Ohio) Star [Edited]*

(i) Name the march being discussed above. Which movement did this march lead to? In which year was that movement launched? (3)

(ii) The movement which began with this march made a considerable impact on the social and political surroundings of the country. Analyse this statement by mentioning any three impacts. (3)

(iii) What were the key assurances in the Gandhi-Irwin Pact that led Gandhiji to call off the Civil Disobedience Movement? (4)

Ans. (i) The march being discussed is the Dandi March. It led to the Civil Disobedience Movement. The Civil Disobedience Movement was launched on 12th March, 1930.

(ii) The movement which began with this march had a considerable impact in following ways

- Firstly, it pushed the Indian struggle for independence into the limelight of Western media.
- Secondly, it brought women and depressed classes directly in touch with the freedom movement.
- Thirdly, it showed the power of non-violent protest as a tool for fighting.

(iii) For answer, refer Q.1 of Long Answer Type Questions.

Q.2 With reference to the picture given below, answer the following questions. (ICSE 2019)

(i) (a) Identify the Memorial built for those who were killed in this incident.

(b) Where did this incident take place ?

(c) Which movement did Gandhiji launch in 1920 as a response to this incident? (3)

(ii) Explain briefly why Mahatma Gandhi withdraw this movement in 1922? (ICSE 2023) (3)

(iii) State any four impacts of the movement. (4)

Ans. (i) (a) This monument was established in 1951 by the Government of India in Amritsar, to commemorate the Jallianwala Bagh massacre.

(b) The incident took place in the Jallianwala Bagh on 13th April, 1919 where a large number of people assembled on the day of Baisakhi.

(c) Mahatma Gandhi started Non-Cooperation Movement in 1920 as a response to this incident.

(ii) For answer, refer Q.2 of Short Answer Type Questions.

(iii) The impacts of the Non-Cooperation Movement were as follows

(a) The Indian national movement, for the first time in history, acquired a real mass base with the participation of different sections of the Indian society.

(b) It instilled a new confidence among the people and transformed the Congress from a deliberative assembly into a moral fighting force.

(c) It fostered Hindu-Muslim unity by merging the Khilafat Movement with this movement.

(d) It led to the formation of the Swaraj party under the leadership of C.R. Das and Motilal Nehru.

Q.3 Look at the picture and answer the following questions.

Indian Express

MAHATMA GANDHI, MAULANA AZAD AND NEHRU ARRESTED

ALL THE LEADERS TAKEN TO POONA

(i) During which movement, the leaders mention above in the picture were arrested? Give any two causes of that movement. (3)

(ii) Give any three effects of the movement launched by Gandhiji in 1942 that was significant to the last phase of the national movement of India. (3)

(iii) "The Quit India Movement was a turning point in India's struggle for independence". Justify the statement. (4)

Ans. (i) The leaders mentioned in the given picture were arrested during the Quit India movement launched by Gandhiji on 8th August, 1942. The causes of the Quit India movement were

- **Failure of the Cripps Mission** (1942) The British Government's proposal for India's post-war constitutional status was rejected by Indian leaders, as it fell short of guaranteeing complete independence.
- **World War II Impact** The British pulled India into the war without consulting Indian leaders, leading to widespread dissatisfaction and demand for immediate independence.

(ii) Three effects of the Quit India Movement launched by Gandhiji in 1942 that was significant to the last phase of the National Movement of India were as follows

(a) This movement developed the feeling of political awakening and consciousness among masses. It showed Indian's anger and hatred against imperialism.

(b) The mass upsurge in this movement shook the basic foundations of the British Raj . It was evident that the British would no longer be able to rule India against the wishes of Indians.

(c) This movement clearly indicated the capacity of the Indian people for sacrifice and determined struggle. It displayed the depth of national feelings.

(iii) The statement, "The Quit India Movement was a turning point in India's struggle for independence", can be justified with the following points

- **Clear Demand for Independence** Unlike earlier movements, the Quit India Movement launched in 1942 directly called for an immediate end to British rule. This marked a decisive shift from negotiations to a bold demand for full independence, intensifying the freedom struggle.
- **Mass Participation** People from all sections of society-workers, farmers, students and women-actively participated, demonstrating national unity against colonial rule.
- **Weakening of British Control** The mass protests, strikes, and uprisings disrupted the colonial administration and highlighted the declining authority of the British in India.
- **World War Effect** After World War II, Britain faced economic exhaustion and global pressure to decolonise. The movement's impact made it clear that the Indian demand for independence could no longer be suppressed, compelling Britain to engage in negotiations which ultimately lead to India's independence in 1947.

Q.4 Look at the given picture and answer the questions that follows. **(ICSE 2025)**

Tears of Blood : When 1,650 Bullets Changed India Forever
–The Times of India, April 2019

(i) **Identify the above incident. Which Gandhian movement did it lead to? Which incident to the suspension of that movement?**

(ii) **Mention any three repressive provisions of the Rowlatt Act.**

iii) **Mention the following**

(a) **Any two causes of the Quit India Movement.**

(b) **Any two causes of the Civil Disobedience Movement.**

Ans. (i) The incident described is the Jallianwala Bagh Massacre on 13th April 1919, when General Dyer ordered troops to fire on a peaceful gathering in Amritsar, killing thousands. This incident led to nationwide outrage and was a major cause of the Non-Cooperation Movement (1920-1922) launched by Mahatma Gandhi.

The movement was later suspended due to the Chauri Chaura Incident (1922), where violent protesters burned a police station, killing policemen. Gandhiji, being a strong advocate of non-violence, called off the movement to prevent further bloodshed.

(ii) The Rowlatt Act was passed by the Imperial Legislative Council in March 1919 and was strongly opposed by Indian leaders. Three repressive provisions of the Rowlatt Act were

(a) **Arrest without Warrant** The government could arrest and detain any person suspected of anti-British activities without a trial for up to two years.

(b) **In Camera Trials** Trials could be conducted in secret (closed-door hearings) without allowing the accused to know the evidence against them.

(c) **Curb on Freedoms** The Act restricted freedom of speech, press and movement and protests against the government were considered illegal.

(iii) (a) Two causes of the Quit India Movement were

- **Failure of the Cripps Mission (1942)** The British government sent the Cripps Mission to offer Dominion Status after World War II, but Congress rejected it as it did not promise full independence.
- **Japanese Threat** The Japanese Army was advancing towards India, increasing fears of an invasion. Indian leaders saw this as a chance to force the British to leave India immediately.

(b) Two causes of the Civil Disobedience Movement were

- **Simon Commission Boycott (1927)** The Simon Commission was sent to review India's political situation, but no Indian members were included. This angered Indian leaders, leading to widespread protests.
- **Declaration of Purna Swaraj (1929)** The Lahore Session of Congress (1929), under Jawaharlal Nehru's presidency, declared Complete Independence (Purna Swaraj) as India's goal, leading to mass protests against British rule.

FORWARD BLOC AND INA

Formation of the Forward Bloc

Forward Bloc was an organised left wing party within the congress. It was formed by Subhash Chandra Bose on 3rd May, 1939 as a result of the different view of Bose and Congress (Gandhiji)

Objective of the Forward Bloc

- The main objective of the Forward Bloc was to unite all the left-wing sections within the Congress and to develop an alternative leadership.
- Its immediate objective was the liberation of India with the support of workers, peasants, youths and all radical organisations.
- Forward Bloc leaders aimed to establish a socialist society, for which they adopted the following meassures
  - State-planning for the re-organisation of agriculture and industry on socialist lines.
  - Abolition of landlordism like Zamindari System, Making the 'Right to Work' as a fundamental right of the citizens.
  - A new monetary and credit system.
  - World peace, disarmament and friendly relations with socialist nations like Russia.

Formation of the Indian National Army (INA)

- The concept of the Indian National Army (INA) originated from Mohan Singh, an Indian officer in the British Indian Army.
- This army consisted of the Indian prisoners of war under Japan.
- The INA was formally established on 1st September, 1942. By the end of 1942, approximately 45,000 Indian POWs had joined the INA.
- The formation of the INA was influenced by Tokyo and Bangkok conferences .

Mohan Singh

Tokyo Conference

Tokyo conference was held between 28th and 30th March, 1942 and it was organised by the efforts of Rash Behari Bose. Some decisions taken in this conference were as follows

- To form an Indian National Army (INA).
- To expand and strengthen Indian Independence league in all Asian countries controlled by Japan.
- To hold a conference of the representatives of Indians at Bangkok in June 1942.

Bangkok Conference

Bangkok Conference was held from 15th June to 23rd June, 1942. Rash Behari Bose was elected as President of the conference. It was attended by more than 150 representatives from East-Asian countries.

Some decisions taken in this conference were as follows

- The Indian Independence League (IIL) would provide support for the Indian National Army (INA).

Rash Behari Bose

- Subhash Chandra Bose was invited to lead the INA.
- Mohan Singh was appointed as the Commander-in-Chief of the INA.
- A council of action was formed to manage the Independence Movement.

Subhash Chandra Bose and INA

- Subhash Chandra Bose took charge of Indian National Army (INA) and became its Supreme Commander in August 1943.
- He set up its headquarters in Rangoon and Singapore and started reorganisation of Indian National Army.
- Subhash Chandra Bose was fondly called Netaji by the soldiers and the civilians. He gave the call to his soldiers, 'Give me blood and I shall give you freedom'. His slogans were, 'Dilli Chalo' and 'Jai Hind'.

Subhash Chandra Bose

Objectives of INA under Subhash Chandra Bose

- Mobilise forces to help Indians regain freedom.
- Prepare Indians both in India and abroad for armed struggle against the British.
- Organise a provisional government of free India.
- Mobilise Indian manpower and money for total war.
- The motto of INA was 'Unity, Faith, Sacrifice'.

Contributions of Subhash Chandra Bose in INA

- Subhash Chandra Bose set up recruitment and training departments to strengthen the army.
- He named INA brigades after famous leaders like Gandhiji, Azad, Nehru, Subhash, and Rani Jhansi.
- He founded the Interim Government of Free India (Arzi Hukumat-e-Azad Hind) in Singapore on 21st October, 1943.
- He moved the headquarters of the provisional government to Rangoon (Myanmar) because it was strategically close to India's Eastern border.
- Japan gave the Andaman and Nicobar Islands to Netaji on 6th November, 1943, marking his first independent territory. Bose renamed the islands as Shaheed and Swaraj Islands.

EXAM ORIENTED QUESTIONS

TYPE - 1 1 Mark

Multiple Choice Questions

Q.1 Which of the following candidates was defeated by Subhash Chandra Bose during the Presidentship of INC at the Tripuri Session in 1939?

(a) Dr. Rajendra Prasad
(b) J.B. Kriplani
(c) Pattabhi Sitaramaiyya
(d) Nellie Sengupta

Ans. (c) Pattabhi Sitaramaiyya

Q.2 Identify the aim which was related to reorganisation of agriculture and industry on socialist lines. **(ISCE Specimen Semester-I 2022)**

(a) Indian National Congress (b) The Indian National Army
(c) The Forward Bloc (d) The Muslim League

Ans. (c) The Forward Bloc

Exp. The Forward Bloc was a political group formed in 1939 by Subhash Chandra Bose, aiming for complete independence from British rule.

Q.3 Identify the contributions of Subhash Chandra Bose.

P : Was the Supreme Commander of INA
Q : Signed the Lucknow Pact
R : Led the Quit India Movement
S : Founded the Forward Bloc **(ICSE 2025)**

(a) P and Q (b) Q and R
(c) P and S (d) R and S

Ans. (c) P and S

Q.4 The Forward Bloc aimed to abolish which of the following?

(a) Zamindari system (b) Dowry system
(c) Sati Pratha (d) Educational system

Ans. (a) Zamindari system

Q.5 Why was Subhash Chandra Bose disqualified from the Indian National Congress?

(a) Due to his support for Muslim League.
(b) Due to ideological differences and formation of Forward Bloc.
(c) Due to his collaboration with the Britishers .
(d) Due to his failure to secure independence for India

Ans. (b) Due to ideological differences and formation of Forward Bloc.

Q.6 Complete the given analogy.

Haripura session : 1938 :: Tripuri Session : ??

(a) 1939 (b) 1940 (c) 1941 (d) 1942

Ans. (a) 1939

Q.7 Which of the following statements was the key objective of the Indian National Army ? **(ICSE 2021)**

(a) To formulate and present the demands to the government.
(b) To make the world aware of the true nature of British rule in India.
(c) Total mobilisation of Indian manpower and money for a total war.
(d) To establish Home Rule in India.

Ans. (c) Total mobilisation of Indian manpower and money for a total war.

Q.8 Which among the following was the founder of the Indian National Army?

(a) Captain G.S. Dhillon (b) Subhash Chandra Bose
(c) Captain Mohan Singh (d) Rash Behari Bose

Ans. (c) Captain Mohan Singh

Exp. Captain Mohan Singh was an Indian Army officer who played a crucial role in the formation of the Azad Hind Fauj (Indian National Army) alongside Subhash Chandra Bose.

Q.9 The Indian National Army (INA) was reformed Initially formed by Indian prisoners of war captured by the Japanese in South-East Asia. The INA aimed to secure India's freedom through armed resistance.
What can be inferred about the impact of the INA's military actions on the British colonial rule?

(a) The INA's military actions directly overthrew British rule in India.
(b) The INA's military actions were insignificant in weakening British control but symbolised resistance.
(c) The INA's military success played a pivotal role in expediting India's independence.
(d) The INA's military actions were ignored by the British authorities.

Ans. (b) The INA's military actions were insignificant in weakening British control but symbolised resistance.

Q.10 Identify the odd one out regarding the formation of the INA.

(a) It was formed in South-East Asia during World War II.
(b) It was created to fight for Indian independence.
(c) It was formed by Indian prisoners of war.
(d) It was founded in 1885 during the Indian freedom struggle.

Ans. (d) It was founded in 1885 during the Indian freedom struggle.

Exp. The Indian National Army (INA) was formed in 1942 by Subhash Chandra Bose with the help of Indian prisoners of war in South-East Asia.

Q.11 Identify which of the following statements are correct?

P : Rani Jhansi was the female regiment of INA.

Q : The INA was initially formed by Indian prisoners of war.

R : The Forward Bloc was founded by Subhash Chandra Bose when he was president of the Indian National Congress.

S : Subhash Chandra Bose collaborated with America to gain support for the INA.

Options

(a) P and Q (b) R and S

(c) P and R (d) Q and S

Ans. (a) P and Q

Q.12 Read the description and identify the person.

He coined the slogan "Give me blood and I shall give you freedom"

(a) Mahatma Gandhi (b) Jawaharlal Nehru

(c) Bal Gangadhar Tilak (d) Subhash Chandra Bose

Ans. (d) Subhash Chandra Bose

Q.13 Read the description and identify the person.

He established the Forward Bloc and coined the slogan, 'Delhi Chalo'. **(ICSE Specimen 2025)**

(a) Mahatma Gandhi (b) Subash Chandra Bose

(c) Bal Gangadhar Tilak (d) Dadabhai Naoroji

Ans. (b) Subash Chandra Bose

TYPE - 2 1 Mark

Assertion-Reason Questions

Q.1 Read the two statements given below about Subhas Chandra Bose and select the option that shows the correct relationship between (A) and (R).

Assertion (A) Subhash Chandra Bose led the Indian National Army (INA) in its fight against British colonial rule during World War II.

Reason (R): Subhash Chandra Bose believed that collaborating with Japan and Nazi Germany would help India in gaining independence from British rule.

(a) R contradicts A

(b) R is the reason for A

(c) A is true but R is false

(d) A and R are independent of each other

Ans. (b) R is the reason for A

Q.2 Read the two statements given below about the Forward Bloc and select the option that shows the correct relationship between (A) and (R).

Assertion (A) The Forward Bloc was formed by Subhash Chandra Bose to challenge the British authorities.

Reason (R) Subhash Chandra Bose was dissatisfied with the Prayer and Petition approach of the Congress.

(a) R contradicts A

(b) R is the reason for A

(c) A is true but R is false

(d) A and R are independent of each other

Ans. (b) R is the reason for A

Q.3 Read the two statements given below about Subhash Chandra Bose and and select the option that shows the correct relationship between A and R.

Assertion (A) Subhash Chandra Bose renamed the Andaman and Nicobar Islands as Shaheed and Swaraj Islands after they were handed over to him by Japan.

Reason (R) The renaming of the islands was done to honor the contributions of Mahatma Gandhi and his followers in the independence struggle.

(a) R contradicts A (b) R is the reason for A

(c) A is true but R is false

(d) A and R are independent of each other

Ans. (c) A is true but R is false

Q.4 Read the two statements given below about Subhash Chandra Bose and select the option that shows the correct relationship between (A) and (R).

Assertion (A) Subhash Chandra Bose did not agree with Mahatma Gandhi's methods of peaceful protest.

Reason (R) Bose believed that non-violence was too slow and ineffective in removing British colonial rule.

(a) R contradicts A

(b) R is the reason for A

(c) A is true but R is false

(d) A and R are independent of each other

Ans. (b) R is the reason for A

Q.5 Read the two statements given below about Subhash Chandra Bose and select the option that shows the correct relationship between (A) and (R).

Assertion (A) Subhash Chandra Bose believed in the importance of youth in the struggle for India's independence.

Reason (R) Bose believed that the energy, enthusiasm, and dedication of the youth could bring about the radical changes necessary for India's liberation.

(a) R contradicts A (b) R is the reason for A

(c) A is true but R is false

(d) A and R are independent of each other

Ans. (b) R is the reason for A

TYPE - 3 — 2 Marks

Very Short Answer Type Questions

Q.1 Mention any two objectives of the Forward Bloc. **(ICSE 2020, 2025)**

Ans. The two objectives of the Forward Bloc were as follows

(i) To unite all the left-wing sections within the Congress under one head and to develop an alternative leadership.

(ii) To liberate India with the support of workers, peasant, youths and all radical organisations.

Q.2. Imagine you are attending the Bangkok Conference in June 1942. How would you react to the decision to form the Indian National Army and invite Subhash Chandra Bose to lead it?

Ans. If I was attending the Bangkok Conference in June 1942, I would feel a strong sense of pride and hope.

The decision to invite Subhash Chandra Bose to lead the INA would inspire confidence, as his leadership and determination are well-known. I would see this move as an opportunity to unite Indian forces under a powerful, experienced leader who could effectively challenge British rule and bring us closer to achieving the long-awaited freedom for India.

Q.3 Mention any two objectives of the Indian National Army.

Ans. The two important objectives of the Indian National Army were as follows

(i) To organise an armed revolution and to fight the British army with modern arms.

(ii) To organise a provisional government of free India in order to mobilise all the forces effectively.

Q.4 Mention two contributions of INA (Indian National Army) to the Indian National Movement.

Ans. Two contributions of INA to the Indian National Movement were as follows

(i) The INA inspired uprisings in the armed forces of the country. Thus, the Indian Navy rebelled in February, 1946 at Bombay, Calcutta, Madras and Karachi.

(ii) As Hindus, Muslims and Sikhs in the INA fought as Indians, the INA demonstrated that those who waged an armed battle against the British were not all affected by communal division.

Q.5 Answer the following questions.

(i) Who was elected as the President of the Bangkok conference?

(ii) Which organisation was formally inaugurated at this conference?

Ans. (i) Rash Behari Bose was elected as the President of Bangkok Conference.

(ii) Rash Behari Bose hoisted the tricolour flag and formally inaugurated the Indian Independence League.

Q.6 Mention the two slogans which became the motto of the INA and which islands were renamed as 'Shahid' and 'Swaraj'?

Ans. The two slogans that became the war cry of the INA were 'Delhi Chalo' and 'Jai Hind'.

Andaman and Nicobar Islands were renamed as 'Shahid' and 'Swaraj'.

TYPE - 4 — 3 Marks

Short Answer Type Questions

Q.1 Explain the vision of the Forward Bloc leaders for the future of India. What socialist policies did they advocate?

Ans. The Forward Bloc leaders envisioned a future India where all sections of society, including workers, peasants, and youth are united to achieve independence.

They advocated for socialist policies such as state-planned reorganisation of agriculture and industry, abolition of the Zamindari system, and the recognition of the 'Right to Work' as a fundamental right. The Forward Bloc sought to build a just and equitable society based on these principles.

Q.2 With reference to the Indian National Army, answer the following.

What were the three decisions taken at the Tokyo Conference?

Ans. Three decisions taken at the Tokyo Conference were as follows

- To form an Indian National Army (INA).
- To expand and strengthen Indian Independence league in all Asian countries controlled by Japan.
- To hold a conference of the representatives of Indians at Bangkok in June 1942.

Q.3 Explain about the formation of Indian Independence League and Indian National Army.

Ans. Indian Independence League (IIL) was formed as a result of associations started by people living in South-Asia territories with the objective of working for the liberation of India. Rash Behari Bose was the leader of IIL. It aimed to fight for the attainment of complete and immediate independence of India.

In the Tokyo conference (28th and 31st March, 1942) of the Indian Independence League, decision about the formation of an Indian National Army (INA) was taken.

Then, the Indian National Army (INA) or Azad Hind Fauj was formed by Indian Nationalists on 1st September, 1942 in South-East Asia during the Second World War.

TYPE - 5 — 4 Marks

Long Answer Type Questions

Q.1 The heroism of the Indians was revealed by the courage of Subash Chandra Bose and the Indian National Army. With reference to this, answer the following questions. **(ICSE 2023)**

Who was the founder of the Indian National Army ? Mention any three of its objectives.

Ans. Subhash Chandra Bose was the founder of the Indian National Army. The main objectives of the Indian National Army were as follows

- To organise an armed revolution and to fight the British army with modern arms.
- To organise a provisional government of free India in order to mobilise all forces effectively.
- Total mobilisation of India's manpower and money for a total war was one of the main objectives of INA.

Q.2 **With reference to the Indian National Army, answer the following questions.**

Explain the measures taken by Subhash Chandra Bose to establish a Socialist Society.

Ans. The Forward Bloc leaders including Subash Chandra Bose adopted following measures to establish Socialist Society

- State-planning for the reorganisation of agriculture and industry on socialist lines.
- Abolition of landlordism, i.e. Zamindari System and making the 'Right to Work' as a fundamental right of the citizens.
- World peace, disarmament and friendly relations with socialist nations like Russia.
- Bose emphasised social equality, including the empowerment of women and the removal of caste-based discrimination

TYPE - 6 — 10 Marks

Structured Questions

Q.1 With reference to the picture given below answer the following.

(i) When was the Provisional Government of Free India established, and who was its leader? Also, explain the role of the Indian National Army (INA) in the struggle for India's independence. **(3)**

(ii) Explain any four contribution of Subhash Chandra Bose in INA. **(4)**

(iii) Identify the personality shown in the picture above, mention any two reason behind his resignation from the congress. **(3)**

Ans. (i) The Provisional Government of Free India was established on 21st October, 1943, in Singapore and its leader was Subhash Chandra Bose. It was also known as the Arzi Hukumat-e-Azad Hind, it was formed to lead India's struggle for independence from British rule.

The Indian National Army (INA), led by Bose, was its military arm. It was made up of Indian prisoners of war and volunteers who joined forces with Japan to fight against the British in South-East Asia. The INA became an important symbol of resistance, showing the strength of the Indian struggle for freedom.

(ii) The contributions of Subhash Chandra Bose in INA were as follows

(a) Subhash Chandra Bose set up recruitment and training departments to strengthen the army.

(b) Subhash Chandra Bose named INA brigades after famous leaders like Gandhiji, Azad, Nehru, Subhash, and Rani Jhansi.

(c) Bose founded the Provisional Government of Free India (Azad Hind) in Singapore on 21st October, 1943.

(d) Bose moved the headquarters of the Provisional Government to Rangoon (Myanmar) because it was strategically close to India's Eastern border.

(iii) The picture belongs to Subhash Chandra Bose, one of the most respected and prominent leaders of Indian Freedom Movement. He is popularly known as 'Netaji'.

Subhash Chandra Bose resigned from the Indian National Congress due to:

(a) **Ideological Differences** Bose disagreed with the Congress leadership's moderate approach and believed in more direct, forceful methods for India's independence.

(b) **Election Dispute** Subhash Chandra Bose resigned from the Congress after defeating Gandhiji's candidate, Pattabhi Sitaramayya, in the Tripuri Session of 1939. He faced intense opposition from Gandhiji and his followers, which made it difficult for him to carry out his responsibilities effectively.

8

INDEPENDENCE AND PARTITION OF INDIA

- After the Second World War (May 1945), India's freedom struggle faced major challenges because Quit India Movement and the partition demand from Muslim League created unrest.
- A constitutional deadlock had also persisted since the Congress ministries resigned in 1939. To address this, **Lord Wavell**, who became Viceroy in 1943, introduced the Wavell Plan on 25th June, 1945.
- The Wavell Plan was not acceptable to both Indian National Congress and Muslim League thus ultimately get failed.

The Cabinet Mission Plan

- On 15th March, 1946, British Prime Minister Clement Attlee announced in the House of Commons that a Cabinet Mission would be sent to India to facilitate the process of transfer of power and to help the Indian leaders to decide the form of government that would suit them.
- The Cabinet Mission arrived in India on 24th March, 1946 consisted of three Cabinet members.
  (i) Mr Pethic Lawrence (the Secretary of State)
  (ii) Sir Stafford Cripps (President of the Board of Trade)
  (iii) Mr AV Alexander (the First Lord of Admiralty).

Provisions of The Cabinet Mission Plan

For Federal Union

- India should be a union or a federation of all the British Provinces and Indian states.
- The union government would deal with foreign affairs, defence and communications.
- All subjects other than union subjects and all residuary powers would vest in the provinces.
- The union would have its own executive and legislature composed of members elected by and sent by all provinces.

For British Provinces

- The existing provincial assemblies were to be organised into three groups as
  (i) **Group A** It would consist of Madras, Bombay, Central Provinces, United Provinces, Bihar and Orissa.
  (ii) **Group B** It would consist of Punjab, North-West Frontier Province and Sindh.
  (iii) **Group C** It would have Bengal and Assam.
- The provinces could choose the subjects to be shared in common. Delhi, Ajmer-Marwar and Coorg joined Group A, while Baluchistan joined Group B.
- Each group would create its own Constitution with input from other provinces in the group. A province could switch groups by a majority vote in its legislature.

For Constituent Assembly

- A Constituent Assembly would be elected by the provincial assemblies through proportional representation, with voting in three groups: General, Muslims and Sikhs.
- This assembly would consist of 389 members-292 from Provincial Assemblies, 4 from Chief Commissioner's provinces, and 93 from Princely States.

- The Provincial Legislative Assemblies would elect the members of the Constituent Assembly.
- The Constituent Assembly would sign a treaty with Britain to address specific issues related to the transfer of power.

Other Provisions

- An interim government at the centre would be formed on the basis of equality between the representatives of the Hindus, Sikhs and Muslims. It would have 14 members representing all communities.
- It was proposed that for the time being, the Viceroy would reconstitute his Executive Council consisting of representatives of all communities.
- India would be free to remain within the British Commonwealth or separate from it.
- However, this plan also failed due to the conflicting goals of the Congress and the Muslim League.

Lord Mountbatten

The Mountbatten Plan

- Lord Mountbatten succeeded Lord Wavell and became new Viceroy and Governor-General in 1947.
- He discussed with the leaders of both the Congress and the Muslim League to resolve the conflict between them. However, he could not unite these major parties and realised that partition of the country was inevitable.
- He discussed plan for the partition of India, also known as Mountbatten Plan, with 'big seven' leaders. These were Jawaharlal Nehru, Sardar Vallabhbhai Patel, Kripalani, Jinnah, Liaquat Ali, Abdul Rab Nishtar and Baldev Singh. This plan was announced on 3rd June, 1947.

Provisions of Mountbatten Plan

- India would be divided into two dominions, i.e. India and Pakistan.
- It was up to the two dominions to decide what relations they would have with the British Commonwealth and with each other.
- A boundary commission was to be set up to determine the boundaries of the two nations.
- A referendum or plebiscite would be held in the North-West frontier province and in Sylhet district (Muslim majority) to find out whether the people in the area wanted to join India or not.
- The Princely states would have the choice of joining either of the two dominions or to remain independent.
- The provinces of Assam, Bengal and Punjab were also to be divided.
- The Muslim majority district of Sylhet would be decide by referendum whether to join East Bengal or remain in Assam.
- The existing Constituent Assembly would continue to work and draft the Constitution of free India. Pakistan would have a separate Assembly.

Muhammad Ali Jinnah

Acceptance of the Mountbatten Plan

The Mountbatten Plan had a mixed reaction for its acceptance from both the Muslim League and Congress.

Muslim League's Reaction

- Muslim league accepted the plan on 10th June, 1947.
- Jinnah complained about the small and undeveloped Pakistan after the division of Punjab and Bengal.

Congress's Reaction

Congress wanted a united India but accepted partition on 15th June, 1947 due to the following reasons

- To avoid large-scale riots and violence.
- Patel thought a smaller, united India was better than a disorganised, divided India.
- British 'Divide and Rule' policy had deepened divisions between Hindus and Muslims.
- Delay in power transfer could lead to civil war.

- Partition could help build a secular and democratic India.
- Congress realised that working with the Muslim League was difficult after the 1946 interim government.

The Indian Independence Act, 1947

- Clement Attlee introduced the Indian Independence Bill in the House of Commons on 4th July, 1947 which was passed on 18th July, 1947.
- The Indian Independence Act was a short document, consisting of less than 20 sections and 3 schedules.
- The Indian Independence Act marked the end of the British rule led to the beginning of journey of two new nations India and Pakistan.
- On 26th January, 1950, India became a Republic, and Dr. Rajendra Prasad became its first President. The Constituent Assembly thus became the Parliament of India.

Provisions of the Indian Independence Act

For Two Dominion

- The Independence Act provided for the creation of two independent dominions namely India and Pakistan from 15th August, 1947.
- The territories of Pakistan were to include the areas covered by the provinces of East Bengal, West Bengal, West Punjab, Sind, Baluchistan and the North-West Frontier Province (NWFP).
- Each dominion would have a Governor-General appointed by the British King, who would act as the constitutional head and represent the king for the government of the dominion.
- Provincial governors would act on the advice of elected ministers. Both dominions and provinces were to follow the Government of India Act of 1935 until a new Constitution was created.
- The Constituent Assemblies of both dominions would serve as the Central Legislatures with full legislative powers, acting as sovereign bodies for making laws in their respective dominions.

For Secretary of the State and Division of Army and Assets

- The office of the Secretary of State for India and his advisors was abolished. The affairs relating to the dominion of India and Pakistan were to be conducted in future by the Secretary of the Commonwealth Relations Department.
- Provisions were made for the division of the Indian army between the two dominions.
- Steps were to be taken to share the assets and liabilities between the two dominions.

For Partition

- Bengal and Punjab would be divided if so desired by the people through Plebiscite.
- A plebiscite would be held in North-West Frontier Province (NWFP) and in Sylhet district which was a Muslim majority area in East Bengal

End of the British Parliament Power

- The legislative authority of the British Parliament would cease from 15th August, 1947.
- All treaties and agreements between the British Government and Indian rulers or tribal areas would lapse.
- The Governor-General was vested with necessary powers for bringing Indian independence into effective operation. He was given the powers to modify or adopt the Government of India Act, 1935 by 31st March, 1948.
- The title of the Emperor of India was dropped from the royal style.
- The right of the King to veto laws was abolished and it was given to the Governor-General.
- C. Rajagopalachari was the first and last Governor-General of India before the office was abolished in 1950.

C. Rajagopalachari

EXAM ORIENTED QUESTIONS

TYPE - 1 — 1 Mark

Multiple Choice Questions

Q.1 Who among of the following was the Prime Minister of Britain during World War II ?

(a) Sir Stafford Cripps
(b) Mr. Winston Churchill
(c) Mr. Clement Attlee
(d) Mr. A.V. Alexander

Ans. (b) Mr. Winston Churchill

Q.2 Complete the given analogy.
Approval of Wavell Plan : Shimla ::Approval of the Mountbatten Plan :?

(a) India
(b) England
(c) USA
(d) USSR

Ans. (b) England

Exp. The Mountbatten Plan was approved in June 1947, and outlined the partition of India into two independent dominions, India and Pakistan.

Q.3 Complete the given analogy about Cabinet Mission Plan.
Group 'A' Province : Madras : : Group 'B' Province : ?

(a) Uttar Pradesh
(b) Bihar
(c) Punjab
(d) Assam

Ans. (c) Punjab

Q.4 Which of the following statements is not correct about the Cabinet Mission Plan?

(a) The Cabinet Mission proposed a federal structure for India with the partition of provinces based on religion.
(b) The plan suggested a central government with control over defense, foreign affairs and communications.
(c) The Cabinet Mission Plan aimed to set up a Constituent Assembly for the framing of the Indian Constitution.
(d) The plan proposed a single unified Indian state with no separate Muslim-majority provinces.

Ans. (a) The Cabinet Mission proposed a federal structure for India with the partition of provinces based on religion.

Q.5 Identify the incorrect statement regarding the Cabinet Mission's recommendations for the provinces in India.

(a) The provinces were to be grouped into three sections.
(b) The provinces were given autonomy on mostly matters.
(c) The union would have its own executive and legislature composed of members elected by and sent by all provinces.
(d) All powers will be vested in the union only.

Ans. (c) The union would have its own executive and legislature composed of members elected by and sent by all provinces.

Q.6 Which of the following was a reason for the acceptance of the Mountbatten Plan?
(ICSE Semester-I 2022)

(a) The British forced the Congress to accept the plan.
(b) The Muslim League would cooperate in the governance.
(c) The only alternative to partition was a federation with a weak centre.
(d) The Princely States wanted to accept the plan.

Ans. (c) The only alternative to partition was a federation with a weak centre.

Q.7 Which of the following statements is correct about the Constituent Assembly of India?

(a) It was formed to draft the constitution of independent India.
(b) It was created by the British government to resolve the issues of communal tensions.
(c) It was a temporary body set up for the purpose of drafting a national election code.
(d) It was formed after the independence of India to represent different princely states.

Ans. (a) It was formed to draft the constitution of independent India.

Q.8 Which of the following is not a clause of the Indian Independence Act of 1947?

(a) All treaties made with the British would lapse.
(b) The army and assets would belong only to India.
(c) The Constituent Assemblies would serve as Central Legislatures.
(d) The Princely States were free to associate themselves with either dominion.

Ans. (b) The army and assets would belong only to India.

Q.9 Which of these was not a provision of the Indian Independence Act, 1947?

(ICSE Specimen Semester-I 2021)

(a) There would be a Governor-General for each dominion.
(b) There would be no division of the army.
(c) The office of the Secretary of State was abolished.
(d) The jurisdiction of the British Parliament would end.

Ans. (b) There would be no division of the army.

Q.10 Identify the odd one events related to India's independence struggle during 1947.

(a) Mountbatten Plan
(b) Indian Independence Act
(c) Cripps Mission
(d) Partition of India

Ans. (c) Cripps Mission

Exp. The Cripps Mission took place in 1942 and was an attempt by the British Government to secure Indian support during World War II. It is not directly related to events in 1947, which marked the independence and partition of India.

Q.11 Which act ended the British rule and beginning of Independent India as highlighted in the Newspaper heading below?

Help the Refugees

The Hindustan Times

INDIA INDEPENDENT : BRITISH RULE ENDS

CONSTITUENT ASSEMBLY TAKES OVER

MOUNTBATTEN'S APPOINTMENT AS GOVERNOR-GENERAL ENDORSED

COLOURFUL CEREMONY MARKS BIRTH OF NATION

NEW STAR RISES IN THE EAST

LEADERS TELL NATION OF TASKS AHEAD

Attlee's Greetings To Nehru

Governors Sworn In As Free India Is Born

THE PLEDGE

(a) Government of India Act, 1935
(b) Government of India Act, 1942
(c) Indian Independence Act, 1947
(d) Indian Independence Act, 1942

Ans. (c) Indian Independence Act, 1947.

Q.12 Read the details given below and identify which of the following pairs are correct.

P : The Cabinet Mission Plan was introduced to resolve the constitutional deadlock and prepare for independence.

Q : The partition of India led to the creation of India and Bangladesh as two independent nations.

R : A.V. Alexander was part of the Cabinet Mission Plan to India.

S : Wavell Plan was not accepted by both Congress and Muslim League.

Options

(a) P and Q (b) R and S
(c) P and S (d) Q and S

Ans. (b) R and S

Q.13 Which of the following reactions of Congress leaders is not correct about the Mountbatten Plan?

(a) Jawaharlal Nehru accepted the partition of India as inevitable to avoid further communal violence.
(b) Sardar Vallabhbhai Patel opposed creation of Pakistan.
(c) Maulana Azad and some Muslim leaders opposed partition but accepted it.
(d) Gandhi ji was not against the Partition.

Ans. (b) Sardar Vallabhbhai Patel opposed creation of Pakistan.

TYPE - 2 1 Mark

Assertion-Reason Questions

Q.1 Read the two statements given below about the Cabinet Mission Plan and select the option that shows the correct relationship between (A) and (R).

Assertion (A) The Cabinet Mission Plan was introduced to prepare India for transfer of power to India.

Reason (R) The Cabinet Mission succeeded to resolve the political issues regarding the governance of India, leading to fulfilment of demand for a separate Pakistan.

(a) R contradicts A
(b) R is the reason for A
(c) A is true but R is false
(d) A and (R) are independent of each other

Ans. (c) A is true but R is false

Q.2 Read the two statements given below about the Cabinet Mission Plan and select the option that shows the correct relationship between (A) and (R).

Assertion (A) The Cabinet Mission Plan suggested the formation of a Constituent Assembly for drafting the Constitution of India.

Reason (R) The plan proposed that the Constituent Assembly be formed through indirect elections, with members chosen by provincial assemblies.

(a) R contradicts A
(b) R is the reason for A
(c) A is true but R is false
(d) A and R are independent of each other

Ans. (b) R is the reason for A

Q.3 Read the two statements given below about the Mountbatten Plan and select the option that shows the correct relationship between (A) and (R).

Assertion (A) The Mountbatten Plan of 1947 led to the partition of India into two nations.

Reason (R) The Mountbatten Plan was accepted by the Indian National Congress and the Muslim League to further spread communal violence.

(a) R contradicts A
(b) R is the reason for A
(c) A is true but R is false
(d) A and R are independent of each other

Ans. (c) A is true but R is false

Q.4. Read the two statements given below about Wavell Plan and select the option that shows the correct relationship between (A) and (R).

Assertion (A) The Wavell Plan offered granting of Dominion Status to India and drafting of their own Constitution by Indians.

Reason (R) The Wavell Plan was rejected by both the Indian National Congress and Muslim League.

(a) R contradicts A
(b) R is the reason for A
(c) A is true but R is false
(d) A and R are independent of each other

Ans. (d) A and R are independent of each other

Q.5 Read the two statements given below about the Indian Independence Act and select the option that shows the correct relationship between (A) and (R).

Assertion (A) The Indian Independence Act abolished the title of Viceroy and replaced it with Governor-General.

Reason (R) The Act was designed to ensure that the new dominions which would be independent and governed by a British representative.

(a) R contradicts A
(b) R is the reason for A
(c) A is true but R is false
(d) A and R are indepenent of each other

Ans. (b) R is the reason for A

TYPE - 3 — 2 Marks

Very Short Answer Type Questions

Q.1 Read the questions and answer the following.

(i) When did the Second World War ended?
(ii) Who was the first Indian Governor-General of India?

Ans. (i) The Second World War ended in May 1945.

(ii) C. Rajagopalachari was the first and last Indian Governor- General of India.

Q.2 Name any two members of the Cabinet Mission.

Ans. Lord Pethick Lawrence and Sir Stafford Cripps were the members of the Cabinet Mission.

Q.3 What were the two proposals related to the Princely States in the Mountbatten Plan?

Ans. The two proposals related to the Princely States in the Mountbatten Plan were as follows

(i) All treaties and agreements made by the British with reference to states would lapse from 15th August, 1947.

(ii) They would be free to associate themselves with either of the two dominions or to remain independent.

Q.4 State two important reasons that caused the British to withdraw from India.

Ans. The British withdrew from India in 1947 due to multiple factors. Two key reasons were as follows

(i) **Economic Strain After World War II** The war left Britain financially weak and making it difficult to sustain control over India.

(ii) **Indian Independence Movement** The massive struggle for freedom led by Mahatma Gandhi and the Indian National Army's resistance under Subhash Chandra Bose weakened British authority.

Q.5 Read the questions and answer the following.

(i) Name the last Viceroy of India.
(ii) State any one of the provisions of the Indian Independence Act of 1947.

Ans. (i) Lord Mountbatten was the last British Viceroy of India.

(ii) One of the provisions of the Indian Independence Act, 1947, was the partition of British India into two independent nations, India and Pakistan.

Q.6 Imagine you are a young Indian living in 1947 when the Indian Independence Act has just been passed by the British Parliament. The Act grants India independence, but it also divides the country into two separate dominions, India and Pakistan.

How would you motivate them to focus on the positive aspects of the Indian Independence Act, despite the challenges of partition?

Ans. I would motivate them by saying that the Indian Independence Act marks the beginning of a new era for our country. After centuries of British rule we are finally free to govern ourselves.

This independence is the result of our collective struggle and it's up to us how to rebuild our nation. We now have the opportunity to shape a better and more prosperous India.

Q.7 **Mention any two provisions of the Cabinet Mission for Constituent Assembly in India.**

Ans. Two major provision of the Cabinet Mission were as follows

(i) The assembly would consist of 389 members in which 292 from Provincial Assemblies, 4 from Chief Commissioner's provinces, and 93 from Princely States.

(ii) The Constituent Assembly would sign a treaty with Britain to address specific issues related to the transfer of power.

Q.8 **Analyse the reaction of Muslim League against the Indian Independence Act of 1947.**

Ans. The Muslim League supported the Indian Independence Act of 1947 as it led to the creation of Pakistan, fulfilling its demand for a separate Muslim state.

Jinnah complained about the small and undeveloped Pakistan after the division of Punjab and Bengal.

Q.9 **Mention any two provisions which were made under Indian Independence Act for army and assets.**

Ans. Two provisions made under Indian Independence Act for army and assets were as follows

(i) Provisions were made for the division of the Indian army between the two dominions.

(ii) Steps were to be taken to share the assets and liabilities between the two dominions.

Q.10 **Name the two areas where provisions for a plebiscite were made under the Indian Independence Act of 1947.**

Ans. North West Frontier Province (NWFP) and Sylhet District (in Assam).

TYPE - 4 — 3 Marks

Short Answer Type Questions

Q.1 **With reference to the transfer of power to India, answer the following question.**

Explain the Cabinet Mission's proposals regarding the setting up of a Constitution making body.

Ans. The Cabinet Mission proposed that a Constituent Assembly would be set up to frame the new Constitution of the Indian Union. It would consist of 389 members from which 296 members would be elected from the British Provinces and 93 members from the Indian states.

After the election, the Constituent Assembly would meet at New Delhi and elect a Chairman. The members would be divided into three groups representing A, B and C to frame their respective Constitution.

Q.2 **Discuss the events that led to the introduction of the Indian Independence Act, 1947. How did this act mark the end of British rule in India?**

Ans. The events leading to the Indian Independence Act, 1947, were shaped by growing demands for independence from the Indian National Congress and Muslim League. After years of protests and negotiations, Britishers realised they could no longer control India. The 1947 Act was introduced after discussions between Indian leaders and the British government, which included the partition of India into two countries, India and Pakistan.

This act marked the end of British rule by granting India its independence and dividing the country, thus ending nearly 200 years of British colonial rule.

Q.3 **The Mountbatten Plan was the final proposal put forward by the British to solve the dead lock between the main political parties in India. In this context, answer the following question.**

Any three developments which paved the way for Mountbatten Plan.

Ans. Three developments which paved the way for Mountbatten Plan were as follows

(i) On 26th October, 1946, representatives of the Muslim League were inducted into the interim government .The government seemed to be helpless by non-cooperation of the members of the Muslim League.

(ii) After consultation with Indian leaders, Mountbatten concluded that he would not unite the major parties.

(iii) Lord Mountbatten personally went to England to inform the British Government about the situation of India and get his plan approved by them.

Q.4 **Analyse the provisions of Independence Act regarding the end of jurisdiction of the British Parliament.**

Ans. The major provisions of the Independence Act were as follows

- The legislative authority of the British Parliament would cease from 15th August, 1947.
- The title of the Emperor of India was dropped from the royal style.
- The right of the King to veto laws was abolished and it was given to the Governor-General.

TYPE - 5 4 Marks

Long Answer Type Questions

Q.1 The period between 1920 to 1947 was marked with major events and reforms that finally led us to our independence. In this context, answer the following question. **(ICSE 2017)**

Mention any four clauses of the Cabinet Mission Plan.

Ans. The four major clause of the Cabinet Mission Plan of 1946 were as follows

(i) **Federal Structure** Proposed a federal system with a central government and provincial autonomy.

(ii) **Constituent Assembly** Suggested the formation of a Constituent Assembly to draft India's future Constitution.

(iii) **Interim Government** Recommended an interim government with representatives from both the Congress and the Muslim League.

(iv) **Muslim Safeguards** Provided special provisions to protect Muslim interests, including separate representation for Muslim-majority provinces.

Q.2 Analyse the major reasons behind the failure of the Cabinet mission Plan in India.

Ans. The failure of the Cabinet Mission Plan was due to several key reasons which were as follows

- **Muslim League's Opposition** The Muslim League which was led by Jinnah rejected the proposal for a united India and insisted on a separate state (Pakistan).
- **Unclear Provisions** The plan's vague provisions on autonomy and central power-sharing created mistrust between Congress and the Muslim League.
- **Unresolved Issues** The plan failed to address crucial issues like minority representation and the status of Princely States.
- **Escalating Tensions** Rising communal tensions and dissatisfaction with British rule made the plan increasingly difficult to implement.

Q.3 Explain about the federal structure proposed by the Cabinet Mission Plan.

Ans. The Cabinet Mission Plan of 1946 proposed a two-tiered federal structure for India. It suggested a Union of India that would include both British provinces and Princely States. The Union would control defense, foreign affairs and communications, while the provinces would have autonomy over all other subjects. This structure aimed to keep India united while giving significant autonomy to Muslim-majority areas. However, differences between the Congress and the Muslim League led to its rejection, ultimately resulting in India's partition.

TYPE - 6 10 Marks

Structured Questions

Q.1 The attempt of the British to pacify the Congress and the Muslim League was clearly visible in the Cabinet Mission proposals but in reality, neither could be pleased. With reference to this, answer the following questions.

(i) What were the four key clauses of the Cabinet Mission Plan? Explain them briefly. (4)

(ii) Explain the reasons for the Muslim League's acceptance and later rejection of the Cabinet Mission Plan. (3)

(iii) Why did the Congress refuse to participate in the formation of the Interim Government under the Cabinet Mission Plan? (3)

Ans. (i) For answer, refer to Q.1 of Long Answer Type Questions.

(ii) The reasons for the Muslim League's acceptance and later rejection of the Cabinet Mission Plan were as follows

- The Muslim League accepted the plan on 6th June, 1946, because it allowed Muslim-majority provinces to stay together, supporting their demand for self-rule.
- The Congress opposed compulsory grouping and the League withdrew its acceptance on 29th July, 1946.
- In protest, the League launched Direct Action Day on 16th August, 1946, leading to widespread communal violence in Calcutta and other areas.

(iii) Congress refused to join the Interim Government due to following reasons

- The Congress opposed the grouping system, as it feared it would lead to the eventual division of India.
- They insisted on a strong central government, whereas the plan allowed significant provincial autonomy.
- The Muslim League's hostility and violent protests further discouraged Congress from participating initially.

Q.2 Answer the questions based on the picture given below.

(i) Identify the event in the above picture. Name the lady seen in the given picture. Mention the year when the event took place. **(3)**

(ii) What were the main provisions of the Indian Independence Act? **(3)**

(iii) Mention the reasons that made the Congress to accept the partition proposals under Mountbatten Plan. **(4)**

Ans. (i) The event is the transfer of power ceremony. Here, Jawaharlal Nehru took the oath as the first Prime Minister of India.

The lady shown in the picture is Edwina Mountbatten, wife of Viceroy Lord Mountbatten. The event took place in 1947.

(ii) For answer, refer to Q.4 of Short Answer Type Questions.

(iii) The reasons which led the Congress to accept the partition proposals under Mountbatten Plan were as follows

- The Congress believed that it could not have the joint administration with the Muslim League as it had bitter experience in interim government of 1946.
- The Congress leaders realised that the extension of the British rule would be harmful to India. By applying the Divide and Rule Policy the Britishers not only divided Hindu and Muslim community in India but they instigated the native rulers of the Indian states to remain independent.
- They felt that further delay in the transfer of power could lead to civil war in India.
- They also thought that partition would rid the Constitution of separate electorates and other undemocratic procedures. India could then evolve a truly secular and democratic polity.

THE FIRST WORLD WAR

- First World War was started on 28th July, 1914 and lasted until 11th November, 1918.
- It was fought between two powerful blocs Triple Alliance or Central Powers (Germany, Austria-Hungary and Italy) and Triple Entente or Allied Powers (Great Britain, France and Russia) that were formed between 19th - 20th century.
- It was fought in different areas called Fronts. The Western Front was between Germany and Northern France.
- It was the result of numerous political tensions and rivalry that existed among the European powers.

Causes of the First World War

Nationalism

- The 19th century became an era of militant nationalism and patriotism which means love for one's own nation and hatred towards other nations.
- Each nation focused on its own national interests which led to the rise of aggressive nationalism in Europe.
- Many nations wanted to reclaim their lost territories. For example
  - France wanted to get back its provinces of Alsace and Lorraine from Germany.
  - Italy wanted to get back the territory of Trentino Trieste from Austria.
  - Balkan states like Serbia wanted to unite their people in a bigger Balkan state
- The Balkans region included countries like Romania, Bulgaria, Albania, Greece, Macedonia, Croatia, Bosnia-Herzegovina, Slovenia, Serbia, and Montenegro.
- Intense competition in economic and defence areas were the cause of growing nationalistic feeling.

Imperialism

- Imperialism occurs when a strong nation takes over a weaker nation or region and dominates its economic, political and cultural life. When a nation was conquered physically it was claimed as a colony.
- England and France built up a huge colonial empire in Asia and Africa by the end of the 19th century.
- The British imperialism focused on expanding trade by using the resources of colonies like India, Sri Lanka, Myanmar, South Africa, Egypt, the Caribbean Islands, and parts of Africa.
- Germany, Italy, Russia, and Japan also worked to grow their influence and increase their colonies in less developed regions like Asia and Africa

Armament Race

- The use of arms and spreading of new types of weapons by every nation made the situation unfavourable for peace.
- Every nation started research and development in defense sector in the name of self-defense. For example,
  - Germany developed its naval power to protect colonies in Africa.
  - Britain also launched its new battleship. It resulted into the naval rivalry between Britain and Germany.
  - France also entered this armament race for its own safety.

Division of Europe

In the early 1900s, Europe had two types of states

- **Single Nation-States** Countries like France, Holland and Germany. These states were united by a common language and culture.

- **Imperial States** It include states like the Austria-Hungarian Empire and Russian Empire. Different cultures and languages were popular in these states.

Sarajevo Crisis

- This crisis was the immediate cause of the First World War. This crisis started when the Archduke or emperor of Austria, Francis Ferdinand was murdered along with his wife at the Bosnia capital of Sarajevo on 28th June, 1914.
- This dual murder was planned by a secret society Union of Death and popularly known as Black Hand.
- On 23rd July, 1914, Austria sent an ultimatum to Serbia and made 11 demands. Some of these were
  - Austria wanted the conspirators to be caught and handed over to the Austrian government.
  - It demanded that all anti–Austrian publications, meetings and educational institutions should be banned.
  - All revolutionary movements aimed against Austria were to be suppressed.
- Serbia agreed to fulfill most of the demands except those that would have led to the loss of its sovereignty. As a result of this Austria declared war against Serbia on 28th July, 1914. Russia supported Serbia in the war.

Results of the First World War

The Allied powers were victorious in the First World War. Some of the major results of the war were as follows

The Treaty of Versailles

On 28th June, 1919, the Treaty of Versailles was signed in Versailles in Paris between Allied powers and Germany. The main terms of the treaty were as follows

- Germany was held responsible for the war and ordered to pay 33 billion dollars as war compensation to the Allies.
- The fertile and mineral rich land of Rhine valley was to be taken by Allied powers for 15 years.
- Germany was forced to give up its colonies and other acquired areas in Africa and Europe.
- The Saar valley (coal mines in German area) was given to France for 15 years. This area was decided to be governed by the League of Nations.
- Danzig became a free port in the Polish territory. Most of the Polish territory held by Germany were returned to the new Republic of Poland.
- A restriction was forced on Germany to keep its military. It was allowed to keep only a small army of 1 lakh soldiers, 15,000 navy men and 24 ships. Airforce and Sabmarines were banned hence severely restricting its military capabilities.
- Countries like Belgium, Poland, Czechoslovakia, Yugoslavia, Estonia, Latvia and Lithuania were declared as independent countries.
- Germany was required to supply a large amount of coal to France, Italy and Belgium for 10 years.

Territorial Rearrangements

The peace treaties led to rearrangement of territories and transformed the political map of the world, particularly Europe in the following ways

- Three ruling dynasties, viz the Romanov in Russia, the Hohenzollern in Germany and the Hapsburg in Austria–Hungary were destroyed.
- In Turkey, the Ottoman Empire came to an end.
- Czechoslovakia, Yugoslavia, Finland, Estonia, Latvia and Lithuania emerged as independent states.
- Austria and Hungary became separate independent states in Europe.
- Alsace- Lorraine was restored to France and Schleswig – Holstein was restored to Denmark.

Formation of League of Nations

- League of Nations was formed on 10th January, 1920 with headquarters at Geneva in Switzerland to prevent further wars.
- It had 42 members during its formation. It had four permanent members i.e. Britain, France, Italy and Japan.
- Germany and the Soviet Union were not allowed to become member of the League of Nations for many years because it was held responsible for the first world war. Later, Germany joined it as permanent member in 1926.
- The rise of dictatorships in Italy and Germany disrupted world peace once again and weakened the League of Nations. As a result, the League of Nations came to an end on 20th April, 1946.

Aims and Objectives of League of Nations

- Preventing wars through collective security and disarmament and settling international disputes through negotiations.
- All the nations of the world were prohibited from entering into any secret alliances.
- The member-states were not supposed to maintain huge armies, warships and destructive armaments.
- All states were to respect each other's independence. The member-states were to take necessary action as directed by the League against any state which tried to disturb world peace and order.

EXAM ORIENTED QUESTIONS

TYPE - 1   1 Mark

Multiple Choice Questions

Q.1 Complete the given analogy.
Beginning of World War I : 28th July, 1914:: End of the War : ?
(a) 5th June, 1918
(b) 11th November, 1918
(c) 5th October, 1918
(d) 11th October, 1918

Ans. (b) 11th November, 1918

Q.2 Identify the odd one out regarding the causes of the First World war.
(a) Archduke Franz Ferdinand
(b) Gavrilo Princip
(c) Black Hand
(d) League of Nations

Ans. (d) League of Nations

Exp. The League of Nations was established in 1920 after the First World War. It was aimed to promote peace, security and cooperation among nations.

Q.3 Which of the following causes of the First World War is connected to this headline? **(ICSE 2025)**

The Washington Times
SUNDAY EVENING EDITION
SERB STUDENT ASSASSINATES ARCHDUKE AND HIS DUCHESS

(a) Imperialism
(b) Aggressive Nationalism
(c) Armament Race
(d) Sarajevo Crisis

Ans. (d) Sarajevo Crisis

Q.4 Which of the following statement is correct about the World War I?
(a) The First World War was fought in different areas known as Fronts.
(b) The United States remained neutral at beginning and end of the war.
(c) The war ended with the signing of the Treaty of Paris in 1918.
(d) The Battle of Waterloo was a major event of World War I.

Ans. (a) The First World War was fought in different areas known as Fronts.

Q.5 Which of the following statements is not correct about World War I alliances?
(a) The Triple Alliance included Germany, Austria-Hungary and Italy.
(b) Russia was part of the Triple Entente.
(c) Triple Entente was formed in 1905.
(d) Britain was part of the Allied Powers.

Ans. (c) Triple Entente was formed in 1905.

Exp. The Triple Entente was an alliance of the First World War. It was formed in 1907 which included countries like France, Russia and Britain.

Q.6 Archduke Franz Ferdinand, heir to the Austro-Hungarian throne, was assassinated along with his wife, Sophie, by Gavrilo Princip, a member of the Serbian nationalist group.

The London Times, 14th October, 2023

Which war was the Immediate cause of the news above?
(a) Second World War
(b) First World War
(c) Afghan War
(d) Israel War

Ans. (b) First World War

Q.7 Identify the pairs which are correct about the First World War events.
P : The assassination of Archduke Franz Ferdinand sparked the conflict in world.
Q : Austria-Hungary seized Serbia with no Military actions.
R : Serbia rejected the ultimatum, and brought it to First World War.
S : Serbia accepted all terms of the ultimatum, leading to peace.

Options
(a) P and R
(b) P and S
(c) Q and S
(d) Q and R

Ans. (a) P and R

Q.8 Complete the given analogy.
Triple Alliance : Central Powers : : Triple Entente : ?
(a) Axis Powers
(b) Allied Powers
(c) Supreme Powers
(d) World Powers

Ans. (b) Allied Powers

Q.9 Which of the following treaties was drafted by the Woodrow Wilson?
(a) Treaty of Versailles
(b) Treaty of Paris
(c) Treaty of Tordesillas
(d) Treaty of Utrecht

Ans. (a) Treaty of Versailles

Exp. The Treaty of Versailles was signed in 1919 and ended the First World War. It forced Germany to accept full responsibility for the war, pay reparations, and cede territory.

Q.10 Which of the following city was the headquarters of the League of Nations?

(a) Paris
(b) London
(c) Geneva
(d) Brussels

Ans. (c) Geneva

Q.11 Identify the countries that were not allowed to become members of the League of Nations initially.

(a) Germany and Soviet Union
(b) Italy and Japan
(c) France and Russia
(d) Germany and France

Ans. (a) Germany and Soviet Union

Exp. Germany and Soviet Union were not allowed to join the League of Nations initially because they were considered responsible for starting the First World War.

Q.12 Which of the following is an immediate impact of the given incident? **(ICSE Specimen 2024)**

Daily
HEIR TO AUSTRIAN THRONE MURDERED.
ARCHDUKE AND HIS WIFE SHOT DEAD IN THE STREET.
DETERMINED PLOT.
BOMB FIRST THROWN AT THEIR CAR.
SECOND ATTEMPT WITHIN AN HOUR.
BOY ASSASSIN.

Source : Daily Express, 29th June, Monday 1914

(a) It led to the supremacy of America
(b) It led to the First World War.
(c) Austria and Hungary became two independent nations.
(d) Democracy replaced monarchy in many countries.

Ans. (b) It led to the First World War.

Q.13 The Treaty of Versailles was signed as a result of the discussions at the ....

(a) Paris conference
(b) Moscow conference
(c) London conference
(d) New York conference

Ans. (a) Paris conference

Q.14 Which of the following were the aims of the League of Nations?

(a) Prohibition of secret treaties and Alliances between members
(b) Prohibition of maintenance of large armed forces by member-states
(c) Promotion of local, cultural and economic cooperation
(d) All of the above

Ans. (d) All of the above

TYPE - 2 1 Mark

Assertion-Reason Questions

Q.1 Read the two statements given below about causes of the World War I and select the option that shows the correct relationship between (A) and (R).

Assertion (A) Nationalism was a major cause of World War I.

Reason (R) Nationalism led to competition between nations and encouraged aggressive foreign policies, particularly in the Balkans.

(a) R contradicts A
(b) R is the reason for A
(c) A is true, but R is false
(d) A and R are independent of each other

Ans. (b) R is the reason for A

Q.2 Read the two statements given below about the League of Nation and select the option that shows the correct relationship between (A) and (R).

Assertion (A) The League of Nations was established in 1920.

Reason (R) The League of Nations was created to prevent future wars and promote international cooperation.

(a) R contradicts A
(b) R is the reason for A
(c) A is true but R is false
(d) A and R are independent of each other

Ans. (b) R is the reason for A

Q.3 Read the two statements given below about World War I and select the option that shows the correct relationship between (A) and (R).

Assertion (A) World War I ended with the signing of the Treaty of Versailles.

Reason (R) The Treaty of Versailles imposed harsh penalties on America including territorial losses and reparations.

(a) R contradicts A
(b) R is the reason for A
(c) A is true but R is false
(d) A and R are independent of each other

Ans. (c) A is true but R is false.

Q.4 Read the two statements given below about World War I and select the option that shows the correct relationship between (A) and (R).

Assertion (A) The Treaty of Versailles was intended to bring lasting peace.

Reason (R) The Treaty of Versailles imposed severe reparations and territorial losses only on Germany, leading to economic instability and resentment.

(a) R contradicts A
(b) R is the reason for A
(c) A is true but R is false
(d) A and R are independent of each other

Ans. (a) R contradicts A

Q.5 Read the two statements given below about impact of the World War I and select the option that shows the correct relationship between (A) and (R).

Assertion (A) The collapse of the Austro-Hungarian and Ottoman Empires contributed to the reshaping of Europe.

Reason (R) The end of these empires led to the creation of new nation-states by altering the political map of China.

(a) R contradicts A

(b) R is the reason for A

(c) A is true, but R is false

(d) A and R are independent of each other

Ans. (c) A is true, but R is false

TYPE - 3 — 2 Marks

Very Short Answer Type Questions

Q.1 Mention the names of the countries which were part of the Allied group in World War I.

Ans. Britain, Russia and France were part of the Allied powers during World War I.

Q.2 Explain the meaning of the term 'imperialism' **(ICSE 2020)**

Ans. Imperialism occurs when a strong nation takes over a weaker nation or region and dominates its economic, political and cultural life.

In 19th century, aggressive and fierce economic competition gave rise to fear, confusion, insecurity and mutual hatred in Europe. This was followed by expansionist policies which led to rise of imperialism and further led to First World War.

Q.3 Name the two alliances formed in Europe before the beginning of the First World War. **(ICSE Specimen 2025, 2024, 2022)**

Ans. Triple Alliance and the Triple Entente were the two alliances which were formed before the beginning of the First World War.

Q.4 Name the two rival blocs formed in Europe before the First World War.

Ans. The two rival blocs formed in Europe before the First World War were as follows

(i) Allied Powers including countries like Britain, France and Russia.

(ii) Imperialist Powers including countries like Germany, Austria and their allies.

Q.5 Mention any two reasons behind the growth of military strength among nations in 19th century.

Ans. Some of the major reason behind the rise of military strength among nations in 19th century were as follows

(i) Nationalism led countries to focus on strengthening their military power to defend their sovereignty

(ii) The Industrial Revolution facilitated mass production of weapons, allowing countries to equip large and modernised armies.

Q.6 State any two objections imposed by the Treaty of Versailles on the German military power.

Ans. The two objections imposed by the Treaty of Versailles on the German military power were as follows

(i) German colonies were forcibly taken away and divided among the victors.

(ii) Germany was burdened with huge war penalty and its military power also got reduced.

Q.7 Mention any two ways in which the Treaty of Versailles affected the German Military Force. **(ICSE 2025)**

Ans. Two ways in which the Treaty of Versailles affected the German military force were

(i) **Reduction in Army Size** The German army was limited to 100,000 soldiers, with no conscription allowed.

(ii) **Ban on Heavy Weapons** Germany was prohibited from having tanks, submarines, and an air force, weakening its military strength.

Q.8 Mention any two important consequences of the First World War.

Ans. The two important consequences of the First World War were as follows

(i) Establishment of the League of Nations.

(ii) Saar valley was returned to France from Germany for 15 years.

Q.9 Name any two nations that emerged as independent states after the First World War.

Ans. Two nations that emerged as independent states after the First World War were

(i) Czechoslovakia (ii) Yugoslavia

Q.10 Read the questions given below and answer the following.

(i) When did the Treaty of Versailles get signed?

(ii) When did the League of Nations get established?

Ans. (i) The Treaty of Versailles was signed on 28th June, 1919. It officially ended World War I.

(ii) The League of Nations was established on 10th January, 1920.

Q.11 **State any two aims of the League of Nations.**

Ans. Two aims of the League of Nations were

(i) To prevent wars through collective security and disarmament.

(ii) To settle international disputes through negotiations and peaceful means.

Q.12 **List any two provisions of the Treaty of Versailles.**

Ans. Two provisions of the Treaty of Versailles were

(i) Germany was held responsible for the war and had to pay 33 billion dollars as war compensation.

(ii) Germany had to give up its colonies and territories in Africa and Europe, including Alsace-Lorraine to France.

TYPE - 4 — 3 Marks

Short Answer Type Questions

Q.1 **Mention any three causes behind the rise of the nationalism and imperialism in the early 20th century in Europe.**

Ans. The three major cause behind the rise of nationalism and imperialism in the early 20th century Europe were as follows

(i) Military strength became the same with national prestige and every country began to increase their military power.

(ii) Every nation thought about its national interest and did not care for the interest of other countries.

(iii) England and France established a huge Colonial Empire in Asia and Africa.

Q.2 **Explain the Sarajevo Crisis and how the assassination of Archduke Franz Ferdinand triggered the outbreak of the First World War.**

Ans. The Sarajevo Crisis began with the assassination of Archduke Franz Ferdinand of Austria and his wife on 28th June, by a Serbian nationalist group called the Black Hand. Austria-Hungary blamed Serbia for the attack and issued an ultimatum with harsh demands.

Serbia agreed to most of the demands but refused some that would weaken its sovereignty. As a result, Austria-Hungary declared war on Serbia. Russia supported Serbia, and soon, due to alliances, other countries like Germany, France, and Britain were drawn into the conflict, leading to the outbreak of the First World War.

Q.3 **How did mutual defense alliances contribute to the escalation of the First World War?**

Ans. Mutual defense alliances made the First World War bigger because they promised that if one country was attacked, others would help defend it. The Triple Alliance (Germany, Austria-Hungary, Italy) and the Triple Entente (Britain, France, Russia) formed these agreements.

When Austria-Hungary declared war on Serbia after the assassination of Archduke Franz Ferdinand, Russia supported Serbia, and soon, Germany, France, and Britain joined the war due to these alliances. This turned a local conflict into a world war, as many countries were pulled into the fighting due to their alliance commitments.

Q.4 **The war that broke out in 1914 was different from the previous wars in many ways. In this context, explain the following point briefly.** **(ICSE 2015)**

How did the Treaty of Versailles seek to cripple Germany's military strength?

Ans. The Treaty of Versailles seek to cripple Germany's strength through its terms which were;

- The German army was disbanded. It was allowed to keep only 1 lakh soldiers. The Airforce and submarines were also banned. Its navy was limited to 15,000 navy men and 24 ships.
- Germany had to pay a war penalty of 33 billion dollars to the Allies in yearly installments for 42 years. This heavy debt crippled Germany and made it impossible to maintain its military strength.

Q.5 **Explain briefly about the territorial rearrangements as a result of First World War.**

Ans. The major territorial rearrangements of the World War I were as follows

- Three ruling dynasties, viz the Romanov in Russia, the Hohenzollern in Germany and the Hapsburg in Austria–Hungary were destroyed.
- In Turkey the Ottoman Empire also came to an end.
- Countries like Czechoslovakia, Yugoslavia, etc. emerged as a independent states.

TYPE - 5 — 4 Marks

Long Answer Type Questions

Q.1 **Explain the role of expansionist policies of European countries in making of the ground for the First World War.**

Ans. The role of expansionist policies in beginning of the First World War were as follows

- **Colonial Rivalries** Competition for colonies, especially in Africa and Asia, caused conflicts between nations.

- **Economic Competition** Germany's industrial growth challenged Britain and intensified tensions.
- **Naval and Military Expansion** Germany's naval buildup threatened Britain led to an arms race among European nations.
- **Global Power Rivalry** Expansionism fostered mistrust and alliances, making a regional conflict which led to the beginning of First World War.

Q.2 Analyse the major cause which were responsible for the beginning of the World War I.

Ans. The major cause responsible for the beginning of the First World War were as follows

- **Militarism** European nations, especially Germany and Britain, engaged in an arms race to increase military power.
- Competition for colonies led to conflicts especially in Africa and Asia.
- **Nationalism** Rising nationalist movements particularly in the Balkans challenged empires. Therefore, France also sought revenge against Germany.
- **Immediate Cause** The assassination of Archduke Franz Ferdinand on 28th June, 1914 led to war on Serbia and beginning of the First World War.

Q.3 The Treaty of Versailles was the end of world War I. Justify this statement with suitable example.

Ans. The Treaty of Versailles is considered as the climax of the World War I due to several factors which were as follows

- **Official End of War** It was signed on 28th June, 1919 and ended the hostilities between nations.
- **War Guilt Clause** Germany was held responsible for the war, leading to harsh penalties.
- **Reparations** Imposed financial reparations on Germany to destabilise its economy.
- **Territorial Losses** Germany lost colonies and territories (e.g., Alsace-Lorraine to France).
- **League of Nations** Established to prevent future conflicts, though Germany was initially excluded.

TYPE - 6 — 10 Marks

Structured Questions

Q.1 With reference to the First World War answer the following questions.

(i) How did the Sarajevo crisis lead to the outbreak of the First World War? Explain the assassination of Archduke Franz Ferdinand? (3)

(ii) Explain the role of imperialism in the lead-up to the First World War. How did competition for colonies affect relations between nations? (3)

(iii) Mention any four ways in which the Treaty of Versailles benefitted France. (4)

Ans. (i) For answer, refer Q.2. of Short Answer Type Questions.

(ii) Imperialism played a major role in the lead-up to the First World War as strong nations competed to control weaker regions for resources, land and trade. This competition created tension between countries like Britain, France, Germany, and Italy. Nations built large empires in Asia, Africa, and other parts of the world, leading to rivalry and distrust. As each nation sought to expand its influence, that made it harder for countries to maintain peaceful relations and eventually contributed to the outbreak of the war.

(iii) The Treaty of Versailles significantly benefitted France in the following ways

(a) **Territorial Gains** France regained Alsace- Lorraine, which had been annexed by Germany after the Franco-Prussian War of 1870.

(b) **Security Enhancement** The Rhineland was demilitarised and created a buffer zone between France and Germany hence reducing the threat of future invasions.

(c) **Reparations** Germany was required to pay substantial reparations, providing economic compensation to France for war damages, particularly in its heavily affected Northern regions.

(d) **Colonial Expansion** France gained control over former German colonies such as mandates in Africa to increases its global influence and resources.

Q.2 The final act of the long-drawn-out negotiations took place at Versailles on Saturday afternoon, and today Germany and the Allies—always with the exception of America—are at peace. Peace is a blessed word, and both the word and the fact are welcome today. So far as Germany is concerned there is for the present an end of strife, and at least a formal return to the decent relations of civilised states.

Editorial : Peace in force (12th January, 1920) The Guardian

(i) Mention any three causes of the World War I which ended with the signing of the treaty being discussed in the passage above. (3)

(ii) Name the organisation which was established in 1920 to maintain peace after this war. Mention any two of its objectives. (3)

(iii) Mention any four clauses of the Treaty which affected Germany. (4)

Ans. (i) For answer, refer to Q. 2 of Long Answer Type Questions.

(ii) The League of Nations was established in 1920 to maintain peace after First World War. Two of its objectives were as follows

(a) **Prevention of War** The League aimed to prevent conflicts and wars between nations through diplomacy, negotiation and collective security.

(b) **Promotion of Disarmament** Another objective was the promotion of disarmament to reduce the likelihood of future wars. The League advocated for arms reduction and limitation to maintain global peace.

(iii) The four major clauses of the Treaty of Versailles were as follows

(a) It was declared guilty of aggression and had to pay war reparation of 33 billion dollars.

(b) The area of the Rhine valley was de-militarised and the German territory, (West of Rhine) was to be occupied by the Allied troops for 15 years.

(c) Germany lost all colonies to the Allies.

(d) The German force was restricted to 1 lakh, the Navy to 15,000 men and 24 ships.

Q.3 Look at the Picture and answer the following questions. **(ICSE Specimen 2025)**

(i) Describe the incident depicted in the cartoon. **(3)**

(ii) Mention any three points to analyse how Europe was rearranged as a consequence of the war caused by this incident. **(3)**

(iii) The Germans described the Treaty of Versailles as harsh and humiliating. Give any four reasons that justify this statement. **(4)**

Ans. (i) The cartoon probably depicts the assassination of Archduke Franz Ferdinand of Austria and his wife, Sophie, on 28th june, 1914, in Sarajevo. This act was committed by a member of the Serbian nationalist organisation Black Hand.

The assassination was a trigger for the First World War because it caused Austria-Hungary to declare war on Serbia and setting off a chain reaction among European alliances.

(ii) The major consequences of the incident were as follows

- **Collapse of Empires** The Austro-Hungarian, Ottoman, German, and Russian Empires disintegrated, leading to significant territorial changes in Europe.
- **New Nations Created** Countries such as Czechoslovakia, Yugoslavia Poland, and the Baltic States (Estonia, Latvia, Lithuania) emerged from the remnants of fallen empires.
- **Treaty of Versailles** Germany faced severe territorial losses, military restrictions and reparations, which reshaped the political landscape of Europe and sowed seeds for future conflicts.

(iii) The Germans described the Treaty of Versailles as harsh and humilating. This statement can be justified through the following reasons

(a) **War Guilt Clause** Germany was forced to accept full responsibility for the war, which was seen as unfair and degrading.

(b) **Heavy Reparations** Germany was required to pay an enormous sum in reparations that cripplied its economy.

(c) **Territorial Losses** Germany lost key territories such as Alsace-Lorraine to France, West Prussia to Poland, and its other colonies were also confiscated.

(d) **Military Restrictions** The treaty put limit on the German army to 100,000 troops, and restricted the navy and air force.

10

RISE OF DICTATORSHIP : FASCISM AND NAZISM

- A dictatorship is a type of government where one leader or a small group has total control on government.
- The massive destruction brought by the First World War affected social, political and economic life of Europe.This led to the rise of extreme political parties like Socialist, Communist, Fascist and Nazi parties.
- Mussolini introduced Fascism in Italy and Hitler established Nazism in Germany.

Rise of Fascism in Italy

- Fascism means an anti-democratic type of government, where one man has all the powers of the state.
- Italy was ruled by King Victor Emmanuel III at the beginning of the First World War. In 1919, democracy was introduced in Italy.
- In October 1922, a conference of the Fascist Party was held at Naples. In this conference, Mussolini announced that if the demands of fascists were not fulfilled, he would attack Rome with his volunteers.
- Mussolini put forward the following demands
  - Five members of the Fascist Party to be included in the Cabinet.
  - The government should act firmly on its foreign policy.
  - Economic reforms to be implemented as early as possible.

Mussolini

- However, the Italian government did not show any interest towards these demands. Thus, Mussolini captured Rome in October 1922.

Causes Behind the Rise of Fascism in Italy

- **Dissatisfaction after the Treaty of Versaille** Italy joined the Allies in the First World War to gain territories of Turkey and Germany. However, Italy could not get any port of German and Turkish Colonial empire which affected sentiments of people.
- **Economic conditions in Italy** First World War made Italy weak in economic field. The war disturbed the life of common people including the soldiers. Trade and business also got disturbed that led to large-scale unemployment.
- **Inefficient Government of Italy** Between 1919 and 1922, more than 6 coalition governments were formed in Italy. The governments adopted different policies but could not find any solutions for unemployment, strikes and riots which took place during 1921-22.

- **Threat of Communism in Italy** In Italy, the socialists included the Anarchists, the Communists and the Social Democrats. They created conditions which led to the rise of Fascism such as

  The communists inspired people with their revolutionary ideas. The peasants extorted the land of the landlords and the workmen organised strikes, broke machines and captured factories. People became tired of these things and they wanted a stable government which would establish peace and prosperity for them.
- **Failure of League of Nations** The League of Nations was formed to minimise the possibility of the future wars in Europe. However, it failed to achieve its aims. Many nations were unhappy with this world organisation, because they were compelled to pay huge war penalty, so they never valued the League of Nation.
- **Class Conflict** Class conflicts grew in many countries after the First World War. The main issue in Europe was whether the government and economy would be controlled by the rich aristocrats or the poorer majority. During the war, common people were promised better economic support, but after the war, these promises were not kept.

Rise of Nazism in Germany

Adolf Hitler

- Nazism refers to the ideas and practices of Adolf Hitler and the Nazi Party in Germany.
- In the First World War, Germany fought alongside Austria against the Allies (England, France, and Russia). The US joined the allies in 1917 and led to defeat of Germany in November, 1918.
- On 10th August, 1919 a Constitution was introduced in Weimar and established the Weimar Republic as a democratic nation.
- In the 1932 elections, no party gained majority in the Reichstag (Lower House of the Legislature).
- People lost trust in the democratic system as it couldn't resolve economic issues or prevent unrest.
- President of Germany, Hindenburg offered Chancellorship to Hitler. Hitler then formed his first Nazi Government on 30th January, 1933.
- After Hindenburg's death, Hitler became President, Chancellor, and Dictator of Germany. He adopted the title of Fuhrer.
- Hitler abolished the Constitution, sought lebensraum (living space), and led a regime responsible for the genocide (Mass murder) of 5.5 million Jews and millions of others.
- In 1945, Hitler committed suicide after the defeat of Germany in the Second World War by the Allied powers. This marked the end of Nazism in Germany.

Causes behind the Rise of Nazism in Germany

- **Treaty of Versailles** Germany was forced to give large part of its important territory to France, Belgium, Poland and Denmark. Its overseas colonies were shared by the victorious nations. Many conditions of the treaty gave an opportunity to Hitler to encourage the people, disobey the signed treaty and rose to power.
- **Poor Economic Condition** The foreign nations raised tariffs on the entry of German goods. Thus, the rate of unemployment increased considerably in Germany. Hitler promised to the industrialists that if they support him, he would stop communists and the nationalisation of industries.
- **Anti-Semitic Propaganda** Nazis blamed Jews for Germany's economic issues and defeat in the First World War. This fostered hatred and unity against them. Propaganda spread through media and speeches, creating a common enemy and rallying support for Nazi policies.

- **Resurgence of Militant Nationalism** The Germans did not appreciate the functions of the democratic parliamentary system. They wanted their past prestige and glory back and felt that only a strong leader like Hitler could do this.
- **Absence of Strong Opposition** There was no strong opposition party in Germany that could rise against the Nazi Party. Thus, it became easy for the Nazi Party to gain popularity in Germany.

Comparative Study Between the Ideology of Nazism and Fascism

Differences

- Fascism was in prominence between 1919 and 1945, while Nazism became popular between 1933 to 1945.
- Fascism is a term that was originally referred to the fascists of Italy under Mussolini, while Nazism is an ideological concept of the Nazi Party of Hitler.
- Fascism believes in the corporatism of all elements in the society to form an organic state, while Nazism emphasised on racism.
- Fascism gave more importance to the state, while Nazism considered Aryanism as more important.
- Hitler initiated state-controlled changes like four-year plan, public works program, while Mussolini didn't implement any such plan.

Similarities

- Both supported totalitarian rules.
- Both were against democratic political system.
- Both believed in state supremacy, which could suppress Fundamental Rights and individual freedom.
- Both wanted to uphold the concept of one party and one leader.

EXAM ORIENTED QUESTIONS

TYPE - 1 1 Mark

Multiple Choice Questions

Q.1 Which of the following statements is correct about Dictatorship?

(a) Dictatorship is a form of government where power is held by a single individual or a small group.
(b) In a dictatorship, power is equally distributed among elected representatives.
(c) Dictatorships are always democratic in nature.
(d) In a dictatorship, political opposition is encouraged and supported.

Ans. (a) Dictatorship is a form of government where power is held by a single individual or a small group.

Q.2 Which of the following is a common cause for the rise of dictatorship? **(ICSE 2025)**

(a) Faith in Democracy (b) Economic Crisis
(c) Freedom of Press (d) Political Stability

Ans. (b) Economic Crisis

Q.3 Complete the given analogy.

Fascism : Italy :: Nazism : ?

Options

(a) Russia (b) Germany
(c) India (d) South Africa

Ans. (b) Germany

Q.4 Identify the odd one out from the following statements about Fascism.

(a) Fascism promotes a single-party authoritarian rule.
(b) It emphasises extreme nationalism and loyalty to the state.
(c) Fascism supports equality and democratic values.
(d) It glorifies militarism and the use of violence to achieve goals.

Ans. (c) Fascism supports equality and democratic values

Q.5. Which of the following policies of a dictator ruling over country X is most aligned with the ideologies of Mussolini during his time in power? **(ICSE Specimen 2024)**

(a) Prioritising military expansion.
(b) Promoting environmental sustainability.
(c) Creating a healthcare program for all citizens equally.
(d) Offering financial aid to support the education of students from poor backgrounds.

Ans. (a) Prioritising military expansion.

Q.6 Which of the following statements is correct about the rise of Fascism in Italy?

(a) The rise of Fascism was driven by international cooperation and unity.
(b) Fascism emerged as a movement promoting equality and democratic reforms.
(c) Fascism discouraged militarism and sought peaceful resolutions to conflicts.
(d) The economic instability caused by the war and Great Depression created fertile ground for extremist ideologies.

Ans. (d) The economic instability caused by the war and Great Depression created fertile ground for extremist ideologies.

Q.7 The word Fascism has become so freighted with meaning that it can be difficult to define; today, it is often used as a shallow epithet for any politics one strongly dislikes. *The New York Times, 30th July, 2020*

Which of the following statement can be inferred from the News?

(a) Fascism has a universally agreed definition.
(b) The term 'Fascism' is often used inaccurately in modern political discourse.
(c) Fascism is limited to its historical context and has no modern relevance.
(d) Political disagreements today are less intense compared to the past.

Ans. (b) The term 'Fascism' is often used inaccurately in modern political discourse.

Q.8 Identify the pair of statements which is correct about the Fascism.

P : The word 'Fascism' is related to authoritarian regime of italy.
Q : Nazism is historically tied to authoritarian regime of Mussolini.
R : Fascism was the outcome of the First World War.
S : Treaty of Paris hampered the growth of Germany in early 20th century

Options

(a) P and S
(b) P and R
(c) Q and S
(d) Q and R

Ans. (b) P and R

Q.9 Italy faced severe economic and political instability after World War I. Mussolini, inspired by Fascist ideals, aimed to bring order and strength to the nation. As a follower of Fascism, which of the following actions is Mussolini not likely to support?
(a) Establishing a totalitarian rule with one-party control
(b) Encouraging democratic debates and opposition parties
(c) Using aggressive nationalism to unify the country
(d) Suppressing communist and socialist movements

Ans. (b) Encouraging democratic debates and opposition parties.

Exp. Mussolini believed in Fascism, which rejected democracy and promoted total control. He would oppose democratic debates and opposition parties because Fascism suppressed opposition to ensure absolute power.

Q.10 What was the primary focus of Nazism that differed from Fascism?
(a) Racial superiority
(b) Economic policies
(c) Religious reforms
(d) Expansion of trade

Ans. (a) Racial superiority

Exp. Unlike Fascism, which emphasised state control, Nazism promoted Aryan supremacy, blaming Jews and others for Germany's problems and justifying discrimination and genocide.

Q.11 Which of the following statements is incorrect about Nazism?
(a) Nazism was based on the principles of racial superiority and anti-semitism.
(b) The Nazi regime didn't promoted democratic ideals and individual freedoms.
(c) Adolf Hitler was the leader of the Nazi Party in France.
(d) The Nazi Party used propaganda to manipulate public opinion.

Ans. (c) Adolf Hitler was the leader of the Nazi Party in France.

Q.12 What event allowed Hitler to become the sole leader of Germany?
(a) The Treaty of Versailles
(b) The Great Depression
(c) The death of President Hindenburg
(d) The formation of the League of Nations

Ans. (c) The death of President Hindenburg

Exp. Hitler became the sole leader of Germany after the death of President Hindenburg. With no opposition, he combined the roles of President and Chancellor, declaring himself 'Führer' and establishing total control.

Q.13 Which of the given policies not aligned with the ideologies of the leader seen in the picture? **(ICSE Specimen 2025)**

(a) Prioritising military expansion
(b) Promoting racist policies
(c) Hosting an anti-communist seminar
(d) Holding pro-democracy rallies

Ans. (d) Holding pro-democracy rallies

Q.14 Which of the following was not a common ideology of the dictators? **(ICSE Specimen Semester II 2022)**
(a) Faith in totalitarian rule
(b) One party and one leader
(c) Faith in communism
(d) Aggressive nationalism and imperialism

Ans. (c) Faith in communism

Q.15 Read the following description and identify the person. He was associated with the policy of 'one people, one state, one leader'.
(a) Lenin (b) Hitler
(c) Stalin (d) Mussolini

Ans. (b) Hitler

Exp. Hitler followed the policy of 'One people, One state, One leader' to promote German unity under his dictatorship. He aimed for total control, rejecting democracy and opposing political opposition.

TYPE - 2 1 Mark

Assertion-Reason Questions

Q.1 Read the two statements given below about the rise of Fascism and select the option that shows the correct relationship between (A) and (R).

Assertion (A) Mussolini became the Prime Minister of Italy in 1922.

Reason (R) Mussolini's rise to power was facilitated by the economic instability and widespread discontent in Italy after World War I.

(a) R contradicts A
(b) R is the reason for A
(c) A is true but R is false
(d) A and R are independent of each other

Ans. (b) R is the reason for A

Q.2 Read the two statements given below about the relationship between Fascism and the economy and select the option that shows the correct relationship between (A) and (R).

Assertion (A) Fascism in Italy promoted a controlled economy with state intervention.

Reason (R) Mussolini earlier believed that limited state control over the economy would help in national unity and economic stability.

(a) R contradicts A
(b) R is the reason for A
(c) A is true but R is false
(d) A and R are independent of each other

Ans. (a) R contradicts A

Q.3 Read the two statements given below about Treaty of Versaillies and select the option that shows the correct relationship between (A) and (R).

Assertion (A) The signing of the Treaty of Versailles played a significant role in the rise of Nazism in Germany.

Reason (R) The Treaty forced Germany to give up important territories and overseas colonies, leading to widespread resentment that Hitler used to rise to power.

(a) R contradicts A (b) R is the reason for A
(c) A is true but R is false
(d) A and R are independent of each other

Ans. (b) R is the reason for A

Q.4 Read the two statements given below about the rise of Nazism and select the option that shows the correct relationship between (A) and (R).

Assertion (A) Adolf Hitler became Chancellor of Germany in 1933.

Reason (R) The Nazi Party gained widespread support due to the economic hardships caused by the war.

(a) R contradicts A (b) R is the reason for A
(c) A is true but R is false
(d) A and R are independent of each other

Ans. (b) R is the reason for A

Q.5 Read the two statements given below about Nazi Germany and select the option that shows the correct relationship between (A) and (R).

Assertion (A) Nazi propaganda played a key role in Hitler's rise to power.

Reason (R) The Nazi Party didn't try to manipulate public opinion and gain widespread support.

(a) R contradicts A
(b) R is the reason for A
(c) A is true but R is false
(d) A and R are independent of each other

Ans. (c) A is true but R is false

TYPE - 3 2 Marks

Very Short Answer Type Questions

Q.1 Name the two countries in Europe which came under dictatorship after the First World War. Also name the dictators. **(ICSE Specimen Semester II, 2022)**

Ans. Germany and Italy were two countries of Europe where dictatorship was established.

The two dictators were Benito Mussolini and Adolf Hitler.

Q.2 Explain the meaning of the term 'Fascism'

Ans. Fascism is an authoritarian political ideology that emphasises strong centralised control, dictatorship and the suppression of political opposition.

It promotes extreme nationalism often with a belief in the supremacy of one race or nation over others, and seeks to create a militarised society.

Q.3 Mention any two reasons for the rise of Fascism in Italy due to the threat of Communism.

Ans. Two reasons for the rise of Fascism in Italy due to the threat of Communism were as follows

(i) Communists inspired people with revolutionary ideas, leading to unrest.

(ii) Peasants and workers organised strikes and captured factories, creating lawlessness, therefore people seek a stable government.

Q.4 How did the ineffectiveness of the League of Nations lead to the emergence of dictatorships?

Ans. The League of Nations was created after First World War, to preserve global peace and prevent future conflicts. However, it was ineffective and failed to accomplish its objectives. The League's inability to stop the rise of dictators allowed leaders like Mussolini and Hitler to pursue their expansionist goals unchecked and ultimately resulted into rise of dictatorship.

Q.5 Highlight the meaning and principles of Hitler's Nazism?

Ans. Nazism or national socialism, was the ideology and policies promoted by Adolf Hitler and the Nazi Party (National Socialist German Workers' Party) in Germany. It was characterised by extreme nationalism, racial purity, anti-semitism, and authoritarianism.

Q.6 State any two underlying principles of Fascism.

Ans. The two underlying principles of Fascism were as follows

(i) Centralisation of Powers in a single leader.

(ii) Emphasis on national superiority and unity.

Q.7 **Mention any two demands presented by the Mussolini to the Rome government.**

Ans. The two major demands of the Mussolini to the Rome government were as follows

(i) The government should act firmly on its foreign policy.

(ii) Five members of the Fascist Party to be included in the Cabinet of the Rome government.

Q.8 **Explain how World War I was the major cause behind the rise of Fascism. Mention any two.**

Ans. The two reasons for the rise of Fascism were as follows

(i) **Economic Hardships** Post-war economic devastation led to poverty and unemployment, fueling support for extremist ideologies like Fascism.

(ii) **Political Instability** Weakened political systems and chaos allowed Fascist leaders to gain power by promising strong leadership to Public.

Q.9 **Imagine you are a citizen of Italy and want to promote peace in opposition to Mussolini's aggressive policies. How would you persuade others to adopt peaceful approaches to resolve conflicts rather than resorting to war?**

Ans. As a citizen of Italy, I would advocate for the benefits of peace, emphasising economic stability, prosperity, and global cooperation. I would encourage open dialogue, support strengthening of international organisations like the League of Nations and promote disarmament to prevent unnecessary conflicts.

Q.10 **Italian Fascism and Nazism began, when Mussolini and Hitler capitalised on mass discontentment after World War I to gain power.** *New York Times*

(i) Where was the conference of the Fascist Party held?

(ii) Where was the headquarters of the Nazi Party located?

Ans. (i) The conference of Fascist party was held at Naples in October,1922.

(ii) The headquarters of the Nazi Party was located in Munich, Germany.

TYPE - 4   3 Marks

Short Answer Type Questions

Q.1 **Discuss the economic conditions in Germany after the First World War and their impact on the rise of Hitler and Nazism.**

Ans. After the First World War, Germany faced severe economic problems that were as follows

- The war had destroyed industries, and agriculture production.
- The Treaty of Versailles imposed heavy reparations on Germany, causing inflation and unemployment.

These economic hardships led to widespread dissatisfaction among the people, who were struggling to make ends meet. The economic crisis provided Hitler with an opportunity to gain support. He promised economic recovery, jobs, and stability, which attracted many people to follow him and the Nazi Party.

Q.2 **What was 'lebensraum,' and how did Hitler use this concept to justify his policies?**

Ans. Lebensraum means 'living space' in German. Hitler believed that the German people needed more land to grow and prosper. He argued that this land should come from Eastern Europe, especially from Slavic nations. Hitler used this idea to justify his aggressive expansion policies, aiming to conquer neighbouring countries. By promoting lebensraum, he convinced the German public that the nation's survival and success depended on expanding its territory, which led to the invasion on countries like Poland and the start of World War II.

Q.3 **State any three reasons behind the rise of Nazism in Germany.** **(ICSE 2020, 2019)**

Ans. The three major reasons behind the rise of Nazism were as follows

(i) **Treaty of Versailles** The treaty's harsh terms caused national humiliation in Germany which fueled resentment and support for Hitler's promises.

(ii) **Weak Weimar Republic** Political instability and weak leadership made Germany susceptible to extremist ideologies like Nazism.

(iii) **High Tariff on German Goods** The foreign nations raised tariffs on the entry of German goods which led to high unemployment and inflation in Germany.

Q.4. **Why did the Treaty of Versailles lead to humiliation for the Germans?**

Ans. The defeat in the First World War and the harsh terms of the Treaty of Versailles left Germans feeling humiliated and powerless. Germany had to surrender vast territories to France, Belgium, Poland, and Denmark, while its overseas colonies were taken by the victorious allies.

Germany was also burdened with heavy reparations of 33 billion dollars, and its army was drastically reduced to 100,000 soldiers.

TYPE - 5 4 Marks

Long Answer Type Questions

Q.1 The threat of communism was the major reason behind the rise of Fascism in Italy. Justify the statement.

Ans. The threat of communism was a major reason behind the rise of Fascism in Italy because, after World War I, Italy faced significant social and economic unrest. There were widespread strikes, and many workers to peasants were demanding greater rights and land reforms. This led to fears among the middle and upper classes as well as business owners that a communist revolution might occur similar to the one in Russia.

Mussolini and the Fascist Party capitalised on these fears by promising to restore order and protect private property. They portrayed themselves as the only force capable of preventing a communist uprising. Mussolini's emphasis on strong, authoritarian leadership and his suppression of left-wing groups attracted those who feared the spread of communism, helping the Fascists rise to power.

Q.2. Explain the main reasons behind the failure of the League of Nations in maintaining global peace and preventing conflicts.

Ans. The main reasons behind the failure of the League of Nations in maintaining global peace and preventing conflicts were as follows

- **Weak Sanctions** The League of Nations had little power to take strong action, and because it couldn't enforce its decisions, dictators felt free to do whatever they wanted without fear of consequences.
- **Lack of Unity Among Members** The League of Nations couldn't take strong action against rising dictatorships because the member countries often disagreed, and they needed everyone to agree before making decisions.
- **Appeasement Policy** The League's appeasement approach towards aggressive dictators like Hitler and Mussolini allowed their power to grow, which eventually led to the outbreak of Second World War.

Q.3 Explain how anti-semitic propaganda and militant nationalism helped in the flourishment of Nazism in Germany.

Ans. Anti-semitic propaganda and militant nationalism helped in the flourishment of Nazism in Germany in following ways

Anti-Semitic Propaganda

- Nazis blamed Jews for Germany's economic issues and defeat in WWI and fostered hate against them.
- Propaganda spread through media and speeches, creating a common enemy and rallying support for Nazi policies.

Militant Nationalism

- Nazis emphasised restoring Germany's power and pride after the Treaty of Versailles by appealing to nationalistic sentiments.
- Hitler promised military strength and territorial expansion, which resonated with those seeking revenge and restoration.

Q.4 Explain the similarities between the Fascism and Nazism.

Ans. The similarities between the Fascism and Nazism were as follows

- **Support to Extreme Nationalism** Both Fascism and Nazism promote extreme nationalism by emphasising the supremacy of their nation and the need for its expansion.
- **Totalitarian Leadership** Both ideologies were led by dictatorial leaders who held absolute power and control over the state-Mussolini in Italy and Hitler in Germany.
- **Rejection of Democracy** Both Fascism and Nazism reject democratic values and focused on a single-party system.
- **Militarism** Both ideologies stressed upon the importance of military strength and expansion as a way to enhance national power.

TYPE - 6 10 Marks

Structured Questions

Q.1 Under Hitler's leadership, Germany saw a dramatic recovery through state-controlled economic policies, job creation programs. *The National Archive*

(i) Highlight the economic reforms implemented by Hitler in Nazi Germany. (3)

(ii) Explain the significance of Hitler assuming the title of 'Fuhrer' and its impact on Germany's governance. (3)

(iii) Mark the differences between the ideology of Nazism and Fascism of the Hitler and Mussolini. (4)

Ans. (i) Some of the major economic reforms implemented by Hitler in Nazi Germany were as follows

- **Public Works Programs** Hitler introduced large-scale public work projects, such as the construction of highways which provided jobs and improved infrastructure, thus helped in reduction of unemployment.

- **Rearmament and Military Expansion** Hitler prioritised military rearmament which boosted the economy by creating jobs in defense industries and contributed to the overall economic recovery.
- **State-Controlled Economy** Through the 'Four- Year Plan,' Hitler aimed for economic self-sufficiency, thus reduced Germany's reliance on foreign imports and increased domestic production.

(ii) When Hitler assumed the title of 'Fuhrer' (meaning 'Leader'), it marked the consolidation of his power, combining both the roles of President and Chancellor in Germany. This decision eliminated the democratic framework of the Weimar Republic and gave Hitler total control over the government, bypassing any checks and balances.

By becoming Führer, Hitler centralised authority in his hands, allowing him to pass laws without the need for approval from Parliament. This move greatly impacted Germany's governance by shifting it from a democratic system to a totalitarian regime.

(iii) The major differences between the ideologies of Nazism (Hitler) and Fascism (Mussolini) were as follows

Aspect	Nazism (Hitler)	Fascism (Mussolini)
Racial Ideology	Emphasised Aryan racial supremacy and anti-semitism.	No focus on racial superiority, but emphasised Italian nationalism.
Nationalism	Based on extreme nationalism combined with belief in the superiority of the Aryan race.	Focused on Italian nationalism and restoring the glory of ancient Rome.
Totalitarian Control	Led by Hitler, with absolute control over the state and society.	Mussolini's focus was on creating a disciplined, centralised, and authoritarian state.
Economic System	Promoted domestic economy (economic self-sufficiency) and militarisation.	Favoured corporatism with the state mediating between employers and workers.

Q.2 Look at the picture given below and answer the following questions. **(ICSE 2024)**

(i) **Identify the leader in the above picture. Mention any two of his ideologies. (3)**

(ii) **Mention any three causes for his rise to power. What was the immediate cause of the Second World War? (4)**

(iii) **Mention any three reasons given by this leader to justify his action. (3)**

Ans. (i) The leader shown in the picture is Adolf Hitler, who was the dictator of Germany.

Two of his Ideologies were as follows

(a) **Anti-Semitism** Hitler propagated a strong ideology of hatred against Jews, leading to the Holocaust, where six million Jews were murdered.

(b) **Aryan Supremacy** He believed in the racial superiority of the 'Aryan' race and promoted the idea that Germans were the master race, which justified their expansionist goals.

(ii) The three major causes behind his rise to power were as follows

(a) **Economic Hardship** The Treaty of Versailles and the Great Depression left Germany in severe economic distress, leading to widespread poverty and discontent, which helped in the fame of Hitler.

(b) **Weak Weimar Republic** The democratic government of the Weimar Republic was seen as ineffective and weak, which allowed extremist parties like the Nazis to gain support.

(c) **Hitler's Charismatic Leadership** Hitler was a powerful orator who promised to restore Germany's former glory and provided a solution to the country's problems, which attracted large numbers of supporters.

The immediate cause of the Second World War was Germany's invasion of Poland on 1st September, 1939, which instigated Britain and France to declare war on Germany and beginning of the Second World War.

(iii) The three major reasons given by Hitler to justify his actions were as follows

(a) **Expansionist Policies** Hitler argued that Germany needed more space to expand and secure resources for its growing population, justifying the invasion of neighbouring countries.

(b) **Revenge for the Treaty of Versailles** Hitler believed the Treaty of Versailles had unfairly punished Germany after World War I, and his actions were aimed at reversing its terms and restoring Germany's power.

(c) **Protection of the Aryan Race** Hitler claimed that his actions were necessary to protect the 'pure' Aryan race from what he perceived as threats, including Jews and other minority groups.

Q.3. With reference to the Fascism and Nazism, answer the following questions.

(i) A Constitution was introduced on 10th August, 1919 in Weimar, establishing the Weimar Republic as a democratic nation. How did the conditions of the Weimar Republic lead to the rise of Hitler and the Nazi Party? **(3)**

(ii) In what ways did anti-semitic propaganda and militant nationalism play a role in the spread of Nazism in Germany? **(4)**

(iii) How did the economic struggles in Germany after the First World War contribute to the rise of Hitler and the Nazi Party? **(3)**

Ans. (i) The Weimar Republic faced many challenges, including economic problems, political instability, and the effects of the Treaty of Versailles. The harsh terms of the treaty angered Germans and caused economic hardship, such as high unemployment and inflation. The government struggled to solve these issues, leading people to lose faith in democracy.

This created an opportunity for Hitler and the Nazi Party, who promised to restore Germany's glory and fix the economy. Hitler's powerful leadership and ideas about making Germany great again attracted many people. This support helped him gain power and eventually become the ruler of Germany.

(ii) For answer, refer to Q.3 of Long Answer Type Questions.

(iii) For answer, refer to Q.1 of Short Answer Type Questions.

THE SECOND WORLD WAR

- The Second World War started in 1939 and lasted till 1945. It was fought between Allied Powers (France, UK, The Soviet Union and the US) and Axis Powers (Germany, Italy and Japan).
- The Second World War happened because of the problems caused by the First World War.
- The use of atomic bombs on two Japanese cities made the Second World War even more dangerous and deadly than the First World War.

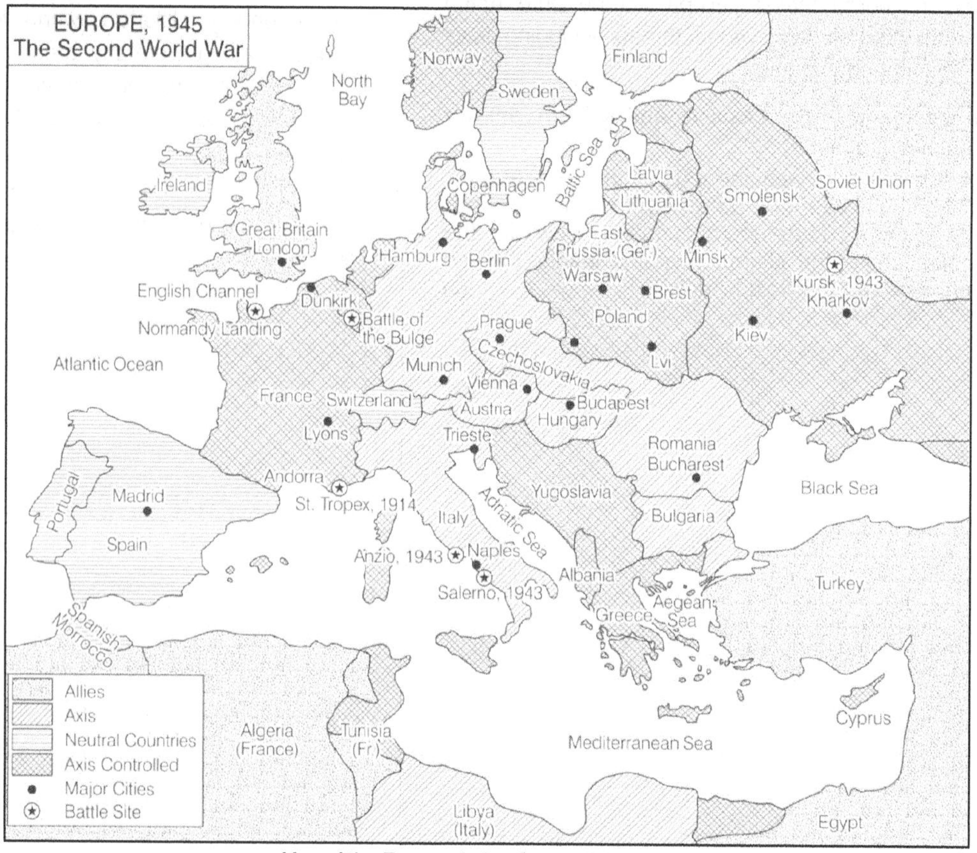

Map of the Europe during Second World War

Causes of The Second World War

Treaty of Versailles

- The Treaty of Versailles was a peace treaty, which was signed at the end of the First World War, but it led to dissatisfaction among the countries especially in Germany and Italy.

- Under this treaty, Germany had to accept responsibility for the First World War and to pay penalty. Germany lost territory and was prohibited from having a large military.
- The humiliation faced by Germany under this treaty paved the way for the spread of ultra-nationalism in Germany.
- Italy was not favoured by allies for the compensation of war. So, the Italians felt that they had won the war but lost the peace.
- The Treaty of Versailles was dictated as treaty imposed by the victorious countries on the defeated countries. Thus, the frustrated people started turning towards totalitarian ideas and authoritarian regimes.

Rise of Fascism and Nazism

- Dictatorship got established in Italy under the powerful leadership of Benito Mussolini.
- Mussolini wanted to bring back the old glory of the Roman Empire. He joined the Anti-Comintern Pact (1937) and made a 10-year alliance with Germany (1939).
- Mussolini changed Italy's administration and followed aggressive policies.
- Adolf Hitler led the Nazi Party and became Germany's dictator in 1934. He broke the military rules of the Treaty of Versailles and increased Germany's military power.
- Hitler aimed to expand Germany's empire and restore its power. He captured Austria in 1938 and later Czechoslovakia.
- The rise of Fascism (in Italy) and Nazism (in Germany) led the world toward another world war.

Policy of Appeasement

- The British Government, led by PM Stanley Baldwin and Neville Chamberlain adopted a policy of appeasement towards Italy and Germany.
- They hoped that by meeting Hitler's demand, he would be satisfied and there would not be any war. However, this only made Hitler bolder and gave him time to build up his army.

Japanese Invasion of China

- Japan and China fought the First World War on the side of the Allies. After the war, Japan became ambitious and started developing its army. In 1931, Japan attacked over China, seized Manchuria and renamed it (Manchukuo).
- China appealed to the League of Nations to declare sanctions against Japan but leading members of League like Britain and France did not pay any attention to it.
- In 1933, Japan left the League of Nations and started occupying the British and American territories in China. These circumstances led to the beginning of another world war.

Failure of the League of Nations

- The League of Nations was created after the First World War to maintain peace in the world. However, the League suffered an initial failure when the USA did not join the League.
- When Italy annexed Abyssinia, Japan annexed Manchuria and Germany annexed Austria and Czechoslovakia, the League of Nations did not take any action against them.

Hitler's Invasion of Poland (Immediate Cause)

The invasion of Poland by the Hitler on 1st September, 1939 led to the beginning of the Second World War. Hitler invaded due to following reasons

- Under the Treaty of Versailles, Germany was divided into two parts. In order to give a land-route to Poland up to the sea, the port of Danzig was handed over to Poland.
- Danzig city was inhabited mainly by the Germans and by occupying Danzig corridor, German could connect with East Prussia.
- In August 1939, Germany signed a Non-Aggression Pact with Russia, but Poland was accused of committing atrocities against Germans who were living there.

Major Events of the Second World War

Attack on Pearl Harbour

- Pearl Harbour (Hawaii) was a US naval base near Honolulu, Hawai. America followed a policy of strict neutrality during the Second World War.
- On 7th December, 1941, Japan under the command of General Tojo, ordered a surprise aerial attack on Pearl Harbour. As a result on 8th December, 1941, the US declared war on Japan.
- The Americans campaigned against Japan to free the islands in the South West Pacific and destroyed many Japanese ships and aircrafts. However, Japan still remained strong in Manchuria (China) and other areas.

Bombings of Hiroshima and Nagasaki

- At the Potsdam conference on 26th July, 1945, the Allied Powers asked Japan to surrender, but Japan refused. As a result, the first atomic bomb was dropped on Hiroshima on 6th August, 1945, and another bomb was dropped on Nagasaki on 9th August, 1945.
- After these bombings, Japan agreed to surrender on the terms of the Potsdam declaration on 10th August, 1945.
- Japan officially surrendered unconditionally on 2nd September, 1945. With this, the Second World War ended.

Consequences of the Second World War

Defeat of Axis Powers

- Germany was divided into zones under the army of each of the Allied Powers.
- The federal republic of Germany (West Germany) was administered by UK, France and the USA with Bonn as the capital. It came under the Capitalist bloc.
- Japan and Italy became very weak. American army occupied Japan in 1952. All the lands acquired or captured by Japan since 1895 were taken away.

Formation of the United Nations

- The immense loss of man and money in the Second World War made every nation serious to prevent any future wars.
- The three big leaders, Frank D Roosevelt (US President), Winston Churchill (Prime Minister of Britain) and Josef Stalin (Premier of Russia) met at Yalta in Crimea in February, 1945 to discuss about international peace. This meeting led to the formation of United Nations on 24th October, 1945.

The Cold War

- Russia (USSR) and USA fought together in the Second World War against the Axis Powers, but a split get formed in ideology between them after the end of the Second World War.
- Both of these countries did not engage in actual fight against each other but an extreme political tension developed between them.
- As a result of this political tension, each of them adopted policies to strengthen themselves and weaken the other with armed conflict. This was known as the Cold War.
- Some of the policies of the Cold War included formation of the military alliances, arms race by gathering nuclear and conventional weapons, economic warfare and proxy wars.

Main Power Blocs of Cold War

(i) The Democratic and Capitalist Bloc It was led by USA called Western bloc or American bloc. They believed in liberal democracy based on capitalism. This bloc comprised of Britain, France, Belgium, Italy, Canada, Australia, Netherlands, Greece, Pakistan, Turkey, etc.

(ii) The Communist Bloc It was led by the USSR, called as Eastern bloc or Soviet bloc. They believed in communism based on Marxist theory. Soviet bloc countries viewed Western bloc democracy as benefiting only the rich and upper middle class.

EXAM ORIENTED QUESTIONS

TYPE - 1 — 1 Mark

Multiple Choice Questions

Q.1 Complete the given analogy about beginning of wars
First World War: 1914 :: Second World War:
(a) 1929 (b) 1939
(c) 1938 (d) 1945

Ans. (b) 1939

Q.2 Identify the odd one out regarding the Allied powers of Second World War.
(a) France (b) Italy
(c) US (d) UK

Ans. (b) Italy

Q.3 Which among the following initially supported Germany but later joined the Allies?
(a) Great Britain (b) Russia
(c) USA (d) France

Ans. (b) Russia

Q.4 The Treaty of Versailles mandated Germany to pay a war compensation of **(ICSE Specimen Semester-II 2022)**
(a) 35 billion dollars (b) 40 billion dollars
(c) 33 billion dollars (d) 50 million pounds

Ans. (c) 33 billion dollars

Q.5 Which of the following was the cause of failure of the League of the Nations?
(a) Lack of cooperation among the member nations.
(b) Some countries wanted to use the League for their own benefits.
(c) There was threat of war between Italy and Greece.
(d) All of the above

Ans. (d) All of the above

Q.6 Hitler attacked Poland because he wanted to **(ICSE Specimen 2023)**
(a) seize the coal mines
(b) militarise the Rhine valley
(c) regain the Danzig port
(d) control the trade

Ans. (c) regain the Danzig port

Exp. The port of Danzig was crucial for Germany because of its location on the Baltic sea, providing easy access for trade and military operations, making it strategically important for Germany's expansion.

Q.7 Complete the given analogy.
Bomb at Hiroshima : 6th August, 1945 : : Bomb at Nagasaki : ?
(a) 7th August, 1945 (b) 8th August, 1945
(c) 9th August, 1945 (d) 10th August, 1945

Ans. (c) 9th August, 1945

Q.8 Which of the following European country remained neutral during World War II?
(a) Switzerland (b) Germany
(c) Italy (d) France

Ans. (a) Switzerland

Exp. Switzerland stayed neutral during the Second World War, meaning it didn't join either side of the war and avoided fighting, despite being surrounded by fighting countries.

Q.9 Identify which of the following pairs are correct.
P : In August 1959, Germany signed a Non-Aggression Pact with Russia.
Q : The Axis Powers consisted of Germany, Italy and USA.
R : The Treaty of Versailles played a major role in World War II
S : The League failed to stop aggressive actions by Axis Powers, leading to war.

Options
(a) P and Q (b) P and R
(c) R and S (d) Q and R

Ans. (c) R and S

Q.10 The German battleship Schleswig-Holstein began to shoot at a military depot in Danzig, Poland. This armed offensive signalled the beginning of a global conflict that lasted six years and involved over 100 million people from 30 countries. *The Hindu, 29th August, 2019*
Identify the war being discussed in the news above.

Options
(a) Crimean War (b) World War I
(c) World War II (d) Cold War

Ans. (c) World War II

Q.11 Identify the cities most affected by American action in World War II. **(ICSE Specimen 2025)**
(a) Rome, Berlin (b) Tokyo, Berlin
(c) Hiroshima, Nagasaki (d) Tokyo, Rome

Ans. (c) Hiroshima, Nagasaki

Q12. Arrange the following events in chronological order.

(i) Treaty of Versailles

(ii) Hitler's invasion of Poland

(iii) Japanese attack on Pearl Harbour

(iv) Japanese invasion of China

(a) (i), (ii), (iii) and (iv) (b) (i), (iv), (ii) and (iii)

(c) (i), (iii), (iv) and (ii) (d) (i), (iv), (iii) and (ii)

Ans. (b) (i), (iv), (ii) and (iii)

Exp. Treaty of Versailles was signed after first World War in 1919.

Japanese invaded China in 1931.

Hitler invaded of Poland on 1st September, 1939.

On 7th December, 1941, Japan attacked the U.S. naval base at Pearl Harbour.

Q.13 Which incident depicted in the below cartoon led to the beginning of the Second World War? **ICSE 2024**

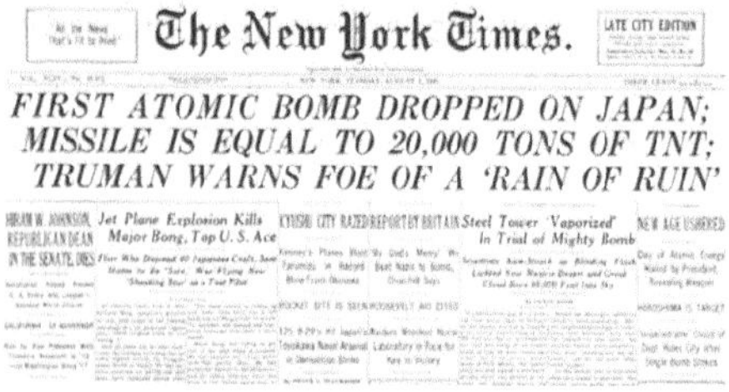
The New York Times.

FIRST ATOMIC BOMB DROPPED ON JAPAN; MISSILE IS EQUAL TO 20,000 TONS OF TNT; TRUMAN WARNS FOE OF A 'RAIN OF RUIN'

(a) Hitler's policy of imperialism

(b) Hitler's attack on Poland

(c) Hitler's annexation of Austria

(d) Hitler's attack on Czechoslovakia

Ans. (b) Hitler's attack on Poland

Q.14 Complete the given analogy.

Democratic bloc : America : : Communist bloc : ?

(a) England (b) France (c) Belgium (d) USSR

Ans. (d) USSR

TYPE - 2 1 Mark

Assertion-Reason Questions

Q.1 Read the two statements given below about The Second World War and select the option that shows the correct relationship between (A) and (R).

Assertion (A) The Axis Powers included Germany, Italy, etc.

Reason (R) These countries formed an alliance to challenge the Allied Powers during World War II.

(a) R contradicts A

(b) R is the reason for A

(c) A is true but R is false

(d) A and R are independent of each other

Ans. (b) R is the reason for A

Q.2 Read the two statements given below about the Treaty of Versailles and select the option that shows the correct relationship between (A) and (R).

Assertion (A) The Treaty of Versailles played a significant role in World War II.

Reason (R) The treaty's harsh conditions led to economic hardship and political instability in Germany, fostering the rise of Mussolini

(a) R contradicts A

(b) R is the reason for A

(c) A is true but R is false

(d) A and R are independent of each other

Ans. (c) A is true but R is false

Q.3 Read the two statements given below about the entry of USA in World War II and select the option that shows the correct relationship between (A) and (R).

Assertion (A) The attack on Pearl Harbour by Japan led to the United States joining of World War II.

Reason (R) The United States had been neutral in the war but the surprise attack forced them to declare war on Japan.

(a) R contradicts A

(b) R is the reason for A

(c) A is true but R is false

(d) A and R are independent of each other

Ans. (b) R is the reason for A

Q.4. Read the two statements given below about the Second World War and select the option that shows the correct relationship between (A) and (R).

Assertion (A) The peace treaties signed after the end of the First World War sowed the seeds for the Second World War.

Reason (R) The Second World War was a continuation of the First World War.

(a) R contradicts A

(b) R is the reason for A

(c) A is true but R is false

(d) A and R are independent of each other

Ans. (b) R is the reason for A

Q.5 Read the two statements given below about the beginning of World War II and select the option that shows the correct relationship between (A) and (R).

Assertion (A) The invasion of Poland by Germany marked the beginning of World War II.

Reason (R) Poland's invasion led to the declaration of war by Britain and France against Germany.

(a) R contradicts A

(b) R is the reason for A

(c) A is true but R is false

(d) A and R are independent of each other

Ans. (b) R is the reason for A

TYPE - 3 2 Marks

Very Short Answer Type Questions

Q.1 Name any two countries that were part of the Axis powers.

Ans. The two countries that were part of the Axis powers were

(i) Germany (ii) Italy

Q.2 Read the extract given below and answer the questions.

The World War II lasted for over 6 years and led to the collapse of Nazi Germany, Japanese and Italian Empires, dissolution of the League of Nations and creation of the United Nations. The Soviet Union and United States emerged as rival superpowers, setting the stage for the nearly half-century long Cold War.

Times of India

(i) When did the Second World War end?

(ii) When did the United Nations come into existence?

Ans. (i) The Second World War ended on 2nd September, 1945.

(ii) The United Nations came into existence on 24th October, 1945.

Q.3 State any two objections imposed by the Treaty of Versailles on the German military power.

Ans. The two major objections imposed by the Treaty of Versailles on the German military power were as follows

(i) The army was restricted to a force of 1 lakh soldiers only.

(ii) The navy was limited to 15,000 men and 24 ships.

Q.4 State the significance of the policy of appeasement as a cause for the Second World War.

Ans. Policy of appeasement is a diplomatic policy of making political or material compromise with enemy power in order to avoid conflict. Britain and France followed this policy and tried to appease Germany and Hitler. They hoped that by meeting Hitler's demand, he would be satisfied and there would not be any war.

Q.5 Mention any two factors which were responsible for the failure of the League of Nations.

Ans. The two factors which were responsible for failure of this League were as follows

(i) Lack of cooperation among the member-nations.

(ii) The League had no army to depend upon.

Q.6 Mention two reasons why Britain and France followed the appeasement towards Germany in 1930s.

Ans. Britain and France followed the appeasement towards Germany in 1930s because

(i) Britain and France felt that the Germany had a real cause of grievances and if their grievances were removed, they would not disturb others.

(ii) Both wanted to check the communist ideology of Russia. So, that they appeased Germany by ignoring its imperialist attitude.

Q.7 Name the two organisations which were formed.

(i) As a consequence of the World War I

(ii) After the World War II

Ans. (i) League of Nation was formed after World War I.

(ii) United Nations (UN) was formed in 1945 by replacing the League of Nations.

Q.8 Why the Cold War emerged after the Second World War? Which two superpowers were the main opponents?

Ans. The Cold War emerged after the Second World War due to the differences in the policies of the countries. The USA and the USSR were the two opponents of the Cold War.

Q.9 Imagine you were a leader in Germany during the time of the Second World War. Why do you think the port of Danzig was so important for Germany? Think about its location and what it could be used for.

Ans. If I were a leader in Germany, I would see the port of Danzig as very important because it gave easy access to the Baltic sea. This would help Germany with trade, allowing goods to move in and out easily. It was also useful for military operations and expansion.

Q.10 Analyse the issue which became the major cause of conflict between Germany and Polland during World War II.

Ans. The major issue between Germany and Poland during World War II was the dispute over Danzig and the Polish corridor. Hitler wanted to annex Danzig, a city with a German population, and gain control of the corridor to connect mainland Germany with East Prussia.

When Poland refused these demands, Germany invaded Poland on 1st September, 1939 leading to the start of World War II.

Q.11 How Germany was divided after the defeat of the Axis powers?

Ans. After the defeat of the Axis powers in World War II, Germany was divided into four zones controlled by the Allied powers-the United States, the Soviet Union, Britain, and France.

Later, in 1949, this division led to the formation of two separate countries: West Germany (Federal Republic of Germany) under democratic rule and East Germany (German Democratic Republic) under communist rule.

Q.12 Name two countries each belonging to the Capitalist Bloc and the Communist Bloc.

Ans. Two countries belonging to the Capitalist Bloc were Britain and France.

Two countries belonging to the Communist Bloc were Poland and Hungary.

TYPE - 4 — 3 Marks

Short Answer Type Questions

Q.1 Mention three causes behind the beginning of the Second World War.

Ans. Three main causes behind the beginning of the Second World War were as follows

(i) **Treaty of Versailles** The harsh conditions imposed on Germany after the First World War created anger and frustration, leading to the rise of Hitler and his aggressive policies.

(ii) **Rise of Fascism and Nazism** Leaders like Mussolini in Italy and Hitler in Germany pushed for expansion and militarisation, aiming to restore their countries' power.

(iii) **Policy of Appeasement** The British and French governments agreed in to Hitler's demands, which encouraged him to take more aggressive actions, ultimately leading to war.

Q.2 With reference to the causes of the Second World War, answer the following question.

Explain how the ideologies of Fascism and Nazism led to the Second World War.

Ans. Fascism and Nazism directly contributed to the outbreak of the Second World War in following ways

- **Fascism** was led by Mussolini in Italy and focused on creating a powerful state through military conquest. Thus, Italy invaded Ethiopia (1935) and later Albania (1939) to expand its empire by ignoring international agreements.
- **Nazism** was led by Hitler in Germany and based on idea of racial superiority, anti-Semitism, and territorial expansion. Hitler aimed to conquer Eastern Europe (Lebensraum) and ignored the Treaty of Versailles by rebuilding Germany's military.
- **Both** regimes rejected democracy and diplomacy, believing in war as a means to achieve national goals. Their aggressive policies and alliance (Rome-Berlin Axis, 1936) encouraged military action, ultimately leading to Germany's invasion of Poland in 1939, which triggered Second World War.

Q.3 Analyse the consequences of the Second World War with reference to the formation of the United Nations.

Ans. The Second World War led to the formation of the United Nations in 1945 because of the devastation caused by the war and the failure of the League of Nations to prevent conflict. World leaders recognised the need for a stronger international organisation to promote peace and cooperation.

The Atlantic Charter (1941) and the Yalta Conference (1945) set the foundation for the UN which aimed to ensure global security, human rights and prevent future wars. The UN replaced the League of Nations and continues to address global challenges.

Q.4 Explain the reasons behind the failure of the League of Nations to maintain peace.

Ans. The League of Nations failed to maintain peace due to several key reasons, which were as follows

- **Lack of Military Power** The League had no army to enforce its decisions thus making it ineffective in stopping aggressors.
- **Absence of Major Powers** The USA never joined the league, while Germany and the USSR were initially excluded which weakened its influence.

Q.5 Explain about the major power blocs formed after the end of the Second World War.

Ans. The major power blocs formed after the end of the Second World War were as follows

(i) **The Democratic and Capitalist Bloc** It was led by USA called Western bloc or American bloc. They believed in liberal democracy based on capitalism. This bloc comprised of Britain, France, Belgium, Italy, Canada, Australia, Netherlands, Greece, Pakistan, Turkey, etc.

(ii) **The Communist Bloc** It was led by the USSR, called as Easter bloc or Soviet bloc. They believed in communism based on Marxist theory. Soviet bloc countries viewed Western democracy as benefiting only the rich and upper middle class.

TYPE - 5 — 4 Marks

Long Answer Type Questions

Q.1 How did the Attack on Pearl Harbour in 1941 impact the United States' involvement in the Second World War?

Ans. The Attack on Pearl Harbor had a profound impact on the United States' involvement in the Second World War which were as follows

- **US Entry into the War** The surprise attack by Japan on the US naval base in Hawaii led to the United States declaring war on Japan the following day. This marked the shift from a policy of neutrality to active participation in the war Second World War.
- **Global Conflict Expansion** Following Japan's attack other allies, (Germany and Italy) also declared war on the United States. This expanded the conflict into a global war with the US.

- **Mobilisation of Resources** The attack united the American public and led to massive mobilisation of military and industrial resources. The US economy shifted to war production, and millions of soldiers were recruited, significantly boosted the Allied war effort.
- **Strategic Importance** The attack on Pearl Harbour prompted the US to focus on defeating Japan in the Pacific theater while also combating Nazi Germany in Europe. It significantly altered the balance of power in the war and accelerated the US's rise as a global superpower.

Q.2 With reference to the World War II, explain the following.

(i) How did the bombings of Hiroshima and Nagasaki influence Japan's decision to surrender and bring an end to the Second World War?

(ii) What were the main consequences of the Second World War on Germany, Italy and Japan.

Ans. (i) The bombings of Hiroshima and Nagasaki in August, 1945 had a major impact on Japan. The destruction caused by the atomic bombs killed thousands of people and caused massive damage to the cities. Japan realised it could not continue the war with such overwhelming power against it. The bombings, along with the Soviet Union call to declare war on Japan, forced Japan to surrender.

On 2nd September, 1945, Japan officially surrendered, which ended the Second World War. The bombings highlighted the devastating power of nuclear weapons.

(ii) The consequences of the Second World War on Germany, Italy and Japan were as follows

- Germany was divided into two parts, with the Allies controlling the West.
- Italy and Japan lost their territories and power. The war caused economic struggles, and the countries faced political changes.
- In Germany, the rise of the Cold War divided the world into two opposing blocs.

Q.3 The Second World War reshape global politics and international relations. Justify the statement with suitable examples.

Ans. The Second World War reshaped global politics in several ways such as

- **Creation of the United Nations** The UN was formed to maintain peace and prevent future conflicts. It becomes a central platform for international diplomacy.
- **Decolonisation** European powers were weakened by the war, leading to independence movements in Asia and Africa.
- **Division of Germany and Europe** Germany was divided into East and West, and symbolised the Cold War as division between communist and capitalist ideologies.
- **New Alliances** Organisations like NATO and economic bodies like the IMF were created, to shape political and economic relations globally.

These changes significantly influenced global politics and international relations throughout the 20th century.

Q.4 Mention how the First World War differ from the Second World War.

Ans. The First World War was different from the Second World War in following ways

Aspect	World War I	World War II
Causes	Caused by imperial rivalries, militarism, alliances, and nationalism, sparked by the assassination of Archduke Franz Ferdinand.	Caused by Nazi desire for more land, fascism, revenge for the Treaty of Versailles, and unresolved issues from WWI.
Duration	It was fought between the period of 1914 to 1918.	It was fought between the period of 1939 to 1945.
Political Context	Focused on European imperial powers competing for global dominance, with rising nationalism and military buildups.	Marked by the rise of fascist regimes (Germany, Italy, Japan), and ideological conflicts between fascism and democracy.
Post-War Impact	The major impacts were collapse of empires, creation of new nations and the establishment of the League of Nations.	The major impacts were division of Germany, creation of the United Nations, and the beginning of the Cold War between the USA and the Soviet Union.

TYPE - 6 — 10 Marks

Structured Questions

Q.1 Look at the picture given below and answer the following questions.

(i) Identify the leader in the above picture. Mention any two of his ideologies. **(3)**

(ii) Invasion of Poland by this leader is often considered the immediate cause of the Second World War. Analyse the reasons behind this invasion and its impact on the global scenario. **(4)**

(iii) Mention any three causes for his rise to power. **(3)**

Ans. (i) The leader shown in this picture is Adolf Hitler. Two major ideologies of him were as follows

(a) **Nazism (Racial Superiority)** Belief in the superiority of the Aryan race and the need for racial purity, leading to the persecution of Jews and other minorities.

(b) **Militarism and Expansionism** Advocacy for territorial expansion (Lebensraum) to create a greater German Empire through military conquest.

(ii) Hitler invaded Poland in 1939 due to the following reasons

- He wanted to reunite Germany and regain lost land under the Treaty of Versailles. Poland controlled the port of Danzig, which was mostly German- speaking area and Hitler wanted to connect Germany with East Prussia.
- The invasion led Britain and France to declare war on Germany, marking the start of the Second World War.
- The attack also revealed the failure of diplomacy and appeasement, triggering to a global conflict by involving many nations, and reshaping the world's political landscape.

(iii) Three major causes behind his rise to power were as follows

(a) **Economic Instability** The Great Depression caused massive unemployment, turned many Germans to Hitler's promise of economic recovery.

(b) **Weak Weimar Republic** The Weimar government was politically unstable, with frequent changes in leadership, making it vulnerable to extremist parties like the Nazis who promised strong, decisive leadership.

(c) **Nazi Propaganda and Leadership** Hitler's powerful speeches and nationalist propaganda, along with his promises to restore Germany's strength and overturn the Treaty of Versailles, helped gain widespread support.

Q.2 **With reference to the Axis powers and Allied powers, Answer the following Questions.**

(i) The Attack on Pearl Harbour in 1941 was a turning point in World War II, leading to a major shift in U.S. involvement. How did this attack influence the United States' role in the Second World War? (4)

(ii) How did the Japanese invasion of China in 1931 contribute to the tensions leading to World War II in the Pacific? (3)

(iii) Why was the Treaty of Versailles (1919) seen as humiliating by many Germans? (3)

Ans. (i) For answer, refer to Q.1 of Long Answer Type Questions.

(ii) The Japanese invasion of China began in 1931 with the invasion of Manchuria etc. Japan sought to expand its empire and control China's resources. The invasion was marked by terrible act, where hundreds of thousands of Chinese civilians were killed.

Even though China was up against a stronger military, both the Nationalist and Communist forces in China fought back and resisted. The invasion weakened China and contributed to the tensions that led to World War II in the Pacific.

(iii) The Treaty of Versailles (1919) was seen as humiliating by many Germans due to the following reasons

- It placed full blame for the First World War on Germany and damaged its national pride.
- Germany had to pay large amounts of money as compensation because of the treaty, which caused its economy to suffer greatly.
- Germany's military strength was limited, reduced under this treaty hence affected the national pride.
- Germany lost significant territories and colonies, thus weakened its power in European nations.

Q.3 Read the passage given and answer the following questions. **(ICSE 2025)**

In an effort to secure resources for its expanding industries, Japan invaded the northern Chinese province of Manchuria. Although many Western nations protested the Japanese action, most members of the League of Nations, including Canada, opposed any form of military intervention to defend Chinese sovereignty. A League of Nations commission, headed by the British diplomat Lord Lytton, was dispatched to Manchuria to investigate.

-Loyal Edmonton Regiment Museum

(i) How did the incident being described above become a cause for the Second World War?

(ii) Mention any three reasons for Hitler's attack on Poland.

(iii) Mention any four reasons for the failure of the League of Nations.

Ans. (i) The Manchurian Incident (1931) exposed the weakness of the League of Nations, as it failed to take strong action against Japan. Despite investigations, no military intervention was made, encouraging aggressive expansionism.

This emboldened other axis powers like Germany and Italy, showing that international bodies would not stop territorial invasions. Hitler and Mussolini saw this as a green light for their own ambitions, leading to further aggression in Europe and Africa. The failure of diplomacy and unchecked invasions ultimately escalated tensions, contributing to World War II.

(ii) Three reasons for Hitler's attack on Poland were

(a) **Reclaiming Lost Territory** Hitler wanted to take back Polish lands that Germany lost after World War I under the Treaty of Versailles.

(b) **Lebensraum (Living Space)** He aimed to expand German territory for its growing population.

(c) **Weak Western Response** Britain and France followed a policy of appeasement, making Hitler believe they would not intervene.

(iii) Four reasons for the failure of the League of Nations were

(a) **Lack of Cooperation Among Member Nations** Countries prioritised their own interests rather than supporting the League's principles of collective security. Even member nations ignored League decisions when it did not suit them.

(b) **Failure to Prevent Aggression** The League remained inactive when Poland seised Lithuania (1920) and Italy refused intervention in the Greece-Italy conflict (1923). This weakened its authority.

(c) **Ineffectiveness Against Expansionist Powers** The League failed to act when Italy annexed Abyssinia, Japan took Manchuria, and Germany took Austria and Czechoslovakia. This encouraged further aggression.

(d) **Loss of Faith in the League** The League's inability to stop conflicts led nations to lose trust in it. Instead of maintaining peace, countries started preparing for war, leading to World War II.

12

UNITED NATIONS AND ITS MAJOR AGENCIES

United Nations (UN)

- United Nations was set-up on 24th October, 1945 at San Francisco.
- The headquarters of United Nations is situated at New York City in the USA.

Objectives of the United Nations

The objectives of the United Nations have been outlined in the Preamble of the UN Charter. The major objectives of the United Nations are

- To maintain international peace and security.
- To develop friendly relations among nations on the basis of equality and self-determination.
- To foster worldwide cooperation in solving economic, social, cultural and humanitarian problems.
- To promote human rights and fundamental freedoms for the people of the world.

UN Logo

Composition and Functions of Important Organs of UN

The United Nations has 6 organs which are

- The General Assembly
- The United Nations Security Council
- The International Court of Justice
- The Secretariat
- The Trusteeship Council
- The Economic and Social Council

Three of these organs are discussed below

The General Assembly

It is also known as the Parliament of the United Nations because all the member nations of UN are member of it.

Composition

- The United Nations General Assembly consists of 193 member states, with each country having one vote.
- The regular session of the General Assembly begins every year on the third Tuesday in September and continues until the third week of December.
- At every new regular session, the assembly elects a new President, 21 Vice-Presidents and the Chairman of each of the 6 main committees of the General Assembly.
- Special Sessions are organised at the request of the Security Counsellor or at the special request by a majority of members.
- Important decisions like appointment, suspension and passing of budget are taken by 2/3rd majority while other normal day to day life decisions are taken by a simple majority.

Functions

- It discusses any question relating to international peace, security and make recommendations on it.

- It discusses and make recommendations on any questions within the scope of the charter or affecting the powers and functions of any organ of the United Nations.
- It appoints the Secretary-General, ICJ judges, etc on the recommendation of the Security Council.
- It considers and approves the United Nations budget and establish the financial assessments of member states.

United Nations Security Council (UNSC)

- UNSC is the executive body of the United Nations which was founded on 24th October, 1945.
- Its headquarters is located at New York, USA.

Composition

- The Council has 15 members: five permanent (China, France, Russia, the UK, and the US) and 10 non-permanent members (5 Afro-Asian, 2 Latin American, 2 Western European, 1 Eastern European).
- Non-permanent members serve a two-year term that are elected by a two-thirds majority of General Assembly.

Veto Power

- The veto power in the UN Security Council means that any of the five permanent members can stop a decision from being passed by giving a negative vote.
- It is used for important issues like peace, security and conflicts.

Functions

- The Security Council ensures global peace and security based on the United Nations' principles and objectives.
- It urges members to use economic sanctions and non-violent measures to prevent or stop aggression.
- It may take military action against an aggressor.
- It recommends the appointment of the Secretary-General to the General Assembly and, together with the Assembly, elects judges for the International Court of Justice.

The International Court of Justice (ICJ)

- It is the principal judicial organ of the UN which was established in June 1945 by the Charter of the UN and began to work in April 1946.
- Its headquarters is located at the Hague (Netherlands).
- It is the only organ of the UN among the 6 organs which is not located in New York in USA.
- Its official languages are English and French.

Composition

- The court has 15 judges, that are elected for a term of 9 years by the UN General Assembly and Security Council sitting separately.
- One-third of the seats are elected every 3 years, and judges can be impeached through other judges vote.
- The President and Vice-President are elected for 3-year terms.

Functions

- The court resolves cases based on international treaties, with consent from involved parties.
- It settles legal disputes between states according to international law.
- The court provides advisory opinions to authorised UN organs and agencies.
- It contributes to the development and clarification of international law and may recommend about settlement methods.

Major Agencies of the UN

There are some specialised agencies that carry out various functions of UN.
The major agencies of the UN are discussed below

The United Nations International Children's Emergency Fund (UNICEF)

- UNICEF was established by the UN General Assembly in 1946 to address children's emergency needs.

UNICEF Logo

- Its mission was expanded in 1950, and the name was changed to United Nations Children's Fund.
- Its headquarters is located at New York.
- UNICEF was awarded the Nobel Peace Prize in 1965 and the Indira Gandhi Peace Prize in 1989.

Functions of UNICEF

- UNICEF focuses on child protection, health, survival and well-being, through immunisation programmes.
- It funds training for health workers, teachers, nutritionists, etc.
- It provides technical supplies and equipment to villages.
- It works to prevent diseases like tuberculosis, malaria, eye and skin diseases.

United Nations Educational, Scientific and Cultural Organisation (UNESCO)

- UNESCO was established on 4th November, 1946 with the main objective to contribute to the peace and security in the world. UNESCO promotes collaboration among nations through education, science, culture and communication.
- Its headquarters is located at Paris.
- All the members of the UN are automatically entitled to the membership of UNESCO.

UNESCO Logo

Functions of UNESCO in Preservation of Cultural Heritage

- UNESCO offers technical support, equipment and funds for preserving monuments like the Taj Mahal and others.
- It works to protect global heritage, including books, artwork and rare manuscripts, and assists in their translation.
- It fosters cultural exchange through initiatives like art exhibitions and travel sponsorships.
- It encourages artistic creation in literature and fine arts.

Functions of UNESCO in Scientific Activities

- It promotes research in the fields like Geology, Mathematics, Physics and Oceanography, etc.
- It helps in correcting the existing imbalances in scientific and technological manpower.
- It organises conferences to bring scientists together.
- It circulates information through journals. Courier is the official monthly magazine of UNESCO.

Functions of UNESCO in Promotion of Education

- It works for removal of illiteracy by encouraging adult education, distance education and open school education into countries.
- It provides financial assistance for the education of disabled children.
- It also lays special emphasis on the education of women and girls.
- It advices about the production of textbooks, syllabus and teacher-training.

World Health Organisation (WHO)

- It was established on 7th April, 1948 with the objective of achieving the highest possible level of health for all.
- Its headquarters is located at Geneva in Switzerland.
- Its main aim is to help the government to raise the standards of public health and medical research.

WHO Logo

Functions of WHO

- It helps countries to improve their health system by building up infrastructure. .
- It launches programmes to immunise children against 6 major diseases such as measles, diphtheria, tetanus, tuberculosis, polio and whooping cough.
- It organises conferences, seminars and training activities for health care personnel.
- It publishes health journals to create health consciousness among people.

EXAM ORIENTED QUESTIONS

TYPE - 1 — 1 Mark

Multiple Choice Questions

Q.1 Which of the following statements is correct regarding the establishment of the United Nations?
(a) The United Nations was set up on 24th October, 1946.
(b) The United Nations was set up on 24th October, 1945.
(c) The United Nations was set up on 24th September, 1945.
(d) The United Nations was set up on 22th September, 1945.

Ans. (b) The United Nations was set up on 24th October, 1945.

Q.2 Complete the given analogy.
First World War : League of Nations :: Second World War : ?
(a) NATO
(b) United Nations
(c) SEATO
(d) Warsaw Pact

Ans. (b) United Nations

Exp. The devastation caused by the Second World War, led to the creation of the United Nations in 1945 to promote peace, security and human rights.

Q.3 Which of the following statements is not correct about the language of the United Nations?
(a) The United Nations has six official languages including French and Spanish.
(b) English is the only working language used in all UN meetings.
(c) All official languages are used in the UN's official documents and meetings.
(d) Any member state can use one of the official languages during the General Assembly.

Ans. (b) English is the only working language used in all UN meetings.

Q.4 Which of the following is not an objective of the United Nations Organisation? **(ICSE 2025)**
(a) Disarm (b) Disengage
(c) Decolonise (d) Develop

Ans. (b) Disengage

Q.5 Identify the odd one out of the following regarding the objective of the UNICEF.
(a) It provides help to children and mothers in case of emergencies.
(b) It maintain international peace and security.
(c) It focuses on improving the health, nutrition and overall well-being as children.
(d) It support access to quality education for all children.

Ans. (b) It maintain international peace and security.

Q.6 "This organ of United Nations provides a platform where all member states can discuss global issues, make decisions on peacekeeping operations, and address humanitarian concerns. It serves as a forum for nations to resolve conflicts diplomatically and cooperatively." *The Indian Express*
Which organ of the United Nations is being referred to in the news above?
(a) Security Council (b) Secretariat
(c) Economic and Social Council (d) General Assembly

Ans. (d) General Assembly

Exp. The General Assembly is where all UN member countries meet to discuss world issues, make decisions on peace, and cooperate on humanitarian matters, just like the news describes.

Q.7 Identify the correct statement about the composition of the General Assembly.
(a) The General Assembly consists of 193 member states, each with one vote.
(b) Only the permanent members of the Security Council can participate in the General Assembly's sessions.
(c) The General Assembly is made up of only 10 member states that are elected every 2 years.
(d) The General Assembly has the authority to make legally binding decisions on all countries.

Ans. (a) The General Assembly consists of 193 member states, each with one vote.

Q.8 Which of the following is not a function of the General Assembly?
(a) Electing the Judges of the International Court of Justice.
(b) Appointing the Secretary-General.
(c) Enforcing economic sanctions against aggressor nations.
(d) Discussing international peace and security issues.

Ans. (c) Enforcing economic sanctions against aggressor nations.

Q.9 Which of the following countries will not be part of this cartoon? **(ICSE Specimen 2025)**

(a) China (b) Japan (c) Russia (d) Britain

Ans. (b) Japan

Exp. The veto power in the UN Security Council is held by five permanent members - the United States, the United Kingdom, France, Russia and China.

Q.10 The non-permanent members of the Security Council are elected by the members of .... **(ICSE Specimen 2022)**

(a) General Assembly
(b) International Court of Justice
(c) The Trusteeship Council
(d) The Secretariat

Ans. (a) General Assembly

Exp. The General Assembly elects 10 non-permanent members of the Security Council for a 2-year term. These members help in making decisions about world peace and security.

Q.11 The International Court of Justice consists of .... Judges. **(ICSE 2023)**

(a) 9 (b) 15 (c) 10 (d) 20

Ans. (b) 15

Q.12 Read the description given below and identify the organisation.

It is the only organ of the UN among the 6 organs which is not located in New York, USA.

(a) WHO (b) UNICEF
(c) UNESCO (d) ICJ

Ans. (d) ICJ

Exp. The International Court of Justice (ICJ) is the principal judicial body of the United Nations which resolves disputes between states and provides advisory opinions on international legal matters.

Q.13 Complete the given analogy.

Headquarter of UN : New York :: Headquarter of ICJ: ?

(a) Geneva (b) The Hague
(c) Vienna (d) Paris

Ans. (b) The Hague

Q.14 Read the details given below and identify which of the following pairs are correct?

P : UNICEF was established in 1945.
Q : UNICEF stands for the United Nations Children Free Environment.
R : UNICEF is an international organisation.
S : UNICEF focuses on child protection, education, and health.

Options

(a) P and Q (b) R and S (c) Q and R (d) S and Q

Ans. (b) R and S

Q.15 Identify the odd one out regarding UNESCO's contributions to scientific activities.

(a) Supporting global water resource management through the research programmes.
(b) Coordinating the technology for the benefits of the mankind.
(c) Administering the World Heritage Sites list to preserve cultural landmarks.
(d) Promoting open access to scientific knowledge and research.

Ans. (c) Administering the World Heritage Sites list to preserve cultural landmarks.

Q.16 Which agency of the United Nations Organisation is associated with this picture? **(ICSE 2025)**

(a) UNESCO (b) UNICEF
(c) WHO (d) ILO

Ans. (a) UNESCO

Q.17 Read the newspaper heading and identify the organisation responsible for issuing global health warnings.

(a) United Nations Educational, Scientific and Cultural Organisation.
(b) United Nations International Children's Emergency Fund.
(c) World Health Organisation.
(d) United Nations High Commissioner for Refugees.

Ans. (c) World Health Organisation.

TYPE - 2 — 1 Mark

Assertion-Reason Questions

Q.1 Read the two statements given below about the United Nations and select the option that shows the correct relationship between (A) and (R).

Assertion (A) The United Nations has 193 member states.

Reason (R) The UN was initially formed with 51 founding members, but it has grown over time through the inclusion of new countries.

(a) R contradicts A
(b) R is the reason for A
(c) A is true but R is false
(d) A and R are independent of each other

Ans. (b) R is the reason for A

Q.2 Read the two statements given below about the United Nations and select the option that shows the correct relationship between (A) and (R).

Assertion (A) The United Nations was founded to promote international cooperation and maintain peace.

Reason (R) The United Nations was created after the success of the League of Nations.

(a) R contradicts A
(b) R is the reason for A
(c) A is true but R is false
(d) A and R are independent of each other

Ans. (c) A is true but R is false

Q.3 Read the two statements given below about the United Nations and select the option that shows the correct relationship between (A) and (R).

Assertion (A) The United Nations promotes human rights through various conventions and treaties.

Reason (R) The universal declaration of human rights, adopted by the UN in 1948, sets out fundamental human rights that should be protected for all people.

(a) R contradicts A
(b) R is the reason for A
(c) A is true but R is false
(d) A and R are independent of each other

Ans. (b) R is the reason for A

Q.4 Read the two statements given below about the United Nations and select the option that shows the correct relationship between (A) and (R).

Assertion (A) The United Nations plays a key role in humanitarian efforts worldwide.

Reason (R) The UN's specialised agencies like WHO, UNICEF and UNHCR are not involved in providing aid and addressing global challenges.

(a) R contradicts A
(b) R is the reason for A
(c) A is true but R is false
(d) A and R are independent of each other

Ans. (c) A is true but R is false

Q.5 Read the two statements given below about the Security Council and select the option that shows the correct relationship between (A) and (R).

Assertion (A) The Security Council is the main decision-making body of the United Nations.

Reason (R) The General Assembly is responsible for maintaining international peace and global order.

(a) R contradicts A
(b) R is the reason for A
(c) A is true but R is false
(d) A and R are independent of each other

Ans. (d) A and R are independent of each other

TYPE - 3 — 2 Marks

Very Short Answer Type Questions

Q.1 State the two main reasons behind the formation of the United Nations.

Ans. The two main reasons behind the formation of the United Nations (UN) were as follows

(i) **To maintain international peace and security** The UN is aimed to prevent future conflicts and promote peaceful resolution of disputes.

(ii) **To promote social and economic cooperation** The UN works to improve living standards, support human rights, and foster international collaboration in solving global issues like poverty, disease and education, etc.

Q.2 When and where was the United Nations formed? What are the official languages of the UN?

Ans. United Nations was formed at San Francisco in USA on 24th October, 1945.

The official languages of the UN are Arabic, Chinese, English, French, Russian and Spanish.

Q.3 Mention the five countries that are the permanent members of the Security Council (UNSC).

Ans. The five permanent members of the Security Council are Britain, France, Russia, China and the United States of America (USA).

Q.4 State the full forms of the following agencies of the United Nations. **(ICSE Specimen 2023)**

(i) UNICEF

(ii) UNESCO

Ans. (i) UNICEF stands for United Nations International Children's Emergency Fund.

(ii) UNESCO stands for United Nations Educational, Scientific and Cultural Organisation.

Q.5 Mention any two objectives of the United Nations.

Ans. The two major objectives of the United Nations are as follows

(i) To maintain international peace and security.

(ii) To develop friendly relations among nations on the basis of equality and self-determination.

Q.6 Imagine you are a member of the United Nations General Assembly. A drought has affected many parts of the world. As a member of the Assembly, what steps would you propose to address the crisis and ensure international cooperation?

Ans. I would propose an immediate and coordinated global response. The first step would be to establish an emergency relief fund to provide food, clean water, medical supplies, and humanitarian assistance to the hardest-hit regions. I would call to member states for making swift contributions, ensuring that aid reaches those most in need. Additionally, I would advocate for long-term solutions to combat the root causes of drought, such as climate change, unsustainable agricultural practices, and water mismanagement.

Q.7 Explain the meaning of the term 'veto power' and which countries have this power?

Ans. Veto power refers to the authority granted to a member of a decision-making body to block or reject a proposal or decision, even if the majority supports it.

In the context of the United Nations Security Council (UNSC) the five permanent members—China, France, Russia, the United Kingdom, and the United States—have veto power

Q.8 Name any two of the ten non-permanent members of the UNSC.

Ans. Two non-permanent members of the United Nations Security Council (UNSC) are Algeria and Denmark.

Q.9 Mention any two qualifications required for becoming a Judge at the International Court of Justice.

Ans. The two qualifications required for becoming a Judge at the International Court of Justice are as follows

(i) Judges must be elected from among persons of high moral character and who possess the qualifications required in their respective countries for appointment to the highest judicial offices.

(ii) A person should be a jurist of recognised competence in international law.

Q.10 Analyse the major functions of the UNICEF in promotion of the scientific activities.

Ans. The UNESCO plays a crucial role in the promotion and advancement of Scientific Activities in following ways

- It promotes research in the fields like Geology, Mathematics, Physics and Oceanography etc.
- It helps in correcting the existing imbalances in scientific and technological manpower.

TYPE - 4 — 3 Marks

Short Answer Type Questions

Q.1 Mention any three powers of the United Nations Security Council.

Ans. The three powers of the United Nations Security Council (UNSC) are as follows

(i) **Maintenance of International Peace and Security** The UNSC has the authority to take action to maintain or restore international peace and security.

(ii) **Imposition of Sanctions** The Security Council can impose economic and diplomatic sanctions on countries.

(iii) **Authorisation of Military Action** The UNSC has the power to authorise the deployment of peacekeeping missions or military intervention to address conflicts or threats to global stability.

Q.2 With reference to the United Nations, explain the following.

(i) Session of the General Assembly

(ii) Composition of the Security Council

Ans. (i) The General Assembly meets once a year for its regular session, typically starting in September, although special sessions can be called anytime as per the need. Decisions are made by a two-thirds majority for most issues like budgetary matters and simple majority for ordinary matters. The presidency of the General Assembly rotates annually among the member states.

(ii) The United Nations Security Council (UNSC) has 15 members. These are divided into following groups

- **Permanent Members** Five permanent members are China, France, Russia, the United Kingdom, and the United States. These countries have veto powers also.
- **10 Non-Permanent Members** These members are elected for two-year terms by the General Assembly and also represent various regions of the world and do not have veto power.

Q.3 **"The United Nations Security Council plays a critical role in maintaining international peace and security. Justify this by mentioning any three powers or functions of the Security Council."**

Ans. The three power of the United Nations Security Council are

(i) It maintains international peace and security in accordance with the principles and purposes of the United Nations.

(ii) It investigates disputes or situations that might lead to international conflicts and recommends solutions.

(iii) It calls on member nations to apply economic sanctions or take military action to prevent or stop acts of aggression.

Q.4 **Mention any three powers of the International Court of Justice (ICJ).**

Ans. The three major powers of the International Court of Justice are as follows

(i) The Court has the power to provide advisory opinions on legal questions referred to it by the United Nations or other in authorised organisations.

(ii) The Court settles legal disputes between states according to international law, such as border disputes, territorial claims, and treaty violations.

(iii) The Court can interpret international treaties and conventions by providing clarifications on their legal meanings.

Q.5 **Explain the major functions of the UNICEF in protection of children rights across the world.**

Ans. UNICEF plays a crucial role in protecting children's rights in following ways, which are as follows

- **Advocacy for Child Rights** Promotes laws and policies to ensure children's safety, education, and healthcare.
- **Emergency Relief** Provides vital assistance to children in conflict zones and disaster-stricken areas.
- **Child Protection** Works to prevent child abuse, exploitation and ensures children's safety worldwide.

Q.6 **Explain about the role of UNESCO in promotion of education worldwide.**

Ans. The UNESCO plays a crucial role in the promotion and advancement of education in following ways

- It works for removal of illiteracy by encouraging adult education, distance education and open school education into countries.
- It provide financial assistance for the education of disabled children.
- It also lays special emphasis on the education of women and girls.

TYPE - 5   4 Marks

Long Answer Type Questions

Q.1 **Analyse those factors which encouraged global leaders to create an international body to ensure peace.**

Ans. Several key factors encouraged global leaders to establish an international organisation to maintain peace such as

- **Devastation of the two World Wars** The massive destruction, loss of lives, and economic collapse caused by World War I and World War II highlighted the urgent need for a global system to prevent future conflicts.
- **Failure of the League of Nations** The League of Nations, formed after the First World War, failed to prevent global conflicts due to its lack of authority and enforcement mechanisms. This failure underscored the necessity of a stronger and more effective organisation.
- **Fear of a Third World War** With rapid advancements in military technology, world leaders feared about another devastating world war. Therefore, a global organisation become necessity.

Q.2 **With reference to the United Nations and its related agencies, answer the following questions.**

Explain any four functions of the WHO.

Ans. The World Health Organisation (WHO) plays a vital role in global public health. Some of its functions are as follows

(i) WHO tracks and assesses global health trends including the spread of diseases and emerging health issues.

(ii) It develops guidelines for health practices, sanitation, and disease prevention to improve global health standards.

(iii) The organisation offers technical support and training to countries for improving their healthcare systems especially in underdeveloped regions.

(iv) WHO coordinates global responses to health emergencies like epidemics and pandemics, ensuring effective action and resource mobilisation.

Q.3 **A momentous achievement for India as Santiniketan, West Bengal, has been officially inscribed on UNESCO's World Heritage List.** *The Indian Express*

Explain any four functions of the UNESCO in preservation of the cultural heritage.

Ans. The four major functions of the UNESCO in preservation of the cultural heritage sites are as follows

(i) It provides technical advice and assistance, equipments and funds for the preservation of monuments like Taj Mahal and other works of art.

(ii) It aims to protect the world inheritance of books, works of art and rare manuscripts. It also helps in translating rare manuscripts.

(iii) It promotes cultural exchange between people of different countries by sponsoring travelling, art exhibitions and similar activities.

(iv) It gives encouragement to artistic creations in Literature and Fine Arts.

TYPE - 6 — 10 Marks

Structured Questions

Q.1 **The United Nations was established to be an effective peace keeping international organisation. In this context, explain the following questions.**

(i) Mention two specialised agencies of the United Nations and explain their functions briefly.

(ii) United Nations was set-up on 24th October, 1945 at San Francisco when the Charter was ratified by 29 Nations including the five permanent members of the Security Council. Discuss the objectives of the United Nations and how they contribute to global cooperation.

(iii) Name the agency that the UN set-up to deliver relief to children and mothers after Second World War. State any three of its functions.

Ans. (i) Two specialised agencies of the United Nations are UNICEF and WHO.

The functions of these agencies are

- **UNICEF** (United Nations International Children's Emergency Fund) It works to protect children's rights, support child health and immunisation, and help children in emergencies. It also provides education and nutrition support to children in need.
- **WHO** (World Health Organisation) It focuses on improving global health by providing medical care resources, promoting disease prevention, and conducting health research. It also organises immunisation programs to prevent major diseases.

(ii) The main objectives of the UN are

- To maintain international peace and security.
- To develop friendly relations among nations based on equality and self-determination.
- To foster worldwide cooperation in solving economic, social, cultural, and humanitarian problems.
- To promote human rights and fundamental freedoms for all.
- To work towards disarmament, decolonisation, and development.

The objectives of the United Nations contribute to global cooperation by providing a platform where countries can address issues like peace, security, and human rights. Through its efforts in resolving conflicts, promoting equality, and tackling global challenges, the UN helps nations collaborate for common goals, ensuring a safer, more just, and more prosperous world for everyone.

(iii) UNICEF is the agency that the UN set-up to deliver relief to children and mothers after Second World War.

For functions of UNICEF, refer to Q.5 of Short Answer Type Questions.

Q.2 **The United Nations Organisation aims to maintain international peace. With reference to its organs and agencies, answer the following.** **(ICSE Specimen 2025)**

(i) What is the composition of the International Court of Justice? **(3)**

(ii) Mention any three functions of the General Assembly. **(3)**

(iii) Gujarat's famed garba dance received the intangible heritage tag. Which agency of the United Nations is authorised to give this tag? Mention any three other contributions of that agency in the preservation of culture. **(4)**

Ans. (i) Composition of the International Court of Justice is as follows

- The International Court of Justice (ICJ) is composed of 15 Judges.
- These Judges are elected by the United Nations General Assembly and the Security Council for a term of 9 years.
- The Judges are chosen from various regions and are highly qualified in international law.

(ii) The three major functions of the General Assembly are as follows

(a) **Deliberating on International Issues** The General Assembly discusses and makes recommendations on important international issues, such as peace and security, disarmament, and human rights.

(b) **Electing Non-Permanent Members to the Security Council** The General Assembly elects 10 non-permanent members to serve in the UN Security Council for two-year terms.

(c) **Approving the UN Budget** The General Assembly approves the annual budget of the United Nations and allocates resources for the work of its agencies and programmes.

(iii) UNESCO is authorised to give this tag. For its contributions, refer to Q.3 of Long Answer Type Questions.

Q.3 Look at the image given below and answer the following questions.

(i) Name the organisation associated with the above emblem. State any two roles of the organisation in maintaining peace across the world. (3)

(ii) Highlight any three major differences between the UNICEF and WHO. (3)

(iii) The UNESCO works for the promotion of educational programmes across the world. Justify the statement. (4)

Ans. (i) The emblem belongs to the United Nations organisation. It was established by the efforts of the three big leaders, Frank D Roosevelt (US President), Winston Churchill (Prime Minister of Britain) and Josef Stalin (Premier of Russia) etc.

The organisation plays a major role in maintaining peace by following ways

(a) The UN works on preventing conflicts by addressing their root causes, including poverty, inequality, and human rights violations, through diplomatic means.

(b) The UN facilitates dialogue between conflicting parties and provides platforms for peaceful negotiations to resolve disputes without resorting to war.

(ii) The three major differences between the UNICEF and WHO are as follows

UNICEF	WHO
Focuses on the welfare, education, and protection of children worldwide.	Works on improving global health and combating diseases.
Provides immunisation and nutrition programmes for children.	Conducts research and advises on global health policies.
Emphasises child rights, education and survival programmes.	Focuses on pandemics, disease control, and public health initiatives.

(iii) The UNESCO plays a crucial role in the promotion and advancement of education globally in following ways

- **Removal of Illiteracy** By promoting adult education, distance education, and open school systems, UNESCO empowers individuals with access to learning opportunities irrespective of their circumstances.
- **Support for Disabled Children** Through financial assistance for the education of disabled children, UNESCO ensures inclusive education for all, breaking barriers for differently-abled learners.
- **Focus on Women and Girls' Education** UNESCO prioritises the education of women and girls, addressing gender disparities and promoting equality in learning opportunities.
- **Encouragement of Scientific Education** Establishing regional training centers enhances the accessibility and quality of scientific education globally.
- **Guidance in Curriculum Development** UNESCO advises on syllabus creation, textbook production, and teacher training, ensuring standardisation and improvement in educational quality.
- **Support for Libraries and Fellowships** By setting up library systems and awarding fellowships, UNESCO fosters a culture of reading, research, and academic excellence.

Q.4 The organs and the agencies of the United Nation Organisation work towards the development of the world. With reference to this, answer the following questions. (ICSE 2025)

(i) What is the composition of the General Assembly?

(ii) Mention any three functions of the International Court of Justice.

(iii) **Give the full form of UNICEF. Mention any three of its functions.**

Ans. (i) The General Assembly is the main deliberative body of the United Nations, where all member countries are represented. It consists of 193 member nations, with each nation having one vote, regardless of size or power. Every member country can send five representatives, but they still hold only one vote. The General Assembly meets annually and can hold special sessions in case of urgent matters.

Important decisions, such as electing non-permanent members of the Security Council or approving the UN budget, require a two-thirds majority, while others are decided by a simple majority.

(ii) The International Court of Justice (ICJ) is the judicial organ of the UN, headquartered in The Hague, Netherlands. Its three main functions are

- **Settling Legal Disputes** It resolves disputes between member nations based on international law.
- **Advisory Opinions** It provides legal advice to the General Assembly, Security Council and UN agencies.
- **Interpreting International Treaties** The ICJ interprets treaties and agreements, ensuring their proper implementation.

(iii) The full form of UNICEF is United Nations International Children's Emergency Fund. Although its name later changed to United Nations Children's Fund, the acronym UNICEF remains the same.

Three major functions of UNICEF are

- **Child Healthcare and Immunisation** It provides vaccines to protect children against diseases like polio, measles and tuberculosis.
- **Education and Literacy Programes** It promotes education for underprivileged children, especially girls and disabled children.
- **Emergency Relief** UNICEF provides food, clean water and medical aid during natural disasters, wars and crises.

13

NON-ALIGNED MOVEMENT

- The Non-Aligned Movement arose after the Second World War (1939-45), which divided the world into two opposing power blocs–one led by the USA and the other by the USSR (former Soviet Union).
- Many newly independent nations in Asia and Africa chose to remain neutral and did not align with either bloc.

Non-Aligned Movement (NAM)

- The Non-Aligned Movement (NAM) is a coalition of developing or newly independent nations, often referred to as 'Third World Nations', that choose not to align formally with any major power bloc.
- It is against military alliances like NATO (North-Atlantic Treaty Organisation), SEATO (South-East Asia Treaty Organisation), Warsaw Pact, etc.
- It emphasise upon the complete freedom of nations to make independent Foreign Policy.

Objectives of NAM

At the beginning, the main objective of NAM was to keep away the newly independent nations of Asia and Africa from the rivalry of the two power blocs and preserve their independence. The other objectives of NAM are

- To remove all those factors and tendencies that could lead to war.
- To strengthen the United Nations Organisation as an organ of world peace.
- To oppose colonialism, imperialism and racial discrimination.

The Main Architects of Non-Aligned Movement

- Non-Alignment as a movement originated when the first Prime Minister of India, Pandit Jawaharlal Nehru, gave the idea of an organisation of newly independent states of Africa and Asia in a radio speech in 1946.
- The main architects of Non-Aligned Movement were
  - (i) Prime Minister Pandit Jawaharlal Nehru of India
  - (ii) President Sukarno of Indonesia
  - (iii) President Josip Broz Tito of Yugoslavia
  - (iv) President Colonel Gamal Abdel Nasser of Egypt
  - (v) President Kwame Nkrumah of Ghana

Role of Jawaharlal Nehru in Non-Aligned Movement

- India under the command of Jawaharlal Nehru was the first nation to adopt the Non-Alignment Policy.
- Nehru highlighted the danger of joining power blocs at the 1947 Asian Relations Conference in New Delhi.
- He opposed alliances like NATO and SEATO, considered them as tools of colonialism and imperialism.
- In 1955, Nehru, along with leaders like Ho Chi Minh and Zhou Enlai organised the Bandung Conference.
- The conference aimed to unite newly independent nations and promote mutual cooperation.

Principles of Panchsheel

- Panchsheel Agreement was an agreement of peaceful co-existence signed by India and China in 1954.
- It included five principles that were emphasised by Prime Minister Jawaharlal Nehru and Premier Zhou Enlai in a broadcast speech at the time of Asian Prime Ministers Conference in Colombo, Sri Lanka after signing the Sino-Indian Agreement in Beijing.
- These principles save sovereignty and territorial integrity of the newly independent nations.
- The five principles of Panchsheel Agreement were as follows
  - (i) Mutual non-interference in each other's internal affairs.
  - (ii) Mutual non-aggression.
  - (iii) Equality for mutual benefit.
  - (iv) Mutual respect for each other's territorial integrity and sovereignty.
  - (v) Peaceful co-existence.

EXAM ORIENTED QUESTIONS

TYPE - 1 — 1 Mark

Multiple Choice Questions

Q.1 The non-alignment means............

(a) staying out of military alliances.
(b) avoiding alignment with global power blocs.
(c) engaging actively in world affairs by preserving independence.
(d) All of the above

Ans. (d) All of the above

Q.2 Which summit is being discussed in the following headlines below?

INDIAN EXPRESS

PM calls for summit of all UN members

Mrs Gandhi elected Chairman

Need for fresh look at major problems

Global pledge against use of nuclear arms sought

(a) Formation of League of Nation
(b) United Nations Summit
(c) Commonwealth Summit
(d) Non-Aligned Movement Summit

Ans. (d) Non Aligned Movement Summit

Exp. The inaugural summit of Non-Aligned Movement (NAM) took place in Belgrade(Yugoslavia), in September 1961.

Q.3 Which of these leaders was an architect of the Non-Aligned Movement? **(ICSE 2023)**

(a) Joseph Stalin
(b) Abdel Nasser
(c) Winston Churchill
(d) Franklin Roosevelt

Exp. Abdel Nasser, the President of Egypt, was one of the main leaders who helped start the Non-Aligned Movement. He worked with leaders like Nehru and Tito to keep nations independent from power blocs.

Q.4 The NAM was established in the midst of the Cold War, when leaders of newly independent countries sought a neutral stance and avoided joining either of the two major power blocs, headed by the United States and the Soviet Union. *UN News*

Who among the following was the key figure in the Non-Aligned Movement?

(a) President Sukarno
(b) Pandit Jawaharlal Nehru
(c) President Josip Broz Tito
(d) President Gamal Abdel Nasser

Ans. (b) Pandit Jawaharlal Nehru

Q.5 Identify the odd one out from the following about NAM's objectives.

(a) To oppose colonialism
(b) To support imperialism
(c) To strengthen the UN for peace
(d) To avoid military alliances

Ans. (b) To support imperialism

Exp. NAM was against imperialism, colonialism, and domination by powerful countries. Its goal was to promote peace, independence, and cooperation among newly independent nations.

Q.6 Read the details given below and identify which of the following pairs are correct.

P : NAM was created as a response to the WW I tensions.

Q : NAM promotes alignment to America.

R : Belgrade hosted the first NAM Summit in 1961.

S : NAM promotes peace, security and political cooperation.

Options

(a) P and S are correct
(b) Q and R are correct
(c) R and S are correct
(d) Q and S are correct

Ans. (c) R and S are correct

Q.7 Which of the following is not a key feature of the Non-Aligned Movement (NAM)?

(a) Opposition to military alliances like NATO and SEATO
(b) Advocacy of colonialism and imperialism
(c) Freedom for countries to take independent foreign policy decisions
(d) Support for the rights of newly independent nations

Ans. (b) Advocacy of colonialism and imperialism

Q.8 Which of the following scenarios describes the Non-Alignment Policy (NAM)? **(ICSE Specimen 2025)**
(a) A country forms a military alliance only with the United States.
(b) A country maintains relations with both factions during the Cold War and does not take sides.
(c) A country is part of a religious movement advocating non-violence.
(d) A country aligns with Soviet Union and receives military aid.

Ans. (b) A country maintains relations with both factions during the Cold War and does not take sides.

Q.9 Which of the following served as a foundation for the Non-Aligned Movement (NAM)?
(a) The principles of the Communist Manifesto
(b) The objectives of the United Nations Charter
(c) The ideals of Panchsheel
(d) The agreements of the Warsaw Pact

Ans. (c) The ideals of Panchsheel

Exp. Panchsheel's five principles, like mutual respect and peaceful coexistence, guided NAM. These principles helped newly independent nations to stay neutral and avoid conflicts between powerful countries after World War II.

Q.10 Which of the following is not a principle of Panchsheel?
(a) No interference in each other's internal matters.
(b) Use of force or hostility.
(c) Fairness and mutual advantage.
(d) Harmonious coexistence.

Ans. (b) Use of force or hostility.

TYPE - 2 — 1 Mark

Assertion-Reason Questions

Q.1 Read the two statements given below about the Non-Aligned Movement and select the option that shows the correct relationship between (A) and (R).

Assertion (A) The Non-Aligned Movement (NAM) was established during the Cold War to avoid alignment with either the USA or the Soviet Union.

Reason (R) NAM sought to promote peace, security, and economic development among newly independent countries.

(a) R contradicts A
(b) R is the reason for A
(c) A is true but R is false
(d) A and R are independent of each other

Ans. (b) R is the reason for A

Q.2 Read the two statements given below about the Non-Aligned Movement and select the option that shows the correct relationship between (A) and (R).

Assertion (A) The Non-Aligned Movement's objective is to maintain neutrality in global conflicts.

Reason (R) The Non-Aligned Movement was formed to support the communist bloc during the Cold War.

(a) R contradicts A
(b) R is the reason for A
(c) A is true but R is false
(d) A and R are independent of each other

Ans. (c) A is true but R is false

Q.3 Read the two statements given below about the non-Aligned Movement and select the option that shows the correct relationship between (A) and (R).

Assertion (A) The Non-Aligned Movement emphasises sovereignty and independence of countries.

Reason (R) NAM encourages its members to take sides in global conflicts to strengthen their political ties.

(a) R contradicts A
(b) R is the reason for A
(c) A is true but R is false
(d) A and R are independent of each other

Ans. (c) A is true but R is false

Q.4 Read the two statements given below about The Panchsheel Agreement and select the option that shows the correct relationship between (A) and (R).

Assertion (A) The Panchsheel Agreement was signed between India and China in 1954 to promote peaceful coexistence.

Reason (R) The Panchsheel Agreement laid down five principles, including non-interference and mutual respect for territorial integrity.

(a) R contradicts A
(b) R is the reason for A
(c) A is true but R is false
(d) A and R are independent of each other

Ans. (b) R is the reason for A

TYPE - 3 — 2 Marks

Very Short Answer Type Questions

Q.1 What is meant by the term Non-Alignment? **(ICSE 2025)**

Ans. Non-Alignment refers to the foreign policy adopted by countries that chose to remain independent and not align with any major power blocs (USA or USSR) during the Cold War. It aimed at peaceful coexistence, economic development and protecting national sovereignty.

Q.2 When and why did the idea of non-alignment arise?

Ans. The idea of non-alignment took shape during the Cold War era. After Second World War, the world became divided into two dominant power groups-one under the leadership of the United States and the other led by the former Soviet Union.

During this time, several newly independent nations in Asia and Africa chose to stay neutral, refraining from aligning with either bloc. This phase of neutrality is termed as non-alignment.

Q.3. Read the questions given below and answer the following

(i) Where was the Non-Aligned Movement formally inaugurated?

(ii) Which leaders were involved in the formulation of the Panchsheel principles?

Ans. (i) The Non-Aligned Movement (NAM) was formally inaugurated in Belgrade, Yugoslavia in 1961.

(ii) The leaders involved in the formulation of the Panchsheel principles were Prime Minister Jawaharlal Nehru and Chinese Premier Zhou Enlai.

Q.4 Mention any two features of Non-Aligned Movement?

Ans. Two features of Non-Aligned Movement are as follows

(i) It is not aligned to any power blocs.

(ii) It is against military alliances like NATO, Warsaw Pact, etc.

Q.5 Who were the architects of NAM? and when was the Panchsheel Agreement signed?

Ans. The main architects of the Non-Aligned Movement (NAM) were Jawaharlal Nehru (India), Gamal Abdel Nasser (Egypt), Kwame Nkrumah (Ghana), and Josip Broz Tito (Yugoslavia).

The Panchsheel Agreement was signed on 29th April, 1954 between India and China.

Q.6 Imagine you are the leader of a newly independent country in the early 1960s. You are considering joining the Non-Aligned Movement (NAM) during the Cold War. How would you explain the advantages of NAM to your people, and how would it benefit your country in the global political landscape?

Ans. I would explain to them that joining the Non-Aligned Movement (NAM) allows us to remain neutral in the ongoing Cold War between the USA and the Soviet Union. This neutrality offers our country the freedom to make independent decisions without the pressure of aligning with any major power.

NAM will also allow us to maintain our sovereignty, and focus on domestic development, especially in areas like education, healthcare and infrastructure.

TYPE - 4 — 3 Marks

Short Answer Type Questions

Q.1 Mention any three objectives of the Non-Aligned Movement. **(ICSE Specimen 2021)**

Ans. The three major objectives of Non-Aligned Movement were as follows

(i) To remove all those factors and tendencies that could lead to war.

(ii) To protect the growing freedom of the newly independent Asian and African countries and help them to keep away from colonial domination.

(iii) To protect human rights and the environment.

Q.2. With reference to the Non-Aligned Movement, explain the following.

(i) Non-Alignment Policy

(ii) Two factors responsible for its formation

Ans. (i) Non-Alignment is the policy through which the developing world states or newly independent nations are not formally aligned with or against any major power bloc.

It is against military alliances like NATO (North-Atlantic Treaty Organisation), SEATO (South-East Asia Treaty Organisation), Warsaw Pact, etc. It is the belief that each country has the complete freedom to take independent Foreign Policy decisions.

(ii) Two factors responsible for the formation of the Non-Alignment Policy were as follows

(a) **Desire for independence** Newly independent countries wanted to avoid alignment with either the USA or the Soviet Union during the Cold War.

(b) **Promotion of peace and security** NAM aimed to foster global peace, non-interference, and disarmament amidst Cold War tensions.

TYPE - 5 4 Marks

Long Answer Type Questions

Q.1 "The Non-Aligned Movement (NAM) has saved the world from the onset of a Third World War". Justify this statement.

Ans. The Non-Aligned Movement (NAM) was instrumental in keeping the Cold War from turning into a world war in the following ways

- NAM kept newly independent nations out of the ideological conflict between the USA and the Soviet Union by promoting neutrality and peaceful coexistence.
- NAM freed nations to prioritise their own development and sovereignty over military alliances.
- NAM continuously promoted diplomatic talks and disarmament, which helped in reducing tensions and chances of direct armed conflicts.
- Thus, NAM made a significant contribution in preserving world peace, stability and averting the start of the Third World War.

Q.2 Analyse the role of Jawaharlal Nehru in beginning of the Non-Aligned Movement.

Ans. The role of Jawaharlal in the beginning of the Non-Aligned Movement were as follows

- **Promoted Neutrality and Sovereignty** Nehru promoted the idea that newly independent countries should avoid alignment either the USA or the Soviet Union to ensure their sovereignty and independence in global affairs.
- **Promoted Peaceful Coexistence** Nehru believed in peaceful coexistence among nations and advocated for diplomacy and non-violence to resolve conflicts especially during the Cold War.
- **Founding of NAM** Nehru played a key role in the establishment of the Non-Aligned Movement, alongside leaders like Tito, Nasser, and Nkrumah, during the Belgrade Conference in 1961.
- **Support for Disarmament** Nehru strongly supported for nuclear disarmament and global peace, making disarmament a core goal of NAM to reduce the risk of global conflicts.

Q.3 With reference to Non-Aligned Movement, answer the following

State the five principles of Panchsheel.

Ans. The five core principles of Panchsheel were as follows

(i) **Respect for sovereignty and territorial integrity** Every nation should honor the independence and borders of other countries.

(ii) **Refraining from aggression** Nations should not engage in military conflict or use force against each other.

(iii) **Non-interference in internal matters** Countries should not interfere in the domestic affairs of other states.

(iv) **Equality and cooperation for mutual benefit** Relationships between nations should be based on fairness and shared advantages.

(v) **Peaceful coexistence** Countries should live in harmony and maintain friendly relations despite ideological differences.

TYPE - 6 10 Marks

Structured Questions

Q.1 Look at the picture given below and answer the following questions.

(i) The picture given is related to which conference? Why the leaders of the third world countries had gathered at this conference? **(3)**

(ii) The people of the developing countries are against the imperialism of the superpowers. Justify the statement. **(3)**

(iii) How world politics changed after the formation of NAM? **(4)**

Ans. (i) The picture is related to the Bandung Conference. The leaders of third world countries gathered at the Bandung Conference in 1955 to

- Promote solidarity among newly independent nations.

- Resist colonialism and imperialism.
- Encourage economic cooperation and development.

The conference was a significant step towards forming the Non-Aligned Movement and independence of Asian and African countries from the two major power blocs.

(ii) The people of developing countries opposed imperialism because it led to exploitation of the weaker nations. Imperialism often leads to the loss of independence, where developing countries are forced to follow the orders of stronger nations. This results in the exploitation of resources, poor living conditions, and the suppression of local cultures. Developing countries want to make their own decisions and control their own resources without interference from superpowers. They seek justice, freedom, and equality, and they strive to build their nations in ways that benefit their people, not foreign powers. Hence, they oppose imperialism.

(iii) The formation of the Non-Aligned Movement (NAM) changed world politics in the following ways

- NAM provided a platform for newly independent nations to advocate for sovereignty, peace, and development.
- It promoted neutrality by allowing countries to avoid aligning with the USA or the Soviet Union during the Cold War.
- NAM called for global disarmament, peaceful conflict resolution, and the de-escalation of Cold War tensions.
- It emphasised economic justice and self-reliance, urging fairer trade terms and addressing poverty and inequality in developing nations.

ICSE Solved Paper 2025

ICSE SOLVED PAPER 2025
(FULLY SOLVED)
HISTORY & CIVICS X

General Instructions

Maximum Marks : 80

Time allowed : Two hours

Answers to this paper must be written on the answer sheet provided separately.

You will **not** be allowed to write during the first **15** minutes.

This time is to be spent in reading the question paper.

The time given at the head of this paper is the time allowed for writing the answers.

Part I is compulsory. All questions from Part I are to be attempted.

A total of **five** questions are to be attempted from **Part II**.

The intended marks for questions or parts of questions are given brackets ().

Part - I

(30 Marks)

Attempt all questions from this Part.

Question 1

Select the correct answers to the questions from the given options. [1]

(i) The Council of Ministers is collectively responsible to the............... .

(a) Lok Sabha (b) President

(c) Rajya Sabha (d) Prime Minister

(ii) Given below are details of a few Indian Citizens. [1]

Person	Age (In years)	Description
W	25	Is a famous journalist
X	45	Is an industrialist
Y	35	Has declared insolvency
Z	50	Has taken citizenship of another country

Select the one who is eligible to be a member of the Rajya Sabha.

(a) X (b) W (c) Y (d) Z

(iii) With reference to the Supreme Court of India, complete the following **[1]**

Advisory Jurisdiction : Advice the President :: Judicial Review : ....

(a) Review its own judgements.

(b) Review the judgements of the High Court.

(c) Review the laws passed by the Parliament.

(d) Review the administration of the Government.

(iv) Observe the given picture. In case of a similar unruly situation in the Lok Sabha, choose the action that may be taken by the Speaker. **[1]**

(a) Adjourn the House for lack of quorum.

(b) Dissolve the Lok Sabha.

(c) Adjourn the House for lack of discipline.

(d) Disqualify the members under Anti-defection law.

(v) If an Adjournment Motion is passed in the Lok Sabha .... **[1]**

(a) the Lok Sabha will be dissolved.

(b) the House will discuss a matter of urgent public importance.

(c) the President ends the session.

(d) the Government will fall.

(vi) Which emergency will be declared by the President if the security of the Nation is under threat? **[1]**

(a) General Emergency

(b) Financial Emergency

(c) Constitutional Emergency

(d) President's Rule

(vii) Read the statements given below and select the option that shows the correct relationship between (A) and (R). **[1]**

Assertion (A) Lord Curzon partitioned Bengal in 1905.

Reason (R) The Nationalists felt that the British wanted to divide the Hindus and the Muslims.

(a) (A) is true and (R) is false.

(b) (R) is true but (A) is false.

(c) Both (A) and (R) are independent of each other.

(d) (A) is the reason for (R).

(viii) Read the description and identify the person. **[1]**

He introduced the Subsidiary Alliance to expand the British control over India.

(a) Lord Dalhousie

(b) Lord Canning

(c) Lord Wellesley

(d) Lord Curzon

(ix) Identify the odd one out of the following Assertive Nationalists Leaders. **[1]**

(a) Bipin Chandra Pal

(b) Lala Lajpat Rai

(c) Dadabhai Naoroji

(d) Bal Gangadhar Tilak

(x) Who among the following is most associated with this picture? [1]

(a) Jyotiba Phule
(b) Raja Ram Mohan Roy
(c) Swami Dayanand Saraswati
(d) Aurobindo Ghosh

(xi) Identify the contributions of Subhash Chandra Bose [1]

P. Was the Supreme Commander of INA
Q. Signed the Lucknow Pact
R. Led the Quit India Movement
S. Founded the Forward Bloc

(a) P and Q
(b) Q and R
(c) P and S
(d) R and S

(xii) The market of a small industrial town *X* has been dominated by many products of foreign companies. The local residents decide to save the Indian industries by helping them increase their sales. Which method of the Assertive Nationalists must they follow to become self-reliant? [1]

(a) Passive Resistance
(b) National Education
(c) Swadeshi
(d) Revivalism

(xiii) Which of the following is not an objective of the United Nations Organisation? [1]

(a) Disarm
(b) Disengage
(c) Decolonise
(d) Develop

(xiv) Which agency of the United Nations Organisation is associated with this picture? [1]

(a) UNESCO
(b) UNICEF
(c) WHO
(d) ILO

(xv) Which of the following is a common cause for the rise of dictatorship? [1]

(a) Faith in Democracy
(b) Economic Crisis
(c) Freedom of Press
(d) Political Stability

(xvi) Which of the following causes of the First World War is connected to this headline? **[1]**

The Washington Times
SUNDAY EVENING EDITION
SERB STUDENT ASSASSINATES ARCHDUKE AND HIS DUCHESS

(a) Imperialism
(b) Aggressive Nationalism
(c) Armament Race
(d) Sarajevo Crisis

Question 2

(i) Mention any two powers of the Prime Minister with reference to the Cabinet. **[2]**

(ii) Imagine you are an Early Nationalist leader. Mention any two methods you would follow to fight against the British. **[2]**

(iii) Mention any two factors that led to the formation of the Muslim League. **[2]**

(iv) Mention any two objectives of the Forward Bloc. **[2]**

(v) Mention any two ways in which the Treaty of Versailles affected the German Miliary Force. **[2]**

(vi) What is meant by the term Non-Alignment? **[2]**

(vii) When a judicial system is correctly calibrated, the law is applied by judges fearlessly, without favour or fear and with respect. That is why judicial security of tenure is so fundamental. It is also why judges must be properly paid without any interference from the Executive or Legislature.
-(The Need for Independent Judiciary) UNODC

From the passage, deduce and mention any two ways in which the Constitution ensures the independence of the Judiciary. **[2]**

Part - II

(50 Marks)

SECTION - A

Attempt any five questions from this Part.

Question 3

The Parliament of India comprises the President and the two houses. With reference to the Indian Parliament, answer the following questions

(i) Mention any three circumstances under which the Parliament can make laws on subjects in the State List. **[3]**

(ii) Explain the following terms **[3]**

(a) Question Hour (b) Quorum

(c) No-confidence Motion

(iii) When can the term of the Lok Sabha be extended? **[4]**

Mention any three powers of the Lok Sabha which show its superiority over the Rajya Sabha.

Question 4

The Executive Power of the country is in the President and Vice President. With reference to this, answer the following questions

(i) Explain the impeachment process through which the Parliament can remove the President from power. **[3]**

(ii) Mention any three powers of the Vice President in her/his role as the Chairman of the Rajya Sabha. **[3]**

(iii) With reference to the powers of President, mention **[4]**

(a) any two Financial Powers

(b) any two Executive Powers

Question 5

The High Courts of India are the highest courts of appeal in each state. With reference to the High Courts of India, answer the following questions

(i) What is meant by the term Original Jurisdiction of the High Court? Mention any two cases which fall under this jurisdiction. **[3]**

(ii) Mention any two advantages of the Lok Adalat. Mention any one difference between the Sessions Court and the Court of the District Judge. **[3]**

(iii) Explain the following with reference to the High Court. **[4]**

(a) Revisory Jurisdiction

(b) Court of Record

SECTION-B

(30 Marks)

Attempt any three questions from this Section.

Question 6

The Revolt of 1857 was conscious beginning of the independence struggle against the British. With reference to this, answer the following questions

(i) What was the Doctrine of Lapse? Who introduced it? **[3]**

(ii) The British Government interfered in the social and religious matters of the Indians. Mention any three socio religious causes to justify this statement. **[3]**

(iii) Mention any four military causes which led to this revolt. **[4]**

Question 7

The oppressive British colonial rule led to the growth of nationalism in India. With reference to this answer the following questions

(i) The repressive policies of Lord Lytton became a catalyst to the growth of nationalism. Mention any three of his repressive policies to justify this statement. **[3]**

(ii) Mention any three ways in which the Press promoted nationalism. **[3]**

(iii) Who presided over the second session of the Indian National Congress? Mention any three objectives of the Congress. **[4]**

Q.8Look at the given picture and answer the questions that follows.

Tears of Blood : When 1,650 Bullets Changed India Forever
–The Times of India, April 2019

(i) Identify the above incident. Which Gandhian movement did it lead to? Which incident led to the suspension of that movement? **[3]**

(ii) Mention any three repressive provisions of the Rowlatt Act. **[3]**

(iii) Mention the following. **[4]**

(a) Any two causes of the Quit India Movement.

(b) Any two causes of the Civil Disobedience Movement.

Question 9

Read the passage given and answer the following questions.

In an effort to secure resources for its expanding industries, Japan invaded the Northern Chinese province of Manchuria. Although many Western nations protested the Japanese action, most members of the League of Nations, including Canada, opposed any form of military intervention to defend Chinese sovereignty. A League of Nations commission, headed by the British diplomat Lord Lytton, was dispatched to Manchuria to investigate. *—Loyal Edmonton Regiment Museum*

(i) How did the incident being described above become a cause for the Second World War? **[3]**

(ii) Mention any three reasons for Hitler's attack on Poland. **[3]**

(iii) Mention any four reasons for the failure of the League of Nations. **[4]**

Question 10

The organs and the agencies of the United Nation Organisation work towards the development of the world. With reference to this, answer the following questions.

(i) What is the composition of the General Assembly? **[3]**

(ii) Mention any three functions of the International Court of Justice. **[3]**

(iii) Give the full form of UNICEF. Mention any three of its functions. **[4]**

Answers

1. (i) (a) (ii) (a) (iii) (c) (iv) (c) (v) (b)
(vi) (a) (vii) (d) (viii) (a) (ix) (c) (x) (a)
(xi) (c) (xii) (c) (xiii) (b) (xiv) (a) (xv) (b)
(xvi) (d)

2. (i) Two powers of the Prime Minister with reference to the cabinet are
   - **Appointment and Allocation of Portfolios** The Prime Minister selects ministers and assigns them specific departments.
   - **Presiding Over Cabinet Meetings** The Prime Minister leads discussions and ensures decisions align with government policies.

   (ii) Two methods I would follow to fight against the British are
   - **Petitions and Appeals** I submit petitions and requests to the British government to demand reforms and justice.
   - **Public Meetings and Speeches** I organise meetings to raise awareness and encourage Indians to demand their rights peacefully.

   (iii) Two factors that led to the formation of the Muslim League are
   - **British Policy of Divide and Rule** The British encouraged communal divisions to weaken the nationalist movement.
   - **Muslim Fear of Hindu Domination** Some Muslim leaders felt that their political and economic interests needed separate representation.

   (iv) Two objectives of the Forward Bloc were
   - **Complete Independence** To achieve full and immediate independence from British rule.
   - **Radical, Social and Economic Reforms** To work for the upliftment of the poor through socialist policies and economic equality.

   (v) Two ways in which the Treaty of Versailles affected the German military force were
   - **Reduction in Army Size** The German army was limited to 100,000 soldiers, with no conscription allowed.
   - **Ban on Heavy Weapons** Germany was prohibited from having tanks, submarines and an air force, weakening its military strength.

   (vi) Non-Alignment refers to the foreign policy adopted by countries that chose to remain independent and not align with any major power blocs (USA or USSR) during the Cold War. It aimed at peaceful coexistence, economic development, and protecting national sovereignty.

(vii) Two ways in which the Constitution ensures the independence of the Judiciary are

- **Security of Tenure** Judges cannot be removed arbitrarily; they can only be removed through impeachment on grounds of proven misconduct.
- **Financial Independence** Judges' salaries and allowances are charged on the Consolidated Fund of India, ensuring they are not controlled by the Executive or Legislature.

3. (i) Three circumstances under which Parliament can make laws on subjects in the State List are

- **During a National Emergency** Under Article 249, Parliament can legislate on State List subjects when an emergency is declared.
- **When Rajya Sabha Passes a Resolution** If the Rajya Sabha declares, by a two-thirds majority, that a subject in the State List is of national importance, Parliament can legislate on it.
- **When States Request Parliament** If two or more states pass resolutions requesting Parliament to make a law on a State List subject, Parliament can legislate on it.

(ii) (a) **Question Hour** The first hour of a Parliamentary sitting where members ask questions to ministers regarding government policies and decisions.

(b) **Quorum** The minimum number of members required to be present in either House for proceedings to take place. In Lok Sabha, it is 1/10th of total number of members.

(c) **No-confidence Motion** A motion moved in Lok Sabha to test if the government still has majority support. If passed, the government must resign.

(iii) The term of the Lok Sabha can be extended by one year at a time during a National Emergency under Article 352.

Three powers of Lok Sabha that show its superiority over Rajya Sabha are

- **Control Over the Executive** The Council of Ministers is responsible to the Lok Sabha and it can be removed through a No-confidence Motion.
- **Financial Supremacy** Money Bills can only be introduced in the Lok Sabha and the Rajya Sabha cannot amend or reject them.
- **Final Decision in Case of Disagreements** In case of a disagreement over an Ordinary Bill, a joint session is held, where the Lok Sabha's larger strength ensures its dominance.

4. (i) The President of India can be removed through impeachment under Article 61 for violating the Constitution. The process involves

- **A charge** is initiated in either House of Parliament with one-fourth of the members signing a notice.
- **Investigation** The charges are investigated and the President is given an opportunity to defend.
- **Two-thirds Majority Required** If both Houses pass the resolution with a two-thirds majority, the President is removed from office.

(ii) Three powers of the Vice President as Chairman of the Rajya Sabha are

- **Presiding Over Sessions** The Vice President conducts and maintains order in the Rajya Sabha.
- **Deciding on Points of Order** The Vice President interprets rules of procedure and ensures smooth functioning of debates.
- **Casting Vote in Case of a Tie** If there is a tie in voting, the Vice President (as Chairman) casts the deciding vote.

These powers make the Vice President an important figure in the parliamentary system, ensuring efficiency and impartiality.

(iii) (a) Two financial powers of the President are

- **Money Bills Require Presidential Recommendation** No Money Bill can be introduced in Parliament without the President's approval.
- **Control Over the Contingency Fund** The President authorises emergency expenditures from the Contingency Fund of India.

(b) Two executive powers of the President are

- **Appointment Powers** The President appoints the Prime Minister, Governors, Chief Justice, Judges and other key officials.
- **Administration of Union Territories** The President directly administers Union Territories through Lieutenant Governors or Administrators.

5. (i) The Original Jurisdiction of a High Court refers to cases that can be directly filed in the High Court, rather than coming through an appeal from lower courts.

Two cases under this jurisdiction are

- **Disputes involving Fundamental Rights** The High Court can issue writs under Article 226 to protect citizens' rights.
- **Cases involving State Government and Individuals** The High Court can hear cases between the state government and private parties.

(ii) Two advantages of Lok Adalat are

- **Speedy and Low-Cost Justice** Cases are resolved quickly without expensive court procedures.
- **Binding Decisions with No Appeal** The decision of Lok Adalat is final, preventing unnecessary delays.

The difference between Sessions Court and the Court of the District Judge can be seen as

Session Court	**Court of the District Judge**
It deals with criminal cases like murder, robbery and serious offenses.	It handles civil cases like property disputes and contracts.

(iii) (a) **Revisory Jurisdiction** The High Court has the power of Revisory Jurisdiction, which allows it to review and correct decisions made by lower courts if they contain legal errors. If a subordinate court exceeds its authority or fails to follow proper legal procedures, the High Court can call for records, examine the case and make necessary corrections. This ensures that justice is administered fairly and that lower courts function within their prescribed limits. However, the High Court does not re-examine evidence but only checks for procedural and legal correctness.

(b) **Court of Record** The High Court is a Court of Record, meaning its judgements, decisions and legal proceedings are permanently recorded and can be used as legal precedents in future cases. These records hold binding authority over lower courts. Additionally, as a Court of Record, the High Court has the power to punish for contempt of court if someone disrespects or disobeys its rulings, ensuring the dignity of the judiciary.

6. (i) The Doctrine of Lapse was a policy introduced by Lord Dalhousie, the Governor-General of India. According to this doctrine, if a ruling king died without a biological heir, his kingdom would automatically be annexed by the British East India Company. Adopted sons were not recognised as legitimate heirs. Using this policy, the British annexed several princely states, including Satara, Jhansi, Nagpur and Awadh. This caused widespread resentment among Indian rulers and was one of the major political causes of the Revolt of 1857.

(ii) The British government interfered in the social and religious matters of Indians, which led to widespread dissatisfaction. The three socio-religious causes to justify this statement are

- **Interference in Religious Practices** The British banned Sati (1829) and discouraged child marriage, which was seen as an attack on Hindu customs and traditions.
- **Promotion of Christian Missionaries** The British encouraged Christian conversions, making Indians fear that their religion and cultural practices were under threat.
- **Social Discrimination** Indians were treated as inferior to the British, facing racial discrimination in jobs and administration, which created resentment among the people.

(iii) Four military causes which led to this revolt were

- **Discontent Among Sepoys** Indian soldiers (sepoys) were paid less, treated unfairly and had fewer promotion opportunities compared to British soldiers.
- **General Service Enlistment Act (1856)** This act forced sepoys to serve overseas, which was against Hindu religious beliefs, as crossing the sea (Kala Pani) was considered impure.
- **Greased Cartridge Incident** The new Enfield rifle cartridges were rumored to be greased with cow and pig fat, offending both Hindus and Muslims. Sepoys who refused to use them were punished, increasing their anger.
- **Annexation of Awadh** Many sepoys were from Awadh, which was annexed under the Doctrine of Lapse, leading to resentment among soldiers who had family ties to the region.

7. (i) Lord Lytton's repressive policies fueled nationalist sentiments in India. The three policies that became a catalyst for the growth of nationalism are

- **Vernacular Press Act (1878)** This act restricted the Indian press from publishing material against British rule, suppressing freedom of speech and limiting nationalist expressions.
- **Arms Act (1878)** This law prohibited Indians from possessing weapons without British permission, while Europeans were exempted, creating a sense of discrimination and weakening Indian resistance.
- **Extravagant Expenditure on Delhi Durbar** (1877) Despite a severe famine, Lytton hosted a lavish Delhi Durbar to celebrate Queen Victoria's title as Empress of India, showing British insensitivity toward the suffering of Indians.

(ii) Three ways in which the Indian press promoted nationalism were

- **Exposing British Policies** Newspapers like Kesari and The Hindu criticised British exploitation and called for reforms.
- **Uniting Indians** The press spread awareness about freedom movements, inspiring people across India to fight for independence.
- **Encouraging Political Participation** Nationalist leaders used newspapers to mobilise public opinion and urge Indians to join protests, boycotts and the Swadeshi movement.

(iii) The second session of the Indian National Congress (INC) was presided over by Dadabhai Naoroji in 1886 in Calcutta.

The Indian National Congress (INC) was formed in 1885 by A.O. Hume with the goal of achieving political rights and self-governance for Indians. Its three key objectives were

- **Promoting National Unity** The INC aimed to bring together Indians from different regions, religions and communities to develop a common national identity.
- **Political Awareness and Representation** It worked to educate Indians about their rights and demanded greater representation in government through constitutional means.
- **Social and Economic Reforms** The Congress sought to address issues like poverty, taxation and economic exploitation caused by British rule while promoting Indian industries and education.

8. (i) The incident described is the Jallianwala Bagh Massacre on 13th April, 1919, when General Dyer ordered troops to fire on a peaceful gathering in Amritsar, killing thousands. This incident led to nationwide outrage and was a major cause of the Non-Cooperation Movement (1920-1922) launched by Mahatma Gandhi.

The movement was later suspended due to the Chauri Chaura Incident (1922), where violent protesters burned a police station, killing policemen. Gandhiji, being a strong advocate of non-violence, called off the movement to prevent further bloodshed.

(ii) The Rowlatt Act was passed by the Imperial Legislative Council in March 1919 and was strongly opposed by Indian leaders. Three repressive provisions of the Rowlatt Act were

- **Arrest without Warrant** The government could arrest and detain any person suspected of anti-British activities without a trial for up to two years.
- **In Camera Trials** Trials could be conducted in secret (closed-door hearings) without allowing the accused to know the evidence against them.
- **Curb on Freedoms** The Act restricted freedom of speech, press, and movement and protests against the government were considered illegal.

(iii) (a) Two causes of the Quit India Movement were

- **Failure of the Cripps Mission** (1942) The British government sent the Cripps Mission to offer Dominion Status after World War II, but Congress rejected it as it did not promise full independence.
- **Japanese Threat** The Japanese Army was advancing towards India, increasing fears of an invasion. Indian leaders saw this as a chance to force the British to leave India immediately.

(b) Two causes of the Civil Disobedience Movement were

- **Simon Commission Boycott** (1927) The Simon Commission was sent to review India's political situation, but no Indian members were included. This angered Indian leaders, leading to widespread protests.
- **Declaration of Purna Swaraj** (1929) The Lahore Session of Congress (1929), under Jawaharlal Nehru's presidency, declared Complete Independence (Purna Swaraj) as India's goal, leading to mass protests against British rule.

9. (i) The Manchurian Incident (1931) exposed the weakness of the League of Nations, as it failed to take strong action against Japan. Despite investigations, no military intervention was made, encouraging aggressive expansionism. This emboldened other axis powers like Germany and Italy, showing that international bodies would not stop territorial invasions. Hitler and Mussolini saw this as a green light for their own ambitions, leading to further aggression in Europe and Africa. The failure of diplomacy and unchecked invasions ultimately escalated tensions, contributing to World War II.

(ii) Three reasons for Hitler's attack on Poland were

- **Reclaiming Lost Territory** Hitler wanted to take back Polish lands that Germany lost after World War I under the Treaty of Versailles.
- **Lebensraum** (Living Space) He aimed to expand German territory for its growing population.
- **Weak Western Response** Britain and France followed a policy of appeasement, making Hitler believe they would not intervene.

(iii) Four reasons for the failure of the League of Nations were

- **Lack of Cooperation Among Member Nations** Countries prioritised their own interests rather than supporting the League's principles of collective security. Even member nations ignored League decisions when it did not suit them.
- **Failure to Prevent Aggression** The League remained inactive when Poland seised Lithuania (1920) and Italy refused intervention in the Greece-Italy conflict (1923). This weakened its authority.
- **Ineffectiveness Against Expansionist Powers** The League failed to act when Italy annexed Abyssinia, Japan took Manchuria and Germany took Austria and Czechoslovakia. This encouraged further aggression.
- **Loss of Faith in the League** The League's inability to stop conflicts led nations to lose trust in it. Instead of maintaining peace, countries started preparing for war, leading to World War II.

10. (i) The General Assembly is the main deliberative body of the United Nations, where all member countries are represented. It consists of 193 member nations, with each nation having one vote, regardless of size or power. Every member country can send five representatives, but they still hold only one vote. The General Assembly meets annually and can hold special sessions in case of urgent matters. Important decisions, such as electing non-permanent members of the Security Council or approving the UN budget, require a two-thirds majority, while others are decided by a simple majority.

(ii) The International Court of Justice (ICJ) is the judicial organ of the UN, headquartered in The Hague, Netherlands. Its three main functions are

- **Settling Legal Disputes** It resolves disputes between member nations based on international law.
- **Advisory Opinions** It provides legal advice to the General Assembly, Security Council and UN agencies.
- **Interpreting International Treaties** The ICJ interprets treaties and agreements, ensuring their proper implementation.

(iii) The full form of UNICEF is United Nations International Children's Emergency Fund. Although its name later changed to United Nations Children's Fund, the acronym UNICEF remains the same.

Three major functions of UNICEF are

- **Child Healthcare and Immunisation** It provides vaccines to protect children against diseases like polio, measles and tuberculosis.
- **Education and Literacy Programs** It promotes education for underprivileged children, especially girls and disabled children.
- **Emergency Relief** UNICEF provides food, clean water and medical aid during natural disasters, wars and crises.

ICSE Latest Specimen Paper

ICSE LATEST SPECIMEN PAPER
(FULLY SOLVED)
HISTORY & CIVICS X

General Instructions

Maximum Marks : 80

Time allowed : Two hours

Answers to this paper must be written on the answer sheet provided separately.

You will **not** be allowed to write during the first **15** minutes.

This time is to be spent in reading the question paper.

The time given at the head of this paper is the time allowed for writing the answers.

Part I is compulsory. All questions from Part I are to be attempted.

A total of **five** questions are to be attempted from **Part II**.

The intended marks for questions or parts of questions are given brackets ().

Part - I

(30 Marks)

Attempt all questions from this Part.

Question 1

Choose the correct answers to the questions from the given options. **(16)**

(Do not copy the question, write the correct answers only.)

(i) On 19th May, 2023, the President of India exercised legislative power under Article 123 of the Constitution, during the period Parliament was in recess, to promulgate The Government of National Capital Territory of Delhi Ordinance, 2023. *–The Hindu, 26th May, 2023*

What information about an ordinance can be obtain from the above passage? **(1)**

(a) The ordinance must be approved within six weeks.

(b) Only the Cabinet can prepare an ordinance.

(c) It is issued when the Parliament is not functioning.

(d) If the Parliament does not approve it within six weeks it becomes inoperative. **[Application]**

(ii) Given below are details of few Indian citizens.

Person	Age [In years]	Description
W	34	Is a Professor in the Government College
X	35	Has taken up the citizenship of the United States of America
Y	27	Is a reputed sportsperson
Z	36	Is a scientist

Select the person who fulfils the eligibility criteria to become the President of India. **[Understanding] (1)**

(a) W (b) X

(c) Y (d) Z

(iii) Who made the amendment which resulted in the below headline? **[Application] (1)**

THE TIMES OF INDIA

In Historic Move Within 100 Days Of Modi-2, Govt Bifurcates State Into 2 UTs, Defangs Article 370 & Scraps 35A

KASHMIR IS NOW UNION'S TERRITORY

J&K To Lose Special Status, Centre To Directly Rule Ladakh

INDIA'S NORTH POLE SHIFTS TO CENTRE

Why now? PM, Shah felt political tide and timing favoured action

(a) The Supreme Court (b) The President

(c) The Parliament (d) The Prime Minister

(iv) Residents of Jodhpur, X and Y got married in the year 2014 and after 4 months of wedlock, petty family issues and arguments resulted in their separation for 6 years. The matter was placed before the Bench of Lok Adalat Family Court, Jodhpur wherein all efforts were made to reunite the family again. With constant efforts of counselling parties agreed to live together and withdraw their Divorce Petition

Case Study, Lok Adalat, District - Jodhpur.

Which advantage of the Lok Adalat is highlighted in the above case? **[Application] (1)**

(a) Saves money (b) Speedy justice

(c) Works on the spirit of compromise (d) Reduces the burden on High Courts

(v) District Judge : Cases :: Sessions Judge : Criminal Cases **[Recall] (1)**

(a) Advisory (b) Civil

(c) Constitutional (d) Appellate

(vi) Identify the exclusive powers of the Rajya Sabha.

P : Can introduce a new All India Service

Q : Can impeach the President

R : Can never be dissolved as a whole

S : Can introduce a Money Bill **[Recall] (1)**

(a) P and Q (b) R and S (c) P and R (d) Q and S

(vii) Read the two statements given below about the Civil Disobedience Movement and select the option that shows the correct relationship between (A) and (R).

Assertion (A) The Civil Disobedience Movement was renewed by Mahatma Gandhi.

Reason (R) The Second Round Table Conference was a failure. **[Analysis] (1)**

(a) R contradicts A (b) R is the reason for A

(c) A is true but R is false (d) A and R are independent of each other

(viii) The government of Country X has introduced a law similar to Ilbert Bill introduced in 1883. Who will be impacted by this Bill? **[Understanding] (1)**

(a) The Farmers (b) The Artisans

(c) The Soldiers (d) The Judges

(ix) The area in which Anand stays has had no water supply for three days in spite of repeated complaints. The residents have a meeting and discuss a few methods to resolve this problem. Being a follower of the beliefs and methods of the Early Nationalists, which of the following methods is Anand not likely to approve? **[Application] (1)**

(a) Peaceful procession by the residents

(b) Follow the method of boycott

(c) Write a petition to the government

(d) Write an article in the newspaper highlighting the problem.

(x) Which of the given policies is not aligned with the ideologies of the leader seen in the picture? **[Understanding] (1)**

(a) Prioritising military expansion
(b) Promoting racist policies
(c) Hosting an anti-communist seminar
(d) Holding pro-democracy rallies

(xi) Identify the odd one out of the following objectives of the Muslim League. **[Analysis] (1)**

(a) To promote among Muslims of India, support for the British.

(b) To promote cultural and socio-economic cooperation among Muslims.

(c) To protect and advance political rights and interests of the Muslims.

(d) To present the needs and demands of the Muslims to the government.

(xii) Your school has organised a poster making competition on the topic - Education empowerment for girls in India. Which of the following leaders would most likely be part of the poster? **[Understanding] (1)**

(a) Surendranath Banerjee
(b) Pherozeshah Mehta
(c) Dadabhai Naoroji
(d) Jyotiba Phule

(xiii) Read the description and identify the person–

He established the Forward Bloc and coined the slogan, 'Delhi Chalo'. **[Recall] (1)**

(a) Mahatma Gandhi
(b) Subhash Chandra Bose
(c) Bal Gangadhar Tilak
(d) Dadabhai Naoroji

(xiv) Which of the following countries will not be part of this cartoon? **[Application] (1)**

(a) China
(b) Japan
(c) Russia
(d) Britain

(xv) Identify the cities most affected by American action in World War II. **[Recall] (1)**

(a) Rome, Berlin
(b) Tokyo, Berlin
(c) Hiroshima, Nagasaki
(d) Tokyo, Rome

(xvi) Which of the following scenarios describes the Non-Alignment Policy (NAM)? **[Understanding] (1)**

(a) A country forms a military alliance only with the United States.
(b) A country maintains relations with both factions during the Cold War and does not take sides.
(c) A country is part of a religious movement advocating non-violence.
(d) A country aligns with Soviet Union and receives military aid.

Question 2

Read the extract given below and answer the question which follows.

Congress member's adjournment motion disallowed. The notice, along with another moved demanding a discussion on China, was disallowed in the Lok Sabha.

The Times of India, 10th Feb, 2023

(i) Who can allow or disallow the above motion? What does this motion mean? **[Understanding] (2)**

(ii) Which category of power is being exercised by the President in the following. **[Recall] (2)**

(a) Approval of Bills

(b) Appointment of the Supreme Court judges

(iii) Imagine you were an artisan, in the year 1856. Mention any two ways in which the economic policies of the British would have affected you. **[Understanding] (2)**

(iv) Give two reasons for the acceptance of the Mountbatten Plan by the Congress. **[Recall] (2)**

(v) Mention any two leaders of the Assertive Nationalists. **[Recall] (2)**

(vi) Mention any two objectives of the League of Nations. **[Recall] (2)**

(vii) Name the two alliances formed in Europe before the beginning of the First World War. **[Recall] (2)**

Part - II

(50 Marks)

SECTION - A

Attempt any five questions from this Part.

Question 3

The Union Legislature of India is not only the law-making body, but the center of all democratic political process. With reference to the Parliament, answer the following questions.

(i) The Lok Sabha is more powerful than the Rajya Sabha. Justify this by mentioning any three points. **[Analysis] (3)**

(ii) Rajya Sabha adjourned sine die, overall productivity at 79 percent.

–Deccan Herald, 21st December, 2023

Who can adjourn the above session? Explain the composition of this house. **[Recall] (3)**

(iii) Mention any four legislative powers of the Parliament. **[Recall] (4)**

Question 4

The President is the nominal head of the executive, the first citizen of the country, as well as the commander-in-chief of the Indian Armed Forces. With reference to this, answer the following questions.

(i) The President is the nominal head of the country and cannot act independently.

Mention any three legislative powers of the President which justifies the nominal position. **[Understanding] (3)**

(ii) Mention any three financial powers of the President. **[Recall] (3)**

(iii) Describe the procedure of impeachment of the President. **[Recall] (4)**

Question 5

The Supreme Court of India is the supreme judicial authority and the highest court of the Republic of India. It is the final court of appeal for all civil and criminal cases. With reference to the Supreme Court, answer the following questions.

(i) Who appoints the judges of the Supreme Court?

Mention any two qualifications required for a person to be appointed as a judge of the Supreme Court. **[Recall] (3)**

(ii) Under Article 129, the Supreme Court of India is called a Court of Record.

Justify this statement with any three points. **[Analysis] (3)**

(iii) Explain the following terms.

(a) Revisory Jurisdiction (b) Advisory Jurisdiction **[Recall] (4)**

SECTION-B (30 Marks)

Attempt any three questions from this Section.

Question 6

The Indian Rebellion of 1857 was a major uprising against the rule of the British East India Company, which functioned as a sovereign power on behalf of the British Crown. With reference to this, answer the following questions.

(i) The British used many policies of expansion. Mention any three such policies. **[Recall] (3)**

(ii) How did the failure of this Revolt impact the Mughals and the Peshwas? **[Recall] (3)**

(iii) The India army was reorganised after 1858, to prevent the reoccurrence of another uprising. Analyse this statement by stating any four changes made in the army after the Revolt. **[Analysis] (4)**

Question 7

Nationalism refers to the feeling of oneness that emerges when people consider themselves as one nation. With reference to the growth of nationalism, answer the following.

(i) Name the first President of Congress. Mention any two of its objectives. **[Recall] (3)**

(ii) The press played an important role in the growth of Indian Nationalism. Thus, the British saw the need for curbs on the press. Mention any three points to analyse the role of the press in the growth of nationalism. **[Analysis] (3)**

(iii) Lord Lytton's repressive policies led to the growth of Nationalism. Mention any four policies enforced by him. **[Recall] (4)**

Question 8

Read the excerpt given below and answer the questions that follow

The March, which took place in India, was led by Mohandas Gandhi to protest British rule in India. During the march, thousands of Indians followed Gandhi from his religious retreat near Ahmedabad to the Arabian Sea coast, a distance of some 240 miles. The march resulted in the arrest of nearly 60,000 people, including Gandhi himself. *–The Marion (Ohio) Star [Edited]*

(i) Name the march being discussed above. Which movement did this march lead to? In which year was that movement launched? **[Recall] (3)**

(ii) The movement which began with this march made a considerable impact on the social and political surroundings of the country. Analyse this statement by mentioning any three impacts. **[Analysis] (3)**

(iii) Mention any four clauses of the Gandhi Irwin Pact. **[Recall] (4)**

Question 9

Look at the picture given and answer the following questions. **[Recall] (3)**

(i) Describe the incident depicted in the cartoon.

(ii) Mention any three points to analyse how Europe was rearranged as a consequence of the war caused by this incident. Consequence of the war caused by this incident. **[Recall] (3)**

(iii) The Germans described the Treaty of Versailles as harsh and humiliating.

Give any four reasons that justify this statement. **[Analysis] (4)**

Question 10

The United Nations Organisation aims to maintain international peace. With reference to its organs and agencies, answer the following.

(i) What is the composition of the International Court of Justice? **[Recall] (3)**

(ii) Mention any three functions of the General Assembly. **[Recall] (3)**

(iii) Gujarat's famed garba dance received the intangible heritage tag. Which agency of the United Nations is authorized to give this tag? Mention any three other contributions of that agency in the preservation of culture.

[Application & Recall] (4)

Answers

1. (i) (c) It is issued when the Parliament is not functioning.

(ii) (d) 2

(iii) (c) The Parliament

(iv) (c) Works on the spirit of compromise

(v) (b) Civil

(vi) (c) P and R

(vii) (b) R is the reason for A

(viii) (d) The Judges

(ix) (b) Follow the method of boycott

(x) (d) Holding pro-democracy rallies

(xi) (a) To promote among Muslims of India, support for the British.

(xii) (d) Jyotiba Phule

(xiii) (b) Subhash Chandra Bose

(xiv) (b) Japan

(xv) (c) Hiroshima, Nagasaki

(xvi) (b) A country maintains relations with both factions during the Cold War and does not take sides.

2. (i) The Speaker of the Lok Sabha has the authority to allow or disallow an adjournment motion. This power is crucial for maintaining order and focusing the discussion in the house.

An adjournment motion is used to temporarily stop proceedings to discuss a matter of urgent public importance. The discussion must be specific and is intended to draw the government's attention to a particular issue that needs immediate attention.

(ii) (a) The President of India exercises legislative powers under Article 111 of the Constitution to approve bills passed by both houses of Parliament.

(b) The President exercises executive power to appoints judges to the Supreme Court of India under Article 124 of the Constitution.

(iii) An artisan in the year 1856 would have been affected by the British policies in the following ways

- **Reduced demand for local goods** As an artisan in 1856, British economic policies such as the promotion of British-made goods would have severely affected his/her livelihood by reducing the demand for locally made products.
- **Taxation and raw material supply** One would likely face heavy taxes imposed by the British, which would diminish their earnings. Additionally, the colonial focus on raw material exportation would limit his/her access to necessary resources, further impacting his/her ability to produce and sell.

(iv) Two reasons for the acceptance of the Mountbatten Plan by the Congress were

(a) **Immediate Transfer of Power** One of the primary reasons Congress accepted the Mountbatten Plan was the provision for immediate transfer of power from British to Indian hands, which promised a quicker end to British rule.

(b) **Avoidance of Civil War** The plan proposed the partition of India into two dominions, which, despite being a painful decision, was seen by Congress leaders as a necessary compromise to prevent a civil war between different communal groups.

(v) Two leaders of the Assertive Nationalists were

(a) **Bal Gangadhar Tilak** Often referred to as 'Lokmanya, Tilak' was a prominent leader of the Assertive Nationalists, advocating for Swaraj as a birthright of Indians. He initiated the Shivaji festival in 1896 to inspire nationalism in addition to the Ganesh festival.

(b) **Lala Lajpat Rai** He was also called 'Punjab Kesari' and 'Lion of Punjab' and was instrumental in the freedom struggle and was known for his advocacy of aggressive policies against British rule. Along with Bipin Chandra Pal and Bal Gangadhar Tilak, he formed the Lal-Bal-Pal trio of extremist leaders.

(vi) Following are the two main objectives of League of Nations.

(a) **Prevention of wars** The League of Nations aimed to maintain peace and prevent wars through collective security and disarmament and settling international disputes through negotiation and arbitration.

(b) **Promotion of international cooperation** The league of Nations aimed to foster cooperation among nations in solving international problems of an economic, social, or humanitarian nature and to achieve international peace and security.

(vii) Before the beginning of the First World War, two major alliances were formed in Europe. These were

(a) **The Triple Entente** This alliance, established in the early 20th century, included France, Russia and the United Kingdom. It was formed through a series of agreements that aimed to counterbalance the growing strength of the Triple Alliance and provide mutual support and cooperation among the member nations.

(b) **The Triple Alliance** This alliance was formed in 1882 and comprised and Germany, Austria-Hungary and Italy. It was intended primarily as a defensive pact, where each member promised to support the others in case of an attack by two or more powers, or in case of aggression by France against Germany or Italy.

3. (i) The Lok Sabha is more powerful than the Rajya Sabha because it has

- **Legislative Power over Money Bills** The Lok Sabha holds exclusive powers to introduce and make decisions on money bills. While the Rajya Sabha can suggest amendments, it cannot reject or indefinitely withhold its approval of money bills, which must be returned within 14 days.
- **Major Role in Government Formation** The Lok Sabha is directly involved in the formation of the government, as the Prime Minister and the majority of the cabinet ministers are typically from the Lok Sabha. This house reflects the direct choice of the electorate.
- **Motion of No-Confidence** Only the Lok Sabha has the power to move and pass a motion of no confidence against the sitting government. If such a motion passes, it necessitates the resignation of the entire cabinet, underscoring the greater political power of the Lok Sabha.

(ii) The session of the Rajya Sabha can be adjourned sine die by the Chairman of the Rajya Sabha, who is the Vice-President of India. This type of adjournment marks the end of a session without any definite date for resumption.

The Rajya Sabha, or the Upper House of Parliament, is composed of representatives from the states and union territories. 238 members are elected by the state legislative assemblies, and 12 members are nominated by the President of India.

The total membership is limited by the Constitution, which allocates seats based on the population of each state and territory.

(iii) The four legislative powers of the Parliament are as follows

(a) **Amendment of the Constitution** Parliament can amend the Constitution, subject to the provisions of Article 368.

(b) **Passing Laws** Parliament can legislate on subjects listed in the Union List and, under certain circumstances, on the Concurrent List shared with states.

(c) **National Emergency** During a national emergency, Parliament assumes the power to make laws on any subject, including those normally reserved for states.

(d) **Creation or Abolition of States** Parliament can pass laws changing the boundaries of states or creating new ones.

4. (i) The three legislative powers of the President that justify the nominal position are as follows

- **Bill Assent** The President has the power to give assent to bills passed by Parliament, which is required for a bill to become law. This role is largely ceremonial as refusal to assent is rare and usually done on the advice of the cabinet.
- **Ordinance Issuance** The President can issue ordinances under article 123, when Parliament or any of the two houses are not in session, which have the same force as laws passed by Parliament.
- **Summoning and Proroguing Parliament** The President summons and prorogues the sessions of Parliament, but these actions are typically performed on the advice of the Prime Minister and the cabinet.

(ii) The three financial powers of the President are as follows

(a) **Budget Presentation** The budget is presented in the Parliament with the President's prior recommendation, necessary for any proposals involving expenditure from the Consolidated Fund of India.

(b) **Financial Bills** No financial bills involving expenditure can be introduced in Parliament without the President's recommendation.

(c) **Contingency Fund** The President is the custodian of the Contingency Fund of India (Article 267(1) of the Indian Constitution), allowing him to make advances to meet unforeseen expenses.

(iii) Impeachment procedure of the President is discussed below

- **Initiation** The process can be initiated by either house of Parliament i.e Rajya Sabha or Lok Sabha. The motion to impeach must be supported by at least one-fourth of the total number of members of that house.

- **Investigation** The charges are investigated, and the President has the right to appear and to be represented at the investigation.
- **Decision** For the impeachment to succeed, it must be passed by a two-thirds majority of the total membership of each house of the Parliament.

This rigorous procedure emphasises the stability of the executive head and ensures that impeachment is a measure of last resort based on substantial misdeeds or incapacity.

5. (i) Appointment and Qualifications of Supreme Court Judges.

The Judges of the Supreme Court are appointed by the President of India after consulting the Chief Justice of the Supreme Court.

The qualifications required for being a Supreme Court Judge are

(a) **Experience in the Judiciary** A person must have been a judge of one or more high courts for at least five years, or an advocate there for at least ten years.

(b) **Distinguished Jurist** Alternatively, a person must be a distinguished jurist in the opinion of the President, recognised for their expertise and contributions to the legal field.

(ii) Under Article 129, the Supreme Court of India is called a Court of Record. This statement can be justified the rough the following points

(a) **Permanent Record Keeping** As a Court of Record, all judgments, proceedings, and acts of the Supreme Court are recorded for perpetual memory and testimony. These records are recognised as legal precedents and authoritative references.

(b) **Power to Punish for Contempt** The Court of Record status grants the Supreme Court the authority to punish for contempt of itself. This power helps maintain the respect and authority of the court.

(c) **Precedential Value** Decisions made by the Supreme Court as a Court of Record are binding on all lower courts within the territory of India. This ensures consistency and predictability in the application of the law across the country.

(iii) (a) Revisory jurisdiction refers to the power of the Supreme Court to review, revisit and possibly overturn its own decisions or those of lower courts. This jurisdiction is exercised to correct errors or injustices in judgments and to ensure that justice is served in accordance with law and evolving legal standards.

(b) Under Article 143 of the Constitution, the President of India can seek the advice of the Supreme Court on any question of law or fact that is of public importance or that which involves interpretation of the Constitution. This is known as the Advisory Jurisdiction. While the advice provided by the Supreme Court is generally respected, it is not binding on the President. This jurisdiction helps in clarifying legal issues and aiding executive decisions with judicial insight.

6. (i) The three British Policies of expansion were as follows

(a) **Doctrine of Lapse** Introduced by Lord Dalhousie, this policy allowed the British to annex any princely state where the ruler died without a direct heir.

(b) **Subsidiary Alliance** This strategy, pioneered by Lord Wellesley, involved placing British forces in a princely state and making it a protectorate of the British Empire, effectively controlling its external affairs.

(c) **Direct Conquest** Several regions of India were directly conquered through military force, expanding British territorial holdings and control over resources.

(ii) The impacts of the failure of Revolt of 1857 on the Mughals and Peshwas were

- **End of the Mughal Empire** The failure of the Revolt marked the end of the Mughal Empire, with Emperor Bahadur Shah II being deposed and exiled. This effectively eliminated the Mughal Empire as a political entity and symbol of authority in India.
- **Decline of the Peshwas** The Peshwas, who were leaders of the Maratha Empire, also faced decline as their power had been waning through earlier defeats. After the Revolt, any remaining influence or claims to authority by the Peshwas were further diminished, consolidating British dominance.

(iii) The Indian army was reorganised after the Revolt of 1857 in the following ways

- **Reduction of Indian Troops** The proportion of Indian soldiers in the army was reduced, and the number of European troops was increased to prevent future revolts.
- **Strategic Placement of Troops** The artillery units, which were crucial in any military engagement, were placed under direct British control and Indians were largely removed from these key positions.
- **Enhanced Segregation** The troops were reorganised based on ethnicity and religion to divide and rule by fostering distrust among different groups.
- **Improved Communication** The British improved infrastructure, like roads and telegraphs, to facilitate faster movement and communication of their forces across the country.

7. (i) The first President of the Indian National Congress was Womesh Chunder Bonnerjee.

The Objectives of Congress were

(a) **Promote Political Education and Unity** One of the main objectives was to promote political education among Indians and to foster a sense of unity against colonial rule.

(b) **Formulate and Present Demands** The Congress aimed to provide a platform for all Indians to discuss public matters and to formulate demands for greater civil and political rights from the British administration.

(ii) The role of the Press in the Growth of Nationalism was

(a) **Educating the Masses** Newspapers and periodicals played a critical role in educating the masses about political ideas and the impacts of colonial policies.

(b) **Fostering Unity** The press helped in creating a shared sense of identity and purpose among diverse linguistic and cultural groups across India.

(c) **Exposing Injustices** The press was instrumental in exposing the injustices and exploitation under British rule, which galvanised support for nationalist movements.

(iii) The four policies enforced by Lord Lytton's were

(a) **Vernacular Press Act (1878)** This act aimed to curb the freedom of the Indian press, particularly vernacular newspapers, to prevent the spread of nationalist ideas.

(b) **Arms Act (1878)** This law prohibited Indians from possessing arms without a licence.

(c) **Reduction of Maximum Age for Civil Service Examinations** Lord Lytton reduced the maximum age for appearing in civil service exams, making it difficult for Indians to enter the service.

(d) **Imperial Assemblies** Lord Lytton hosted luxurious assemblies and durbar to reinforce the might of the British Empire, even during famines and hardships faced by Indians, showing a stark disconnect and fueling resentment.

8. (i) The Salt March, also known as the Dandi March, is one of the most iconic events in the history of India's struggle for independence.

This march was a key part of the Civil Disobedience Movement, where Indians were encouraged to disobey British laws non-violently to press for independence.

The Civil Disobedience Movement was officially launched in 1930 following the culmination of the Salt March. The march itself began on 12th March, 1930.

(ii) The impacts of the Civil Disobedience Movement were as follows

- **Increased National Unity** The Civil Disobedience Movement, sparked by the Salt March, played a crucial role in bringing together Indians from different backgrounds. It transcended regional, caste and religious boundaries, creating a widespread collective consciousness against British rule. This unity was pivotal in strengthening the national movement and making it a mass movement rather than being limited to the intellectuals and the elite.
- **Economic Impact** By boycotting British goods, refusing to pay taxes, and halting other economic activities that benefited the British economically, the movement delivered a blow to the British economy in India.
  These boycotts were effective in reducing the revenue the British could extract from India.
- **International Attention** The non-violent nature of the protest drew widespread international attention, particularly from the Western world. Reports of British repression during the movement helped gain sympathy for the Indian cause, boosting support for Indian independence on an international level.

(iii) The four clauses of the Gandhi-Irwin Pact were

(a) **Release of Political Prisoners** A significant achievement of the pact was the release of thousands of political prisoners who were imprisoned for participating in the Civil Disobedience Movement. However, those convicted of violence were not included in this amnesty, which was a point of contention among some nationalists.

(b) **Salt Manufacture** The agreement allowed the collection and manufacture of salt by the coastal communities, which was crucial since the Salt March was specifically initiated against the salt tax imposed by the British.

(c) **Return of Confiscated Properties** Under the pact, the British agreed to return the confiscated lands and properties of the satyagrahis, although properties seized directly by the government were not returned. This clause aimed at alleviating some of the financial strains on the protesters who had sacrificed much in their fight against British laws.

(d) **Right to Peaceful Protests** The pact acknowledged the right of Indians to conduct peaceful protests. It also allowed Gandhi to represent the Indian National Congress at the Round Table Conference in London, marking a significant step toward negotiations for Indian self-rule.

9. (i) The cartoon likely illustrates the assassination of Archduke Franz Ferdinand of Austria in Sarajevo.

This event occurred on 28th June, 1914, when the heir to the Austro-Hungarian throne was assassinated by Gavrilo Princip, a Bosnian Serb nationalist.

This assassination is widely acknowledged as the spark that ignited the First World War I, leading to the mobilisation of allied and central powers into one of the deadliest conflicts in human history.

(ii) Europe was rearranged as a consequence of the first world war in the following ways

(a) **New Nations Formed** The map of Europe was dramatically redrawn with several new nations emerging, such as Czechoslovakia, Poland and Yugoslavia, as multi-ethnic empires like Austro-Hungarian and Ottoman were dismantled.

(b) **Territorial Losses for Central Powers** Countries like Germany and Austria-Hungary lost significant territories to neighbouring states and new nations, altering the political landscape of Europe.

(c) **New Blocks Formed** There were formation of new blocks in Europe along with other non-European countries for example; UK sided with USA etc.

(iii) The Treaty of Versailles was viewed as Harsh and humiliating by Germans due to the following reasons

(a) **Territorial Losses** Germany lost significant territories, such as Alsace-Lorraine to France and parts of Prussia to the new Polish state, reducing its size and economic power.

(b) **War Guilt Clause** Article 231, known as the War Guilt Clause, forced Germany to accept sole responsibility for starting the war, a point of national humiliation.

(c) **Reparations** Germany was required to pay huge reparations, which strained its economy and contributed to severe economic hardships during the interwar period.

(d) **Military Restrictions** The treaty drastically limited the size and capability of the German military, undermining national defence and pride.

10. (i) The International Court of Justice (ICJ) is composed of 15 judges elected to nine-year terms by the United Nations General Assembly and the Security Council. These judges represent the principal legal systems of the world and no two judges may be from the same country, ensuring a diversity of legal traditions.

(ii) The three functions of the General Assembly are

(a) **Legislative Functions** The General Assembly passes resolutions that influence international law and practices.

(b) **Budgetary Functions** It approves the budget of the United Nations and determines the financial contributions of member states.

(c) **Electoral Functions** The General Assembly elects non-permanent members of the Security Council, judges of the International Court of Justice and other key officials within the UN system.

(iii) UNESCO (United Nations Educational, Scientific and Cultural Organisation) is authorised to give the intangible heritage tag.

The contributions of UNESCO in the preservation of culture are as follows

(a) **World Heritage Sites** It identifies and preserves cultural sites and natural wonders around the world that are of outstanding value to humanity.

(b) **Preserves Heritage** It aims at preserving the rich cultural heritage of the countries and focuses on preserving its significance.

(c) **Intangible Heritage** It also maintains a list of Intangible heritage for example, Garba, Vedic Chanting etc from India to preserve their cultural significance.

Sample Question Paper

SAMPLE QUESTION PAPER
(UNSOLVED)
HISTORY & CIVICS X

General Instructions

Maximum Marks : 80

Time allowed : Two hours

Answers to this paper must be written on the answer sheet provided separately.

You will **not** be allowed to write during the first **15** minutes.

This time is to be spent in reading the question paper.

The time given at the head of this paper is the time allowed for writing the answers.

Part I is compulsory. All questions from Part I are to be attempted.

A total of **five** questions are to be attempted from **Part II**.

The intended marks for questions or parts of questions are given brackets ().

Part - I

(30 Marks)

Attempt all questions from this Part.

Question 1

Select the correct answers to the questions from the given options. **(1)**

(i) The Speaker of the Lok Sabha is elected by the ....

(a) President (b) Rajya Sabha

(c) Members of Lok Sabha (d) Prime Minister

(ii) Identify the odd one out regarding the President's veto powers: **(1)**

(a) Pocket Veto (b) Absolute Veto

(c) Suspensive Veto (d) Judicial Veto

(iii) The number of seats in the Lok Sabha - the lower house of parliament representing directly elected MPs - has risen from 494 to 543 and has remained constant since then. The freeze means that despite India's growing population since 1971. *-BBC 17th March 2025,*

The number of members allocated to different states in the Lok Sabha is based on which of the following? **(1)**

(a) Area of the State (b) Population of the State

(c) Literacy Rate of the State (d) Economic Status of the State

(iv) Look at the given cartoon image of the Lok Sabha in session. **(1)**

The person sitting in the central elevated chair is responsible for maintaining order in the House. Who is this person?

(a) President of India
(b) Prime Minister of India
(c) Speaker of the Lok Sabha
(d) Leader of the Opposition

(v) Given below are details of a few individuals regarding their eligibility for appointment as the Prime Minister of India. **(1)**

Person	**Age** (in years)	**Description**
W	21	Member of Rajya Sabha
X	50	Has taken citizenship of another country
Y	35	Has been convicted of a criminal offence
Z	45	Member of Lok Sabha

Who among them is eligible to be appointed as the Prime Minister of India?

(a) W
(b) X
(c) Y
(d) Z

(vi) With reference to the Supreme Court of India, complete the following. **(1)**

Advisory Jurisdiction : Advises the President :: Judicial Review : ?

(a) Reviews its own judgments
(b) Reviews the judgments of the High Court
(c) Reviews the laws passed by the Parliament
(d) Reviews the administration of the Government

(vii) Which of the following titles is most likely associated with the leader seen in the picture? **(1)**

(a) The Father of Indian Unrest
(b) The Governor-General of India
(c) The Commander of British Forces
(d) The Viceroy of India

(viii) Your school is organising a debate on the impact of social reform movements in India. Which of the following leaders would most likely be mentioned for his efforts in abolishing Sati and promoting widow remarriage? **(1)**

(a) Swami Vivekananda (b) Jyotiba Phule

(c) Raja Ram Mohan Roy (d) Dadabhai Naoroji

(ix) Read the description and identify the person. **(1)**

After the failure of the revolt, he was exiled to Rangoon by the British.

(a) Bahadur Shah Zafar (b) Nana Sahib

(c) Tantia Tope (d) Baji Rao II

(x) The United Nations General Assembly is discussing ways to handle a humanitarian crisis caused by a natural disaster. Countries propose different methods to provide aid and support to the affected region. As a representative following the principles of the UN, which of the following actions is least likely to be taken? **(1)**

(a) Sending emergency medical and food supplies

(b) Deploying peacekeeping forces to provide relief

(c) Encouraging international cooperation for rebuilding efforts

(d) Imposing trade restrictions on the affected country

(xi) Identify the country where Fascism emerged as a dominant political ideology in the early 20th century. **(1)**

(a) Germany (b) Italy

(c) Russia (d) Spain

(xii) Which of the following scenarios describes the Swadeshi Movement? **(1)**

(a) A person exclusively buys British-made goods to support trade relations.

(b) A group of activists promote the use of Indian-made products and boycott foreign goods.

(c) A government official enforces strict British policies on Indian industries.

(d) A leader advocates for complete reliance on imported goods for economic growth.

(xiii) Which of the following event led to the headline below? **(1)**

(a) Sarajevo Crisis (b) Treaty of Versailles

(c) Munich Agreement (d) Cuban Missile Crisis

(xiv) Read the two statements given below about the Partition of Bengal and select the option that shows the correct relationship between (A) and (R). **(1)**

Assertion (A) The Partition of Bengal led to widespread protests and the rise of the Swadeshi Movement.

Reason (R) The British government wanted to create a Mohammedan province where Islam and its followers could be predominant.

(a) (R) contradicts (A) (b) (R) is the reason for (A)

(c) (A) is true but (R) is false (d) (A) and (R) are independent of each other

(xv) What is the primary role of the International Court of Justice (ICJ)? **(1)**

(a) Conducting criminal trials of individuals accused of war crimes.

(b) Resolving legal disputes between member nations according to international law.

(c) Monitoring human rights violations across the world.

(d) Conducting financial audits of UN peacekeeping missions.

(xvi) Identify the key objectives of the Forward Bloc **(1)**

P: Establishment of a socialist society

Q: Support for British rule during World War II

R: Abolition of the Zamindari system

S: Opposition to large-scale industrialisation

(a) P and Q (b) R and S

(c) P and R (d) Q and S

Question 2

(i) Give two reasons why the early nationalists demanded protection for Indian industries. **(1)**

(ii) The All India Forward Bloc is a political party in India with a rich history and a commitment to socialist principles. Established on 3rd May, 1939, by Netaji Subhas Chandra Bose, the party was formed as a breakaway faction of the Indian National Congress. *- India Today*

Who opposed the leadership of Subhash Chandra Bose in the Congress, leading to the formation of the Forward Bloc? What was the key reason for this opposition? **(2)**

(iii) State any two functions of the Prime Minister in relation to the Council of Ministers. **(2)**

(iv) Which British strategy is reflected in the following actions? **(2)**

(a) Encouraging Muslims to set-up a separate political organisation

(b) Justifying the Partition of Bengal to create a Muslim-majority province.

(v) Imagine you are a judge of the Supreme Court of India. Mention any two powers you would exercise to uphold justice. **(2)**

(vi) Mention any two principles of the Panchsheel Agreement. **(2)**

(vii) Mention any two major causes that led to the outbreak of war in Europe in 1914. **(2)**

Question 3

The High Courts in India play a crucial role in upholding justice and ensuring the implementation of constitutional provisions. With reference to this, answer the following questions

(i) The High Courts have multiple jurisdictions that allow them to exercise their authority effectively. Mention any three types of jurisdiction of a High Court. **(3)**

(ii) The process of appointing High Court judges involves consultation with various authorities. Explain the procedure for appointing the Chief Justice and other judges of a High Court. **(3)**

(iii) The High Courts in India possess the power of Judicial Review to ensure the constitutionality of laws. Analyse this statement by explaining any four grounds on which a law can be declared unconstitutional by a High Court. **(4)**

Question 4

The President of India holds a crucial position in the country's governance, with various powers and responsibilities. With reference to the office of the President, answer the following questions

(i) Explain the term of office of the President and the conditions under which it can be terminated before completion. **(3)**

(ii) Mention any three legislative powers of the President. **(3)**

(iii) With reference to the powers of the President, mention **(4)**

(a) two diplomatic powers (b) two military powers

Question 5

The Indian Parliament consists of the President and the two Houses. With reference to the Indian Parliament, answer the following questions.

(i) Mention any three unitary features of the Indian Constitution. **(3)**

(ii) Explain the following terms. **(3)**

(a) Single Citizenship (b) Integrated Judiciary

(c) Unequal Representation in Rajya Sabha

(iii) Under what circumstances can a member's seat in the Lok Sabha become vacant? Mention any four conditions. **(4)**

Question 6

Look at the given picture and answer the questions that follows.

(i) Name the organisation to which this logo belongs. Explain any three key objectives of this organisation. **(3)**

(ii) This organisation was established in 1945 with specific objectives. Mention any three reasons that led to its formation. **(3)**

(iii) This organisation works through various agencies to achieve its goals. Mention any four functions of this organisation. **(4)**

Question 7

The Growth of Nationalism in India was influenced by various factors. With reference to this, answer the following questions.

(i) Explain any three economic policies of the British that led to the rise of nationalism in India. **(3)**

(ii) How did the socio-religious reform movements contribute to the growth of nationalism? Give two examples. **(3)**

(iii) The British introduced Western education in India with their own interests in mind, but it played a significant role in the rise of nationalism. Analyse this statement by stating any four ways in which Western education contributed to the national movement. **(4)**

Question 8

The Non-Cooperation movement democratised India's freedom struggle and saw the participation of women, peasants, workers, students and people from all castes and religions. It energised the Congress leadership and base. The British were stunned. *- Hindustan Times, 22nd Aug, 2022*

(i) Mention any three major causes that led to the initiation of the above movement. **(3)**

(ii) Explain any three significant programmes undertaken during the Non-Cooperation Movement. **(3)**

(iii) Describe the impact of the Non-Cooperation Movement on Indian society and politics. **(4)**

Question 9

The Revolt of 1857 was a turning point in Indian history. With reference to the causes and consequences of the Revolt, answer the following.

(i) The British followed various policies to expand their territorial power in India. Name any two policies and briefly explain them. **(3)**

(ii) The British justified the annexation of Awadh on the pretext of 'good governance,' but it led to widespread dissatisfaction among the people. Analyse any three reasons why the annexation of Awadh created resentment among Indians. **(3)**

(iii) The economic exploitation by the British severely affected different sections of Indian society. Mention any four ways in which the British drained India's wealth. **(4)**

Question 10

The Second World War reshaped global politics and economies, leading to significant changes in world order. With reference to the war, answer the following questions.

(i) The Treaty of Versailles was a major cause of the Second World War. Justify this by mentioning any three points. **(3)**

(ii) "Germany invades Poland; Britain and France declare war."

-BBC

Who led Germany at the time of this invasion? Explain his ideology and its impact on world politics. **(3)**

(iii) Mention any four consequences of the Second World War. **(4)**